CONVEYANCE
OF
ETERNAL LOVE

By: Christine J. Haven

© 2007 Christine J. Haven
All Rights Reserved.
No part of this publication may be reproduced, stored in a retrieval system, or transmitted, in any form or by any means, electronic, mechanical, photocopying, recording, or otherwise, without the written permission of the author.

First published by Owl Creek Press

ISBN: 978-0-6151-7990-2

Printed in the United States of America

Dedication

Scholared theologians of all religions place their personal concepts as if demands from God above all people.

And the Angel Jo said, "When one asks and you answer, that is not domination because they were seeking the knowledge that you possess. You have asked and We have answered."

I do not beat on doors to force anyone to read what God's Angels have said. You have decided to read this book. Therefore, this book is dedicated to you, the one who is thinking "Outside the Box" of life of what we were taught by other humans, for you are the one who is seeking the true understandings of God and His Angels.

Lift Your Soul
Feel Free
Live Free
Touch Free
Love Free
And You Shall Be Free

CHAPTERS

Preamble 1
The Guider a Ministry as Directed by the Angel Gabrael 4
Understanding God's Master Plan 6
Applied Quantum Theory 8
The Cycle of The Universe.. 11
How We View and Understand Life 13
All Religions Evolved From Metaphysics and Spiritualism 17
Understanding Religions 21
Religious Withdrawal 29
Life Everlasting 33
Does "God" Exist? 36
Is God Dead? 38
Living God's Will 41
Which God to Follow 45
Directions of God 49
Choosing What We Follow 53
Pretense of Knowledge 56
The Call to Perfection 62
Insight 64
Right of Choice 66
The Gift of Choice 74
Understanding The Gift of Choice 77
You Control Your Choices 81
Understanding The Growth of Life 87
The Direction of Civilization 90
The Challenge of Life 93
The Structure of Life 96

Spiritual Origin of Man 98
Re-incarnation 100
You Are Reaping What You Have Sowed 104
People Do What Pleases Themselves.. 107
Only Take What You Can Carry 109
The Confusion of The World 111
Prophets and Prophecy... 114
False Prophets.. 127
Prophets... 131
How I Became a Prophet... 133
Fools Learn From Fools 138
What is Right for Humankind... 142
Who Will Be Determined Righteous?... 146
Do Not Infringe Upon Others... 150
Do as He Did, Not as They Say.. 153
Individual Salvation... 159
A Body of Doctrinal & Practical Divinity...................................... 161
The Angel Uriel.. 165
A Common Trait.. 171
Feeding The Beast 177
Basic Human Rights.. 181
Socialism as a Vehicle for Progress... 187
Separation of Church and State... 190
The Myth of the Separation of Church and State.......................... 194
Confusion of Separation of Church and State............................... 201
The First Amendment.. 204
Are You Saved?... 206
Catholic Religion Hypocrisy... 208
Cardinal Law's Statement On Sexual Abuse Of Minors By Clergy.... 215
Cardinal Law: Abuse Policy Must Wait.. 219
Religious Reform... 222
The Nature of God... 225
Other Belief Systems... 229
Do You Follow The Father?.. 278
Understanding God.. 282
Expanding Our Directions... 285
Jesus and His Religious Teachings.. 287
Faith and Belief.. 318
Beautiful Front Lawns... 326
The Book of Gabreal Is Opened... 329
Revelation.. 332

Understanding The Book of Revelation 335
The Book of Revelation, part I 338
The Book of Revelation, part II 345
The Book of Revelation, part III 347
The Book of Revelation, part IV 349
The Book of Revelation, part V 353
The Book of Revelation, part VI 356
The Book of Revelation, part VII 359
The Book of Revelation, part VIII 362
God's Angels Said to The Jew 365
God Said to The Christians 367
God's Words to All Muslims 369
God's Angels Said to All The People 372
The Messiah is Coming 374
The Apocalypse is Upon Us 376
What Is Judaism? 378
Why Islam Resembles Judaism 384
Why No Peace 390
Homeland for Martyrs 393
Know Your Enemy 396
Reply to an Open Letter from bin Laden to All Americans 398
Muslims See War as The New World Crusade 415
Muslim Terrorists Do Not Follow Their Religion 420
Suicide 424
Palestinians Against The Israelis 428
Islamic Terrorist 431
Fighting Terrorists 433
Understanding Our Enemy 435
The World's 1,300 Year Old War 453
World Conflict 455
Violence in The World 458
Terrorism 460
Who is Right 467
The Enemy Within 471
God's Angels Words are The Truth 473
Individual Feelings 475
We Lead You Not Into Temptation 478
The Choices of God's Angel within 480
Gift of Choices 483
The Light and The Darkness 486
The Covenant - A Promise Between God and The People 490

God's Messenger to The Covenant	497
Follow Jesus' Way of Life	501
And The Angel Michael Said unto Me…	504
Do Not Fear	506
Blessed are Those Who…	508
Final Secrets of Fatima	510
Leash The Dog	514
And if Anyone Wishes to Move a Mountain…	517
Live a Righteous Life	519
We Bring Only Love to All	521
Foolish People	524
Confused and Ignorant People…	527
"Love Them"	529
Do Not Brood	531
Marriage and Family	533
Going Back	537
The Dog Returns to Its Vomit	540
The Transition Continues	542
Understanding Prayer	544
Confession and Forgiveness	550
A World Without Santa Claus	552
Santa Claus is Coming to Town	554
The Christmas Season	556
Christmas Love	558
My Christmas with The Angels	560
Christmas 2001 with the Angels of God	562
Christmas 2002 with The Angels	565
The Glory of Christmas	569
My Last Christmas here on Earth	571
The Angels Final Teachings to Me	573
And I prayed, "Why…"	575
My Final Message	577

Preamble

As I sit on the swing on the patio, gazing out across the beautiful gardens of our back yard, I am at peace within as I feel the love of the Angels that surround me. It hardly seems like eleven years have passed since the Angel Joleen had entered our lives.

David, my husband of thirty-two years, had never been what you would call a religious person by far. I was one always looking for the truth. There was something in me that just couldn't grasp certain ways of thinking of the different churches which I attended. I felt like I wasn't whole with God. I didn't know what was missing, but I seem to have more questions than I was getting answers.

When David and I would get into discussions of death and Heaven and Hell, he would always tell me that he would never bow down to anyone, not God, not the Devil, not anyone or anything. I would ask him what he intended to do when he died and he would always respond that he was going to just stay right here on earth. I would just shake my head and smile. I always knew that there was something more, but I just didn't feel like I knew the complete truth about it.

I recall, when I was a very young child, being in Sunday School. We were talking about Heaven and God's love for us. Our teacher was telling us how lovely Heaven was and that someday when we die, we will all meet again in Heaven. Then she told us how nobody would really know each other, but we would all love each other. I remember raising my hand and asking her if my mommy would know me. She told me no, my mommy would not know me as her little girl, but that she would still love me and I would still love her. Well, I decided right then and there that this Heaven place was no place for me.

As trivial as it may seem, that answer to my question totally devastated me. I guess it was at that point, even though I could not have been more than four or five years old, that I started really questioning things in my mind.

Once I became an adult and could make my own decisions on which church I wanted to attend, I seemed to be on a mission. There was a void in me that I could not seem to fill. I loved God with all my heart, but I found myself being even more confused on other aspects of religion.

Then in 1996, David slowly began divulging the story of his love affair with Joan Lee Harris back in 1965 and about his search to find her. As our book, *Holly Graduel* reveals, this was the beginning of his quest to find God through the Angels Joleen, Gabrael, Michael and Jesus.

I cannot tell you how blessed I have been to have been allowed to travel this road with David. He has been able, through the inspiration of the Angels, to show me the truth. I no longer feel that void within me. David answered my questions as I asked them. Sometimes it was difficult for me to understand things. I have learned that if I just let my Angel within guide me and keep an open heart, I have a better understanding of things.

Sometimes, I would let the old teachings of my younger days take a hold of me and then I would become frustrated. I would find myself questioning things again and becoming irritable. I was turning into a person that I did not like. In actuality, I was allowing the evils of this world to get to me. I was letting the dog lead instead of my Angel within.

David would see this and begin talking to me about God's love and the Angels that surround us. He would remind me to turn it all over to God. I have found that God does keep his promise to us to be there beside us and guide as. All he asks of us is love all others and have no domination over them.

Christine J. Haven

And now, in David's own words, here is God's *Conveyance of Eternal Love.*

The Guider a Ministry as Directed by the Angel Gabrael

Bringing all Religions Together under the One True God.
The Guider promotes and propagates the one true God and His Divine Love that is above all religions and their man-made gods. Thus, I expose the domination and lies that men have imposed upon their fellow humans in the name of God as told to me, the Guider, a Messenger of God, by the Angels Joleen, Gabrael, Michael and Jesus.
Men have taken their communications with God and polluted His desires with their concepts as they turned their Gods into cults, then other men translated the early Prophets words to fit their agendas as they built religions that dominate over others. There is not any one religion that pleases God more than another because all religions are man-made, and all religions are designed out of corruption of a few to control the majority, but actually God has given each individual choice in pursuit of his happiness.
There is one God - Ultimate, Infinite and Eternal Source - who created all that is: the universes, energy, matter, and all living creatures, including humankind in its many expressions on Earth, and the varying forms and expressions of sentient life throughout all of creation.
A part of God resides in, and is part of, all creation.
All humankind are equal. All are the children of God, created in and of Prefect Love. There is no rank among God's children - morally, intellectually or spiritually. Man's concept of rank is

designed to separate and categorize humankind for the purpose of promulgating control over many by a few.

A base human desire to dominate others manifests through an insistence on establishing moral precepts for others to follow and on issuing directives for "proper thinking" at the expense of each individual's own search for peace within as it is revealed to him by his Higher Source.

God admonishes all of humankind to love one another unconditionally and without reservation, and to have no domination over any other, in any way. Such loving-kindness when expressed leads to peace within, to salvation, and ultimately to everlasting life.

There is no one true religion, for religions are developed by man, each in support of a particular group's belief system, with its own agenda and its own moral compass guiding that agenda.

The systems of teaching, the doctrines, and the dogmas of organized religions emanate from the thoughts and ideas of man, coming out of a presumption to know the fullness of God and to speak for God or in God's name. These are set forth in catechisms designed to keep followers "in line" through domination and the threat of spiritual estrangement from God.

Religions have drawn God in man's image rather than understanding and acknowledging that man is made in God's image. Religions have made God small. Through their dogmas and codes of belief, they have presumed to limit what God is, to announce what God thinks, and to proclaim what pleases and displeases God.

God does not favor one religion over another, one code of beliefs over another, or one form of worship over another. God has given each individual who is seeking peace within an inner knowing as to the path he is to follow during his lifetime.

We cannot be responsible if the words of God that the Guider, David A. Haven, has received from the Angels are not inline with what you have been taught. Therefore, if God's Messages offend you in your beliefs, then maybe you should take a better look at your religion and rather its teachings came from God or man. For God and His Angels do not lie! And this is not a place to debate religion, it is a place to learn about God, and comprehend His Master plan, and understand true Monotheism - one God above all other gods.

Understanding God's Master Plan

As we entered into 2003, People often asked me if I have read this book or that because many things that I have written line-up with many other writers. I refrain from reading others writings because I do not wish to contaminate my teachings from God's Angels with other men's thoughts. However, many do need to know that others have the same thoughts and ideas as theirs. But yet, we need not know what others think if we truly listen to what God is telling us. The comfort of knowing others think as you merely strengthens your belief in a Spiritual or religious system whereas I do not need to reinforce my belief in God from others.

At this time, I would like to reflect back to the understanding of: God, our existence and the cycle of time.

Christianity followed the beliefs of Judaism about God placing intelligence into the first man and woman, Adam and Eve. This is proven in the story of the Apple; When God told Adam and Eve not to eat from the Tree of Knowledge, He actually placed intelligence into them to comprehend, understand, and the ability to reason that there would be a consequence if they did not follow His words.

The Islamic religion came into existence around the 700s AD, and Muhammad said, God placed intelligence into the first insect. This was a new theory and its proof came from seeing life, including the insect in the world that contain some kind of intelligence.

Each of these two theories of intelligence was back by "facts of their beliefs" of that day while the Islamic theory proved more species than human had intelligence.

Then, God's Angels told me that He instilled intelligence into the first one-cell animal. Today, with the use of microscope, we can truly see that all life contains some kind intelligence.

Each of the three teaching of intelligence raised the level of average of intelligence in the human species and brought us closer to God. Quantum Theory and Physics - working together while changing from one form to another in a peaceful manner, thus - is God - is Love.

Peaceful Manner - the lifestyle of nature. God created all, even what we consider as bad and/or evil. God created bad and evil to give each his individual choice to choose between doing good or bad. The intelligence that He placed in that first one-cell animal gives us the comprehension, understanding and reasoning to know what our actions will bring. Whereas, animals live mostly for personal survival, and while the "lifestyle" of all species of plants is to root out the other for its survival.

(God created the concept of "Evil" whereas humankind created the actions of "Evil.")

Applied Quantum Theory

If the cycle of plant and animal life would continue without interference from the human species, someday the world would end up with only one type of animal and/or one type of plant species living. Therefore, we should not judge if it is right for one animal to kill another for food or to sustain life. But we must understand that killing one of another species for food is needed in the cycle of life of the animal and insect, while we should also understand that it is wrong to kill another human' for killing another of the same species is wrong. Because when one kills another of his own species, he is diminishing the populous of his species, but when one kills one from another species for food, he is continuing the cycle of his species.

We cannot force our "teachings" upon others, we can only inspire them to seek the truth, for if we force our knowledge upon others we are killing the thoughts of the individuals. Our doctrines (the things God's Angels have told and shown me) cannot be forced upon another, for each must seek for personal and individual doctrines that are symbolic for his understanding, comprehension and reasoning. For if we force and/or push our doctrines upon others, we are no better (righteous) than they as we try to place them under domination. But, we can help raise the level of intelligence of the human species by teaching the proven facts in their belief systems and religions; all religions speak of Love to all, and this is what we need to inspire in them.

Animal instincts of survival drive individuals to force their beliefs upon others. This is truly demonstrated in the business world by companies taking over other companies. If this continues, someday, we will end up with one person owning and in charge of all we buy and consume. And, if we continue to allow our animal instincts to lead, there will come a time when only one person is alive and is living in a world where no one else exist.

In the knowledge of mathematics, it is thought that there is a mathematical formula for life in this third dimensional realm, and it is said that once it is found it will be a one-digit equation.

The formula and equation to this mathematical question is zero. For zero plus zero always equal zero. No matter how many you place together as digits, the answer is always zero, and no matter how many you take away, you always end up with zero. While the symbol for zero is a continuous line that connects back to itself - the cycle of life, never ending life that contains nothing that we can feel, see, touch, smell or taste, and yet, it is opposite to what it is placed on and what it contains because you would not see it if it were the same color, and because it only contains energy while what you see is the line that makes the zero - the circle of life.

God can be symbolized as "0" because He is never-ending Love that continues out and returns as Divine Love - Parts of His energy that we know as Angels enters into our hearts and experiences the endurances (joys and distasteful things) of life. After our deaths, God's Angels ascend back to Him, and we embrace Him, thus, Divine Love returns to Him.

God contains energy of Love that cannot be seen, held, felt, tasted or smelled, but only experienced - He contains out-flowing energy of Love while animals - humans can only experience things that the animal can see, hold, taste, feel and smell - the human contains only selfish (drawn inward) energy. The Angels (parts of God) attempt to turn our selfish energy into Divine Love, but the human has the final choice of his actions.

Whatever you sow, you shall reap. Do good to others, and good shall be returned to you. Do bad to others, and you shall receive bad from others. Allow the Angel within you to lead and he shall lead you to God - Eternal Heaven. Follow your feelings of the animal and it shall lead you to Satan - evil and Eternal Hell. For the cycle of life and the afterlife is the circle, the symbol of "zero."

The symbol "zero" that I refer to as God is a line that is arced - a continuous curve that returns back to its point of origin. This line is the geological location of Time, for the line is the cycle of Time. All that happens has its individual location on this line, and we live on that line.

One night as the Angel Joleen and I talked, I asked her to return the next night at 10:00 pm, and she said she would. The next night, she did not appear until after 11:00 pm, and when I asked her why she did not come at our appointed time, she replied that she was busy taking children to the Light. (But yet, I recalled that she and I had traveled back into the past and into the future, but we never interacted with people during those times, we only interacted with people during the present time.) Once she missed our appointed time, she could only go back to view the things that happened during the time of 10:00 pm, and she could not enter that time and interact with me at that location.

Angels and humans who are traveling in "out-of-body experiences" can travel to other places at this present time, or they can go back into the past or into the future, but they can only inter-act with people during the present time. Therefore, people "out-of-body," dead or alive, and Angels cannot change the past or future. Therefore, one cannot change his Hell to Heaven after death by removing past sins or changing his attitude that contributed to his Hell. Angels (parts of God) - Energy do not live on the line of time, the line of time is life (as we know it) and this third dimension.

The Cycle of The Universe

The Universe is traveling on this continuous curve. And soon after the Big Bang, it began its journey. It passed the speed of light as it continues to travel faster and faster. The faster it travels, the smaller it becomes, and while the distances between planets, stars, etc. and including space become smaller, it seems as if everything is growing further apart. It is the total of the Universe that is traveling on this curve, not just one or a few of the planets and stars. But as we stand on this planet in this Universe, we see all things at comparative the same continuous distances. Once the Universe returns back to its point of origin, the Universe will collapse back into itself, and this cycle of life will end, and then, another cycle will start.
    Nothing exist except God's Master Plan, even you and I and all that surround us is part of God's Master Plan, too. When this cycle ends, everything will be gone except the energy that we contain, that is our Souls. Life will not continue in God's Heaven. Our Souls, the energy that we created here in life will remain in God; Our lives stories will remain there with the Angels. Therefore, all that we did in life remain as part of God's energy forever, until He judges our past life and decides if our lifes were righteous or not.
    There may be other cycles occurring at this same time, and there may have been hundreds of cycles before, but we live in what is called this, the fifth cycle.
    Life is simple, but everything is part of God's Master Plan, and we confuse it because all life is inter-woven, and you cannot

examine one single piece of life and understand it. For all actions have re-actions - past, present and future, and in total, all pieces combine to form all of Life - God.

After God placed intelligence into that first one-cell animal, all things to come was laid down in God's master plan - the domino chain-action effect - things that your ancestors believed in, thought and did contributed to your beliefs, thinking and attitude.

Your ancestry goes back to the time that God placed intelligence into that first one-cell animal. That one-cell animal influenced what you think and do today, and while the one-cell animal's comprehension, understanding and reasoning combines with the new knowledge that you obtain and learn will influence your children of the future - the never-ending cycle of life.

We are here to enjoy, and experience, and to learn in knowledge that helps us understand life and death. Life may not seem grand, but to God all life is grandeur, for God did not promise us Heaven here on Earth, but He did promise us our individual pursuit of happiness.

How We View and Understand Life

As the pendulum of time swings farther into the darkness of evil, the thoughts of more move deeper into selfishness as they force their beliefs upon others who fall pray to Domination. But yet, we must see life not as the only life but merely as a small part of life that is continued everlasting after life. Therefore, when we speak of life here on earth, it is no more comparative than a bad moment in our daily life. And those who cannot stand to hear or speak of the End of Time are self-centered fools that do not know our lives as God Wills will prevail.

During the mid-80s, I became ill with EB Virus (kissing disease, now known as the Yuppie Flu,) I was hospitalized many times and disabled for 10 months as I watched my doctors and hospitals bills soare. (My part of my medical bills were well over $40,000.00, and they wanted payment in full immediately and therefore I had to declare bankruptcy.)

It was at this time that I tried to decide what is "Quality of Life" and when does it end. For I had decided that when quality of life ended for me, I would commit suicide.

As time went by, I found many others were suffering from EV as well as I. I soon found others who were sicker than I, and somewhere without much energy left in my body I started an EV Virus support help group. And soon thereafter, I realized that I could not keep saying, "poor me." I had to get on with life, no matter how bad I felt or how much energy I had...I just had to DO IT.

Thinking that I would soon die, I felt I must do whatever I really wanted to do before I died. And I recalled as a teenager I used to love riding motorcycles, so therefore, I decided to ride a motorcycle again, but not just ride, I wanted to ride around the world on a motorcycle. I was soon writing and calling companies for sponsorship for my ride.

Oh yea, I had a TV station that would air the beginning and ending of my world ride on their News. I had a magazine who would send a writer and photographer with me and who would use my ride in a series in their magazine. I had a motorcycle rebuilding company who would give me the motorcycle that I wanted to ride, a 1937 Indian Chief, and I had parts manufactures that would give me all the parts and supplies that I needed.

What stopped my ride around the world? Money. I did not have the money to support my family nor myself during the ride. It was then I realized that I needed to get back to work. So still suffering with EB Virus, somehow daily I forced myself to get up out of bed and go to work.

(Once a person has EB Virus, you never get over it. The Virus is in all people, but does not become active until your immune system gets run down from depression, or from fatigue, or when you suffer from any other disease as the flu or a cold.)

Today I still suffer from its many symptoms and still have to continue to force myself to get up daily. But I was able to work for over 15 more years before heart disease forced me to retire.

My story shows that we live for the moment alone, and while we should live life of this moment to its fullest enjoyment and experience, for those days and months that I was down and disabled is only a short time compared to the total time the world has given us life. But yet, this time is not the only length to our individual lives, for our lives shall continue to remain forever with God if you allow your life's story to live as His wills.

And for those who look at the End of Time as doom and gloom, do not understand God or life just as I did not understand when I was disabled.

And I have found the answer to the question, "When does the quality of life ends." It never ends; if one can only watch a sunset, or only see a sunrise, or only taste any of the wonderful food that God has given us, or can only smell coffee brewing, or only hearing the sweet sounds of children playing, then one has quality of life.

As we as a civilization enter into a world of darkness and evil, we need to see that there are things to continue to live for. Many will die in the days to come, but even in their last moments of life before Everlasting Life there are things that make life worth living. Money does not make life worth living; Love for others is the true key to "Quality of Life" as God's will, but for the human the simple things that we enjoy may be the "Quality of Life" that we need to continue our endeavors of life.

But yet, all people view the "Quality of Life" differently, for that is part of the Gift of Choice as given to each as individuals by God.

Personal perspectives - the relative importance of facts, or matter, or beliefs systems, from any specific point of view, can be misjudged by not understanding the complete situation. And if one continues to comprehend, in his opinion, situations without taking in all facts involved in the situations but continues to judge, then one's judgment becomes malice motivated, and then all of his perspectives become twisted and warped from the evil within himself.

The three major religions - Christianity, Muslim and Jewish religions all claim that their Messiah shall come before the End of Time and His appearance will indicate the end is near. And while each religion state their Messiah will place their religion above all other religions, and that their religion will rule the world.

It was prophesied that the Muslim Messiah will appear during the time when a Lunar Eclipse occurs one the first day of Ramadan and a Solar Eclipse occurs during the middle of that Ramadan. This double Eclipse will happen this coming November - this coming Ramadan.

Do I believe the Muslim Messiah is coming? NO!

But many Muslim Terrorists will believe that their Messiah is here when the double Eclipse occurs, and will use this prophesy to fight for control of the world. Last year, I heard many discussions between Muslims about is bin Laden the prophesied Messiah. You must understand that Terrorists will try to use the appearance of their Messiah (bin Laden or any other) to fight the Jews and Christians throughout the world.

The warped perspectives of the Terrorists and most Muslims demand a country without any boundaries. (That means a country that is continuous, stretching around the world in which the Muslim religion in the only beliefs system that is practiced and followed.)

Therefore, when we see the Palestinians crying for land for a country, and when we see them begging for part of Jerusalem for their capital; they are merely trying to take over Israel. And if they are allowed these lands, they will continue their push until they have taken over the world.

All Religions Evolved From Metaphysics and Spiritualism

The word "Metaphysics" means; The branch of philosophy that investigates principles of reality transcending those of any particular science, traditionally including cosmology and ontology.

The word "Spiritual" means;

1. Of, pertaining to, like, or consisting of spirit, as distinguished from matter; incorporeal.

2. Affecting the immaterial nature or soul of man.

3. Of or pertaining to God; Holy.

4. Sacred or religious; not lay or temporal; ecclesiastical: spiritual authorities: distinguished from secular.

The words "Metaphysics" and "Spiritual" may be used when describing encounters with God or His Angels of those who lived the stories in the Old Testament, and those who witnessed Jesus' life, and Jesus himself, and the words "Metaphysics" and "Spiritual" could be used when describing events occurring in the past of many people's lives around the world. But in reality, "religious" events have been occurring from the dawn of time and throughout time and even today. These people that I speak of, claim to have communicated with God. And some of these people have written books about their communications with God, but many more have not recorded their communications. The important thing that I see is that most of what those who have written or said, lines up and overlaps with each other and with many parts of the different bibles. Therefore, all these messages seem to be coming from the same source; the Creator.

All the written and spoken communications with God tell of love, inter-peace, Heaven, afterlife and a Creator or God, and all indicate they are being told to help people and not to harm people.

Most who truly follow a major religion will say, "God or Jesus do not communicate with humans today." Why? Did those who lived in the days of The Old Testament hear God say, "I have said all that is needed"?

Did all people who lived in the time of Jesus believe he was communicating with God - the Father? Did Jesus say all that was needed forever or did he say the things that were needed just for those who lived during his days?

Jesus said he would return, but did he say he would be in body? He only said something like, "All men will see me." The only way all men around the world could see him at the same time is if he is in Spirit and not in body! For then, he could be in all places at the same time!

I have seen and talked with Jesus. I know of others who have seen him as well. Has he returned and now it is just a matter of time before all men see him?

In one conversation with God's Angels, I said, "I had other questions, but I cannot remember what they were."

They replied, "They must not have been important."

I have not asked Jesus if he has returned for the end of time as the Christian Bible said he would, for it is not important to me.

Each of us has our own "end of time." The end of time for the world should not be important to you nor should the knowledge of your end of time be important to you, for you should only focus on finding happiness and inner-peace during your life and not afterward.

Recently, on the ULC Forum, I posted the question, "What will I find in Heaven?"

Each of us are different, and we all have different things that will give us the inner-peace that we seek during our lives; I was trying to cause people to search their hearts for what would make them happy. The questions that I lay before them were to help each realize that Heaven in the afterlife will not make them happy here on earth; I try to help people find what brings them inner-peace and happiness, for God does not command us to have inner-peace and happiness based on our knowledge of Him. But He does demand that we have inner-peace and happiness when we join with Him in Heaven.

Most people have been taught that only communications human can have with those from the Other Side are evil. It is insane for anyone, who is religious or otherwise, to think God or His Angels DO NOT communicate with people today. And many whom I tell that I communicate with God's Angels, warn me, "You must test them."

I need not test those who lead me toward the Father with love. Just as I need not to test those who try to lead me away from God with hatred and jealousy in their hearts. For I know that most religious people only embrace their religion and not the Father while God's Angels and the Father embrace human inner-peace with love. But above all, I did not need Entities from the Other Side to convince or guide me to be bad and evil, I was bad and evil before they came into my life, THEY directed me to God, THEY turned me from bad to good, THEY helped me find my Salvation. Therefore, should I "test" them, the ones who helped me?

Concerning in the recent Catholic Priest Sexual Abuse Scandal, did you hear those who committed the acts, or the Bishops, or the Pope, say anything about the predators going to Hell? Did any of them say anything about what God might do to the offenders? Does anyone who commits an evil act toward another believe God exist? Those who run the Catholic religion and Catholic churches only have hatred and lust in their hearts. They lead people away from the Father, for they do not believe in God nor do they have love for Him. We need not "test" the Catholic religion for we know where their hearts are.

Around the end of the first millennium, the Christians carried out crusades against the Muslims for control over Jerusalem. The first crusade was successful because they did it for God, but men did not keep God in their hearts and allowed Jerusalem to fall back into the hands of the Muslims. And then, their crusades that followed failed because they were for the Church and the evil that dwelled in their hearts, and not for the love of God.

God allows us whatever we wish.

The first crusade; The people desired God's Will.

And the crusades that followed; The people wanted fulfillment of lustful things in their hearts.

Those who hold God in their hearts and their actions, God communicates with them. And for those who hold their religion above God, He allows them to worship their god.

So…where is your Heaven? Is it where you wish it to be? Is it where you are now?

What is your Heaven? Is your Heaven all the earthy things that you desire and hope someday to own such as a mansion on a street paved with gold, or is your Heaven the image of you down on your knees worshipping God forever, or is it the inner-peace you find in God's house - your heart?

Both; Metaphysics and Spiritualism are appropriate descriptive words used for describing conversations with God. But, today, both; Metaphysics and Spiritualism along with religions have doctrines (guide-lines) that were written by men for control over others that people believe must be followed in order for God to communicate with us. And these doctrines speak of things that humans think God desires or disapproves of.

Therefore, it does not matter if you follow Metaphysics, Spiritually, Jesus or any religion or some other doctrines. What counts is what is in your heart and how you embrace God. For Scripture of any religion is recorded doctrines of spiritual and metaphysic events that occurred during the time of history. And from these events Judaism, Christianity and Islam have risen. And events of Metaphysics and Spiritually continue to happen today just as they did in the life of the (Judaism, Christianity and Islamic) bible stories. Therefore, I communicate with God's Angels, and all who are of Metaphysics and Spiritually are "writing" the new words from God.

Understanding Religions

And Jesus said unto me, "Many understand religions, but few speak the truth. People place their personal thoughts into others' thoughts on religions, so that each individually choose their beliefs based on what a few believe."

In keeping with the request of Jesus, the following is the writing of John Roberts of Sydney, Australia.

The Divine Origin of Man

Being thoughts on comparative religion and the relationship of Mankind to the Creator.

Introduction

Men have always pondered the question of the existence of God (or Gods) and the relationship, if any, which exists between Mankind and its Creator. This is a necessary and healthy practice, for it stimulates the intellect and promotes the continuous refinement of ideas on this most important of all subjects. Such curiosity has resulted in the formulation of many religious systems. Each differs in its concepts and approach to the question of how best to live or relate to one's fellows. Should the tendency to question belief become restricted, as in the case of totalitarian religious systems, the parent body becomes moribund and stagnant, as is apparent in the case of all the major religions of the present day. These notes are an attempt to place in perspective the writer's ideas regarding the major world-

religions: their strengths and weaknesses.

Religious Practice

Religious practice varies widely, from the simple totemism of the Australian Aborigines, to the complex theology of the Catholic Church: from the simple worship of the Great Spirit by indigenous Americans, to the intellectual philosophy of Buddhism.

The Aborigines visualize a "Dream Time", in the remote past, when their own particular world was created. Common animals and objects take on spiritual significance and animals figure largely in the mythology of the creation. There is no concept of a Creator Spirit, as such, and a great deal of superstitious speculation appears to be present, in regard to their beliefs as to the nature of death and the beyond. Much of Aboriginal ritual is devoted to placating the spirits of the dead. Isolated, as they were for countless thousands of years from other emerging civilizations, the Aborigines remained in a virtually static evolutionary condition. It would be true to assert that Aboriginal "religion" was, perhaps, the most primitive form to be found on Earth. Since the advent of the White Man, of course, they have been the object of much ardent proselytising on the part of both Catholic and Protestant Churches. Tribal Aborigines display a uniquely simple spirituality. Much of their traditional life remains hidden from the prying eyes of the newcomers.

The Jewish religion, of course, forms the basis upon which the two world-religions, Christianity and Islam, were engrafted. The Jews initially worshipped their tribal God, Yaweh or Elohim. He was a typical tribal deity and strictly partial to the tribe of the Israelites. Over a period of perhaps a thousand years, the Jewish idea of God developed into the concept of a Deity who is the Creator of all things. This is a strictly Unitarian concept: the Jewish God is omnipotent, omniscient, compassionate and, ultimately, a caring and concerned Deity, who particularly cares for the Jewish people. Happily, the Jews were commanded by their early leader, Moses, to refrain from constructing images or idols, representing their Deity. This rule prevented them from deteriorating into a polytheist tribe. Thus, the Jewish idea of God becomes an abstract, intangible concept, in spite of the tendency to anthropomorphise their God. The great Temple of Jerusalem contained no idols or other images of created things, which might detract from contemplation of the true nature of God.

Christine J. Haven

Whilst Islam has remained, essentially, a united faith, having only two main streams, the Sunni's and the Shia's, Christianity is glaringly divided, primarily into Catholic, Eastern-Catholic (Orthodox) and Protestant Camps. The Catholic and Orthodox Faiths differ only in respect of a highly technical question as to the nature of the Christ and His relationship to the Father: the doctrine of "Transsubstantiation". I do not propose to go into a discussion of Arianism, which I am not qualified to canvas.

Protestant Christianity is split into a myriad sects, all teaching similar doctrines, in essence, yet differing widely in their approach to the question of worship and practice. Such differences range from the Anglo-Catholicism of certain extreme sections of the English Church, which is indistinguishable from Catholicism, to the strict puritanism of the Quakers and Calvinists.

Within the Christian World, the Church of England has now found a place for the Unbeliever. The situation prevails within the Anglican Communion wherein a Clergyman may deny the existence of God, yet still insist upon his right to remain in Holy Orders. This takes the concept of the Career-minded Clergyman to its natural conclusion: the Agnostic Priest: a person dedicated to the service of a God, of whose existence he has no sound conviction. One would not expect to hear highly inspirational words proceeding from the mouth of such a Minister.

As a child, I observed the inspirational destitution of many young clergymen, as they struggled vainly to express themselves during the mindless formalism of the Anglican Church Service. In contrast, I recall the lofty and nobly expressed idealism of Garfield Williams, a former Dean of Manchester. Williams was greatly influenced by the writings of Paul the Apostle. He thundered forth his Sermons with such force of inspiration as to leave an indelible impression upon the mind of at least one small boy of 12 or so years. Williams' Calvinism was no barrier to the flow of his lofty and powerfully expressed ideas. He was truly inspired.

One interesting branch of Protestantism is Unitarianism, which acknowledges the essential Unity of the Deity and rejects the doctrine of the Trinity. I believe that Unitarians accept the other major points of Christian doctrine.

The outlook of many lesser Calvinistic Sects is circumspect: hardly reflecting the lovely precepts of the Founder. If God is comprehended at all by these people, it is as an essentially all-powerful, rather childish personality, endowed with most of the weaker attributes of the Human Race. All mankind is at the mercy of this selfish deity, who grants salvation by indiscriminate "Grace" to an infinitely small segment of humanity: the remainder, regardless of works, being consigned to perdition.

Islam, the second world-religion, acknowledges the unity of all things in Creation: that everything, mankind included, is inseparably linked to the Creator. This is a noble and very practical idea and one, which led, no doubt, to the rapid growth of Islam in the 7th Century AD.

There is no Priesthood in Islam, another highly commendable rule, although certain individuals do assume the role of "prayer-leader" or Immam. Not being a Muslim myself, I do not know exactly how prayer is conducted in the mosque, but the sight of rows of individuals with their foreheads to the ground leaves one with a sense of the devotion of Muslims to the cause: with a sense of the depth of their religious feelings.

Regarding the image of Islam in the Western world: one is hardly encouraged to seek deep spiritual significance, when faced with the pronouncements of Ayatollah's, calling for the destruction of their opponents. The voice of healthy criticism is prematurely stifled by the threat of vengeance for real or imagined insults to the teachings or the person of the "Prophet". "Kill God's enemies!" is the catchphrase. The absence of a progressive and spiritually enlightened influence in Islam must spell its inevitable decline as a force in human affairs. This in spite of the activity of the Fundamentalists. Hate must always be a destructive rather than a creative element in any philosophical system.

Prior to the commencement of the Christian Crusades in the 12th Century, relations between the Saracens and the Christians were tolerably good. Islam recognized the special relationship that existed between those faiths based upon the Old Testament and the New Testament. The Prophet Muhammad expressly commanded tolerance of Christian and Jewish religious practice in the conquered lands. (The People of the Book). However, the barbarous behaviour of the

Christian Crusaders towards Jews and Muslims alike, in the Holy Land, quickly soured relations between East and West. This unhappy development was not improved by the activities of Colonialist European powers, during the period of 17th to 19th-Century colonial expansion.

It must be conceded that prevailing hostility towards Westernisation of Muslim communities is partly, if not largely, the result of the failure of many Western Nations to maintain proper moral standards within their own spheres. The extent of the decadence which has developed increasingly in nominally Christian lands, in recent years, is appalling, with a rapid decline in moral standards. Strict Muslims are, naturally, anxious to avoid a breakdown of their own standards on such questions as drug-addiction, alcoholism, homosexuality and pornography.

As a result of such fears, the appalling suppression of the rights of women in Islam is certain to have a retarding effect upon the progress of the Islamic nations. This is particularly evident in Afghanistan, where restrictions on the activities of women, both culturally and intellectually, are so severe as to stifle all aspirations of women to lead a useful and constructive life. Women are beaten unmercifully, in public, for the slightest breach of the rules regarding dress or deportment, imposed by their male counterparts. Some have been killed for trivial offences. Many professional females have been forced to discontinue working and remain imprisoned in their homes.

Similar, but not so oppressive, restrictions were imposed on women in Iran, in the 70's, following the revolution which deposed the Shah. Hopefully, recent liberal developments in that country may eventually result in an improvement in the lot of women in Iran. The same cannot be said for the Islamic lands of Algeria and Morocco, in which women are increasingly being subjected to unreasonable pressure to conform to strict Islamic codes of dress and behaviour.

The Hindu religious system has created a distinct hierarchy of Gods and Goddesses, with the principle God, Brahma being the supreme source of all things. Two lesser Gods, Vishnu and Krishna, are of great importance in this hierarchy, whilst thousands of minor deities, exhibiting certain divine attributes, are worshipped throughout India. Never having visited India, I cannot comment further upon the specific beliefs of the Hindu's, although the principle writings of Hinduism, the Mahabharata (Bhagavad-Gita), reveal a quite enlightened spiritual philosophy.

Militant Hinduism can be criticised for its intolerant attitude towards other minority religions and, particularly, its antagonism towards the Musselmen. There is no doubt that antagonism has been smouldering between Muslim and Hindu for centuries, following the Muslim conquest of much of India in the 16th Century. Even during the Raj, the British found it impossible to control outbreaks of sectarian violence between Hindu and Muslim. This hostility has now found its full scope in the violent war being conducted, sporadically, between India and Pakistan, on the question of Kashmir.

Concepts of Deity

Human beings certainly worship many versions of Deity. The Christian has a vague idea of a God in Three Persons (God the Father, God and Son (In the person of Jesus) and God the Holy Spirit. This, in spite of argument to the contrary, is a polytheist religion, albeit not quite so complex as the Hindu faith. Of course, early Christianity developed in Rome, notoriously Pagan and worshipping numerous Gods. It was inevitable that Christians would be influenced, throughout centuries of growth, by rubbing shoulders with Roman Pagans. The net result is the Catholic Church as we perceive it today: not greatly differing from the old religion in many respects: worshipping three aspects of God and many Saints.

The Jew, of course, worships his own limited form of a Supreme God, Jahweh, all powerful, yet merciful: sometimes cruel but justly so. He is intolerant and demands total obedience to his laws. He is particularly partial to the Jewish people and looks after them very well.

The Islamic God is substantially the same deity as that conceived by the Jews, but reveals a distinct fondness for the people of Islam. The prophet Muhammad, is the last and greatest of the prophets, since when revelation has ceased.

Anthropomorphic images of God leave Mankind at the mercy of a domineering and vindictive Deity, who regards the objects of His creative activity with indifference and contempt. Such a God is highly convenient in times of human conflict, when He can be invoked to support the nefarious ambitions of those who conduct aggressive *warfare against their neighbours. Very free use has been made of the claim to have the support of Deity in the course of warfare and other bloody persecutions, throughout the history of mankind.*

The Hindu's worship, essentially the Supreme Being, Brahma and to this extent, I suppose, Hinduism is essentially monotheistic. However, intruding into the vision of the supremely divine intelligence, is an host of lesser deities, too numerous to detail, who I suppose, all represent certain aspects of Deity. Whilst not by any means an authority on the Hindu (or any other) religion, I would imagine that from the higher Caste Hindu's down to the lower, underprivileged Caste's, there is a great variety of forms of belief and worship.

Buddhism, classed as a religion, is perhaps more a philosophy of living than a strictly religious idea. Certainly, in its variations, it has a religious significance of some importance.

In China, Confucianism and Taoism were the principle philosophies for many centuries and, like Buddhism, were systems of moral philosophy rather than religious doctrines. Running side by side with these ideas were the nature-religions of the masses, including the recognition of the survival of the soul after death. Even today, Chinese Buddhism incorporates a belief in a form of spiritual communion, in which presents and offerings are made to the spirits of the ancestors. A commendable practice, yet hardly necessary, as those who have passed into the spirit-world have no need of physical objects of any nature.

Buddhism, originally an offshoot of Hinduism, offers solutions to the problems of daily living. It accepts the concept of Brahma: a somewhat abstract Creator Spirit, but does not conceive of a God in the form familiar to Western minds. Buddhism, in its original form was a religion of "Reason" rather than of "Faith": of intellect rather than emotion. The vacuum for lay Buddhists is filled by Buddha: whose huge images are calculated to induce an emotive response. One cannot deny the overpowering effect of the sight of a massive statue of the Buddha. One is left with an impression of the All-seeing eye of the Buddha.

A distinction needs to be drawn between the lofty, barely comprehensible, concepts of Gautama and the modern practice of

Buddhism, which necessarily concentrates upon the practical and daily aspects of life, without, apparently, questioning too deeply the value of its procedures. The absence of a personal Deity in Buddhist teachings is perhaps an indication of a reaction on the part of the Founder to the excesses of the Hindu Pantheon. The Buddha himself has, to some extent, evolved into a Demi-God.

(I have been criticised recently (1999) for this view of Buddhist belief, on the grounds that Buddhists do not accept the idea of Brahma. My understanding of the original teachings of Gautama was that: although brought up as an Hindu, he formulated his own philosophy, without emphasis upon the nature of Brahma, rather than by adopting a form of direct denial. I also believe that he taught that "Enlightenment" is synonymous with "Annihilation", which leads to the loss of individual consciousness in the merging of the enlightened soul with Brahma. I mean no disrespect to Buddhists but cannot overlook the undoubted fact that there is a vast gulf between the high-minded philosophical speculations of the intelligentsia and the practical day-to-day religious ideas of the masses. (This principle applies to all religious practice, of course.) From my limited reading on Buddhism, it appears to me that there are wide discrepancies in the religious practices of Buddhists world-wide and that it would be hard to generalise as to what, precisely, Buddhists really believe. What I have myself observed, is Buddhists at prayer, rather than at meditation. If Buddhists pray, to whom or to what do they offer their invocations? Buddhism, like all religious practices, must shed itself of superfluous ritual and grossly superstitious practices, if it is to find credibility in Western minds. (4.5.99.)

Buddhism propounds ways towards the attainment of enlightenment through disciplinary exercises, meditation and good-conduct, in order to acquire "Merit". It advocates Monastic withdrawal from the world, as a way of avoiding contamination and to facilitate a more rapid transition to the state of Nirvana (or total inner harmony). The attainment of enlightenment results in Union with Brahma and release from the perpetual cycle of re-birth, which is said to be the lot of the generality of the Human Race.

Religious Withdrawal

The following is another writing by learned John Roberts of Sydney, Australia.

The idea of the avoidance of contamination has appealed to people of all religious persuasions. Methods of acquiring "Merit" appear to be artificial and, in my opinion, to some extent futile.

Buddhism acknowledges that man is weak and incapable of leading a "good" life under the normal circumstances of human intercourse. Yet how is genuineness of character to be assessed, if not within the normal range of human experience? How easy is it to withdraw from life's responsibilities and seek the freedom from temptation and lust, which the monastic life offers? What finer test of a person's mettle is there than the response of the individual to the demands of family life? It is surely only within the framework of normal community activity that the calibre of individual conduct is seen in its true perspective. This criticism of the principle of withdrawal applies irrespective of the particular Faith involved. I would not deny that a period of withdrawal from the worldly life could be beneficial, as is customary in Siam, (Thailand) where most young men traditionally entered a Monastery to experience the life of a monk for a period of some months. Such a retirement would enable a youth to reflect upon his life and, perhaps, assist him in the planning of his future career.

It seems to me that conduct of any kind, necessarily, has good or evil consequences, in varying degree, and this is the product of human activity. If the result of selfish motivation, then the normal consequences flow to the perpetrator of the action: on the principle that everyone is the product of his or her own activity. That this is another form of the law of "Karma" is perhaps correct, with the proviso that the consequences are immediate and not operative at some future time or in a later incarnation. To suggest that Karma accumulated in previous incarnations, affects one's lifestyle in the present seems ludicrous to the Christian, who does not in any event accept the doctrine of the laws of Reincarnation and Karma.

The existence of the "Prayer Wheel" in Buddhist ritual, in which prayers are conveniently repeated with each turn of the wheel, calls to mind the admonition of Jesus of Nazareth regarding "Vain Repetitions" (Matt. Ch 6 v 7). One could, perhaps, be excused if sceptical regarding the degree of "Merit" to be obtained by turning a prayer wheel.

Another form of apparently useless activity is the practice of certain Indian Sadhu's (Holy Men), members of the Jain Sect, who adopt self-mortification as a way to salvation. Some adopt and maintain difficult and painful physical postures for years, until the muscles become atrophied and paralysis ensues. In this manner do they effectively mutilate themselves, in the hope of obtaining merit through self-inflicted suffering. What a dreadful waste and misunderstanding of the Spiritual Law! Apart from this unfortunate practice, the beliefs of the Jains appear to be of a highly evolved nature. Many advanced Jains adopt nudity as a way of expressing their rejection of worldly standards. Such a practice also has doubtful value, being in the nature of a symbolic device. In the relatively warm climate of India this may be tolerable but in colder regions would be quite impracticable.

Prayer

Of course, my reference to "vain repetitions" is equally applicable to the pathetic "prayers" used by all the major Christian sects, in endless and futile repetition. This simply means that there is, in such instances, a failure to appreciate the meaning and significance of prayer, as a means of communication with the Deity or with those Ministering Spirits in the Spirit-World, whose task is to act as helpmates to struggling men and women of this world. What is more pathetic, is that this practice totally ignores the express mandate of Jesus. What is known as "The Lord's Prayer" is just such a vain repetition, although originally a simple demonstration of the nature of prayer.

Within the Spiritualist Movement, we now have the phenomenon of the "Great Invocation", so-called, which purports to be a mystical and collective vehicle of worship. This prayer is recited in many meetings, as a matter of course and is, in effect, a classical example of an utterly useless vain-repetition. When will men and women start to think about what they are repeating?

It is an unfortunate fact that most Westerners have totally lost the capacity for prayer. This is definitely true of the Spiritualist Movement today. There is a failure to understand that this simple procedure is the channel by which mankind communicates with its Creator: by the simple offering of oneself in acknowledgement: in gratitude for the gift of life; for material and spiritual gifts and for the modest intellect with which we are endowed. In the place of prayer is substituted the idea that "meditation" will achieve the desired result: the development of spiritual gifts.

It is true of all religions that a lofty concept on the part of the founder soon gives way to ignorant and superstitious practices when subjected to the interpretation of later adherents. The semi-literate masses need to be supplied with physical evidence of spiritual ideas in the form of images, ritual, rich priestly vestments and pre-fabricated prayers, before religion becomes comprehensible to them.

Love as the Divine Attribute

Mahatma Ghandi proclaimed himself to be a member of all the great religions of India and attempted to destroy sectarian divisions by this approach. He recognized the essential truth underlying each and every approach to the Godhead. However, he could not overcome the bigotry and hatred of centuries of smouldering conflict, which eventually resulted in the division of his country and a resultant bloodbath in the slaughter of thousands of Muslims and Hindus.

Jewish (and, hence, Muslim and to some extent Christian) ideas as to the "Nature" of God have produced a Deity who is limited in every degree. Yaweh and Allah both suffer from the consequences of having been created in Man's image and not the reverse. (One has to concede that the Jewish Prophet, Isaiah, made a considerable contribution towards the development of the idea of God, as a loving and compassionate Deity.)

The Christian concept has been modified by the confusing doctrine of the Trinity, but at least the Christian God has acquired some attributes as a result of the activity of Jesus, which can be considered to be progressive in nature. The existence of the "Holy Spirit", as forming part of this collective Deity is an acknowledgement of the fact that God is active in the superintendence of His work of Creation.

In fact, the net result of the Ministry of Jesus is the transformation of the more vengeful and terrifying aspects of Yahweh's personality into attributes consistent with an enlightened concept of the nature of God. God is Perfect. Man is commanded to be, likewise, Perfect: to follow the example of his Creator. (Matt. Ch 5, v 48).

"Love" was to be the cornerstone of the new establishment. (John Ch 13, v 34). Love is the Divine attribute! The injunction towards universal love was very soon disregarded by the followers of Jesus, as is evident from a perusal of the Acts of the Apostles. From time to time, however, the precept has been understood and observed by those gentler disciples of the Master. Happily, his words remain as an inspiration for later generations of Christians.

Life Everlasting

Another chapter by learned John Roberts of Sydney, Australia.
The message that Jesus was commanded to give to Mankind, was a promise of "Life everlasting". (John Ch 12 v 50). This is a promise indeed: no longer a prospect of annihilation or worse. The precise nature of this, "Life everlasting" remains indistinct, yet the fact was that Jesus emphasized that he had been sent with this specific injunction to declare the promise to mankind. To me, it means the certainty of an immediate resurrection upon the physical death, for all humankind. The nature of the future life is to depend very largely upon the quality of the life of the body; i.e. the degree of spiritual maturity attained by the individual.

But, the words used and spoken back then, do not mean the same today. "Life Everlasting" actually meant our Souls, (our record experiences, all that we did in our lives, will be remembered forever in God's thoughts of life) our lives do not continue, only our past life remains and lives forever.

Thus it is clear that Jesus added a wonderful new dimension to Mankind's concept of the Creator God. More importantly, to the relationship which exists between God and Man. No longer is mankind a plaything with which God diverts His leisure moments. Jesus informs us that we are God's children. Accordingly, we can no longer be subject to the doctrine of Original Sin, which is seen to be absurd. Indeed, how can this be when Jesus expressly commands us to seek the perfection of God? There was here no suggestion of a future Vicarious Atonement but an unconditional commandment, "Be ye, therefore, Perfect!" (Matt Ch 5, v 48).

I have recently read an essay by a learned Jew on the question of the historicity of Jesus. ("Refuting Missionaries" by one, Hayyim ben Yehoshua). The essay denies the validity of any historical evidence for the existence of Jesus of Nazareth and claims that he is a composite drawn from three historical figures of the pre-Christian era. He goes on to affirm the fictitious nature of much of the writings of the New Testament.

This is, no doubt, a reasonable argument, in as much as little is known of the factual history of the times and, particularly, of the period prior to the sack of Jerusalem in AD 70. However, modern Spiritualist experience is able to confirm much of the recorded history of the life of Jesus and the events recorded in the Acts of the Apostles and the letters of Paul, but documents of Jesus' life and death can be found in recorded Roman history even still today. In essence, it does not matter a great deal whether Jesus and Paul were fictitious figures or not. What is important is the recorded message they (or the actual originators of the doctrines) left to humanity, and this was a message, primarily to Jews as well as Gentiles. The Sermon on the Mount stands as irrefutable evidence of the wisdom of this individual, whosoever he may have been. The record of the events subsequent to the death of Jesus and the outpouring of the Spirit, at Pentecost, are fully confirmed in the experience of Spiritualists today. Like the first Christians, Spiritualists are maligned and calumniated by the ignorant, as were the followers of the Nazarene.

Sadly, the Christian Church in two thousand years of implementation of the teachings of Jesus, has fallen far short of the mark in maintaining his standards. Indeed, it could be safely affirmed that Jesus has been totally disregarded, except as a nominal figurehead. Images of long dead Gods and Goddesses have been invoked in shoring-up the edifice of Holy Mother Church. Astarte (Ashtoreth), Minerva, The Earth-Mother, (Queen of Heaven), symbol of fertility and fruitfulness has become Our Lady, Mother of our Lord. This lady is venerated and worshipped as freely as of old. In place of the old Gods, stand the images of the Saints, many of whom are *frauds:* e.g., St. George, St. Christopher. *(Many have, in recent years, been demoted, in recognition of the fact that they were figments of someone's all too vivid imagination). Rich vestments and cloth-of-gold are much in evidence.*

Solemn processions are held, with pomp and ceremony, during which images of the Saints are displayed to the masses: just what they need to keep them entertained and in awe of the splendour of the occasion. The service itself is ritualistic: tinkling bells, holy water, incense: the Mystery of the Eucharist: the bloodless sacrifice of the Mass. This ritual is a legacy from the animal sacrifices of Ancient Rome and has nothing whatever to do with the true Holy Communion, which is the Communion of Spirit.

Fortunately for the sanity of the average person, many priests and ministers sincerely endeavour to instil into the minds of their parishioners the Christian principles of love and service to their fellows.

Does "God" Exist?

By learned John Roberts of Sydney, Australia.

How does one approach the question of the Existence of God? Philosophy has proved conclusively that God does not exist. God has been defined as, "The greatest conceivable being!" This definition in itself is misleading, as it seems clear to me that such a definition falls far short of a comprehensive idea of Deity. It is also perhaps true to suggest that one could not begin to conceive the nature of God, such being beyond human capacity. That being so, then all further argument is futile. If, however, one is convinced of the fact of the resurrection: the continuance of life beyond the physical death, then must all doubt as to the existence of a Divine Intelligence be laid aside.

Referring to the doctrine of the resurrection from the dead, (1 Corinthians Ch 15 verse 12): the Apostle Paul, suggested that: if there is no truth in the doctrine that Christ rose from the dead then, "is our preaching vain and your faith also is vain". He emphasized the importance of the Doctrine, when he said, "If after the manner of men I have fought with Beasts at Ephesus, what will it profit me if the dead rise not?" (v 32). All his striving would have been futile, if there was no truth in this teaching. Happily, one is able to affirm the truth of the Resurrection and, consequently, the existence of God.

What then is the purpose of maintaining or striving after high personal standards? If there is no guiding or directing hand, how is *one to benefit from "good-works" or how can the very concept of "goodness" be any different from our concept of "evil"?*

What is the point of working for the good of mankind?

Clearly, if there is no moral or progressive advantage in being better, rather than worse, why should one be concerned at all?

The answer lies in the self-evident truth that constructive activity of any kind has advantages over destructive behaviour and results in greater security and hence, greater happiness for men and women. Destructive behaviour produces nothing of use or utility and is, prima-facie, less desirable than good works. The same can be said in respect of all activity of any nature or degree. Man is capable of evaluating for himself the quality of his own behaviour and also that of his peers. It, therefore, follows that belief in the existence of Deity is not essential for the development of sound moral ideas or the leading of a spiritual life.

But an enlightened religious belief helps a person to understand why he has been granted the gift of life and points the way ahead.

Is God Dead?

During the aftermath of September the 11th, many donated millions of dollars to victims and their families. About two months later, most of this money had not been delivered to its intended recipients. Now, we hear that most of those millions of dollars will be used for other programs, and if anyone wishes to have their money back, just ask and it will be returned.

At most funerals, a preacher speaks of all the good things about the deceased, and about all the good deeds that person did in his or her life. Any Sunday, one can enter a Christian Church, a house of God, and hear a preacher talking about and worshipping Jesus. Thus, the preacher speaks of all the good things that Jesus did in his life as though he is dead. The preacher may also speak of God, but only what occurred during the lives of the people of the Old Testament, as if God does not exist anymore.

Around 325AD, the old Roman Church canonized the Christian Bible. In other words, they decided what stories of history should be included or deleted from the Bible and also, what things meant in the Bible; such as Jesus is God. Therefore, Christians do not follow God but instead they follow their religions which came a Bible that was conceived by the old Roman Church. Therefore, they are following another man's ideas and concepts of God.

Christians of today, act as if they do not think God is involved in our lives anymore. Today, peoples' daily lives do not contain God.

They act as if God died on the cross with Jesus, or He just does not care about us anymore. The church leaders ask for more money to build bigger and better churches. Maybe they think if they build a bigger and better church, God will Bless them more than those who go to a little or poor churches.

Keep this thought in mind and let's go back to the aftermath of September 11th for a minute. So why did all those people give money to the victims and their families who suffered on September, 11th?

Was it from the goodness of their hearts (the Angel-within, that is part of God) or from guilt? Or maybe, they were trying to show others that they are Christians. God surely does not need for us to prove ourselves to Him.

I did not give money to those funds that were suppose to help the victims and their families. Sure, I felt sadden by the actions that took so many lives. I give to those who need help, but most do not need help of money, they need love and help to rise themselves in self respect, then, they can help themselves. But, now let's get back to what I was talking about; is God dead?

I understand that in the Book of James of the New Testament, it says; "I said," and "He said," and then, "I said," and "he said," that is a conversation between Jesus and James, and not a preacher standing up in front, on a stage, telling a group of people what he thinks.

In the Book of James, it indicates James and Jesus had a conversation. In other words, Jesus allowed others to join in and ask questions and have input into their conversation. He was equal to the people that he was talking with. The preachers place themselves above the people and refuse questions and input into their sermon.

In the Bible, it talks of; beware of walking up onto an Altar and allowing others to see that you are no better than they. Whenever a preacher climbs up onto the stage and gives a sermon, he has placed himself higher, as if closer to God than his congregation, and his actions allow others to see he is no better than they.

Yes, God is dead in the churches and that is because the preachers will not let Him live in their hearts! And the flock shall follow its shepherd. Therefore, all who listens to the preachers who refuses input and question during his sermon consider God as if He is dead. I believe that Jesus only did one sermon and that was the Sermon on the Mound.

So, whom does the Christian preacher follow? God or the old Roman Church?

Is God in your daily life?

Is God alive in you?

There is a church named something like the Spiritual Temple. They claim they have been talking to the deceased for over a hundred years. And yet, they refuse to consider that Angels and Jesus have communicated with me, while other churches also refuse to discuss about God's Angels and Jesus visiting me. If Jesus visited others after his resurrection, then can he not visit you, or I, or whomever he wishes? But many people do believe that the Virgin Mother, Mary had been seen by some today. Why? Is Jesus and God dead? Is Mary the only one alive today?

Those who attend church today, only go for the religion and not for God nor Jesus. They only go to hear that God and Jesus once lived and to hear the preacher's comments about God's involvement with those of the Bible.

Yes, God is dead in most churches and in the hearts of many who attend church, and in most of those who claim to be Christians, for they have placed Jesus - the Son of God, above the Father. And most Catholics have placed their Saints and the Virgin Mother Mary above both, Jesus and God, as demonstrated when they pray and/or worship to Mary and/or the Saints.

The Messages from God's Angels and the things that I speak about are revealed for you to see and recall the things that indicate that They are alive and involved into our daily lives. If you remember Their touch - things They have done in your life, then They are real and stand beside you. If you cannot remember Their touch, then They are dead, for you are of the dead.

And I pray, "Dear Father, thank you for another day and all that You have given me today, for the guidness, protection and inspiration that You have allowed Your Angels to grant me and my family throughout the past, this day and for all the days to come. I shall try to live by Your Inspirations that has been shown to me. Please forgive me as I forgive others whenever the dog becomes unleashed. Amen."

Living God's Will

All wars are caused and driven by different beliefs of people. The present day war against Terrorism is no different, for it also is driven by the two religious beliefs of Muslims and Christians. And while the war of terrorism in Isreal is a war of different beliefs systems, it is not driven by two beliefs systems, but one - the Islamic Religion.

The war in Isreal is driven by two different beliefs systems trying to occupy and control the same land. The Jewish beliefs are that of pacifist; they do not force others to join in their religion nor do they force other religions out while on the other hand, Muslims demand that others submit to their god and they force others out of their holy places and change them into Islamic holy places.

The present day World Conflict is not a war merely against Terrorism, but is a war between Christianity and Islamic rule of the world.

Islam is not the religion of God, for it is a religion created by man.

The Islamic religion is not just a religious belief system, it is also a governmental system; If one who is not Muslim lives in a Islamic community or country, he cannot take part in governmental affairs - he cannot take part in deciding or voting on the laws that govern the land of the town or the country in which he resides, and he can only worship his God as described in the Islamic laws, for to the Muslim, he is an infidel - one who has not submitted to Allah - one who is less than a dog!

Islamic governments teaches only the Qur'an and basic math in their public education systems.

All Islamic governments have a spiritual leader who dicates and rules over the country. This spiritual leader is not voted into office by the people, he is appointed by a governmental board of spiritual leaders.

The spiritual leader rules directly by what he interprets is written into the Qur'an.
And it is the commandment from Allah for all Muslims to convert all the people to Islam - to persuade by convincing or forcing them to submit to the Islamic God - Allah. They will not stop until their religion covers the world and the world is one country without boundaries and this is indicated presently in the destruction of the southern border in the United States of America.

Christianity is not the religion of God, for it is the religion created by man. No matter what we say, the U.S.A. is a Christian country. We have Christian views and standards; Freedom for all, each person may pursue his individual happiness, we claim that we allow other religions their place in our communities; we allow others of different religions to paricipate in governmental affairs and any one can be elected into political office. But Christian values and beliefs are forced onto the people by Christians who ruthlessly demand you to change your religion when they forcefully continually to speak to you about Jesus "Christ" and your salvation without your consent to talk with them about your belief system. And as I said, "We say that we allow different religions into our communities," we do, but Christians will continue to pound their beliefs into the ears of people of different religions until they submit to "Jesus as Lord!" and it is their, the Christian church leaders, concept to spread Christianity around the world for the salvation of all the people and the world - a world that is controlled by Christian concepts and values.

As we watch the events unfold in Iraq, we can see that our country, the U.S.A., is trying to place a democracy government, Christian values, over Iraq. This may sound well and good if you are

Christian, but the Iraqi people are Muslims and they want and will only accept an Islamic government.

Christian and Muslim cannot live in peace or harmony on the same planet; They have drawn a great line between them that divides them about whose God is the true God. And while the Jew could live in peace and harmony with others of different religions but the Christian and Muslim will not allow others to live peacefully without trying to convert the others of different religions than their own.

The Jewish people are truly God's "Chosen People" - the people who are the center of the World's Conflict, for the Muslims say that all Jews must be driven out of Israel or destroyed, and because Israel was the beginning of the Muslim fight for control of the world.

The Muslims proclaim that the Jew is the cause for their problems. But the true Islamic god's - Muhammad, and not Allah's concepts is their problem. Allah (the arab word for God) proclaims Love for all and not just Muslims.

This World Conflict that we face today has been going on since Muhammad first communicated with Gabrael - approximately 1,400 years ago. God did not bring this conflict to the World. God created Muhammad so he could choose which direction he wished to travel and he chose evilness. Muhammad created the World Conflict for his self-interest.

The word "Israelites" - Israelis as described in the dictionary means descendants of Jacob, the choosen son of Abraham, were given the land of Israel by God.

The word "Muslim" as described in the dictionary means a believer in Islam. Muslims claim to be the descendants of Ishmeal, the bastard son of Abraham, and they claim they are the true owners of Israel.

Islam has stolen the "Monotheism doctrine or belief," that there is one God, and they have placed their God, Allah, as that God. Therefore, if God did give the Israelites Israel, it was Allah who gave the Israelis the land! And whereas, Muslims try to steal Israel from the Israelis as Islam has stolen everything that it presently owns and has. Muhammad was confused and thought as most Muslims think today. But yes, God through His Angel, Gabrael, may have communicated with Muhammad and tried to change him, but it did not work. And therefore, today do you think we can change the views of Muslims?

It will never be won by either side until each Muslims realizes what Muhammad has done and until every Christian realizes that their religious leaders of old and present placed their self-interest into their religion and above God.

As the World Conflict deepens, we shall see new diseases and illnesses come forth from modernized pollution while weather conditions worsen that also will bring more deaths as the people of all religions cry out, "Why," to their man-made gods.

Which God to Follow

As we enter into the month of Ramadan, the Islamic Terrorists have truly demonstrated that each, including them, have freedom of choosing between right and wrong doing. For Islam states that in the month of Ramadan, all Muslims need to fast from eating, drinking and sex, and all Muslims must do good deeds to all others.

Doing good deeds to all others does not mean to Kill Israelis citizens or other people around the world! Therefore, the Islamic Terrorists are not of Allah, but of the DOG! For they follow their human desires instead of Allah's desires.

The Muslims religion speaks of God's Messenger of the Covenant, the one who will be bringing all religions together under one God, and yet, it says their religion, Islam is the religion that will be placed above all other religions as the true religion of God. If this is so, then, God has chosen Islam as His true religion. WRONG! Islam is just another religion that will line up with all religions under God. He does not prefer Islam over any other religion, for all religions are man-made.

But God has given the Muslim the choice of following Him or the Dog feeling of the human. What fools the Muslim is who follows his human feelings, for they know nothing of God.

God through His Angels have placed guards around my home to keep out the evil energy, and you know, to this day, I have not yet seen Muhammad in our house.

Interesting... Islam means to "Submit." The word "Submit" means to go with, even if it is against your will. Well, God is not like that. He allows all to follow their personal desires, even if their personal desires are against God's.

Muslims read the Qur'an over and over again until its words have brainwashed the reader into believing that it is true. How sad to think that any religion must enforce itself upon humans like that.

"Oh Foolish Ones, Muhammad was a fake! He did not see the true Angels as he said he did. He communicated with Satan that he has in his heart. He wanted to be better than the Jew and the Christian, and then he created a false God that he named "Allah" above his man-made religion.

"Muhammad lied to himself, and then to all those who wanted something better than the God that the Jew and Christian worshipped, and yet, the Jew and the Christian do not Embrace their God, for they placed a (their) false God above the true Creator - the Father.

"Islam is full of lies, and all those who follow it are corrupted by the lies that Muhammad proclaimed as true.

"Repent! Repent! Muslim, get down on your knees and "Pray" to the true God above all, that He does not destroy you and all that you think is yours.

"Repent! Repent! Jew, get down upon your knees and "Pray" to the true God above all, that He does not destroy you and all that you think is yours.

"Repent! Repent! Christian, get down on your knees and "Pray" to the true God above all, that He does not destroy you and all that you think is yours.

"For NO religion is better than another! For all of you have followed your false Gods far enough! For it is time for your Salvation - find your direction to the Righteous God above all."

And Jesus said, "Pick up your cross, and follow me."

"Pick up your cross," means to "Leash the dog (human) feelings," for the feelings of the dog are those things that kill you either spiritually or bodily. The "Cross" meant; the thing(s) that will kill you either spiritually or bodily.

"Follow me," means to live the lifestyle that Jesus demonstrated to be Righteous.

And then, Jesus said, "My yoke is light," which meant; he did not do many or none of the evil feelings of the dog - human evil feelings.

These two statements of Jesus, expresses that we have the choice to be good or bad, for Jesus, Son of God, did not or does not force his beliefs or his Father's Will upon us. Therefore, should we, the children of God be any different (have different concepts) than our Father? We should follow the lifestyle that Jesus demonstrated to be Righteous.

(In keeping with our topic of "The Gift of Choice," and to help understand our choosing of a god that we follow, I need to reiterate the creation of man-made gods.)

There is one true God that is above all gods that we have placed above our man-made religions, which are above man. But yet, all religions worship the same God that is at the top. Men have taken communications that they have had with God's Angels (part of God), and changed His words into containing man's thoughts, ideas and concepts and formed gods into their images of what God desires, wants and wills.

Each of the major religions; Christianity and Jewish religions came from direct contact by man with God's Angels. Both speak of their individual Messiah coming to earth as he, their Messiah, places their religion over other religions as the true religion of God's. Whereas, all Metaphysics, and all Spiritualism, and all other beliefs systems have been created by man, come directly or indirectly for some part of the communications that man has had with God. Now, I did not say only the major religions listed above were the only communications man had with God. There are many other conversations men have had with God that are not recorded as communications with God through His Angels. And as with the major religions, all belief systems are corrupted with man's concepts, thoughts and ideas of what God is thinking, and how He looks, and what He wants. Therefore, all beliefs systems have human created god above them, though they worship the same God, who is above their man-made gods.

In the conception of (God allowing man to create) his own religion, whatever religion one wishes to follow is okay as long as it contains and follows what God desires; To love are others and have no domination toward others. For if your religion contains and follows His desires then you shall find your Salvation. But all men have concluded that their religion is the true religion of God, and to know God you must know their belief system (religion), and follow it alone. Therefore, all men have placed their beliefs system (religion) above the true one God. Even those who plead that they truly follow what is Righteous are lost, for they turn and twist their "God concept" into what is right for them. But yet, that is their choice as given to them by God.

One does not need to know any bible to know God. Bibles only contain the accounts of God's interactions with humans, and they (bibles) are only recorded history of human love and hatred for itself.

Directions of God

The three major religons; Christianity, Judaism and Islam, all three religons came forth from supposedly conversations or encounters with the Father (Creator) or His Angels, while each of these religions are mostly based on man's concepts of Him, and what they believe He desires and thinks.

Yahweh is believed to be the Creator and Father in the Judaism religions, but man has placed his demands and laws upon people through his concepts of Yahweh in the Torah.

God is named as the Father and Creator in the Old Testament of the Christian religion, but man has placed his demands and laws upon the people through his concept of God in the Bible. The New Testament placed Jesus as the Father, according to the old Roman Church, but they missed Jesus' teaching of "Love of all others and have no domination toward them." Today, all Christian churchs teach only what Jesus did in His lifetime and not how He demonstrated how we should live together in the congergation of humanity.

Allah is claimed to be the Father and Creator in the Islam religion, but man has placed his demands and laws upon the people through Muhammad's concept and his Qur'an.

Each of these religions places man as His slave, and demands that the human act accordingly to His wishes or be doomed in some type of Hell forever. Do you really think that the father or the Creator of everything would NEED us to go through life, a place where we have free choices, to be His slaves forever? Of course Not!

The pages of each of these religion's Scriptures indicate that the Father is a LOVING God, and not an EVIL DICTATOR! Man's concept of a God has made the Father into an Evil God who demands His creation - man to do as He says.

The Old Testament, which is the foundation to Christianity, truly shows the changes of God's desire for humans to follow.

In the New Testament of the Christian Bible, the recorded history of Jesus tells of a loving Jesus, who is said to be the Son of God. But once again, man has taken his concepts that protrays Jesus as God - turned Jesus into the Lord.

My Funk and Wagnalls Standard Desk Dictionary says, "In Monotheism, God is the ruler of life and the universe." Muslims claim Monotheism as their own, and state Allah is the ruler of life and the universe.

In the correct order of their creation; first came Judaism, Christianity, and then Islam. Each gave a new direction for God's children to follow, but each contained concepts created by human. Even the New Testament, which should have turned the direction of religion from human self-interest toward God, did not work. The New Testament, the lifestyle that Jesus lived, should have brought the people to look outward in a loving and caring manner for others as he demonstrated, but it did not work.

The people needed a "GOD" that was above them, one they could never be close to, but one they could only worship as one would worship a golden calf! Some one or something that was worth more than them! So the people placed Jesus upon a throne and called him "LORD"! And now they worship Jesus as if he is God!

As the Angel Jesus and I watched a program on televion about him, he said, "I did not intend man to call me Lord, or to worship me as God."

Jesus did not preach the religion of Christianity, he taught Judaism without the laws and rules that it contained. He spoke of Love to all of the Father's children and not love just for those who followed him. Jesus did not create Christianity, those who followed him created Christianity out of the things that they thought he said.

We cannot even communicate with other humans and get a complete understanding of what they are talking about, therefore, we surely should understand that when we communicate with the Father or His Angels, there is lost understanding of what they said as we turn their thoughts into our concepts. And that is what has happened with all of those who communicated with humans in the past such as Moses, Jacob and Muhammad. We do not try to analyse each converstation that we have with each person throughout each day of our lives, but yet, we try to analyse each and every word of all those conversations that the Father or His Angels had with each individual years ago. Times have changed, words mean other things today than what they meant years ago, and the needs of humans are different now then they were years ago. The Old Testament and New Testament truly shows the changes God gave humans in their direction of life; examples, first, God did not allow people to eat meat and then He said they could, and the people were first told to perform sacrifices to Him and then told not to, and then Jesus came along and demonstrated to the people that they needed to love each other. And then, if we wish to discuss Islam in the concept of God instructing people how to live; Muhammad came along and he DEMANDED that the people revert back to the old ways of God, as conceived by Man!

The true word of the Father is LOVE!

The true concept of the Father is LOVE!

The true meaning of the Father is LOVE!

The true meaning of life is to experience and enjoy LOVE!

We cannot expect the world to LOVE if we do not show LOVE! We cannot do as we please and expect all others to LOVE us! We are part of the world! We come from the dead and shall return to death! Love is not give and TAKE! LOVE is to give and RECEIVE what is given to you! Embrace the Father by thanking Him for all that He has given you! Do not pray for earthly goods, the Father knows what you need and should have, and you shall receive just that; Follow Evil by being Evil and you shall receive Evil things. Follow Jesus by giving Love and you shall receive Love, and then you have embraced the Father with LOVE!

Judaism, Christianity and Islam all speak of love somewhere is their text, but man has placed his desires and thoughts upon most of their pages. Follow the religion and god that fits your needs, but keep the Love that the Father has placed in their Scriptures in your heart for all others, and you will do fine. And whenever you see or hear someone say something or do something that you disagree with, do not argue with them or become angry with them. Show them love by walking away, for when you argue with someone you are only trying to prove you are right and they are wrong. They do not know and understand as you nor do you know and understand as they. Therefore, allow them to be at the place they are suppose to be at this time in their life. Do not allow hatred to grow within youself. Do not judge another for their thoughts, or concepts, or lifestyle, or actions, but judge their thoughts, or concepts, of lifestyle, or actions to be correct or wrong for you to do.

Choosing What We Follow

Whenever one researches a belief system, and selects only parts and pieces to believe and follow, he then has created his own personal belief system that contains a god that he has created above it. There is no true Christian because no individual Christian truly follows the complete Christian doctrines as they were and are written, but we have "Die Hard Born Again Christians" who create their own and personal religion because each and every Christian merely follows and believes only bits and pieces of the Christian Bible. (These "Die Hard Born Again Christians" are the ones who claim they truly follow the Christian doctrines, but merely follow what they believe to be righteous.) While this concept of creating one's own religion does not pertain only to Christianity, but to all others religions as well.

To illustrate, the "late" Rev. Kirby Hensley who was the founder of Universal Life Church, which has ordained millions of people to minister their own religions, created his own and personal religion from his Christian understanding of God. And this is truly demonstrated in the later writings of the Rev. Hensley where he stated that he is God, but yet, he claimed to be Christian. I cannot remember reading anywhere in the Christian Bible anything about the Rev. Hensley being God. And therefore, if we proclaim that we follow Rev. Hensley's doctrines then we also must believe him to be God, unless we wish to create our own religion by only believing in bits and pieces of the Reverend's made religion and add our personal beliefs to his. If so, then we have created our own religion and placed the God that we have created above it.

One can tell if he has created his God when his God likes and is displeased by the same things that makes him (the person) happy or angry. When this happens, this human has a-lined his God with himself.

God has created the person when the person was inspired by God to repent (change) his views of the past as God a-lines the person with Him. For when this occurs, the person only needs to know parts and pieces of each religion are true and the rest of all religious doctrines are corrupted and/or are polluted by man's concepts, ideas and thoughts of what he (man) believes is God's will.

The All Mighty Father that is above all, including all religions and their man-made Gods, who allows us to create our personal belief systems (religions) and to place whatever God we chose above it. Because He has given each their personal choice to chose whatever they wish, and that is God's "Gift of Choice." Therefore, God communicates with each as that individual wishes God to communicate with him.

All religions are man-made, and all contain rules and laws to control the majority by a few that proclaim they truly know God, as they demand us to worship their God or Jesus Christ. Whereas, I do not "worship" God or Jesus, I embrace them and all of God's Angels as well, for I love them as they love you and me.

Is it wrong to follow an established religion or to create your own? No! But that is not my concept of living a righteous life for God, and one that I do not wish to follow. And if we condemn another, we have condemned ourselves as well.

In conversations with the Angels the other day, I was concerned about my actions toward others, and I asked them, why do I feel the way I do. And they answered, "Your transition is almost over. This is your biggest challenge. You now think as an Angel, but you are still allowing your human feelings to fluster you. Then your feelings of frustration lash towards others because you see what they are doing and they do not understand their actions. When you allow anger to lead your words, you are shutting us out. When you start to become flustered, look to your right and I am there. Then, use your words of Wisdom. Plant the seed of Knowledge within them and if it does not grow, they are not ready for the truth."

Pretense of Knowledge

This past October marked my seventh years of acknowledged communications with God's Angels. Each day of each of those seven years contain lessons of inspiration and guiding taught to me by God through His Angels. And from those teachings, I have written two books and weekly messages that total well over one million words, and that does not include all the personal emails, phone calls, face-to-face conversations and letters with individuals, and messages given in-person directly to groups. And throughout all of God's teachings to me as throughout all the messages that I have given to individuals, and groups, and on my websites, the messages are consistent with Love, for God has not faltered in His Love to each of us.

In the Old Scriptures, God instructs people the righteous things to do. In the New Testament, Jesus attempts to inspire the people to do the right things, and in the New Testament, the Devil trys to demand Jesus to follow him instead of the Father. And from these great writings, people claim that the Devil is very deceitful and sometimes he may say he is God or God's Angels for his motives are always to bring humans under his command.

In the story of Islam, Gabrael appears to Muhammad in a CAVE! In human concepts, a cave is a place where no one can hear what is being said nor can see who is inside; a place even hidden from God and His Angels. Therefore, a cave is a place where the Devil would pretend to be God, or as in the converstaions with Muhammad, claim to be Gabrael.

If you read the Qur'an or any part of it, you will discover that 90% of it directs people to follow the desires of the flesh. The Devil is very deceitful and may say things that sound like Love to all, but his words always return to following his, the Devil's demands, whereas following the desires of the flesh gives the Devil jurisdiction over the human and the human soul.

And you will also find that over the centuries, many relgions that claim to be Christian or otherwise, were truly following the Devil instead of following God. True indication of false religions can be seen as religions that condone suicide or the killing of others, and those who speak the words from their belief systems while their clergy follow their personal beliefs such as child abuse, or other self-gratifying, or other self-interest beliefs systems. These things are all of the flesh.

In a recent conversation with the Angel Joleen, she said, "Each must walk his own path." The individual's path is the things that we have chosen for ourselves as individuals - the directions of our individual life.

And the Angel Joleen said, "God - the Father - the Creator gives His childern their rights to decide which direction to travel during their lives. The Devil - Evil energy uses force to control and places demands upon God's children. ALL religions that use the concepts that we as God's children are His slaves, are of Evil. ALL religions that use the concepts that we as God's children must bow to Him, are of Evil. All religions that place their clergy above its congregation or any person above others, are of Evil.

"Any religion that claims God wills suicide, is of Evil. Any religion that claims God proclaims that we suffer, is of Evil. Any religion that claims God demands that we conform to His demands, is of Evil."

God's true will and His true desire and His true wish is that we live the life that we choose as individuals.

Do not tell others what God thinks, what He desires, what He wills, or what He wishes unless you are God! Thus, do not place demands upon others under the pretense of knowledge of God.

"Under the pretense of knowledge of God."

Lets take a deeper look into the Catholic knowldge of God and what the Catholic clergy think God wills. The following are two new articles about concerns of the Catholic Church.

November 11, 2002
Bishops Weigh Same-Sex Unions
Statement
By RACHEL ZOLL, AP Religion Writer

WASHINGTON - *A committee of bishops proposed Tuesday that the nation's Roman Catholic leaders issue a statement condemning same-sex unions and reinforcing church teaching that gay sex is a sin.*

Catholic opposition to homosexual marriage is well known. However, the committee that drafted the document said it felt a need to restate the church's position as gay unions begin gaining recognition in society.

"Already, one state in our nation has established the category of civil union and, for the purpose of rights and benefits, has recognized it as the equivalent of marriage for homosexual persons," said Bishop J. Kevin Boland of the Diocese of Savannah, Ga., who introduced the measure.

The bishops will debate the statement and decide whether to approve it later in their meeting, which runs through Thursday.

Later Tuesday, the bishops were to hear an update from the National Review Board, a lay watchdog panel they appointed last year at the height of the clergy sex abuse scandal. The board was to discuss the progress that dioceses are making toward protecting children in the church.

The marriage document, called "Between Man and Woman: Questions and Answers About Marriage and Same-Sex Unions," defines marriage as a "lifelong union of a man and a woman." It states that approving a union of a same-gender couple "contradicts the nature of marriage."

"It is not based on the natural complementarity of male and female. It cannot cooperate with God to create new life," the statement says.

The document also states that authorizing same-sex marriage "would grant official public approval to homosexual activity and would treat it as if it were morally neutral."

The authors of the statement said the church's position was not unfair to homosexuals because Christians have an obligation to "give witness to the whole moral truth." And, the committee said, gays can obtain benefits, such as designating each other as beneficiaries of their wills, without granting their unions the same status as marriage.

Bishops Consider Sanctions for Politicians

Mon Nov 10, 9:08 PM ET

By RACHEL ZOLL, Associated Press Writer

WASHINGTON - The nation's Roman Catholic bishops said Monday they are considering whether to recommend sanctions for Catholic politicians who favor policies contrary to church teaching on abortion and other issues.

A task force of bishops will take up the idea of a church punishment as it develops guidelines on how prelates should respond to Catholic lawmakers who do not uphold church values in their work.

Bishop Joseph Galante, a task force member, said some dioceses already ban from church property elected officials who support abortion rights.

Asked what other sanctions may be available, he said it was an issue canon law experts and theologians would have to research.

For example, he said that under church law, Catholics who have a direct role in an abortion can be excommunicated.

Moral theologians would have to decide whether a Catholic politician who votes for abortion rights facilitated the procedure and should therefore be excommunicated, said Galante, coadjutor of Dallas.

The Vatican and U.S. bishops have for years urged Catholic legislators to consider their faith when they vote. No date has been set for the American guidelines to be completed.

"I'm tired of hearing Catholic politicians saying `I'm personally opposed to abortion, but I don't want to impose my moral judgments on anyone else,'" Galante said. "Politicians make moral judgments all the time. That's a weaseling out of something."

What is the difference between a homosexual relationship of two consenting adults or one adult and a child of the same sex?

The Catholic clergy say it is wrong for two of the same sex to marry, but they say that if one of their clergy has sexually abused a child (of the same sex), he will be assigned to another area and church. They claim sex between two people of the same sex is a SIN.

Then is it a sin when the adult rapes (abuses) a child of the same sex? Whenever clergy, a person who claims to speak for God, rapes or sexual abuses a child or adult, he has spiritually killed that person! God has given each person (adult) his choice to choose whatever he wishes. That includes the person that he, the child or adult, wishes to spend his life with. (A child cannot choose if he wishes to be homosexual or not because he does not know truly about life yet.) But when an adult forces himself upon a child or another adult, he is not doing it because he loves the child or adult, he is doing it because of his desires of the flesh - a sin against the child or adult and God!

The fact that the Catholic clergy, that has been discovered, having sex with minors has had sex with not merely one child but many, this truly indicates that the person enjoys sex with children, and as the Catholic church claims; sex with many is a Sin against the people and God! The Catholic church claims homosexual marriages are wrong because homosexuals in their congregation do not procreate more Catholics. Thus, the Catholic church will lose future money.

The Catholic clergy say it is wrong for politicians for follow what is in their hearts and not what their clergy tells them God desires.

ALL POLITICIANS ARE VOTED INTO OFFICE BY THEIR PEERS OF THE AREA THEY REPRESENT, AND THEY ARE TO VOTE WHAT THE MAJORITY IN THEIR DISTRICT WANT, NOT WHAT THEIR CHURCH LEADERS DEMAND THEM TO FOLLOW!

Therefore, who or what does the Catholic church Love, or follow, or believes in? God or themselves.

If politicians are excommunicated because they did not vote the way their religious leaders teaches, then should not the Catholic clergy who do not follow what their higher leaders say also be excommunicated? Excommunicated - removed from the church.

The Pope and the others who run the Vatican and Catholic religion, have placed their religion above all else, even above God! The Catholic religion has become the most powerful entity upon the earth and those, including the Pope, who run it believe they are closer to God than all the people.

Whenever one places the title "Father" in front of his name, and is addressed with that title "Father," the addressee is then acknowledging that person as "Father." Excuse me! Each person has only two Fathers; the man who procreated him, and the Father of Creation. Which Father is a Catholic clergy to you?

I have no church or religion that I follow. I follow God's Angels (that includes Jesus); I love all people, God's Angels and Him, and I believe in God, His Angels and the afterlife of Heaven and Hell.

The Call to Perfection

The solution to the problems of human relationships and the resolution of the age-old conflicts which arise between competing nations, lies in the call of the Nazarene to Perfection. His words testify to the true value of the Human Soul. They reveal the essential spirituality of Man: the relationship which exists between Mankind and the Creator-Spirit: a relationship of parent and offspring. The Quaker, George Fox, saw the importance of these words as a verification of the true Spiritual status of Man. "Be YE, therefore, Perfect: as YOUR Heavenly Father is Perfect". (Matthew Ch 5, v 48). Gone in a flash are those spurious doctrines of the Fall and Vicarious Atonement: gone Pre-destination and Election. The Kingdom of Heaven is open to all, without reservation or consideration of numbers. Jesus comes into his true nobility and stature, not as a Heavenly King and Judge of Men but as a Messenger of Light, sent into a dark and ignorant world, from whence he soon left it, but not without leaving a message of true comfort.

The Sermon on the Mount remains as testimony to his recognition of the Spiritual law: which demands that one have a loving concern for one's fellows.

It is, perhaps, unfortunate for the subsequent development of sectarian divisions in the Western World, that Christianity was subject to the influence of Polytheism for so long, before becoming the predominant faith of the Roman world. The adoption of the Platonic doctrine of the Trinity, as well as the related and Pagan doctrine of the Ministry (Worship) of the Saints, had unfortunate consequences for future generations of Christians. Had these erroneous developments not occurred, the Prophet Muhammad would not have subsequently been compelled to reject these "Fundamental" Christian concepts, when developing his own ideas of a Cosmos based on the Unity of Creation, as a whole. Whilst the Prophet was right to reject such patently Pagan doctrines: he unfortunately modelled his concept of the Creator (Allah) upon the monotheistic and somewhat threatening image of the Jewish God, Yahweh. Thus Muhammad sees God as all-powerful but Merciful. Power is qualified by mercy, which is not synonymous with love. Had Christianity retained the Monotheist concept of the Universal God when developing its Theology and not insisted on deifying Jesus, Islam might have been a very different Faith from what it is today. After all, Jesus never claimed to be the "Only begotten Son of God", nor, indeed, did he ever refer to the concept of a Tri-partite Deity. (The passage at St. John's Gospel, Ch 3, v 16, which commences with the words, "For God so loved the world...." is in the nature of commentary by the writer of the document. Indeed, this probably applies to the whole of verses Nos. 13 to 21 of this Chapter). Had the Prophet, Muhammad, not been obliged to reject much Christian doctrine, the Christian concept of a "Loving" God might well have had a place in Islamic philosophy.

There is no doubt, in this writer's mind, as to the spiritual nature of the early visions of Muhammad, who experienced a brilliant illumination whilst meditating in the Arabian Desert, somewhere around 600AD.

Insight

A knowledge of the value of the human soul assists in resolving the complex questions of human relationships. No longer is one free to indulge oneself freely, without regard for personal responsibilities. One definitely has obligations towards others, which must be fulfilled if there is to be any progress, either for the individual or the Race. It is a question of personal responsibility and the end product of a life spent in either constructive or destructive conduct.

I do believe in "God" in the sense and to the extent to which I am capable of conceiving the Divine Nature. I do so directly as the result of certain dream-experiences, which I recorded many years ago, in which I felt myself to be the recipient of Divine Love, poured upon me from a source of Light, Love and Power. Such momentary illumination was accompanied by a sensation of Paternal and loving Care: Compassion and Love; of forgiveness and concern for the children of Earth. I had these dreams, initially, at a time of doubt and uncertainty in my youth. As a result, I developed a firm conviction in the existence and omnipresent Love of a Creator Spirit. Such a belief provides great advantages for the believer, who has the support and foundation of Divine Guidance as a stabilizing factor in his or her life. It also reinforces one's ideas as to the development of sound moral principles, as a guide throughout life's tortuous vicissitudes. In other words: one should choose to do good rather than evil, as such is productive of further good and is beneficial not only to the individual but to the Community as a whole. Not only is there an external advantage in good works, but the individual himself benefits internally by the consciousness of personal progress, which naturally results from activity of a selfless nature. It is part and parcel of the march towards personal salvation: not by faith, indeed, but by the progressive development of character: by works.

Thus it will be apparent that my own belief as to the existence and nature of God arises not as a result of reasoned argument, but merely from my subconscious and subjective experiences or feelings. It is, therefore, of no value for the purpose of evidence as to its validity. In spite of this logical flaw, it may still be of interest for me to outline my thoughts on the concept of the Divine Origin of Man.

Right of Choice

    I, as the Bishop of Jesus' House of Jacob, do officate over weddings. And before I do a wedding, I interview the bride and groom-to-be, and if I feel in my heart that they are compatible, I will officate over their wedding. And sometimes, I may see differences between them that may be problems for them during their marriage. We then discuss the issues before their wedding, and then other times, I may refuse to officate over their wedding if I feel their marriage will not work. I do not discrimate between heterosexual, or same-sex, or marriages of different races, for if two people truly love each other it is not my place or concern to keep them apart for they have already joined in the eyes of God - the Father without my or the government's blessings.
    Our missions in life are not to chose for others or decide what is right for others, our mission is to help each other as we enjoy and experience life. And those who try to force their beliefs upon others are going against God. The following article indicates the true directions of people of different religions concerning marriage, and something that we as citizens, should try to stop their demands upon us and our fellow humans.

Opponents Of Gay Marriage Divided
Sat Nov 29, 10:43 AM E
By Alan Cooperman, Washington Post Staff Writer

A broad array of religious groups and conservative political activists has united behind the idea of a constitutional amendment against gay marriage. But the fledgling coalition is deeply divided about what, exactly, the amendment should say.

At issue are not merely the fine details of legislative wording but the amendment's very purpose: Should it ban only same-sex marriage, or also take aim at Vermont-style civil unions and California-style partnerships that some opponents say amount to marriage in all but name?

Underneath that dispute, moreover, are differing calculations about what language would appeal to the general public, and what would excite grass-roots conservatives. "It's purity versus pragmatism," said Glenn T. Stanton, a senior analyst at Focus on the Family, one of the groups leading the charge against gay marriage. "Do we go for everything that we want, or take the best we think we can get?"

Although they are early in the process of trying to win a two-thirds vote in both houses of Congress and ratification by three-quarters of the states, some conservatives worry that the political clock is ticking and the drive to amend the Constitution will be doomed unless they can reach consensus.

Since the Supreme Court overturned a Texas law against sodomy in June and the highest court in Massachusetts declared Nov. 18 that same-sex couples have a right to marry, conservative groups have acted with a new urgency, vowing to make gay marriage a major election issue in 2004 and calling for passage of a constitutional amendment by 2006, an extremely fast timetable by historic standards.

At least three versions of the amendment are circulating in Washington. The leading text, and the only one introduced in Congress, is two sentences: "Marriage in the United States shall consist only of the union of a man and a woman. Neither this constitution or the constitution of any state, nor state or federal law, shall be construed to require that marital status or the legal incidents thereof be conferred upon unmarried couples or groups."

Matt Daniels, president of the Alliance for Marriage, a bipartisan coalition of religious and political leaders backing that language, said the first sentence would ban gay marriage and the second is designed to stop courts from finding a constitutional right to same-sex unions.

But he said nothing in the text is meant to prevent state legislatures from establishing civil unions, as Vermont's did in 2000, or from conferring a range of domestic benefits on same-sex partners, as California lawmakers did this year.

"What the polls show is that people make a clear distinction at marriage," Daniels said. If some states want to allow civil unions, he added, "that's life (news - Y! TV) in a democracy."

Since it was introduced in May as House Joint Resolution 56 by Rep. Marilyn Musgrave (R-Colo.), the Alliance for Marriage's language has gained more than 100 co-sponsors. Identical wording was introduced in the Senate last week by three Republicans, Wayne Allard (Colo.), Jeff Sessions (Ala.) and Sam Brownback (Kan.).

Some legal experts have argued that, regardless of Daniels's explanations and the congressional sponsors' intentions, the second sentence of the proposed amendment could gut civil unions by making them unenforceable in the courts. As a result, Daniels said, his alliance is working on another version that would make "minor changes in the text to make it explicit and undeniably clear that we are not seeking to invalidate legislatively created civil unions or partnership arrangements."

The alliance assembled by Daniels cuts across traditional party lines and includes Catholic, Jewish and Muslim leaders as well as ministers in historically black Protestant denominations.

Meanwhile, another powerful coalition of religious leaders is pushing for language that clearly would block Vermont-style civil unions. Known as the Arlington Group because it first met in July at an apartment complex in suburban Virginia, it unites the heads of almost every major political advocacy organization on the Christian right, including James Dobson of Focus on the Family, Gary Bauer (news - web sites) of American Values, William J. Bennett of Empower America, Tony Perkins of the Family Research Council, Sandy Rios of Concerned Women for America and Paul Weyrich of the Free Congress Foundation.

At an Oct. 15 session spearheaded by Charles W. Colson, the former Nixon White House staffer who now heads Prison Fellowship

Ministries, key members of the Arlington Group and several evangelical Christian leaders unanimously decided to push for adding a third sentence to the proposed amendment: "Neither the federal government nor any state shall predicate benefits, privileges, rights or immunities on the existence, recognition or presumption of non-marital sexual relationships."

That wording, according to Colson, would bar the creation of any form of "substitute marriage" specifically for gays. He said state legislatures still could establish civil unions, but only if they conferred the same benefits on "any two people who live together," such as "an unmarried heterosexual couple or two old spinsters." Vermont's law would not meet that test.

Some conservatives question whether the Arlington Group's language would hold up in court. Dale Carpenter, a gay Republican who is an associate professor of law at the University of Minnesota, said the attempt to block legislatures from doling out benefits on a "sexual" basis would misfire, because the civil unions law in Vermont does not require gay couples to claim they are in a sexual relationship.

"This third sentence doesn't really accomplish anything, except to expose the extent to which some religious conservatives are fixated on gay sex," Carpenter said.

Much of the debate within the anti-gay marriage movement revolves around what is politically feasible. In the current edition of the Weekly Standard, Maggie Gallagher, president of the Institute for Marriage and Public Policy and one of the movement's intellectual flag-bearers, calls civil unions an "unwise step" but argues that gay marriage is far worse.

"Which is why," she declared, "I cannot join any coalition willing to fight only for the whole loaf but certain to go down to 'noble' defeat."

Several members of the Arlington Group said that if it becomes clear that a constitutional amendment designed to block civil unions has no chance of getting through Congress, they would unite behind the Alliance for Marriage's less ambitious wording. But Colson said their fear is that language that protects marriage "in name only" would not fire up enough grass-roots evangelical support to win ratification by 38 state legislatures.

The Rev. Don Wildmon, chairman of the Mississippi-based American Family Association and formal convener of the Arlington Group, insisted that there is no bad blood between the two conservative camps. He noted that Daniels, of the Alliance for Marriage, attended the Arlington Group's November meeting.

But Daniels said that for the previous four months, "they deliberately excluded us from the meetings."

The "whole purpose of the Arlington Group has been to try to move the Federal Marriage Amendment from the position that the Alliance for Marriage has adopted toward targeting lgislatively adopted civil unions or partnership arrangements," he said.

A few times in the U.S. history, people have tried to ban alcohol, but each time they tried to ban alcohol in one complete step, the bans did not work but taught people to go little step by little step to get things band from another's use.

During the 70s, a few paranoid people decided they did not like the smell of tobacco burning. They started the push to ban others from smoking. First they pressured restaurants to put in non-smoking areas, and then slowly they convinced others that tobacco smoke was bad for them. Thus by getting their foot in the door and forcing restaurants to put in non-smoking areas, they continued to push the door open wider until making smoking all but illegal today.

Tobacco is a drug...its a downer...it calms its user. Smokers would not fight the anti-smoking people, therefore, allowing the banning of smoking to enter their world.

Muslim terrorists are using little steps by little steps to remove all Israelis from Israel; they fight and use suicide bombers to tirer the Isrealis into submissions of giving pieces and bits of land to the Palestinians, and after getting a little, they go for more. The ideology of the Palestinians are not to stop until all of Isreal is theirs and all Isrealis are dead or removed from Isreal. This no different from what the anti-smoking groups did to the smokers; All non-smoking groups declare not to stop until smoking is illegal and no one smokes.

Groups against same-sex marriage declare not to stop their fight until their beliefs in marriage prevail and only heterosexuals can marry. (The same tactics used by anti-smoking and Terrorists groups.)

And presently other groups are trying to stop us from using sugar by stating our children are too fat. Sugar by itself does not make people fat, eating does! (Again, this is the same ideas of forcing people not to eat sugar as the Terrorists, anti-smoking groups and groups againt gay rights.)

Soon, groups will be saying that fat people should not have children because they do not know the correct foods to eat and if they have childern they will not teach their children good eating habits and their childern will also be overweight and that will cost us more money for health care because of their health issues.

The other day around 6 o'clock as I hurriedly finished putting up outside Christmas lights a young black man walked up our front walk. (I have seen kids of all colors selling products in my neighborhood before, and knew he was a salesman.) From atop the ladder on which I stood, I said to him, "Does it look like I want to buy anything? I am busy, just leave!"

He said something stupid like, "You might want what I am selling."

I told him, "I'm busy...leave now. Get off my property!"

He just stood there staring at me.

Again, I told him, "Get off my property!"

As he turned to leave, he said, "Oh, you are just prejudice and that is why you won't buy from me."

He wanted me to stop putting up the lights and give him my total attention.

Whenever someone calls you on the telephone, they expect you to stop whatever you are doing and talk with them, even if you are sitting on the toilet! The caller may be just a telemarketer, but he expects you to stop whatever you are doing and give him your immediate attention.

Over the last few years, I have heard from young white girls that young black men are using the line, "You won't go out with me because you are prejudice," to get a date with white girls. Thus forcing white girls to go out with them.

If we are not forced to marry another of our same sex, why do we care if others marry their same sex?

If we are not forced to smoke, then why should we care if

others smoke?

(Don't even try to force onto me the concept, "One is forced to smoke if another who is smoking is in the same area." If that is true then also is, "One who passes gas (farts) in the same area of another is forcing poison gas upon another," passed gas is a biological hazard and that gas is more dangerous to our bodies than tobacco smoke. Think about it, passed gas carries particles of human waste that are released into the atmosphere that enter into other humans, and passed gas is methane gas which is highly combustible.)

If we are not forced to lose weight, why do we care if others are over-weight?

And if we are not forced to date people, or buy from people, of another race, why do we care if others do or do not not want to buy from blacks, or do not or want to date blacks?

(I will not buy anything from a door-to-door salesman or from people who call me. And in my younger years before marriage, I have dated black women.)

Jihad is taught in Islamic schools, but yet we allow Islamic schools in the U.S. and while we have removed Christian teaching of Love from our public schools, then why do we allow Muslims to teach Islam in our public schools paid for by our tax money?

There are plans to build a black baseball hall of Fame, but are not famous black baseball players found in our present Baseball Hall of Fame?

People use what they interpret of RIGHT to get their way. Their interpretation of RIGHT is part of their belief system. Oh yes, belief systems goes far beyond religious beliefs. And we need to get past our personal beliefs and understand that not all people believe or think as we do.

Concerning abortion, God's Angels say, "There are 4 reasons for abortion; in the case of rape, in the resolute of incest, if the mother's life is endangered because of the pregnancy or child's birth, or if the unborn child could not substain himself because of defects; In those cases, the child is being forced upon others and removing their or his choices, then the pregnancy should be aborted." But yet, God allows us to decide when we as individuals should allow abortion into our lives.

Whomever trys to force their beliefs upon others are doing it because of their desires of the flesh, and God does not back their actions, for God has given each individual his right to make his own decisions in life (as long as his personal decision does not harm or hurt others), and no man shall take that away from them. Laws created by man should only stop people from controlling others.

("Controlling others" means forcing others to live a life style or doing things that a few believe is correct for them, and it also means injurying or harming others.)

At one time, as written into the Scriptures, we needed to populate the world with people. Homosexuality was wrong, but today we have too many people in the world and it would be better if more people would be homosexual, for then we would have less children being born and less people to feed and house. And maybe those children born would be out of love and be loved instead as today where most children are abused by their parents.

I have friends who are homosexual and they are welcome in my home. The ones who have partners as married do not flaunt their affection for each other in my presence as my heterosexual friends do in my presence. I respect their feelings as they respect mine.

(Did you notice that the news article above does not use the word "homosexual" but only "Gay."...Interesting.)

The Gift of Choice

To help illustrate "the Gift of Choices" in the "chain-reaction" of life, image if you will, setting dominos in a formation so that the first roll of dominos contains only one domino, the second roll has two dominos side by side, the third roll has three side by side, and so forth until millions of millions of dominos are arranged in this order. Now think of each domino as representing an ancestor (person and/or animal) in the evolution of human life. And think of this domino formation as the span of total life here on earth, and near the end of this formation and onto the end of this formation, the dominos represent humans.

As we knock over the first domino at the beginning of this formation, it will touch another and knock over the next row of two others, and in turn they will knock over more, and this "chain-reaction" of knocking down the dominos will continue until the complete formation of dominos are laying down.

Now, imagine that the distances between each of the standing dominos and the location that each domino will obtain when it falls as the time that each person lives, and during that time all that each domino's (person's life) experiences influence the next domino (next of kin) that follows it.

Once that first domino was set in place, and as all the others were placed in this formation, and as the first domino was touched as to knock it down, the chain-reactions of all of the other dominos as to what direction, and to what other dominos it would come in contact with, and to where each domino would final lay, is known to God.

We, as the dominos in this chain-reaction, believe that we have control over which direction our individual lives will go, but our life's directions was known by God before the start of time. All of our individual choices as indicated as "Gods Gift of Choice," are merely the things that we do that was influenced and directed by what occurred in our ancestors and our past life up until this present time. The things that we will do in the future are influenced by those things as well as what we presently do, and all is known by God. Therefore, we are at the correct place in knowledge, and location of time, and geological location, that it was planned for us to be.

"God's Gift of Choice" is our experiencing of the unknown, and that is what life is all about - experiencing as we enjoy life. And it is this "experiencing life;" the recorded experience on energy that is the Soul. The Soul is that part of you that will live forever with God, for each person is made up of two parts: 1. Energy that allows solid matter to think and also gives our bodies movement - that is the Soul, and 2. Matter which will return to which it came from - earth. These two things must come together to form a living being.

And while we live, even though our life's adventures are known to God, our choices of doing good or evil will either help our Angel-within to glow brightly or dim, depending on which you chose. And the attitude of your character is influenced by your ancestors and your past life experiences, will be placed upon your Soul. And after your death, it shall be forever engraved upon the Angel-within. But you may change the attitude of your character, and if you do allow changes in yourself, it was a known factor at the beginning of time.

Another way to view the "Concept of Life," is to think of your Soul as being a file that contains your life's experiences, and the Angel-within as a disk, and God as the Master Computer. After you die, your file (Soul) is transferred to the disk (the Angel-within), and the Angel-within takes your file to God where the Soul (your life's experiences) are downloaded into the congregation of God - His Angels. For God is all Angels in congregation. Therefore, until your life ends, your file is not complete and may be changed, but once life is over, your Soul stands as the Memory of You that will live forever in God, as well as the feelings that you had toward others will influence your descendants in their life, and that is your everlasting Heaven or Hell that you shall live in forever.

Therefore, we do not have control over the future. We merely have the control over the future as was known by God before the start of time. For we cannot control what others do and think. We only control what we as individuals think and do.

Understanding The Gift of Choice

One of the many things that I have learned under the teachings from God's Angels is our misunderstanding God's Gift of Choices.

Of the three big religions; The Torah teaches the rules and laws of Yahweh, the Christian Bible teaches we shall not judge and Islam teaches Muslims to submit to Allah. Why? Because all three human made religions have placed human demands above the true God. It is my job as directed by God's Angels to explain the religions, and to help you understand that all religions worship the same God, and to even help you realize that the word "worship" and its action toward God should be replaced with "Embrace."

Humans cannot comprehend Creation other than the realm of physics of this dimension. For humans to think that they understand Creator, religious leaders of old, have designed religious doctrines that contain their religious understanding of gods to help them to reinforce their beliefs of the Creator of the physics of this dimension and physics in this dimension that we live. But we are not discussing Creation in this chapter, we are talking about the Creator of this physical dimension and His role (Desire) within this dimension which is "The Gift of Choices."

Whenever you make a promise with another, it is also a promise to yourself that was your choice that you made. A great example of this is when Jesus once asked, "Whose face is on this coin?" And he was told, "It is Ceaser." Jesus then replied, "Give Ceaser what is his."

Jesus did not mean to give Ceaser the coins because his face was imprinted upon them, he meant; give Ceaser what you promised to give him, his tax money!

You may be able to cheat another, but you cannot cheat and lie to yourself by changing or making up new rules that imply only to you, or by disregarding your commitments to another.

Just because you think you live righteously does not mean that you actually live righteous because you cannot change the rules to fit your needs or desires. And backing out of a deal or promise to another is you not wanting to take responsibility for your actions and desires. No one twisted your arm to make you agree on a deal or promise just as no one twisted your arm or forced you to accept a gift. A slap for a slap is the same as a love for a love.

The choices that we make comes from the "Gift of Choices" that God has given to each of us as individuals, even though some or all of your choices concerning life may be wrong. Nevertheless, they are your choices.

God created the concept of Evil when He created everything, evil was needed for you to understand the difference between living righteously or living in Sin. Man created the actions of Evil. It was the human choice to create the actions of Evil, and to follow the type of actions that he desires to.

The human body cannot support two different Energies at the same time, thus from the moment of birth, the Energy known as the Angel-within, has about a three day time spand to be selected and enter the newly born child. And from this point in time that the Angel-within first enters the child, the Energy of the Angel-within is acceptable to the human body so that no other Angel nor Energy of either good or bad can enter that body at any time throughout that human's life without the body fighting that Energy as it if were a virus.

The Angel-within is part of God. This Angel-within is the part of God that may or may not dwell within His vessel - your body. If you do not accept the Angel-within to share your life, then you are No-thing to God, and are no more than a dog to God.

The Angel-within does not need to constantly remain in the human body. He may leave and return as often as he wishes, or he may stand along side the body as long as he wishes. For the Angel-within is your pathway to God if you chose him to be.

All young children see things that most adults cannot see. But, usually as the child grows, we as adults tell them, "There is nothing there, you are seeing things!" We as adults "teach" the children that the Angels of God - Entities are not real. We make the childern believe what we believe. We have forced our choice of not seeing Angels - Entites upon our children. We have removed their choice and have removed their pathway to God, and once we have done this, the Angel-within - that is part of God that should be living within each human, is removed and He will stand beside that human until that human allows Him to enter once again.

You see, as humans - children of God, have the choice to accept God or to refuse Him. If we refuse Him, then He has no part in our lives. Thus, God has given us the choice of accepting Him or refusing Him, and our beliefs have direct influence on the actions of our Angel-within. Therefore, the Angel-within knows the same choices that you present to him. The corruption of doing evil in a promise or aggreement that you contain, the Angel-within contains, for you have placed that corruption upon the Angel-within.

When Abraham decided that God had told him to sarifice his son, Isaac, Abraham agreed and promised to kill his son. And then, it was then that Abraham realized what he agreed to do. But Abraham stood up to his agreement and he took Isaac into the mountains to be sarificed. And then God demanded Abraham not to harm his son.

God was not testing Albraham's faith. God does not need to test anyone's faith because He knows what is in our heart.

(This story was acted out because it was the only way for God to reiterate "The Gift of Chioces" to the people back then.)

For it was Abraham's faith in his promise and in himself. that caused him to understand that he and God had a promise to sarifice his son. And therefore, God gave Abraham his personal decision to believe in whatever he wished just as God has given us all our individual choices.

Before Abraham could kill his son, God intervened and said,

that He would not uphold Abraham to the promise but instead replace His side of the promise with something better; people will not have to sarifice any more aminals to Him.

In a recent conversation with a preacher, when our conversation turned to judging. I said, "Daily we judge if things that others do is right for us to do."

The preacher relplied, "We should not judge anything, Jesus, is the only person that can judge others."

Excuse me, daily we decide, what to do and how to act and all kinds of other things. And that is only part of the "Gift of Choices" that God have given to all His children.

"And you shall reap the rewards of your choices."

You Control Your Choices

A Few days ago, I was helping a neighbor find the bad bulb in his outdoor Christmas lights that caused that strand of lights not to light. As we removed and check the bulbs, we talked about the "Do-gooders" (Baptist church goers) who weekly come through our neighborhood.

My neighbor said, "I am tired of answering my door only to find them wanting to tell me about Jesus. If I wanted to find God, I would go looking for Him. I do not need them coming to my door and forcing their religion on me."

Most religions try to dominate others into joining their congregation, and most of the Christianity religions are the worst (beside the Muslims) about trying to dominate others by attempting to convert people. But while, all who claim to be Christians are not true Christians!

A true Christian is one who follows the Bible, and believes everything that is written in it, without question or doubt of what it says. Of all the Christians that I have ever met or knew, all say, "Oh, I don't believe in that or this."

All three major religions - Christianity, Jewish and Islam religion use somewhat the Old Testament. Therefore, in my opinion, the Old Testament needs to be read, and to understand as historical facts that God and His Angels did come into contact with people, and to see how the people lived back then. And it is also my opinion that a Christian is one who truly follows and believes every word in it, and tries to live the lifestyle that Jesus demonstrated in the New Testament. And if you do not follow and believe all that is written into the Old and New Testament, than you are not a Christian. But, if you are Spiritualist, you will follow and try to live the lifestyle that Jesus demonstrated as Righteous. But, if you do not follow all that is written into the Bible while claiming to be a true Christian, then you have created your own religion (that follows only parts and pieces of the Old and New testament) and then have created your own God above it.

I am not a Christian because I do not believe all that is written into the New Testament. I am a Spiritualist because I try to follow the lifestyle that Jesus demonstrated as Righteous.

Spiritual concepts go beyond (or I should say "above") religions. Jesus preached Spiritual concepts because his teachings went beyond the religions of that day. But his teachings and words were turned into the religions of Christianity that many follow the New Testament up until today.

Is Christianity evil?

No, as long as the one who follows it does not try to dominate others.

Christianity is no different than any other religion; it has its pros and cons. And as a Christian or as a follower of any other religion, you need to administer to those who seek God or are dissatisfied with their God, and not to those who have a belief system that they are satisfied with.

There are many stories written in the New Testament that show that is exactly what Jesus did.

But above all, God created the concept of evil. Human created the actions of evil.

Whenever we think of Heaven, we see a place of harmony and peace, a place where there is no evil actions toward another. But the clergy has taught us that war between good and evil rages in Heaven.

DO THEY NOT KNOW THAT GOD IS THE SUPREME BEING!

He has the power to make Heaven however He wishes, and He has the power to control or remove any evil from His Heaven. Do you think He wants war in His peaceful Heaven?

God created man in His image, but we have manifested an image of a God who looks like an elderly man sitting on a throne who is surrounded by people who are all down on their knees worshipping Him forever.

First of all, if He wanted us to be His slaves, He would have created us as His slaves without ever going through life. Secondly, God created us, we did not create Him, and therefore, we do not know what He looks like or thinks.

God created us in His image. If He placed evil in us then there is evil in Him. God did not place evilness in humans. He placed the knowledge of the concept of evil in us because all that He created includes the concept of evil.

Whereas, religions needs warriors to defend their beliefs and bring forth more worshippers, while God does not need warriors or worshippers. God uses people in peaceful means, as demonstrated throughout the pages of the Old Testament and New Testament, to get His words of Love to the people.

One particular message that Jesus gave to a group of people was totally misunderstood; It is written that Jesus said, "For you, the only way to the Father is through me." Let me explain his statement to you. If one wishes to become a doctor, one must know and understand the language in which he is studying under, and for the group of people that Jesus was addressing, he was using the language that they must understand what he was saying for them to go further. Therefore, when Jesus made this statement, he was saying, "You must know and understand what I say and do, and you must follow what I say and do in order to find your way to the Father." But yet, Christians will try to push their belief that the only way to God is by worshipping Jesus, but the only person that Jesus prayed to was God. Then should we be "worshipping" Jesus or God? And whereas, Jesus said he was the son of God, but Christians claim him to be God. Did Jesus really say he was the Son of God or a son of God? This we will never know, but it is irrelative because Jesus prayed to God and not himself. So who are we to worship or to pray to, God or Jesus?

It is pusillanimous for any beliefs system follower to think his beliefs may not be that of the true God. Wars have been fought over people's ideology concepts of God. These "Holy Wars" are brought forth by man, and are against God as well as being against humankind's pursuit of happiness. But these "Holy Wars" will continue until each as individuals "clean out their houses of evil thoughts of domination toward others." But it is written that peace will not come to the world until the end. So, can we live in the world without world peace? We must! We can only find peace in ourselves while we are embracing the God of our choice; A God who proclaims - Love all others and have no domination toward them, for we shall not know God until we are "living" on The Other Side. And until that time comes to each of us, we only must know how to live in harmony with others. God has given each of us his individual choice on how to live with others.

Is it your concern if another' choice is wrong? No!

You can only bring peace into yourself. You cannot force Salvation and peace onto another. You are only responsible for keeping your house clean. But, it is also your responsibility to see that others do not dominate others or you. For each of us are our brothers and sisters keeper of their peace. But if our brothers and sisters would rather live in poverty, that is their choice and we should not try to force a lifestyle upon them that they do not want. It is our only responsibility to inspire them to rise above poverty, and we should not let them starve or die because of the weather conditions. The act of continuing of giving food or money to the needy is not the answer. Inspiring them as teaching them how to take care of themselves is the answer.

Do not allow others to pull you down to their level of understanding God nor their level of life.

The Gift of Choice was given to you by God. Please use it wisely.

Follow that which is in your heart as you lift your Soul toward the Father.

"The Gates To Heaven are Narrow and Not Many Will Enter"

The Lifestyle that Jesus lived is what we should follow and try to live the same. That lifestyle truly demonstrates how to control and remove the evil that is contained in humans. For if this evil if allowed to live, it will grow into our enemies that lives within each of us.

I do not like the word "Pacifist," but it is the only word that closely resembles the concept needed to live a righteous life. Jesus' lifestyle demonstrated this is the only way for a child of God to live.

Many times, I have seen that when anger or hatred is around us, God's Angels remains happy as they laugh and play without ever noticing this evilness that surrounds us. We cannot allow the anger or hatefulness that is in others to contaminate us. For if we allow their evil feelings to control our thoughts, then we are allowing their evilness to grow within us.

An example of this; I used to stand on my front porch and when a speeding car would pass by, I would think, "Slow down before you kill someone…this is a residential area." Then soon, I started thinking, "YOU FOOL, SLOW DOWN, STUPID, BEFORE YOU KILL SOMEONE!" Before long it escalated into me yelling at the speeding cars, "Hey STUPID, slow down or I will kill YOU!"

An innocent thought conceived from caring for the safety of others, can turn into hatefulness, and that will grow into evilness, and this evilness will turn you from God to only thoughts of yourself - thoughts that are turned inward instead of outward as Love for others. When I yelled, "Hey STUPID, slow down or I will kill YOU!" at the speeding motorist, I was not caring about anyone being hit and injured by the speeding car, I was only concerned by the driver driving too fast - something (the actions of the drivers) that I was trying to control.

Human life is short, and it should not matter to us what others do or think. Our only concern is to keep God in our life and thoughts, as we try to live as directed by God's Concept of life.

Whereas, when Jesus told a group how to get to the Father, he also told a prostitute, "Go on your way, and do not do that anymore." He did not get caught-up in her life; he stayed focused on his direction in life just as he did not get caught-up in the lives of the group when he told them their only way to the Father.

A few days ago, as I talked to my youngest son about this concept of being a pacifist that I just learned, he commented, "Sometimes movies pretty well hit the target and never realize what they said In the movie 'Field of Dreams,' Ray tells James Earl Jones that he is a pacifist, and then toward the end of the film and as the ball players offer Jones to come with them into the corn field, Ray is angry because he cannot go, Jones tells Ray, 'You are not ready.'"

In history it is indicated that most of Jesus' disciples and some of his followers were 'ready' to enter the Gates of Heaven because they allowed others to do with them whatever they wished, for the ending part of their life's story contained no anger or hatred toward those who harmed them; Jesus had inspired them to follow him.

You are in control of only your thoughts and actions. You cannot and do not control others. Allow others to do whatever they wish, for they will be judged for what they did when they lived. You shall be judged on only what you did during your life and not by what others have done. Jesus did not hate others who brought great pain unto him in his last days nor did he hate them for killing him in a crucifixion, and now he shines brightly in Heaven beside God.

How will you shine in Heaven?

The "Gift of Choice" is yours.

Understanding The Growth of Life

The other evening as the Angel Joleen and I talked, she said, "All that we have told you was to help prepare you for your final Challenge, but our teachings will help others if they desire.

"The Old Scriptures were needed as you would help a small child, Jesus's teachings were as you would help an older child, Muhammad's instructions were like those received by a teenager from his peers. What we have taught you were like those things learned by one who is graduating from high school - those things taught to young adults.

"The Old Scriptures were instructions to a young and innocent people who could not understand the total meaning of God. And there were changes in the things that God told people through those years as the changes you would tell a young child as he grew in his early years.

"Jesus' teachings spoke of love for all as the things you woud teach an older child who is entering puberty.

"Muhammad's demands came from evilness, and hatred, and domination over others that dwelled within him - a human - the dog, the animal that he was. These are things he, and then his followers, forced upon others.

"Our teachings to you, came from the Divine Love of God, to one of His children - you. Through us, He has explained life and afterlife to you. You have been inspired by Love and you have seen the devil, and you have seen yourself, and now you know that you make the final choices in your life and not in other' lives nor do they make the choices for you, for you are in charge of your decisions in life and of your life.

"We did not design your teachings for you to be like Jesus. He was part human and part Angel - God, You are human with an Angel within. You once asked me if you should change your name to Jacob, and the reason for your question was when we communicated with your Angel within, we spoke to "Jacob." But you thought we were calling you "Jacob." If you recall, I told you "No, because you, the human, was named David and you are not your Angel within who is named Jacob.

"Some people will think of you as being like Jesus, but you are not, for you are human. Some people thought Muhammad was like Jesus, but he was not, for he was human, too. People built religions upon Jesus' teachings and they labeled them Christianity. People made a religion that followed Muhammad's beliefs. Some will build religions following their beliefs in you. And those may be corrupted as all the other religions are. But those who truly believe and undertsand what you have written will be helped in their lives and their final Challenge of Life.

"We have taught you that God is Loving, He cares for His children - His Creation. Fathers do not place their children into salvery, and as with all true father's, He allows His children to select for themselves. But when a child is young, you must teach them without giving them their choices. Once they become older with knowledge, they are given more choices, for Maturity brings freedom of choices.

"We could not force the truth upon you. You cannot force the truth upon others. They must find it for themselves. But you may help them if they seek your advice, for then your words will help others by inspiring them to reach toward God - the Father - the Creator.

"When a human walks upon the altar and acts like he is closer to God than his brothers and sisters, people will see through his falsehood and realize that he does not know God and lose their faith in God because of what he said and that he did not follow his own words about God.

"You will be human until you return Home, and during this time, you will continue to tell people that you are no closer to God than they, for we also continue to communicate with them, but most refuse us as Muhammad and others have refused our words in the past.

"God's Love is not for those who kill others for their own pleasures and possessions or for the ideas of Muhammad and his followers. The evils of Islam have been released upon the earth. God did not release them, the animals - humans of darkness have done that. Dance and sing as children and refuse the offerings of religions."

The Direction of Civilization

From the dawn of life until your birth, all your ancestors lived long enough to procreate life. And to each generation, it concidered itself modern and thought of past generations as primitive just as we do today and as the generations to come will view our generation.

Wars and conflicts of religious beliefs has been of interest throughout time as all wars and disputes are the center of every battle between humans in each generation. Ours is not any different nor will any future generation be different from the past.

The other evening while writing on my computer as the Angel Gabrael stood beside me, he said, "Technology as communication of computers is the Beast."

I really did not understand what he meant, but now after some time has past, I can see what he meant; Intelligence as in electronics has made the world smaller in that we now see and learn of world conflicts and wars within seconds of when they occur. Instead of another' problems being only their own, now their problems and turmoil has come into our worlds.

In the past, knowledge of others and world events was limited to conveyed by word of mouth to other towns and countries, and even to other continents if the news was that important. Whereas during the life of Jesus most of the world never heard of him or of the lifestyle that he taught and lived, nor did other parts of the world learn of his life and death until centuries later. No knowledge of world wars and conflicts was natural for people of the past generations until the last century, and it was in the first part of the 20th century, with the invention of the radio, people began learning some about issues that concerned others in different parts of the world. Still those issues of concern occurred in lands far away so their problems did not invade the comforts of the listeners.

During the latter part of the 20th century and with the invention of the telephone and television and then the computer, the news of world events could be heard around the globe within seconds. Thus, the world became smaller where people's selfgratifying concepts and controlling beliefs to dominate others could spread like wildfire. Did you think that we are really any different than past generations?

Our needs and wants are the same as theirs, but we need only to experience and enjoy of our lives, too. The concern of others should not influence our happiness.

Jesus did not preach to live under the Christian religion; he merely removed most of the rules and laws of the Jewish religion in the beliefs that he taught and he demonstrated a loving lifestyle that we need to live.

Insects such as Ants, live in a world ruled by a Queen, and in the animal world, an elder male rules. And in human societies of Islamic tribal rules are near the concepts of animal rules and the insect world, as indicated by ruling factors in Iraq and Afghanistan; Where death and abuse of humans run rampant, and to those who live in Iraq and Afghanistian, living under control by a few is righteous and natural.

History always writes the winner of each war as righteous. If in the outcome of wars in history were different, the events of history would have changed the direction of life. But life would have still been enjoyed and experienced by each individual. Whereas, if Hitler would have won the Second World War, history would have written that England and the U.S.A. were evil and the enemies of the world that needed to be destroyed. And today, we would have been living under Nazi rule. But would that be much different or wrong?

We are raised to believe our society and government, which are part of our belief system, is righteous alone. Whereas, we cannot compare the belief system of another to ours that we as individuals know is better. You or I cannot say our society and government is better that an Islam controlled country. We can only say that we prefer to live in our society rather than an Islamic society because we understand ours better.

Does it matter if our children or grandchildren live under Christian or Islamic rule or whatever new religion that will come along? Our forefathers decided that we should not live in a society that condones slavery, we did not. We could not decide which society we should have been born under, but we can deside what society we want to raise our children under.

If Thomas Jefferson could come back to life, he would not like what we have done to the world or in the changes we have made in this great country that he helped founded. If we could return centuries from now, it would be no different in our thoughts. Therefore, whatever the direction civilization takes is not our concern. We can only be concerned in the direction we as individuals take during our lives.

Our only concern is to enjoy and experience the life that we wish to live. Move if you do not like the society in which you live. Allow all others their choice of belief systems and lifestyle that they wish to live, and then you are following God's Will.

The Challenge of Life

We have two dogs; one is a 2 year old Bullmastiff, who is named Alvin, the other is a 9 year old Lhasa Apso who is named Nick. For the last 4 or 5 years, Nick has suffered from seizures and is on medication, and around the middle of September of this year, Nick started to shake and by the middle of October, he has having difficultly standing, and eating, and he began to walk into the walls and the furniture because he was going blind. It was appearent that Nick was dying.

Saturday, the 18th of October, after my wife went to sleep, the Angel Joleen and I sat on the edge of the bed and talked.

I said to her, "You once told me, I was becoming a Master and that I could raise the dead but wouldn't. Do you recall that?"

She replied, "Yes."

Then I said, "You also told me, I could heal people, too."

"Yes" she said, "I remember that conversation."

I said, "Nick is dying...I would like him not to die now. I want him to live his full life...just another 4 or 5 years."

She said, "He has more time, he will not die yet."

I asked, "Can I heal him?"

She replied, "No."

Then I asked, "Can you heal him?"

Again she answered, "No."

Then I asked, "Can Jesus heal him?"

Again she replied, "No."

Then I said, "He is just a dog, his life will not change the world. He only gives us affection. Cannot we heal him so that he will live a full life?"

She replied, "You and I will help him... there it is done."

We talked some more about other things including "My biggest challenge is yet to come," and then I went to sleep.

The next morning, Nick was doing better, and within a few days, he was his old-self as he ran and played again.

I began to think about "My biggest challenge is yet to come." I decided that I needed to remove myself from evil in a fast from evil for 40 days. I decided to buy a motorhome and camp-out on the 160 acres of land that we own in Wyoming for 40 days, where I would stop smoking, and stop using some words that we as human consider bad, stop thinking bad thoughts of others and lose weight - fast from evil. Wthin a few days, I realized that my understanding of "My biggest challenge" was wrong; My biggest challenge is my acceptence of myself. For whenever we leave this world and return to The Other Side, if we do not accept our life here, we will place ourselves in Hell forever, but if we accept our lives here, then we place ourselves in Heaven forever. Therefore, "My biggest challenge" is to repent from my past as to accept all that I did in the past and move forward and toward God. If one cannot repent and accept his past mistakes and continues to dwell (live) on them, he cannot move forward. But yes, I should repent; change my view of the past. I should stop smoking, using bad words and thinking bad things of others for these things nurture evil within each of us.

The words we use in conversations with God or His Angels can make a big difference in what was said or what we interpret was said. The lost context of my words to the Angel Joleen made a complete different meaning to my request.

One of the greatest examples of not understanding God's messages that turned into a religion is Muhammad's conversations with Gabreal. Islam which means to "submit," and Muslim which means "submitter," and Qur'an which means "recite," all are true indictors of a religion that forces people into following its leaders concepts. (Religions - the control of the marjority by a few.)

Suicide is murder of one's self, and suicide is the ONLY sin that is not forgiven by God, but, murder of one's self will not be forgiven by God. Also Spiritual suicide or murder of another is not forgiven by God! Suicide bombers are not forgiven for killing themselves or others.

The Islamic belief claims, "One must come to Allah by the age of 40 or he is lost forever." Therefore, no matter what a person does before his 40th birthday, is not recognized by Allah because all that he does before that age is for himself, the dog. Therefore, if one claims to be a suicide bomber, and kills himself and/or others before he is 40, he is not recognized as a martyr by God and goes to Hell for a length of time as proclaimed by Allah, and then after his sentence is over, he will go to Heaven forever because his is a Muslim and all Muslims are righteous.

We have just entered the Ramadan, and this Islamic holy month stands for fasting from three things during the daylight hours; no drinking, no eating and no SEX! But the other 12 hours of the day, Muslims party with drink, food and sex. Oh yes, even in the hours of daylight or darkness is the days of Ramadan, they still can fight and kill, still steal and still do try to gain control over the world. All that Muhammad was told, he turned toward his personal feelings of the dog that he was, but his evil religion was part of God's Master plan; We needed the choice of evil religions to determine which direction that we as individuals desired to travel.

One could say life is like school that prepares us for our afterlife and our final "test" is our "Greatest Challenge" (acceptence of ourselves) in life occurs as soon as one passes over to The Other Side.

I plan on passing my "Challenge." Do you?

Nick was not my first healing that I witnessed nor will it be my last, but I know that one cannot heal if that illness or disability is needed in the present or future experience of themselves or others because we cannot change God's Master plan.

The Structure of Life

Today my friend, I would like to keep telling you more about what I learned at the church convention that I recently attended. These things that I learned were not spoken at the convention, but God inspired me to understand the "Structure of Life" at the convention. Now I am talking about life as we know it here on earth, okay?

There are four levels that all people live by. Some may only see and recognize only three levels while others may see only one or two levels. But I am attempting to explain about the four level system of life.

We are all equal; no one person is better or worse than another. All religions are equal; no religion is better or worse than any other religion. All Gods of religions are equal while none of these Gods is better or worse than any other God. And then, we have at the very top is the one and true God - the Supreme One.

At the bottom of this ladder, you have people who are all equal. One step up from people, you have religions. Our religion is the step to our Gods. So just above our man created religions we have man created individual Gods, then just above them you have the Supreme One.

Everything below the Supreme One belongs to Him - all Gods, all religion and all people are His - the Supreme One created all.

We, the people, create and/or have created our own religions and Gods for us. The Supreme One has given us the choices to create and believe in anything that we wish to. And this is the cause of the problem that we presently see in Israel. Both sides fighting are saying that they worship and follow the real and only God. But in reality both sides are fighting for their belief of their man-made God, and not for the Supreme One who is above all religions.

The name "God" has become contaminated because whenever you hear the word "God" you automatically think of your individual religious beliefs and your God. And everyone always thinks of their individual "God" at the top. Therefore, I must say God is not at the top, but the Supreme One is at the top!

The Supreme One has given us all our individual decision of our choices. Our choices are the direct cause for our actions toward others and ourselves, too. All righteous actions and decisions are of God because they allow all others their individual choices without Domination. Therefore, we should all Love all people and have no Domination toward others. Then we are living life as the Supreme One wished us to live - allowing all others to decide their life and belief for themselves.

If another seeks your opinion and beliefs, then give them your concepts, but do not push your opinion and beliefs unto others.

Let us Pray:

"My Lord, lead me in the direction of life that Jesus has shown us to be righteous. Teach us a Love for a Love as we walk through this world of the Dead. We need to understand that when we remove this clothing (our bodies) then we shall be "born again" and not until then. Help us to live a life without corruption in this world of corruption. Help us try to replace our eyes with eyes of our hearts, replace our hands with hands of our hearts and replace our feet with feet of our hearts, so then we can see Love, hold Love and walk in Love with You as You did and still do with us. Amen."

Spiritual Origin of Man

From the concept of the concern and love of the Creator for the work of His Hand, it is not hard to reach a conclusion as to the Divine Origin of Man. The fact is that man has a spiritual (Divine) origin, with the innate potential for spiritual progression. No matter how degraded he may become, there will always be the opportunity for reformation. No-matter what calamities he, through ignorance and selfishness, may inflict upon his fellows, ultimately the good must prevail over the evil. This is true because in spite of the gift of "Free Will", which is God's gift to humanity, there will always be the yearning and striving of the majority of men and women away from evil, towards the good.

Eventually good must prevail, because people instinctively recognize that order must take precedence over chaos. We live in a barren and wicked world, in which selfishness is predominant. Concern for one's communal responsibilities is being denigrated by those in Public life, whose task is surely to enhance the happiness and wellbeing of the people. There is a great need for loving persons to actively state their concept of truth: that Mankind is an Unity and each one bears responsibilities towards his neighbor.

Within each and every human being: indeed, within all forms of Creation, there is that which is indestructible and Divine. Religion is but the striving of Mankind towards an understanding of this truth, no-matter how varied its form or confused its approach. There is no such thing as "True Religion": to make such an assertion is to close the door to knowledge. One can only comprehend the true nature of things to a limited degree. It is not possible for Man to encompass within his understanding the Universal Whole. The best we can do is to seek a measure of personal illumination: to approach as far as possible to a perception of Truth. To understand and obey the Call to Perfection is to fulfil one's high potentiality: to perceive the Divine origin of Man and to march forward in fulfilment of the ultimate destiny of Mankind.

Re-incarnation

In his first letter to Corinthians, Chapter 2, the Apostle Paul refers to the fact that things of the spirit cannot be physically perceived but are only evident to the spiritual person. In verse 14, he says: "But the natural man receiveth not the things of the Spirit of God: for they are foolishness unto him: neither can he know them, because they are spiritually discerned".

Hindu/Buddhist tradition suggests that all forms of life spring from Brahma, the Creator Spirit, or Principal of the Heavenly Hierarchy. It suggests that all are subject to the continuous cycle of birth, death and re-birth; the latter being instantaneous upon death, so that there is no break or intermission from this continuum until one finally achieves the state of Nirvana or perpetual Bliss. Thus, individual life forms evolve through aeons of growth and development from lesser to higher forms. After, presumably, numerous incarnations in the form of a Human-Being, and subject to there being no regressive development, the soul eventually reaches the point at which re-union with Brahma occurs. Henceforth, the soul is no longer subject to the law of rebirth in the physical world.

One may not disagree with the concept of a gradual refinement of the individual personality in a movement towards perfection, which is the basis of the doctrine of Re-incarnation. In this sense, all Human endeavour tending towards the guidance and improvement of the Species is beneficial for Mankind and is directed towards a common end: the spiritual elevation of the Race.

The concept of a lengthy evolutionary process, necessitating continuous re-birth in the physical world has some appeal. It is an hypothesis which is readily understood and comprehended by everyone. "If you don't succeed this time around, then maybe the next time may possibly be better". One can belabour the idea of the continuity of life in a Spiritual World from now until Doomsday, without convincing people that it is going to be fun; as they have no concept of the Spiritual World. The world we know is a different affair and for this reason many people are prepared to lend credence to the doctrine of Re-incarnation as a possibility, if not a fact.

The Christian world rejects the idea of Re-incarnation, as such a system would conflict with its doctrines regarding the Second-Coming of Christ and the establishment of a Heaven upon Earth. A moment's reflection will convince any reasonably intelligent person that these ideas are fatuous, as is much of the doctrine developed upon the teachings of Jesus of Nazareth.

Christianity also rejects the related doctrine of the Transmigration of Souls, which acknowledges the possibility of regression to a lower life form in a subsequent re-incarnation. It would be abhorrent to Western minds to contemplate the possibility of one's next life taking the form of an insect or other animal somewhat lower down the evolutionary scale. One must definitely reject this doctrine, even if one toys around with that of Re-incarnation. I prefer to reject both doctrines; believing, as I do, in the existence of a Spirit-world of infinite compass and extent: quite capable of accommodating all the past and future generations of Mankind. I believe that this world is contemporaneous with the Physical Universe and, indeed, forms the very essence and framework upon which the latter is constructed. I believe that death merely releases the soul to an awareness of a greater reality and that there is ample scope for development and growth in the various states of the Spirit-world. Such a scheme obviates the necessity for continuous re-birth in the physical world.

The fact that I also believe in the Communion of Spirit: in the intercourse between Physical and Spirit-worlds also leads me to reject these Hindu-Buddhist doctrines. That there is conflict between the ideas of Resurrection, as understood by Spiritualists, and Reincarnation, as taught by the Eastern Religions, must be obvious to any thinking person. There can be no Spirit-communion between people here on Earth and those who have been immediately re-born into this world on passing hence. The argument for Re-incarnation has evidently been modified in some Spiritualist circles by the proposition that one spends a period of adjustment in the Spirit World, prior to launching upon a further incarnation, but that continuous re-incarnation is inevitable.

Evolution

Whatever the origin of the Universe, no one could be so naive as to imagine that such an infinitely complex, vast and varied Cosmos could be the result of an accidental combination of non-existent elements in a non-existent vacuum in non-existent empty space. One cannot conceive such an idea as "Nothingness", as this is beyond the capacity of Man to imagine. Thus, we are expected to believe that a spontaneous process of evolution commenced some billions of years ago as a result of some completely unplanned and unforeseen combination of chemical processes (which themselves must have been subject to pre-existing laws of physics) but which spontaneously resulted in the formation out of absolutely nothing, initially of the Universe: our own Solar system and finally the Earth itself, as a nursery for developing life-forms. The answer to the question of the origin of all things is simply that we do not know, nor can we ever really comprehend the nature of a beginning. I freely confess that my mental equipment is inadequate to enable me to embrace these questions with any degree of satisfaction. What is clear, is that there must have been a supreme intelligence as an underlying force to establish the initial laws upon which the framework of the Universe was constructed.

Laws can never be said to create themselves. As to the "Big Bang" theory: very well, perhaps things did originate in this way and proceed to develop into the Universe as we know it. Matter, in a recognizable form may have had to exist prior to that event. There is no argument here, even though the theory has to be speculative, based upon our limited capacity to "observe" the Universe today. The pre-existing laws must have existed: matter as we see it must have a beginning or at least, a preceding history of which we must remain ever ignorant.

One does not personally disagree with the principle of evolution; or with the idea of natural selection: neither of which is incompatible with the concept of a Divine Intelligence as the source of all things. It is only the mind limited in its concept of God and Creation by narrow doctrinal views, which has trouble with the idea of the evolution of the species.

What we do observe in relation to the world and the universe around us, is a highly complex organization which has resulted in the development of Man as the highest life-form on the planet Earth, himself endowed with almost limitless intellectual potential.

It is Mankind's physical and intellectual development that raises him so far above the other life forms on the planet. Not only has he the ability to organize his affairs in a social way but he may even speculate on the things he observes around-about him. He can ask the question, "What is life all about?"

Is it all, indeed, a futile exercise? Is man not just a microbe crawling about on some planet, deluding himself that he is of greater value and importance than the other life forms, which he observes around about him? Perhaps! Yet may he not be permitted to exercise his mind in recording his experiences and perhaps contributing to the sum total of human progress? Is it not desirable for him to pursue life in a positive and intelligent manner: recognizing Mankind's collective dependability and seeking to understand and share the experiences of others? If this is the proper course, should we not pursue it zealously and thereby try to make a contribution to the evolution of humankind?

You Are Reaping What You Have Sowed

From the dawn of time, God had called them who seem unlikely to His service, but if you listen to the established religions, this is false. Even Metaphysics and Spiritualist of today, state only they who are schooled in the subjects of Metaphysics and Spiritualism have knowledge of those subjects, (in other words) God, nor His Angels, nor Spirits, nor Entities will contact anyone who has not been taught under their established rules and guide-lines. Therefore, all religions, and Metaphysics, and Spiritualisms of today are Blasphemous to God because man has put his thoughts, ideas and concepts into what pleases God and what He does not like, and has placed them above the Supreme One.

God is very capable of communicating to each of us, and He does have individual contact with all His children. He does not need any one person to tell another what He thinks!

Religions are designed as institutions to be a profitable business of a belief system. (The word "system" means; their institution leads in the directions of life of the followers - the flow of order of life.) Metaphysics and Spiritual material are written to be a profitable business for its writers, publishers and distributors, and for the merchants who sell the materials.

All God showed St. John the "Divine," was for his salvation alone, and what I was shown was also for my Salvation, but God's Angels also said, "Write what you have seen and heard, for your writings will help others, too." Do you not think St. John was told the same thing? For all that an individual is shown or told may be for his personal Salvation, but others can also use it for their Salvation as well.

Whenever humans place price tags on the words of God that he has received, those words turn Blasphemous to God because humans demand money from things they know because if necessary, humans will change as they have been known to change the words from God to make their revelations (spiritual encounters) better than the others.

The words that I have received from God's Angels are not that different than others who claim they have communicated with God. The only difference in what I have received is God's Angels speaking only of "Love to all" because none of the Angels talk of hatred toward others as you find in all religions.

And I say to the people of the earth:

"Oh, foolish ones, follow not those who do not see or know of God, but instead, follow your heart and allow God to enter you, and listen to Him as He speaks of Love. Leash your human feelings that are of evil energy as you lift your Soul in repentance. Convert your beliefs from your religion to knowledge of God who dwells within you. Do not allow yourself to be the slave, and do not attempt to master others, but only be the master of your feelings.

"God's Love for you has been revealed since the start of time, and yet, you refuse Him. You would rather follow another human, one who says he knows what the Father desires of you, one who has placed himself above you and above God.

"Your ways have always been wicked, and now you try to turn your brothers and sisters away from the Father's conversations with them. You attempt to know more than He. You attempt to control all others with your lies. You attempt to create a world under the Creator - YOU. You attempt to bring peace and everlasting life, but you do not live in peace or everlasting life.

"When Moses came down from the mountain, he destroyed two tablets that contained ten promises of Joy that you would have received from God if you would have agreed to follow His ten Commandments, and your actions are worst now than before. God refused to give you His ten promises as a Father refuses to grant his children rewards when they have been bad.

"You have brought the things that you hate upon yourselves. You have brought Satan to the world. You have changed God's Creation into your world of your personal inter-feelings - you have created Satan and Lucifer and have turned them loose upon the earth. You have created the gods that you have placed above your man-made religions and beliefs. You have destroyed the earth, and soon you will destroy the world.

"As you witness your world decay, ask your rabbis, "Why?" Your rabbis know the answer, but they will not tell you the answer because they refuse the truth, for they also refuse God.

Ask your clergy, "Why?" They do not know the answer, but they too refuse the truth because they refuse God and worship the Son instead, for they have placed him above the Father.

Pray to Allah, and ask him, "Why?" He will not answer because he is a man-made god that lives only in the hearts of his believers.

Ask, "Why?" To your great writers of Metaphysics and Spiritualisms, and they will not answer because they know not, for they worship the money that they reap from their 'inspirations.'

"Weep as you pray to your gods as your world falls around you. For you have condemned your children, you taught them not to love, but to lust what the other has. You have darken their hearts, for you taught them your religion is above God, and you taught them to steal, and to lie, and to kill their brothers and sisters – the children of God, and you taught them their only brothers and sisters are of the same color as them, and you taught them their only brothers and sisters are those who follow your religion, but above all; you have taught them the Father will not communicate with them because they are not worthy.

"All that I have told you was for your Salvation. If you refuse what I have said, it is not my problem or worry or concern, for my words do not try to place you into domination. I as the world and the Father shall allow you to make the decision yourself, for you shall live with your decision forever."

People Do What Pleases Themselves

The Angels said to me, "In general, most people do not plan to hurt others. Yes, you do have those who kill, rape and torture for personal gain or for pleasure, but in general, most do not plan on hurting others. But I am talking about daily hurts in life that people do to each other.

"People have personal agendas and thoughts on things that pleases them and these things are their main concerns, and once you enter into their world, you become merely an object for them to enjoy and communicate their feelings to. While some may ask for your thoughts or feelings on different subjects, their concepts of life evolve around them in their universe, for they are at the center of their universe and not yours. Therefore they see everything around them is for their use alone, and that includes you.

"Love is God, God is Love, God is the Father, the Father is the Creator, The Father - God - the Creator - Love is The Creation, humans only know animal love of acts of procreation...that is NOT Love as the Creator intended it to be. For Love is for all of the Creator and not only the little part of it that is nearest you. Love is for all of Creation, that includes all of Creation, even the trees, insects, the earth, rocks, the sky, and all animals besides all that lives as humans...everything. But yes, love of the act of procreation is needed to the lasting of life, but Love from the living for the congregation of all of creation must continue for life to continue, but it shall not.

"Therefore, you should love all of Creation as you understand that all humans are confused and they love only those things and people that pleases them and while they hurt but without intention, all that enters into their universe."

Only Take What You Can Carry

This chapter illustrates how many of the Islamic Religion are trying to carry more than they can handle.

From the mid 80s to approximately 1996, I was researching and looking for a certain hidden (lost) treasure, and around the year 2001, the Angels said to me, "Since you have an honest heart, and since you know where the treasure is but you are sure of your faith, I will stand there and point to where it is buried, and you are allowed to enter and bring out all that you can carry in one trip. (The treasure is said to be over 27 million dollars in gold, silver and jewels.) I thought about going after the treasure, but since God takes care of my needs, I could not justify my need for the treasure.

Recently, I decided that if I go and retrieve the part of this treasure as indicated by the Angels, this would prove my communication with God's Angels, and therefore, it would prove that God does exist.

The Angels also said that I could take whomever I wished in the recovery of the part of the treasure. So, in conversation with a friend, I told him about this treasure and what God's Angels said about recovering my part of it. My friend thought for a few days, and then said, "Take Only the Treasure that you Can Carry…in life do the same thing. Take only the wealth (money) that you need…but I need billions…"

(He will not be going with me.)

Now I understand the concept "Only Take What You Can Carry" even further, it means, "Take on only what you can handle" - If you can love your offspring, then have children. If you can handle a bigger home, get it. If you can handle the things involved in marriage, then get married. The concept of "taking only what you can carry" means, "Do not become the slave of earthly goods…Take only what you will enjoy…"

The Confusion of The World

From the start of time, when the Father first implanted Comprehension into the first one-cell animal that one day would evolve into man, man has been confused about the Creator - the Father. Through man's primitive intelligence and even into today's ignorant intelligences of man, he cannot comprehend anything that is smarter than he, nor can he comprehend any being that was designed or was created better than he, for he, man, cannot believe that he is not the supreme being in the universe.

The greatest example of man's stupidity of modern time is humans listening and trying to communicate with ETs, and expect them to communicate with us, and yet, what do we as a primitive race of animal have to offer a civilization that may be able to travel to other planets and/or distant stars.

Throughout time, man has believed that the Father created us to look like Him, and while each religion believes its the only true religion of the Supreme Being - the Creator, Beliefs of individuals has grown into the false religions of the day, and THAT INCLUDES ALL RELIGIONS! The Father - a Loving God did not create one religion that is better or more righteous than another because men created all religions. The Father created all life and us, for the individuals to enjoy and experience life. He did not create life or us to kill each other or the ones who do not believe our personal religion is not the correct religion of God.

Through the pages of the Old Testament, we find stories about people killing or defeating others as instructed and helped by God. These stories may have been exaggerated for the day. We do know people will expand their stories for the interest of the listener. And as such as sacrifice - offerings to God, were needed and important in the first part of the Old Testament, but later God instructed people not to preform offerings to Him anymore. But the most important part of the Old Testament is that God or His Angels communicated with people.

The New Testament, the story of Jesus' life changed the way we should worship God and the way we needed to live - a life filled with Love. Jesus did not worship God, we should do as he did - Embrace the Father (God) with Love and not place Him upon a throne. Jesus talked (prayed to) with the Father. Even after the death of Jesus, people communicated with Angels and Jesus, too. Therefore, God, Jesus and His other Angels are still alive and will communicate with you.

Jesus healed and brought people back from death, for all those miracles were needed just as his death was needed for the creation of Christanity.

Can people heal others today? Yes, they can, but some people are not to be healed. Their illnesses or deaths are needed, and also, all die at the correct time and place that they were suppose to. We cannot tempt or place demands upon the Father. You should not pray to God to save someone or to heal them, only pray that God will protect them and comfort them into His arms. Prayers are no more than saying "Thank You" to God for all that He has given each individual in his life. Once you begin to give "Thanks" daily to God, you are returning His Love.

A friend of mine who needed a heart transplant asked me to pray that he would be put on the list and receive a new heart. I did not need to pray for him, for I knew the answer immediately.

I answered, "You will be placed on the list to receive a new heart, but God may or may not grant you a new organ that pumps blood through your body, and it is up to you if you get a new heart."

Within a few days, his name was placed on the list, and a few weeks later he received the new organ. After getting out of the hospital, he came to my home and we sat and talked.

I told him, "You asked me to pray for you. I knew you would be placed upon the list. I could not tell you the future about you getting a new organ for that was God's decision, and now it is up to you to change your ways to get a new heart and spread the word of God's Love to others." Around the same time that he asked me to pray for him, he also had talked with a group of Christians from some church. They told him that they, their church, would pray for him. After he got his transplant, they demanded that he come to their church and give testimony about their miracle that saved him. We cannot place demands upon God. He did not change his ways, he continued to refuse help from others; he worked in his yard and on his cars, he went to the stores and Malls without a mask to protect himself, 6 weeks after the transplant he was dead.

God knows what will be and what will not be. Love God and accept what He gives you - this wonderful life that we all live. Accept the actions that your decisions create.

Life and Love is "Give and Receive" and not Give and Take! Give from your heart and receive to the heart all that is given to you.

"Treat all other as you wish to be treated."

Once we all learn how to live a life where we give and receive, we shall live in a world of peace without killing or forcing others to believe and follow in our God or religion. Follow Jesus not as the Lord, but as the "Master" who knows God's Will and demonstrated his knowledge by his lifestyle.

Prophets and Prophecy

What is a Prophet?

Many people think of a prophet as any person who sees the future. While the gift of prophecy certainly includes the ability to see the future, a prophet is far more than just a person with that ability.

A prophet is basically a spokesman for God, a person chosen by God to speak to people on God's behalf and convey messages or teachings. Prophets are role models of holiness, scholarship and closeness to God. They should set the standards for the entire community.

The Hebrew word for a prophet, navi (Nun-Bet-Yod-Alef) comes from the term niv sefatayim meaning "fruit of the lips," which emphasizes the prophet's role as a speaker.

The Talmud teaches that there were hundreds of thousands of prophets: twice as many as the number of people who left Egypt, which was 600,000. But most of the prophets conveyed messages that were intended solely for their own generation and were not reported in scripture. Scripture identifies only 55 prophets of Israel.

A prophet is not necessarily a man. Scripture records the stories of seven female prophets, listed below, and the Talmud reports that Sarah's prophetic ability was superior to Abraham's.

A prophet is not necessarily a Jew. The Talmud reports that there were prophets among the gentiles (most notably Balaam, whose story is told in Numbers 22), although they were not as elevated as the prophets of Israel (as the story of Balaam demonstrates).

And some of the prophets, such as Jonah, were sent on missions to speak to the gentiles.

According to some views, prophecy is not a gift that is arbitrarily conferred upon people; rather, it is the culmination of a person's spiritual and ethical development. When a person reaches a sufficient level of spiritual and ethical achievement, the Shechinah (Divine Spirit) comes to rest upon him or her. Likewise, the gift of prophecy leaves the person if that person lapses from his or her spiritual and ethical perfection.

The noted greatest of the prophets was Moses. It is said that Moses saw all that all of the other prophets combined saw, and more. Moses saw the whole of the Torah, including the Prophets and the Writings that were written hundreds of years later. All subsequent prophecy was merely an expression of what Moses had already seen. Thus, it is taught that nothing in the Prophets or the Writings can be in conflict with Moses's writings, because Moses saw it all in advance.

The Talmud states that the writings of the prophets will not be necessary in the World to Come, because in that day, all people will be mentally, spiritually and ethically perfect, and all will have the gift of prophecy.

The Role of Women

The role of women in traditional Judaism has been grossly misrepresented and misunderstood. The position of women is not nearly as lowly as many modern people think; in fact, the position of women in halakhah (Jewish Law) that dates back to the biblical period is in many ways better than the position of women under American Civil Law as recently as a century ago. Most of the important feminist leaders of the 20th century (Gloria Steinem, for example) are Jewish women, and some commentators have suggested that this is no coincidence: the respect accorded to women in Jewish tradition was a part of their ethnic culture.

In traditional Judaism, women are for the most part seen as separate but equal. Women's obligations and responsibilities are different from men's, but no less important.

(In fact, in some ways, women's responsibilities are

considered more important, as we shall see).

The equality of men and women begins at the highest possible level: God. In Judaism, unlike Christianity, God has never been viewed as exclusively male or masculine. Judaism has always maintained that God has both masculine and feminine qualities. As the Angels explained it to me, "God has no body, no genitalia."

Therefore the very idea that God is male or female is patently absurd. We refer to God using masculine terms simply for convenience's sake, because Hebrew has no neutral gender; God is no more male than a table is.

Both man and woman were created in the image of God. According to most Jewish scholars, "man" was created in Gen. 1:27 with dual gender, and was later separated into male and female.

According to traditional Judaism, women are endowed with a greater degree of "binah" (intuition, understanding, intelligence) than men. The rabbis inferred this from the fact that woman was "built" (Gen. 2:22) rather than "formed" (Gen. 2:7), and the Hebrew root of "build" has the same consonants as the word "binah." It has been said that the matriarchs (Sarah, Rebecca, Rachel and Leah) were superior to the patriarchs (Abraham, Isaac and Jacob) in prophesy. Women did not participate in the idolatry regarding the golden calf. Some traditional sources suggest that women are closer to God's ideal than men.

Women have held positions of respect in Judaism since biblical times. Miriam is considered one of the liberators of the Children of Israel, along with her brothers Moses and Aaron. One of the Judges (Deborah) was a woman. Seven of the 55 prophets of the Bible were women.

The Ten Commandments require respect for both mother and father. Note that the father comes first in Ex. 20:12, but the mother comes first in Lev. 19:3.

There were many learned women of note. The Talmud and later rabbinical writings speak of the wisdom of Berurya, the wife of Rabbi Meir. In several instances, her opinions on halakhah (Jewish Law) were accepted over those of her male contemporaries. In the ketubah (marriage contract) of Rabbi Akiba's son, the wife is obligated to teach the husband Torah! Many rabbis over the centuries have been known to consult their wives on matters of Jewish Law relating to the woman's role, such as laws of kashrut and women's cycles. The wife of a rabbi is referred to as a rebbetzin, practically a title of her own, which should give some idea of her significance in Jewish life.

There can be no doubt, however, that the Talmud also has many negative things to say about women. Various rabbis at various times describe women as lazy, jealous, vain and gluttonous, prone to gossip and particularly prone to the occult and witchcraft. Men are repeatedly advised against associating with women, although that is as much because of man's lust as it is because of any shortcomings in women. Women are discouraged from pursuing higher education or religious pursuits, but this seems to be primarily because women who engage in such pursuits might neglect their primary duties as wives and mothers. The rabbis are not concerned that women are not spiritual enough, but rather are concerned that women might become too spiritually devoted.

The rights of women in traditional Judaism are much greater than they were in the rest of Western civilization until this century. Women had the right to buy, sell, and own property, and make their own contracts, rights which women in Western countries (including America) did not have until about 100 years ago. In fact, Proverbs 31:10-31, which is read at Jewish weddings, speaks repeatedly of business acumen as a trait to be prized in women (v. 11, 13, 16, and 18 especially).

Women have the right to be consulted with regard to their marriage. Marital sex is regarded as the woman's right, and not the man's. Men do not have the right to beat or mistreat their wives, a right that was recognized by law in many Western countries until a few hundred years ago. In cases of rape, a woman is generally presumed not to have consented to the intercourse, even if she enjoyed it, even if she consented after the sexual act began and declined a rescue! This is in sharp contrast to American society, where even today rape victims often have to overcome public suspicion that they "asked for it" or "wanted it." Traditional Judaism recognizes that forced sexual relations within the context of marriage are rape and are not permitted; in many states in America, rape within marriage is still not a criminal act.

There is no question that in traditional Judaism, the primary role of a woman is as wife and mother, keeper of the household. However, Judaism has great respect for the importance of that role. The Talmud says that when a pious man marries a wicked woman, the man becomes wicked, but when a wicked man marries a pious woman, the man becomes pious. Women are exempted from all positive commandments ("thou shalts" as opposed to "thou shalt nots") that are time-related (that is, commandments that must be performed at a specific time of the day or year), because the woman's duties as wife and mother are so important that they cannot be postponed to fulfill a commandment. After all, a woman cannot be expected to just drop a crying baby when the time comes to perform a commandment.

It is this exemption from certain commandments that has led to the greatest misunderstanding of the role of women in Judaism. First, many people make the mistake of thinking that this exemption is a prohibition. On the contrary, although women are not obligated to perform time-based positive commandments, they are generally permitted to observe such commandments if they choose. Second, because this exemption diminishes the role of women in the synagogue, many people perceive that women have no role in Jewish religious life. This misconception derives from the mistaken assumption that Jewish religious life revolves around the synagogue. It does not; it revolves around the home, where the woman's role is every bit as important as the man's.

The Role of Women in the Synagogue

To understand the limited role of women in synagogue life, it is important to understand the nature of commandments in Judaism and the separation of men and women.

Judaism recognizes that it is mankind's nature to rebel against authority; thus, one who does something because he is commanded to is regarded with greater merit than one who does something because he chooses to. The person who refrains from pork because it is a commandment has more merit than the person who refrains from pork because he doesn't like the taste. In addition, the commandments, burdens, obligations, that were given to the Jewish people are regarded as a privilege, and the more commandments one is obliged to observe, the more privileged one is.

Because women are not obligated to perform certain commandments, their observance of those commandments does not "count" for group purposes. Thus, a woman's voluntary attendance at daily worship services does not count toward a minyan (the 10 people necessary to recite certain prayers), a woman's voluntary recitation of certain prayers does not count on behalf of the group (thus women cannot lead services), and a woman's voluntary reading from the Torah does not count towards the community's obligation to read from the Torah.

In addition, because women are not obligated to perform as many commandments as men are, women are regarded as less privileged. It is in this light that one must understand the man's prayer thanking God for "not making me a woman." The prayer does not indicate that it is bad to be a woman, but only that men are fortunate to be privileged to have more obligations. The corresponding women's prayer, thanking God for making me "according to His Will," is not a statement of resignation to a lower status (hardly an appropriate sentiment for prayer!) On the contrary, this prayer should be understood as thanking God for giving women greater binah, for making women closer to God's idea of spiritual perfection, and for all the joys of being a woman generally.

The second thing that must be understood is the separation of men and women during prayer. According to Jewish Law, men and women must be separated during prayer, usually by a wall or curtain called a mechitzah or by placing women in a second floor balcony. There are two reasons for this: first, your mind is supposed to be on prayer, not on the pretty girl praying near you. Second, many pagan religious ceremonies at the time Judaism was founded involved sexual activity and orgies, and the separation prevents or at least discourages this.

The combination of this exemption from certain commandments and this separation often has the result that women have an extremely inferior place in the synagogue. The women's section is poorly climate controlled, and women cannot see (sometimes can't even hear!) what's going on in the men's section where the services are being led. Women are not obligated by Jewish law to attend formal religious services, and cannot participate in many aspects of the services (traditional Jewish services have a very high degree of "audience participation" -- and I'm not just talking about community readings, I'm talking about actively taking part in running the service). Because of these issues, many Orthodox women rarely attend services, and some of those who do attend spend much of the time talking and not paying attention.

This restriction on participation in synagogue life does not mean that women are excluded from the Jewish religion, because the Jewish religion is not just something that happens in synagogues. Judaism is something that permeates every aspect of your life, every thing that you do, from the time you wake up in the morning to the time you go to bed, from what you eat and how you dress to how you conduct business. Prayer services are only a small, though important, part of the Jewish religion.

Love and Brotherhood

Many people think of Judaism as the religion of cold, harsh laws, to be contrasted with Christianity, the religion of love and brotherhood. This is an unfair characterization of both Judaism and Jewish law. Laws are at the heart of Judaism, but a large part of Jewish law is about love and brotherhood, the relationship between man and his neighbors. Jewish Law commands us to eat only kosher food, not to turn on lights on shabbat, and not to wear wool woven with linen, but it also commands us to love both Jews and strangers, to give aid to the poor and needy, and to do no wrong to anyone in speech or in business. In fact, acts of love and kindness are so much a part of Jewish Law that the word "mitzvah" (literally, "commandment") is commonly used to mean any good deed.

The Talmud tells a story of Rabbi Hillel, who lived around the time of Jesus. A pagan came to him saying that he would convert to Judaism if Hillel could teach him the whole of the Torah in the time he could stand on one foot.

Hillel replied, "What is hateful to yourself, do not do to your fellow man. That is the whole Torah; the rest is just commentary. Go and study it."

The "Golden Rule" is not an idea that began with Christianity. It was a fundamental part of Judaism long before Hillel or Jesus. It is a common-sense application of the Torah commandment to love your neighbor as yourself (Lev. 19:18), which Rabbi Akiba described as the essence of the Torah.

The true difference between Judaism and Christianity lies in Hillel's last comment: Go and study it. Judaism is not content to leave love and brotherhood as a general ideal, to be fulfilled as each individual sees fit; Judaism spells out, in intricate detail, how we are meant to show that love.

Jewish Law includes within it a blueprint for a just and ethical society, where no one takes from another or harms another or takes advantage of another, but everyone gives to one another and helps one another and protects one another. Again, these are not merely high ideals; the means for fulfilling these ideals are spelled out in the 613 commandments.

Everyone knows that the Ten Commandments command us not to murder. The full scope of Jewish Law goes much farther in requiring us to protect our fellow man. We are commanded not to leave a condition that may cause harm, to construct our homes in ways that will prevent people from being harmed, and to help a person whose life is in danger. These commandments regarding the preservation of life are so important in Judaism that they override all of the ritual observances that people think are the most important part of Judaism.

We are commanded to help those in need, both in physical need and financial need. The Torah commands us to help a neighbor with his burden, and help load or unload his beast, to give money to the poor and needy, and not to turn them away empty handed. See Tzedakah: Charity.

Jewish law forbids Jews from cheating another or taking advantage of another. Jewish Law regarding business ethics and practices is extensive. It regulates conduct between a businessman and his customer (for example, not to use false weights and measures, not to do wrong in buying and selling, not to charge interest) and between a business man and his employee (to pay wages promptly, to allow a worker in the field to eat the produce he is harvesting, and not to take produce other than what you can eat from the employer while harvesting).

Entire books have been written on the subject of Jewish Laws against wronging another person in speech. They are commanded not to tell lies about a person, nor even uncomplimentary things that are true. They are commanded to speak the truth, to fulfill our promises, and not to deceive others.

Contrary to what many people think, most of these laws regarding treatment of others apply not only to our treatment of our fellow Jews, but also to our treatment of gentiles, and in many cases even to our treatment of animals. In fact, some of the laws instituted by the sages even extend kind treatment to inanimate objects. The bread on the shabbat table is covered during the blessing over the wine, so that it's "feelings" are not hurt by having the wine take precedence over it. Of course, we do not believe that bread actually has feelings, but this practice helps to instill an enormous sensitivity to others. If we can show concern for a loaf of bread, how can we fail to show concern for our fellow man?

The Messianic Idea in Judaism

Belief in the eventual coming of the moshiach is a basic and fundamental part of traditional Judaism. It is part of Rambam's 13 Principles of Faith, the minimum requirements of Jewish belief. In the Shemoneh Esrei prayer, recited three times daily, we pray for all of the elements of the coming of the moshiach: ingathering of the exiles; restoration of the religious courts of justice; an end of wickedness, sin and heresy; reward to the righteous; rebuilding of Jerusalem; restoration of the line of King David; and restoration of Temple service.

Modern scholars suggest that the messianic concept was introduced later in the history of Judaism, during the age of the prophets. They note that the messianic concept is not mentioned anywhere in the Torah (the first five books of the Bible).

However, traditional Judaism maintains that the messianic idea has always been a part of Judaism. The moshiach is not mentioned explicitly in the Torah, because the Torah was written in terms that all people could understand, and the abstract concept of a distant, spiritual, future reward was beyond the comprehension of some people. However, the Torah contains several references to "the End of Days" (achareet ha-yameem), which is the time of the moshiach; thus, the concept of moshiach was known in the most ancient times.

The term "moshiach" literally means "the anointed one," and refers to the ancient practice of anointing kings with oil when they took the throne. The moshiach is the one who will be anointed as king in the End of Days.

The word "moshiach" does not mean "savior." The notion of an innocent, divine or semi-divine being who will sacrifice himself to save us from the consequences of our own sins is a purely Christian concept that has no basis in Jewish thought. Unfortunately, this Christian concept has become so deeply ingrained in the English word "messiah" that this English word can no longer be used to refer to the Jewish concept. The word "moshiach" will be used throughout this page.

The Moshiach

The moshiach will be a great political leader descended from King David (Jeremiah 23:5). The moshiach is often referred to as "moshiach ben David" (moshiach, son of David). He will be well-versed in Jewish Law, and observant of its commandments. (Isaiah 11:2-5) He will be a charismatic leader, inspiring others to follow his example. He will be a great military leader, who will win battles for Israel. He will be a great judge, who makes righteous decisions (Jeremiah 33:15). But above all, he will be a human being, not a god, demi-god or other supernatural being.

It has been said that in every generation, a person is born with the potential to be the moshiach. If the time is right for the messianic age within that person's lifetime, then that person will be the moshiach. But if that person dies before he completes the mission of the moshiach, then that person is not the moshiach.

When will the Moshiach Come?

There are a wide variety of opinions on the subject of when the moshiach will come. Some of Judaism's greatest minds have cursed those who try to predict the time of the moshiach's coming, because errors in such predictions could cause people to lose faith in the messianic idea or in Judaism itself. This actually happened in the 17th century, when Shabbatai Tzvi claimed to be the moshiach. When Tzvi converted to Islam under threat of death, many Jews converted with him. Nevertheless, this prohibition has not stopped anyone from speculating about the time when the moshiach will come.

Although some scholars believed that God has set aside a specific date for the coming of the moshiach, most authority suggests that the conduct of mankind will determine the time of the moshiach's coming. In general, it is believed that the moshiach will come in a time when he is most needed (because the world is so sinful), or in a time when he is most deserved (because the world is so good). For example, each of the following has been suggested as the time when the moshiach will come:

1. If Israel repented a single day;
2. If Israel observed a single Shabbat properly;
3. If Israel observed two Shabbats in a row properly;
4. In a generation that is totally innocent or totally guilty;
5. In a generation that loses hope;
6. In a generation where children are totally disrespectful towards their parents and elders;

What Will the Moshiach Do?

Before the time of the moshiach, there shall be war and suffering (Ezekiel 38:16)

The moshiach will bring about the political and spiritual redemption of the Jewish people by bringing us back to Israel and restoring Jerusalem (Isaiah 11:11-12; Jeremiah 23:8; 30:3; Hosea 3:4-5). He will establish a government in Israel that will be the center of all world government, both for Jews and gentiles (Isaiah 2:2-4; 11:10; 42:1). He will rebuild the Temple and re-establish its worship (Jeremiah 33:18). He will restore the religious court system of Israel and establish Jewish law as the law of the land (Jeremiah 33:15).

Olam Ha-Ba: The Messianic Age

The world after the messiah comes is often referred to in Jewish literature as Olam Ha-Ba (oh-LAHM hah-BAH), the World to Come. This term can cause some confusion, because it is also used to refer to a spiritual afterlife. In English, we commonly use the term "messianic age" to refer specifically to the time of the messiah.

Olam Ha-Ba will be characterized by the peaceful co-existence of all people. (Isaiah 2:4) Hatred, intolerance and war will cease to exist. Some authorities suggest that the laws of nature will change, so that predatory beasts will no longer seek prey and agriculture will bring forth supernatural abundance (Isaiah 11:6-11:9).

Others, however, say that these statements are merely an allegory for peace and prosperity.

All of the Jewish people will return from their exile among the nations to their home in Israel (Isaiah 11:11-12; Jeremiah 23:8; 30:3; Hosea 3:4-5). The law of the Jubilee will be reinstated.

In the Olam Ha-Ba, the whole world will recognize the Jewish God as the only true God, and the Jewish religion as the only true religion (Isaiah 2:3; 11:10; Micah 4:2-3; Zechariah 14:9). There will be no murder, robbery, competition or jealousy. There will be no sin (Zephaniah 3:13). Sacrifices will continue to be brought in the Temple, but these will be limited to thanksgiving offerings, because there will be no further need for expiatory offerings.

Judaism and Jesus

Judaism has no specific beliefs about Jesus, just as it has no specific beliefs about Muhammad, Buddah, Confuscius or King Arthur.

In Judaism, Jesus is not a god, a messiah, a prophet, or even a great teacher. We don't even have an official opinion on whether Jesus existed.

Why don't Jews believe that Jesus is the messiah?

Quite simply, because he never did any of the things that the messiah was supposed to do. The Jewish messiah is a warrior-king like David, who will lead the world into an era of perfect peace, prosperity and justice, as the prophets repeatedly and explicitly promised. The Jewish messiah is not a god in human form behind a 2000-year-old IOU for the messianic age.

What About Jesus?

Jews do not believe that Jesus was the moshiach. Assuming that he existed, and assuming that the Christian scriptures are accurate in describing him (both matters that are debatable), he simply did not fulfill the mission of the moshiach as it is described in the biblical passages cited above. Jesus did not do any of the things that the scriptures said the messiah would do.

On the contrary, another Jew born about a century later came far closer to fulfilling the messianic ideal than Jesus did. His name was Shimeon ben Kosiba, known as Bar Kochba (son of a star), and he was a charismatic, brilliant, but brutal warlord.

Rabbi Akiba, one of the greatest scholars in Jewish history, believed that Bar Kochba was the moshiach. Bar Kochba fought a war against the Roman Empire, catching the Tenth Legion by surprise and retaking Jerusalem. He resumed sacrifices at the site of the Temple and made plans to rebuild the Temple. He established a provisional government and began to issue coins in its name. This is what the Jewish people were looking for in a moshiach; Jesus clearly does not fit into this mold. Ultimately, however, the Roman Empire crushed his revolt and killed Bar Kochba. After his death, all acknowledged that he was not the moshiach.

Throughout Jewish history, there have been many people who have claimed to be the moshiach, or whose followers have claimed that they were the moshiach: Shimeon Bar Kochba, Shabbatai Tzvi, Jesus, and many others too numerous to name.

Leo Rosten reports some very entertaining accounts under the heading False Messiahs in his book, The Joys of Yiddish. But all of these people died without fulfilling the mission of the moshiach; therefore, none of them were the moshiach. The moshiach and the Olam Ha-Ba lie in the future, not in the past.

It is interesting to note that Judaism has 613 Commandments that most Jews follow, and these were written by man. While many "things" about life fall outside those Commandments, therefore, most Jews live lifes dominationed by man's thoughts, ideas and concepts.

As I continue to say, "All religions are man's concepts of what pleases and displeases god. God does not dominate! Man dominates in the name of God!"

False Prophets

I am thoroughly confident because the Angels have told me, all people are born with the ability to see and communicate with those of The Other Side, and are able to predict the future. What happens is that during our youth, we are taught by parents and peers, and by religious teachings that it is wrong to do those things. We are taught that it is the devil's work if we can see, communicate or read the future while we are also driven (taught) into corruption of self-interest.

In today's world, many are coming out of the closets and claiming that they have the "Gift" of these supernatural abilities that was given to them by God. Some of these people may have carried the knowledge of their abilities throughout their lives while others may have refreshed their memories of their "Gifts" in latter years. (When they first realized their capabilities is not priority in understanding "Gifts" given by God.)

The Funk and Wagnalls Standard Desk Dictionary describes a "Prophet" as;

1. One who delivers divine messages or interprets the divine will.
2. One who foretells the future; esp., an inspired predictor.
3. A religious leader.

(Why a religious leader would be considered a Prophet is

beyond me.)

The Christian Bible describes a False Prophet as one who is incorrect in his prophecies.

We can find many prophets, ones who claim they can foretell the future, working the psychic hot-lines and also working the internet, while others write columns and books dealing with religion and God. Many of these have demonstrated their abilites to predict the future, or to tell their version of their communications with the The Other Side, with a fair amount of accuracy. But they ALL make mistakes, so are they False Prophets because they laced their human feelings into their predictions or stories? NO!

They are False Prophets because they believe they are better than others because God has given them the "Gift." Whenever one raises himself above the majority as believing he is closer to the Father, he becomes False in his comprehension, and then his perspectives become warped and he begins charging others for use of his "Gift."

Once a person has to produce answers for the inquirers, he will begin to create what is of self-interest instead of what is true - false answers to pay his keep and to pay for his gains in life. And this Power has corrupted many.

There is a man who has written four or five books about his communications with God, who before his books were published, did not have much, and now he has made millions of dollars from his concepts, and today he runs a religious retreat and has a great following on his website and large turnouts at his seminars. His work began for God, and now it has turned into making a profit for himself. He has become a False Prophet.

Another psychic that I found on-line charges $25.00 for answering three of your questions in one email and gives you the answer for you forth question free.

These two psychics are the same as Muhammad - they are False Prophets. The only difference is that Muhammad used the sword to force people to believe in what he said.

All clergy are False Prophets because they must tell you something better than the next preacher to keep you coming back to their church. They must have better words for you to give them your money. They must make their church bigger and better than the rest.

Whenever one tells me about the great and beautiful church they belong to I think, "How nice it is for him to be proud of the church that he attends, but HOW SAD. Does a big and beautiful church make it any closer to God?"

Should all that money be spent on remodeling church or building a new church or go to helping the poor or homeless instead of trying to out-do other churches?

If I have more money than you, does that place me closer to God?

If I only have one dollar and give it to someone who is hungry, and then I have nothing, am I poorer than you?

Most psychics will read tarot cards or tea leaves, or some other kind of item they use for their medium to obtain their answers. Clergy - "preachers" use their Scriptures to obtain their answers. Both try to use their "Knowledge" to enforce their power over the majority. The clergy reads from old writings and twist its words to fit his interpretation of his bible, these words he uses to persuade or to force, the congregation to do as he demands by saying if they do not follow his words, they shall go to Hell forever. The only difference between the clergy and psychics is psychics do not state the part about, "If you do not follow what I say, you will go to Hell forever," while both demand your money for their "knowldge," and they are not any different from the guy who wrote the four or five books about his communications with God! They are ALL false because they predict for money.

Whenever you see or hear of someone charging for telling you God's words or for telling you the future, you can be sure they are False Prophets.

God - the Father provides all that I need.

In January of 2000, Jesus said to me, "We have stood beside you through all of your life. I was there beside you when you had your by-pass operation, I shall stand beside you for the rest of your life. We will guide and take care of you."

I once asked the Angel Joleen, "Why does not Muhammad ever appear...why cannot I see him?"

She answered, "He is not like us...he is different."

In a candid way she was saying, "He is Evil."

We will never know if Muhammad truly communicated with God or His Angels, but by studing the recorded history of Muhammad and his Islam religion, we can see that he used the sword to convert people to his religion. If people refused his religion, he would cut off their heads, so therefore, the children of those that he forced into Islam, were the first Muslims and that was the beginning to Islam!

Muhammad's "bible" - the Qur'an, means to recite; Recite the words that he had written into his "bible." This is the same type of brain-washing as the Russians used in the cold war! Therefore, Muhammad was a False Prophet, and Islam was created by Muhammad for the control of the majority.

Each of us, in our own personal way must find the Salvation that is needed by us. There is No Evil in God or Heaven...we as individuals create the Evil that is within us. What or who we follow is not Evil, its how we interpret old writings and/or how we follow another' concepts determines if we shall live forever with the Father or not. Life is no more than a wink of an eye compared to Eternity. Use your time wisely for someday, life will surely fade away into Eternity for each of us. And when you are gone, how do you wish to be remembered? Lift your Spirit - enjoy and experience life!

I have a wonderful wife and two sons. I have a lovely three bedroom, two story home. I ride a new and paid for motorcycle. I drive a 1973 Silver Shadow Rolls Royce, and my bills are paid. As everyone, I could use more money...but I refuse to sell what was given to me - a gift from God's Angels - the words of God. Now, when I am gone and my writings are put into books, those who publish and print those books will have to be compensated for their work. But I SHALL NOT benefit in monetray gains from the gifts given to me, and therefore, all that I say is true for I have no reason to lie, for I experience life as I enjoy it.

Prophets

To understand "who is a Prophet," we could review the Christian Bible and the Jewish Torah, but the Islamic Qur'an has the best definition of a Prophet. The following is from the teaching of Islam 101; If the whole of mankind and jinns were to gather together to produce the like of the Qur`an, they could not produce the like thereof, even if they backed up each other with help and support.

What is a miracle?

I believe it is necessary that we have a clear picture of what we mean by a miracle. Here are some definitions: "An event that appears so inexplicable by the laws of nature, that it is held to be supernatural in origin or an act of God." Or "A person, thing or event that excites admiring awe." Or "An act beyond human power, an impossibility."

It is logical that greater the impossibility, greater the miracle. For example, should a person expire before our very eyes and is certified dead by a qualified medical man, yet later on a mystic or a saint commands the corpse to 'arise!', and to everybody's astonishment the person gets up and walks away, we would label that as a miracle. But if the resurrection of the dead took place after the corpse had been in the mortuary for three days, then we would acclaim this as a greater miracle. And if the dead was made to arise from the grave, decades or centuries after the body had decomposed and rotted away, then in that case we would label it the greatest miracle of them all!

How I Became a Prophet

Some of you have asked me, how and when did I become a Prophet. I must tell you my true story of God's Love.

I was born and raised across the street from the Nazarene Church in Wooster, Ohio. We did not go to any church nor follow any religion, but on Sunday and Wednesday nights, I would sit outside our home and listen to the Christian music that they played and sung in the church.

In the summer of 1965, I had a love affair with a woman, Joan. She was 32, but indicated that she was 27 years old while I was 20, but claimed that I was 22 years old. We were both married but separated from our spouses at that time.

Joan had breast cancer, but I did not know much about cancer and did not know she was dying. (I did not find out until during the spring of 1997 that she had past on September 1, 1968.)

During our affair, she asked me for a child, and I agreed. We planned on staying together, but during that fall, after reconciliation with my wife, I had to leave town because I worked drilling oil wells and I moved across the state to another area. Realizing I should have stayed with Joan, I was unable to return until months later and when I did return, I was told that she had become pregnant and moved away with another guy. I did not know where to look for her. I had met her mother and sister only once, but I could not even recall her last name, so therefore, not knowing where to look for her, I left.

During the first part of the 90s, I began having heart problems; heart attacks, by-pass, etc. The future did not look good for me, and it was in the spring of 1996 that I decided to find Joan and our child, if we did conceive one. I just wanted to tell her I was sorry for not returning and to ask her for her forgiveness. I knew things between us would never be the same; I was happily married now and in my 50s, and she would be in her 60s. I knew that I could never leave my family for her, and thought she would feel the same about her family, too. I just wanted to see her one more time before I died.

During the summer of 1996 I started my search for her, and upon returning to Marion, Ohio, I was unable to find any trace of Joan. I then decided that maybe hypnosis may jog my memory for her last name or names of her friends or family, or maybe the directions to her sister's home because we did drive to her sister's one time.

While I was under hypnosis, Joan was with me. I was unable to recall the things that I wished, but she told me that even if I found the house in which her sister once lived, it would not do any good because everyone had moved. But, as we talked, I noticed her mouth did not move as she spoke, and I asked her about it.

She answered, "I am dead," as she smiled at me.

Once Joan said she was dead, I was able to accept the fact that she was gone and that I would never see her again in life. But, from that point on, she continued to be beside as we continued our conversations.

She told me about how my wife, Chris, had seen her twice, and my oldest son had seen her four times, and how my youngest son had seen her many times as well.

Not being a religious person, I thought it was kind-of nice having a "friend" on the Other Side that I could talk to.

Then, Joan asked me to ask Chris is she would allow her to enter into her body just for a short time, so that we could be together again. I refused and told Joan to ask Chris herself. Around a week later, as Chris and I started to make love, I found that Chris was doing things as Joan did when we used to make love over thirty years prior. I had never told Chris about Joan because Chris and I were married in 1975, and that was 9 years after Joan and I had been together. Therefore, there was no way Chris could have ever known about Joan.

But there in bed was Chris acting like Joan, and talking about the things we did and places we went in the past. Afterward, Chris told me about how she stood beside our bed as she watched us making love.

As the months passed and Joan being in Chris' body diminished, she slowly introduced me to Gabrael (he says we spell and pronouce his name wrong), then Michael and Jesus.

When Joan and I talked, I could hear her as if only in my mind, so I decided to channel her through Chris. I learned the art of hypnosis and learned how not to lead my questions so that I would recieve answers from Joan and not from Chris. Therefore, I would use both; the answers that I received in thought and the answers that Chris spoke that were recorded to verify Joan's answers. For a period of about 3 years (from the fall of 1996 to the spring of 2000), I recorded our conversations on both audio and video cassettes. I presently have over 30 hours of recorded conversations from which I have written and spoke in excess of 1 million words about The Other Side, Angels and God.

It was the humanly love that we shared when she was alive and her ability to show me love from The Other Side that inspired me to seek God with Divine Love for Him because there was no one else alive or dead that I would listen to about God. Though I was surrounded by "ghosts" my entire life, I refused Salvation until she, the Angel Joleen (Jo, Joan), entered into my life.

We have discussed many things, and she has told me many things about my life and the future of the world that have come to pass, but she said that I was told these things for my Salvation and not many would listen to what I say, but people will come after I am gone and they will spread the words of God that I have written and spoken.

I do not tell you these things for my glorification. I tell you things for the recognition of God. I cannot give you the answer to why others communicate with God, but I do know that unconscious writings and only hearing God or His Angels in one's mind, may not be truthful because our human thoughts, ideas and concepts can pollute our thoughts.

Throughout my life, I have been surrounded by Entities. And through my life, I have told people that I did not want the Entities to leave because I was studying them and wanted to understand them. And boy, did they teach me a bunch throughout the years.

I have learned many things about relaying prophesies to others. One must understand where the prophesy came from; was it from God's Angels or from the concepts of you?

Three of the prophesies that I have told people did not come true exactly as I thought they were told to me. And those three prophesies were about others where I was involved in their lives. But I told these prophesies as if these prophesies were about me as if I was the center of the universe.

A good analogy is; We are "thinking" about moving to Ohio, once we weigh out all the things involved in moving, we may "decide" and will "believe" in our decision, then we "know" the decision is corect for us. Our "belief" to move to Ohio, may not be correct for you. Therefore, when ever a preacher says, "I think," to his congregation, he is merely speaking of things that he is thinking about and not what God really said or thinks.

Whenever I speaks to others about prophesies that I have received, I must understand where the thoughts come from; did the thoughts come from God's Angels or from the "dog" within? We need to be more concerned about what comes out of our mouths instead of what goes in.

I tell you that God is dead in the eyes of most people, but some will listen and believe God is communicating with people today. I guess many people think God finished His communications with us when His Son died on the cross. Yet, the clergy know differently, but they are selling His words, and their product as your salvation and God's Heaven. The clergy cannot allow you to know that you can speak to God directly, for if you do, they will not be in business. The churches and religions have become that which is against God.

The Catholic Church is a good example of how the clergy use God's words to obtain your money and Soul.

How can anyone say they believe in God and claim to follow His words while abusing children?

Is the Catholic religion (Christianity) any better than Islam?

How can Muslims believe that if you die while killing others, you will go to Heaven and be surrounded by 72 virgins (both male and female) for your personal use?

Do not the 72 virgins have a God?

Would He not grant them Heaven, too?

The Jewish people claim that when their Messiah comes, the world will live under their religious laws and rules. Is that not domination?

Does God dominate?

Is He not a loving and forgiving God?

Today, the beliefs in God come directly from inter-feelings of the human. The lust (Sins) of man lead the religions of the world.

People are murdering others for their beliefs in God because people cannot explore the thought that they may be wrong in their concepts of God. People would rather fight and kill or be killed instead of finding out the truth about God - that He also loves all people even those who follow different religions.

How sad it is to know that people regard their thoughts, ideas and concepts – their beliefs, are more precious than life.

God through His Angels have told me the truth. They do not lie. I used channeling while listening to their answers in thoughts to verify their answers.

It was said that Gebrael talked to Muhammad because Christianity had become corrupted. Now God's Angels have talked to me because Islam has become corrupted, too.

I do not intend to change people or save the world. I merely am speading the words that I was told. It is up to you to believe in whatever you wish, but you will find that what I say lines up with the true God above all.

Fools Learn From Fools

As we journey through the world (life) we have been taught that we must learn what others have endured (experienced) by what they have written. Civilization has allowed the individual within its society, to become acquainted with an authority on any given subject by studying the writings of another.

There are three types of learning that we need to understand; the first type are those learned as science such as physics and natural laws. These things incorporate equations and formulas that produce constant answers. The second is those of human knowledge such as engineering, building, medicine and so forth. These teachings stem from trial and error, and may be improved upon by the input through the intelligence of the student. The third is spiritual or other beliefs systems that may be considered as philosophies. These types of teachings all contain concepts, ideas and thoughts from the writers and/or from his sources and/or his investigations.

For whenever we study another' concepts, ideas or thoughts, we merely come to an understanding of what the author believed, endured or experienced. As such, whenever one goes to a school or college and studies these types of philosophies, one is merely learning an established understanding thought process of the author. And while you are in the class, you will be given a test to see if your thinking and/or understanding of the subject lines up with the professor's. After the exam, and if you agreed with what the professor and the authors of the books the professor used in his class, you will be given a passing grade. But, even if the grade that you receive is low but above failing, you are considered as passing the class. And thus, you will be considered as an authority on the subject.

Whereas, many people go to religious colleges for years, and then later become preachers and/or ministers. These people only learned what their teachers have taught them. And while the teachers only teach what they were taught, but the pupil does not retain all that he was taught. Therefore, the teachers who were once pupils also, are only teaching what they remembered.

These newly ordained preachers and ministers (past and present) do not allow God to communicate with them because their teachings did not include the understanding that God continues to communicate with His children. And also, they have been taught that the religious writings that they been studying but did not learn what is correctly interpreted. Is that any different than those who claim to be authorities that post web sites on the internet because they have read a book or two on a certain subject? The only difference is that those who self-proclaim authority are usually self-taught and have taken a thought or two from maybe a few sources and blended them into their belief system. But, the true genesis of a given field, excells their teachings are usually self-taught. Both, the preacher's or minister's ideas and thoughts came from another' concepts, ideas and thoughts. But he has forgotten many important parts because he did not endure or experience what the other had lived. He did not take into account that all the other has said or written came from words that were symbolic for the writer's understanding.

And then, foolish people will find the preacher or minister, and listen to the them and then believe that person knows what they were talking about, and many foolish people believe all that they read or hear.

An example of this concerning religion, the Jewish, Christianity and Muslim religions, all three claim to be the only religion of God. But yet, all three religions have different beliefs that places it above the other two. And today, followers of all three religions are ready and willing to kill all others of other religions to make (force) their religions the true religion of God.

All three of these religions are blasphemous against God because they all use human concepts, ideas and thoughts that created a God and His Will for their personal desires.

In keeping with people claiming "I follow the correct religion of God and you don't," the only way to bring peace to the world is by controlling all others because there can be no peace unless it is as directed by thinking and understanding that you alone know as the truth from God.

God does not condone murder of any type, nor does He believe in suicide. I stand with His Will, therefore I do not condone murder or suicide of any type, and if you ever read me speaking about God and Him demanding us to murder or commit suicide, run as fast as you can from me because then I will be speaking as human from the evil within and not as the Guider, a Messenger of God. The words of God's displeasure against murder and suicide are written throughout my writings, for what I write is for the Glory of God and not for the glory of any human or belief system.

Throughout history, man has created weapons that were considered as weapons of mass destruction. These range from the sword to bows and arrows to gun powder to airplanes that could drop bombs, and then to nuclear, biological and chemical weapons feared by most people of the world today. But nuclear, biological and chemical weapons are not the final end of our creation of weapons of destruction for future use. And you have these weapons to destroy your enemies and try to dominate your enemies by their knowledge that you have these things. You created these things to dominate others who do not believe and follow what you believe. War will not bring peace to the world, it only brings despair and hatred after the war has ended. But God will not change the course of the human race, nor will I try to change your views. God does not need to destroy the world, you - the human and our warped perspectives will do that by ourselves because we will not allow the other to follow his beliefs. And he, our enemy, will not allow us to follow our personal beliefs, so therefore, use our modern weapons that we have to control the thoughts, beliefs and actions of others. Today, the only way for peace is to nuke all those who do not believe or follow your belief system. Kill them all that do not agree with you, for if you do not, they will kill you.

We have built nukes to keep men and women out of harms way, so use them. Drop nukes on Iraq, waste it, and then allow those who remain alive after the bombing to die without your help. For that is your choice, not God's.

The human only knows what he has learned from the foolish ones who lived before him. And he will continue to hate until he is inspired to understand that God is the way of love and that hatred is the way of humans.

Our schools, professors and clergy teach, "I am righteous because I have knowledge as written by man, and God is not knowledge for He is what we have created under our religions. God is not knowledge because we have placed Him in part of our knowledge as created by man. Therefore, you cannot listen to or communicate with God because if He does exist, He would only talk with me and not you. So give me your life, money and your children and I will tell you how He demands you to live."

Our schools, professors, clergy are the true Antichrist of the world. Listen and learn from the Antichrist of our world and allow them to pull you into believing and following their warped perspectives, for that is your choice as given to us by God. I shall not try to force you to love God and follow His Will. The Gates to Heaven are narrow and not many will enter.

I have been taught under God's Angels, from the fall of 1996 through 2004, my Master's in learning to sepaprate my human (dog) feelings from God's teachings. And one of His teachings was; "Whenever you know someone is going to Hell but they claim that they are going to Heaven, don't tell them." Because that is the difference between a true Prophet or a human.

What is Right for Humankind

Throughout the past years of my website, I have written Messages about the Father, His Angels and His Creation. And during those years of my learning, I too, understand more and more. And I as you, during learning will find better words and/or better ways to explain the subject to others. For the Angel Jollen said, "You will not completely understand until you are here on The Other Side."

Often, people in their search of the Father have emailed me asking questions about Him, His Angels and His Creation. I knew that because of all the information contained within our Archives it may be difficult for one to quicky find the answer for their questions. And also, it is time to get away from writing about issues of present day and go back to revealing the Father's Messages as explained to me by His Angels. So therefore, lets get back to understanding the Creator's Will as I will tell you more of what I have learned.

Scientist keep trying to uncover creation of the universe. Whereas they keep seeking the wisdom of where did or does matter originate from.

Energy is the connection between this "plane" or dimensions and the one of the Creator. Energy can and does move from one dimension to another, back and forth as it wishes and/or as needed. It is this Energy that is referred to as the Father or Creator and His Angels as well as bad Energy. The dimension of the Father is a dimension of Energy that can think and comprehend and move about without mass. This Creation (dimension) that we live in also means that we are part of that Creation. (The Father created us.)

We cannot comprehend another dimension until we have been there. Whereas our physical universe and physics do not exist in any other dimensions, and while our understanding of what is natural is completely right here, but our comprehension is not correct in any other dimensions.

(For this discussion, I will refer to this dimension as Creation and the Father's or Creator's dimension as The Other Side.)

All that is of this Creation is made-up of this Energy of either (in human opinion) good or bad, for the Father did not create anything that was not needed. The good and even the bad are needed for us to decide whichever is right for us, whereas, the Father has given each individual our freedom of choice because one must know the difference between good and bad to understand his or her choices and to understand the consequences or rewards of the individual's actions and of each separate action.

On The Other Side, time has location, where one can travel to different locations in time. In Creation, time does not have location and where time is used as past, present and future for humans to experience the future as the unknown factor in the equation (formula) of personal actions.

All the Energy, which is all Angels in Congregation, is the Creator of all in and of this universe, and who is the Father of all the people as indicated by His statement; "Break open a piece of wood and I am there. Turn over a rock and I am there."

Whereas, the Father - His Angels are not just part of everything, for He - They are all of everything. They are not just part of us, for They are all of us. But we are not Them because we were conceived by Them for Them. They do not need us...we need Them for without Them, we are No-thing and do not exist.

The Father did not create us and allow us to live through our lives for us to be down on our knees worshipping Him forever as His slaves. If He merely wanted us as His slaves, there was no need for us to have life. He gave us life so that we could experience the rewards of our choices. As any good Father, He allows us to choose what we think is needed for us as we "Learn from the experiences of others through the endurance of life."

Jesus said, "The only way to the Father is through me," and

after Jesus was killed, he returned and spoke with his desciples. Therefore, when Jesus returned and talked with His desciples, He was an Angel for He was dead (without human body).

But Christians say, "Do not associate or converse with Angels or the deceased (those without human body)," because the Devil - Satan - Lucifer is very deceiving.

Christians also say, "The Devil will portray himself as God and do whatever he must to get you to worship him instead of God."

Daily, preachers will say that God has told them something that needs to be said to the people. Did they truly know with whom they spoke?

The Old Roman Church which now is the Vatican - the Mother Church of the Catholic Religion, removed most mention of Angels from its Bible so people would not worship Angels instead of God as described in their religion, but yet the Old Roman Church, decided and canonized "The Father and Son and the Holy Ghost are one and the same," and Christian preachers will tell you that Jesus and God are one in the same. And still the Catholic Chruch worship and pray to Angels that they now call Saints.

Throughout time, man has taken his agenda and placed it into his concept of the Father's Will and thus, men believe they know the Father and are closer to Him than all others. Human concepts of man are the common reasons for wars and battles of men, whereas, Religions are the procreation of men for the control of the people. And those men have decided that only evil (the Devil, or Satan, or Lucifer) communicates with today's humans while they, the clergy, are the only ones who communicate with the true Father. And while the words "God", "Allah" and "Lord" were designed and are used to control people into visualizing a man as God, or Allah, or Lord as referred to Jesus, who is in control and rules over all the people, and all people must do as the preacher instructs them to do as God's Will.

Therefore, ALL Religions are SINS AGAINST THE FATHER and ALL preachers and ministers are SINNERS AGAINST THE FATHER! Because the Father, the Creator is LOVE WITHOUT DOMINATION, and whereas, all religions promise you Love if you follow its rules and laws, and all preachers and ministers promise you their God's Love if you follow His rules and laws.

Churches are the beast, and the clergy of all religions are one of the Anti-Christ that we have been warned about. Human concepts of what is right for all humans is the evil that conceives thoughts of control and domination over the people. But, the Father has given each individual his or her freedom of choice, and whereas, the Father has given each his or her freedom of choosing whichever belief system they chose to follow. And this is where humans become confused because each see themsevles as the center of their universe and do not understand that they are only part of Creation that is directly part of total LIFE - a place where each individual is part of the congregation of the Father because each person carries a part of the Father within. And that part of the Father is the Energy from The Other Side. And while this part of each, that is the Energy from The Other Side, will live forever with the knowledge of whatever each have choosen to do in their life, for these memories of life will be our individual Heaven or Hell afterlife and will live forever within the individual's Angel.

What is right for Creation is right for you.

Who Will Be Determined Righteous?

During the early 70s, I worked for Santa Fe Drilling Company, drilling oil wells in Libya while I lived on the Island of Malta. I stayed 14 days in the desert and worked 12 hours a day there, and then would fly home to Malta for 7 days off. And it was there in Tripoli, Libya, that I would spend the night at a house that was kept by Santa Fe for its employees who were en-route to or from the desert.

We would leave our drilling location early in the morning and fly to Tripoli, spend the afternoon and night there, and then the next morning catch another flight to Malta, and the same thing in reverse when we were heading back to work.

The house in Tripoli was bare of furniture except for a couch and chair in the living room, beds in the two bedrooms where we slept and a small table and chairs in its dining room. No carpets or rugs nor would you find other furnishings or little nick-knacks that most homes in the U.S have. The kitchen was bare also except for a counter and sink and a stove and refrigerator. The house had a houseboy (an old Muslim man) who was hired by Santa Fe to maintain the house for its employees staying over in Tripoli. He did not cook for the Santa Fe employees nor did he have much conversation with the men who stayed there. Our houseboy would be seen leaving or coming home, or sweeping the floors, or he would be found squatting on the kitchen floor as he prepared his meal.

Whenever we were in Tripoli, we would shop and eat out, and spend the evening talking about our work on the drilling rigs and occasionally playing cards. (Libya was a dry country so we were not allowed to have alcohol there; we did our drinking in Malta.)

There was another ex-pat (a person who lives overseas that worked in a foreign country) who lived in Tripoli with his wife. And since we knew them, they would come over and visit whenever we were in town, and on occasion, if he was out in the field, his wife would come over alone and visit with us. And even though her visits were innocent, whenever she came over by herself, our houseboy would hide and watch us and listen to what was said. Our houseboy reported her visits to the police and they called her in and told her that if she continued to visit us, they would stamp her passport "Prostitute" and kick her out of the country.

If a Muslim accuses you of wrong doing to another Muslim, he is automatically believed right and you are wrong. A Muslim will not humiliate another Muslim, nor will any Muslim allow you - another from any belief system, to deface or disgrace a Muslim. That is part of their religion!

To the Muslim, only Muslims are truthful while all other people are infidels, and the Muslim believe that these "other people" are no better than dogs. But yet, the Islam religion did come from God. Muhammad not only polluted God's words with his personal thoughts, but he also corrupted God's words with his selfish Arab ideas and concepts.

The word "Muslim" means one who submits to God.

The word "Islam" means to submit to God.

The word "Qur'aan" means to recite (remember and be able to speak the exact words that Muhammad claimed Gabrael told him) the words of God.

The word "Allah" is the Arab (word) name for one of the many man-created gods below the true one God who is above all.

The name "Muhammad" is the name of a man who used God for his delights, pleasures and lust of young girls.

But yet, even though Muhammad created an evil religion, it too, still holds words from God that does speak of "love all other and have no domination toward them." Even Muhammad could not erase

God's love. As the same with Christianity, Islam holds as you wish to live, either for God or the evilness within yourself.

If you listen to Muslims speak, they will talk of the nation of Islam, one nation that covers the world. A nation without borders, and this is what is happening to the U.S.A. and to our southern neighbors.

But what do we hear when we listen to Christians talk?

I voted for President Bush, but where is he going with Christianity?

President Bush told Arafat, he needs to convert his government to a democracy. He told North Korea not to work with nuclear power. He told Saddam that he cannot have weapons of mass destruction and that he must leave his country. And Bush said that God told him to defeat the Muslim terrorists.

President Bush is trying to spread Christian theology and concepts around the world. The U.S. is governed by Christian ideas while the Muslim countries are governed by Muslim ideas. Can the Muslim countries convert to Christian style governments and keep its Islam religion?

But yet, the U.S. government has removed prayer from its schools, but will not remove "God" from its Pledge of Allegiance, and continues to use national songs that mention "God," and refuses to remove "God" from its money, and pays a chaplain $75,000.00 per year to open its congress with a prayer daily. (The word "God" as used in the U.S. is the Supreme Being over Christianity.) ...And they talk of allowing Islam into our schools. So in the U.S. are all religions equal?

After 9-11, Bush opened a can of worms that cannot be closed. He started a fight against all Muslims and called it his fight against terrorists. President Bush should have fought the terrorists as Israel does - fight the little fractions and pockets of terrorists that were involved in the 9-11 destruction.

Have you ever seen a bar-room fight? Two people start to fight, and then everyone begins to fight each other, but for different reasons. The Christians, and Jews, and the Muslims will not back down, for this world war is the same as the people in a bar-room brawl.

The U.S. cannot clear its own streets of gang warfare and there is no way that it will clean the world of terrorism. The street gangs leaders are no different than the terrorist leaders around the world - they make their living off of money they are given by others. These leaders are un-capable of making a living from anything else because they know of nothing else but violence. Christians like President Bush have taken their religious teachings and turned them into selfish reasons to control all other religions, and the people who are the true terrorist leaders were taught the Islam religion and to recite the words of Muhammad who was evil.

Islam speaks of Martyrdom, but where is Arafat or bin Laden? Do they stand up to die for their Allah? Therefore, do they really believe in or follow their religion?

To truly defeat Islamic terrorism is to wipe out every Muslim and remove its religion from the face of the world, but then isn't that what Hitler tried to do with the Jews? And if winning the war on terrorism is what President Bush wants...

A Christian started talking about God as he approached my youngest son. My son asked the man, "Do you worship Jesus?" The man answered, "Yes." Then my son asked the man, "Is Jesus God?" the man dropped his head and walked away.

In the Christian Bible, it is indicated that God is to have said, "Do not place any other above me."

If one worships Jesus, he is placing Jesus above God. If the Muslim fights for Islam, then he has placed the religion of Islam above God. Therefore, is Christianity or Islam more righteous?

Both religions came from God, but both were corrupted by man as he (man) polluted God's words as he (man) created his (human) religions.

Do Not Infringe Upon Others

As I sit here in my home here in the U. S. A., and in the comfort of freedom, and in a lifestyle where I have no enemies nearby, I continue to read the news of tragedies caused upon the Israeli people by terrorist. My heart goes out to the Israeli people as I mourn for the innocent that have been murdered by Palestinian bombers who are no more than terrorists.

Daily, as in the past, I view world events on my computer, and it does not take a mind reader to see the Muslim concepts of life are just as corrupted today as they have always been in the past, and as always if one gives them an inch they will take a mile.

Peace will not come by giving the Palestinians land for their country that includes part of Jerusalem for their capital. For if you give them part of Jerusalem, they will begin a fight to take all of Jerusalem, and then they will fight to push all Israelis out of Israel.

Throughout the year prior to the 9-11 terrorist act, I wrote many articles that I posted on my web site; Jesus' House of Jacob, about how the world needs to back Israel in fighting terrorists now or soon the world would be fighting terrorists in their individual homelands.

The terrorists who bomb Israeli citizens are not part of the nation of Islam. The nation of Islam is part of worldwide network of terrorists. Because to be a terrorist, one only needs to be driven by self centered ideas, while Muslims are driven by corruption taught to them by their society as being righteous, whereas, it is simple for the insane of any religion to grasp the Islam religion's concepts for reasons of self-interest.

There is no way for Israel to have peaceful homeland until all Palestinians are removed or placed under the complete control of Israel. And if the world is not willing to help Israel, the people from other places should leave Israel alone and allow them to take care of their Palestinian problem.

President Bush has opened the "box of evil" that cannot be closed. That "box of evil" is not one-sided but contains evil of the Muslim and Christian as well. And as history has shown, he who wins the war shall go down in history as being righteous, and therefore, if the Christian side wins the war on terrorists, Christianity will go down in history as being the righteous religion of God. And can he, President Bush, deny helping Israel in its fight against the Palestinians who are terrorists? If the U.S. does not help fight all terrorists, is it truly fighting terrorists? For if President Bush does not help Israel to delete terrorists then he is merely doing personal battle (things President Bush wanted his Daddy to do to Saddam but didn't) and going to war against Iraq because of his self centered ideas.

The Christians say of those who are not Christians; if they do evil things, they have sinned, but if the evildoer is Christian than he has merely backslid. The Muslims claim those who are not Muslim are the infidel and no better than dogs. And therefore, if a Muslim lies to an infidel, he has not lied, and while if a Muslim lies to another Muslim or if they humiliate another Muslim by calling him a liar, that is Allah's Will.

Both religions put down women by indicating women are lower than men and act as if women are only for the production of MAN-kind and the sexual gratification of man.

The Mormon religion - the last religion formed, states men are to have more than one wife, thus, they too, believe man is above women. But yet, all three religions came from God, but men have placed their individual concepts of men being more God-like or more righteous than women into God's words.

Therefore, all religions that came from God were and are polluted with man's ideas and then corrupted by man's ideas and thoughts of what God Wills.

WHY? Because men cannot remove himself from his image of the Supreme Being - God, is why. For men will always think as men. They cannot allow others to do for themselves - the world will not let the Israelis do what is fit for them. People have been taught to put their noses into places that they should not.

Each individual needs to protect and assure himself of his personal Salvation without placing his beliefs upon others. Whereas, allow others their personal beliefs with love as long as the other's beliefs do not infringe upon yours. Therefore, "Love all others and have no domination toward them."

Do as He Did, Not as They Say

During the first minutes of June 12th, 1944, in Wooster, Ohio, at 205 West South Street, I was born the 10th child of 11 children to Zona and Estil Haven.

Our home... my home was an old house that was divide into a duplex; we had two rooms down and two rooms with a bath up. The other side was three rooms down and two rooms up with a bath. I recall, our house still had the old gas lines sticking out of its walls for gaslights, and we heated our home with our kitchen stove and one gas space heater in the other down stairs room. It would have been a lovely old mansion if it would have been taken care of and painted once in a while, but it wasn't. It was just an old rundown house that didn't even have grass or any vegetation growing in its front yard except for one old pear tree that didn't bear fruit anymore. Inside, we lived with cockroaches and mice, sleeping on the floor, and had little food to eat. Each night, I would lay in fear because of all the little noises that I heard and the ghost that I saw. My parents felt they had done pretty good, considering each only had a third grade education, and moved to Ohio from Kentucky for a better life. I recall, in the late '50s, my Dad was bringing home 50 dollars per week, our rent was taken out before my Dad received his pay; he worked in a junkyard behind our house whose owner was also was our landlord.

I was raised in a house without religion, but across the street stood a Nazarene church. Besides the regular Sunday morning services, each Sunday and Wednesday evening, they held services as well. I recall sitting outside on those evenings and listening to their preacher give his sermons and then hearing the wonderful songs they sung afterward. I loved hearing the organ play with all the voices blending together in songs praising God.

But then, I also remember one Sunday morning, after service as the adults stood around outside and talked with their minister, their children threw stones at the birds in the intersection of the street. One of the boys hit a bird with a stone, the little bird lay there still alive and moving around but could not get up. The adults looked at the bird and then they all laughed as the boys continued throwing stones at the bird until they killed it. No one cared about the life of the bird, but I did.

Another Sunday morning as the adults stood outside the church after services and talked, I was playing with our neighbor kids in our yard. As we played, I ran with a toy small metal ladder sticking out of my mouth. I fell and the little ladder cut me under my tongue. I recall standing up and crying as blood ran from my mouth and down onto my shirt as all the churchgoers pointed at me and laughed. No one cared. After that, sometimes I still would sit outside and listen to their music, but never enjoyed their songs as much anymore.

And during these, my elementary school years, I was made fun of and called names because of the rags that I wore and because of always being dirty. But no one cared... not even the teachers, no one attempted to stop the other kids from tormenting me. But, then in high school, I soon learned how to "take care of myself" by fighting. I stopped the name calling and laughing at me because I cared.

When I was around 14 years old, we bought a house across town and moved, but I never forgot the lies their Christian preacher told his congregation and how they "truly" listened to what he said. For if God and Jesus were real, why didn't the congregation or the preacher believe in and follow what the preacher said?

In my teen years, I started drinking and smoking cigarettes and running wild as I raised hell. And throughout my teen years as through most of my life, I just knew God and Jesus were false. They were just lies told by preachers, to make money from the people who wanted to live forever. For if the preachers didn't even try to live the life that they preached that the congregation should live, that meant that the preachers did not believe in God or Jesus either.

For most of my life, it was "do what was best for me," to hell with the others, and laws were made for others and not me. I recall even telling my Mom once, "F___ God! And F___ Jesus! They are not for me, and when I die, I will NOT bow to God or the Devil, I will stay here on Earth forever!" For I just knew that they were lies to make people live the way society wanted us to live.

But the real truth was that God and Jesus never forgot me. They stood beside me throughout my life and waited for the correct time to enter my life.

No person alive could ever convince me that God and Jesus were not false. It would take someone that I trusted, someone that I loved, a person from beyond, to convince me that God and Jesus existed. And after 52 years of living in my hell of living as I wished, it was during the fall of 1996, that the Entity of a deceased ex-girlfriend, Joan Lee Harris, she had died from breast cancer in September of 1968, entered into my life once again. For Joan was the only person that could convince me that God and Jesus did exist.

Joan was one (ghost) that I was not afraid to see or hear. And at first, it was fun having someone on the other side to visit with. Then, slowly she introduced me to Gabrael, and then they introduced me to Michael, and then all three of them introduced me to Jesus. At first Jesus called himself the Helper, and referred to Joan as the Deliverer, and soon they began to talk about God and life while their words inspired me to ask questions that they answered for me.

As their "teachings" continued, I soon learned that most of what the ministers preached about was false. (The Angels never put anyone down, they said the ministers were just confused.)

I soon realized that ministers do not teach Jesus' lifestyle, but rather, they preach how we should live - forcing others to convert to Christianity. And while most ministers do not believe that the Bible or God's Will should govern their lives but only ours, as is now known with the knowledge of the Catholic sexual child abuse cases.

Known Catholic clergy sex offenders are being moved from one parish to another, but not removed from being a Catholic spokesperson for God. One Cardinal was actually promoted and now works in the Vatican directly under the Pope. But yet, where is the Catholic God, and what does He think about sexual abuse of children? If the minister, a Catholic clergy, can stand up in front of you and speak of God's love for His children and then do ungodly things to children, is he living for God? He must be telling lies, for he does not live what he preaches.

I have yet to hear one Catholic clergy say anything about what God thinks or says about the Catholic clergy child abuse. Have you?

Another spin-off of Christian religion now allows its clergy to live and/or marry the same sex, but yet, its Bible forbids same gender sexual relations, and they condemn those of their congregation who live homosexual lifestyles. Can its clergy live a lifestyle different from righteousness in its Bible and still speak the words of its God?

(Personally, I know that if two of the same sex are truly in love as two heterosexuals should be when they wed, it is not my place to condemn their relationship, for in God's eyes they are already one. And if asked to officiate over their wedding, I will.)

It is recorded in the New Testament, that Jesus talked of things that he disliked. He never said he hated anything. But we hear all ministers saying that he hates this or that. That is not as Jesus lived.

When you allow hatred or even the thought of hating something to enter into your heart, you are allowing hatred to grow within you. When Jesus was being killed and hanging on the cross, he did not hate, in fact, he asked the Father to forgive those who were murdering him, for he would not allow hatred to enter into his heart, thus, he would not let hatred grow within him.

"Those who walk upon the Altar should be careful or otherwise people will look under their gown and see their nakedness." In other words, if you speak the words of God, do not place yourself above the other people (closer to God) because the congregation will someday learn that you are human too, for you also make mistakes as all humans do. Whereas, live as you preach others to live.

Do you believe liars when they do not live the lifestyle that they say you should live?

The Roman Church that is now known as the Catholic Church called for the Crusades to end the control of Muslims over Jerusalem. The Church leaders did not go fight these battles, they told their congregation to go and fight, which they did. Today, Islamic radicals tell their followers to kill Jews and Christians by suicide bombings, and they do. Iraqi Islamic clergy tell their congregation to kill U.S. Soldiers, and they do. The Muslim clergy do not die as martyrs in their "Holy Wars."

All religions have liars that standup and tell their congregation how to live and how to die. Whereas, Christianity is no different. It is not the religion that Jesus preached; it is a religion made up about lies told about Jesus. He was not the Messiah as told in the Old Testament, the one that the Jewish people looked for. Their Messiah was to be a warrior like their King David was, and one who would place Judaism around the world as the religion of the world, and to make Jerusalem the capital of the world. Jesus did not do that.

Christianity is a religion that was founded and started by Jesus' Disciples years after His death. And the books written into the New Testament were written hundreds of years after His death, because then people placed Him upon a pedestal, as we do when someone we love or "worships" dies today.

Jesus did not say the Father and Son and the Holy Ghost were the same, the church said that.

Jesus did not say that He was Lord, the church said that.

Jesus did not say that He was the only Salvation, the church said that.

Jesus did not say to worship Him, the Church said that.

Jesus did not say to pray to him, the church said that.

Jesus did one thing...He showed us how to live...His lifestyle was a demonstration on how we were to live! And His lifestyle demonstrated to whom we should pray to and to give thanks to...THE FATHER!

Christians who are instructed by their preachers to go around knocking on doors while trying to force their religion upon others are no better than the Muslim Terrorists. For Muslims also try to force their religion on all the people. And all religions will fight and kill others to keep their religion growing.

Read the Bible's Old Testament for its historical fact that God did communicate with humans to understand that God still communicates with humans.

Read the Bible's New Testament for its knowledge of how to

live as demonstrated by Jesus.

I have talked with Jesus many times, and know Him very well. He does not lie! And He does not preach how we are to live, for the inspiration that He demonstrated in His lifestyle is the only way of Salvation for me and you.

Do not live as the preachers tell you to live. Live as Jesus demonstrated for us to live, and you shall be fine.

Individual Salvation

In this "Virtual Reality" of life that we live, a realm of a third dimensional plane, we cannot image or comprehend the plane of reality that on which the Angels, and who in congregation are God, and who is all the Energy combined live. All in this dimension, including all life is merely a thought or idea of the Angels. And all this in that we live must be endured as to experience and enjoy as desired by God.

Our lives have a beginning and an ending as all time has a beginning and an ending, but we do not know if Energy (God) has a beginning and ending, but that is not our concern, for our concern is to experience and enjoy life as intended by God. But nevertheless, we as human have created evil actions and have created the difference between good and bad as views of society as directed by God, but He does not contain evil, and whereas, we as human have designed the concept of evil to control our feelings toward others and ourselves as well. And our design of evil has created our individual and personal eternal Hell. Therefore, we have control over our afterlives of Heaven or Hell.

God did not create Satan or Lucifer or the Devil, for Satan, Lucifer and the Devil do not exist. In the minds of human we use Satan, Lucifer and the Devil as the concept of evil as an excuse for our selfish interest. Therefore, there is no evil in Heaven or in God.

Evil only lives in the hearts and minds of men. For the thought of a Satan, Lucifer and/or the Devil is a fictitious entity created by men to control others as the concept of a man-like Supreme Being and/or God was designed by evil men to control others.

We are human and not Angels, we cannot "do" as Angels do, but also we have a part of God inside each of us, (I refer to this piece of God that dwells within each of us as the Angel-within,) and we should allow that Angel-within to lead our lives. But that is not to say that we cannot live as humans, but to blend both together as one.

"Turn the other cheek," does not mean, "to allow your other cheek to be hit also." It means to continue as you were before you were struck. Do not let the evil actions from another turn your feelings into hatred. And whereas, if another wishes to harm you and if you wish, you may allow him to do whatever he wishes because this life that we live is merely a very small part in the Reality of God, and you should not corrupt your Salvation with evil from another. For we have no enemies except for the hatred that dwells within us.

A Body of Doctrinal & Practical Divinity

By John Gill
Doctrinal Divinity~Book 6

The fitness of Christ to be a Redeemer of his people is worthy of notice. As he engaged in it he was every way fit for it; none so fit as he, none fit for it but himself; no creature, man or Angel: no man, for all have sinned, and so everyone needs a redeemer from sin, and can neither redeem himself nor any other; nor could an Angel redeem any of the sons of men; God has put no trust of this kind in those his servants the Angels, knowing that they were unequal to it: the Angel Jacob speaks of Jesus who redeemed him from all Evil, "Was not a created but the uncreated Angel; the Angel and Messenger of the covenant, the Messiah."

All on The Other Side is Energy. It seems that we cannot accept that other forms of intelligent life may exist in other places besides here or earth or in this universe. But yet, Life on The Other Side is another life form that is very different than ours. Life on The Other Side is Energy that is able to comprehend, communicate and move without assistants from solid matter.

This combined Energy is what we conceive as God - the Supreme Being. There is a difference between Angels and deceased people, and that distinction is; Angels are those who returned to the Light (God's Knowledge) after their human deaths while the deceased people (ghost or entities) have not yet gone to God. But there is no rank on The Other Side; all are equal for all are Energy, but yet, they may have different directions. We as humans are all God's children, and therefore we also are all equal. But yet, each human as an Individual, has selected his individual direction (mission - job) in life; I worked drilling oil and gas wells for over 19 years, and then I changed my direction and became a heavy truck and forklift mechanic. While yours was completely different from mine, we are still equal.

This Energy (the Angel-within; that piece or part of God that dwells within each individual) can be felt as our feelings of either good or bad. And while, we as individuals can cover our Angels within with feelings (Energy) of Evil if that is what we follow, or we can glorify that piece or part of God (the Angel-within) that dwells within each of us by personally following a righteous way of life. As when Jacob wrestled with Uriel, Jacob was fighting with the thoughts (the things that he did to his brother) that were driven by his human desires and the Godly feelings of Uriel; to do that which was right. The Energy that is a piece or part of God called Uriel won and from that point forward, Jacob allowed Uriel to lead his life, and therefore, God renamed him Israel and granted him the inheritance that He had promised his grandfather, Abraham. And after Jacob died, his life's experiences were forever recorded upon his Soul, and therefore, most on The Other Side even today still refer to him as Jacob. (Even though God had renamed Jacob Israel), his human birth name was Jacob, and that is what he is forever known as.

The feelings of our actions are like veils that are laid like layers upon our Angel-within now and then forever afterlife. And each layer can be thick or thin depending upon how we handled our life and our missions while alive, but all Angels may have "lived" many lives, so therefore your Angel-within may have layers from different lives that it has "lived." These layers do not necessarily "darken" the Angel-within for layers of righteous living make the Angel-within glow brightly for the Glory of God - the Congregation of Angels - the Energy.

It is the responsibility of each human to help raise his Angel-within nearer to God. Whereas, each should live the best life possible for afterlife we shall remain as we did during life, and therefore, the veils that you have created and placed upon your Angel-within is your Soul that "lives" forever on The Other Side.

In many conversations with the Angels, they call me "Jacob." Wondering if they were speaking to me or not, I asked, "What is my name on The Other Side?"

They replied, "You have many names, but most call you Jacob."

And then I asked, "Should I change my name to Jacob?" They answered, "No, for you were given the name "David" by your Father and Mother when you were born."

Then, I was shown my Angel-within, and he did not want us to look at him, for he was covered with veils of Evil. I felt sorry for him and wanted to help remove those veils, and which I have been doing.

The Energy of Divine Love emits from everything in God's creation for it is God's Creation, and it flows throughout God's creation touching and influencing everything as it moves through everything and those (people that are alive) who do not refuse it.

Each individual has the choice to accept or refuse the One all Mighty God who is above all, and if you truly accept Him, you shall feel His Divine Love flow through you. No other can force you into believing in Him. But most will not place their faith in Him, but continue to worship their man-made Gods who govern their religion and that is okay if that is what you desire, and if the belief system that you follow proclaims, "Love all others and have no domination toward them," then you shall have found your Salvation and the Heaven that you desire.

And while each Angel may be in many places as once, it is possible for one Angel to be the Angel-within for many at the same time. And yet, you are not your Angel-within; you are merely a human who allows an Angel who I refer to as the Angel-within you to lead your life.

During the evening of February 19th of this year as I prepared for bed, I noticed "Alvin," our watchdog and who is a 15 month old Bull Mastiff, and is part of our family, staring toward a corner of our bedroom. Immediately I knew he was looking at the Angel Joleen.

She did not have to say why she was there; I knew the reason for her visit. As I laid down in bed, I felt something that I cannot fully explain; it was the Energy of Divine Love not flowing to me and stopping in me nor was it starting in me and flowing out of me, but it was the flow of Energy of Divine Love through me, for now I was becoming part of God's Creation and not part of God's creation; I have taken another step toward the transition of allowing the Angel Jacob to lead my life. This transition has been ongoing for around one year. Now I was beginning to truly follow the Angels Uriel and Jacob.

As Guider, I help guide people to the God of their choosing. My following the Angel Jacob - allowing him to lead my life; I let him select the direction that he "knows" I need to go. He is the guiding Light (Knowledge of God) in my life, and of which I have been following for the last 7 years, but I did not know it was he who I was following until just two weeks ago. And if you view the Ministry of the Guider, you will see that I guide people to God and not to any specific religion. I only Inspire others with the Knowledge of God.

The Angel Uriel

Before going further, we should understand who is this Angel Uriel that Jacob wrestled with because he is one of the lesser known Angels. First we need to read what is found on: www.iit.edu/~herzdan/uriel.htm

Uriel ("fire of God")
One of the leading angels in noncanonical lore, and ranked variously as a seraph, cherub, regent of the sun, flame of God, angel of the presence, presider over Tartarus (Hades), archangel of salvation (as in II Esdras), etc. In the latter work he acts as heavenly interpreter of Ezra's visions. In Enoch I, he is the angel who "watches over thunder and terror." In The Book of Adam and Eve he presides over repentance.

Uriel "is supposed to be," says Abbot Anscar Vonier in The Teaching of the Catholic Church, "the spirit who stood at the gate of the lost Eden with the fiery sword." The Book of Adam and Eve designates him as this spirit, i.e., one of the "cherubims" of Genesis 3. He is invoked in some of the sancient litanies He has been identified as one of the angels who helped bury Adam annd Abel in Paradise (Dictionary of the Bible); as the dark angel who wrestled with Jacob at Peniel; as the destroyer of the hosts of Sennacherib (II kings 19:35; II Maccabees 15:22); as the messenger sent by God to Noah to warn him of the impending deluge (Enoch I, 10:1-3), all of which feats or missions have been credited to other angels, as elsewhere noted. In the view of Louis Ginzberg, the "prince of lights" in The Manual of Discipline refers to Uriel. In addition, Uriel is said to have disclosed the mysteries of the heavenly areana to Ezra; interpreted prophecies, and led Abraham out of Ur. In later Judaism, says R. H. Charles (The book of Enoch), "we find Uriel instead of Phanuel" as one of the 4 angels of the presence. Uriel is also the angel of the month of September and may be invoked ritually by those born in that month. The Magus claims that alchemy "which is of divine origin" was brought down to earth by Uriel, and that it was Uriel who gave the cabala to man, although this "key to the mystical interpretation of Scripture" is also said to have been the gift of Metatron. Milton describes Uriel as "Regent of the Sun" and the "sharpest sighted spirit of all in Heaven" (Paradise Lost III). Dryden, The State of Innocece, pictures Uriel as descending from heaven in a chariot drawn by white horses. Despite his eminence, Uriel was reprobated at a Church Council in Rome, 745 C.E. Now, however, he is Saint Uriel, and his symbol is an open hand holding a flame. Burne-Jones' painting of Uriel is reproduced as a frontispiece in Duff, First and Second Books of Esdras. The name Uriel derives, it is claimed, from Uriah teh prophhet. In apocryphal and occult works Uriel has been equated or identified with Nuriel, Uyan, Jeremiel, Vretil, Suriel, Puruel, Jehoel, Israfel, and the angel Jacob-Israel. In The Legends of the Jews V, 310 Jacob says: "When I was coming from Mesopotamia of Syria, Uriel, the angel of God, cam forth and spoke: 'I have come down to the earth to make my dwelling among men, and I am called Jacob by name.'"

The meaning of the foregoing puzzling, unless Uriel turned into Jacob after wrestling with the patriarch at Peniel; but the incident as related in Genesis 32 suggests a different interpretation. A commentary on Exodus 4:25 speaks of a "benign angel" attacking Moses for neglecting to observe the covenantial rite of circumcision with regard to the latter's son Gershom, the benign angel being identified as Uriel in Midrash Aggada Exodus, and as Gabriel in The Zohar I, 93b. The latter source reports that Gabriel "came down in a flame of fire, having the appearance of a burning serpent," with the express purpose of destroying Moses "because of his sin." In The

Legends of the Jews II, 328, the angel here is neither Uriel nor Gabriel but 2 angels, the wicked Hemah and Af. Uriel is said to be the angel of vengeance that Prud'hon pictured in his "Divine Vengeance and Justice," a canvas to be found in the Louvre. Uriel, "gliding throught the Ev'n/On a Sun beam" (Paradis Lost IV, 555) is from Hayley, The Poetical Works of John Milton. The Uriel in Percy MacKaye's Uriel and Other Poems is not our angel but William Vaughn Moody, American poet and playwright (1869-1910), to whom the title poem is addressed in memory. The most recent appraisal of Uriel is the one offered by Walter Clyde Curry in Milton's Ontology Cosmology and Physics, where Professor Curry says of Uriel that he "seems to be largely a pious but not too perceptive physicist with inclinations towards atomistic philosophy." To illustrate in what high esteem Uriel was held, we find him described in the 2nd book of the Sibylline Oracles as one of the "immortal angels of the undying God" who, on the day of judgment, will "break the monstrous bars framed of unyielding and unbroken adament of the braxen gates of Hades, and cast them down straightway, and bring forth to judgment all the sorrowful forms, yea, of the ghosts of the ancient Titans and of the giants, and all whom the flood overtook... and all these shall be bring to the judgment seat... and set before God's seat."

Now, lets read what www.sarahsarchangels.com says about the Angel Uriel.

Uriel is the spirit of ministration and peace. He helps turn our worst disappointments into our greatest blessings. He is the Archangel of salvation. The ruler over magick, devotion, alchemy, sudden changes, ("The Winds Of Change"), astrology, universal cosmic consciousness, divine order, distribution of power and universal flow, emergencies, judgment, enlightenment and insights.

The name Uriel means God is my Light; or God is Light; or Radiation of God; or God is the radiating principle of Light; or Fire of God.

Uriel is one of the Archangels of rabbinical angelology. He was sent by God to answer the questions of Esdras (II Esdras iv). He is mentioned in I Enoch and IV Ezra, where he "watches over thunder and terror." In the Midrash 1, Uriel is said to be one of the four guardians of God's throne. In The Book of Adam and Eve he presides over repentance.

Uriel appears in Milton's Paradise Lost where he is the 'Regent of the Sun' and 'sharpest-sighted spirit of all in heaven.'

Uriel is of the leading angels in noncanonical lore, and ranked variously as a Seraph, Cherub, Regent of the Sun, Flame of God, and Angel of the Presence. As one of the most faithful and dedicated members of the host, Uriel was also placed in charge of Tartarus (another name for Hades).

Uriel has been identified as one of the angels who helped bury Adam and Abel in Paradise. He is known as the dark angel who wrestled with Jacob at Peniel; as the destroyer of the hosts of Sennacherib; as the messenger sent by God to Noah to warn him of the impending deluge, (although Raphael is credited with teaching the building of the ark), all of which feats or missions have been credited to other angels. In the view of Louis Ginzberg, the "prince of lights" in The Manual of Discipline, refers to Uriel. In addition, Uriel is said to have disclosed the mysteries of the heavenly arcana to Ezra; interpreted prophecies, and led Abraham out of Ur.

In later Judaism we find Uriel instead of Phanuel" as one of the 4 angels of the presence. The Magus claims that alchemy "which is of divine origin" was brought down to earth by Uriel, and that it was Uriel who gave the cabala to man, although this "key to the mystical interpretation of Scripture" is also said to have been the gift of Metatron.

Legend tells us that Uriel stands at the gate of the Lost Eden with a fiery sword. The Lost Eden is a term describing forgetting to Love God. The fiery sword shows that negative matter (selfish and unpure desires) are destroyed when one truly focuses their love on God. In this legend Uriel reminds humanity to Love God by using the "fire of God" (by using the fiery sword).

Uriel teaches the path of the heart, the fire of pure Love. Without this pure Love and devotion to Spirit, all spiritual study remains an intellectual pursuit, fairy gold. This understanding of true spiritual study is further supported by the tradition that Uriel brought to Earth: Alchemy, the heavenly arcana and was the giver of the Cabala to man.

It is through Noah's devotion and Love of God that Uriel is able to warn him of the flood. Noah's pure love and devotion was the telephone number of Uriel. If Noah had been unable to express divine love and devotion to God, he would have been unable to hear Uriel's warning via the cosmic phone. This is how another attribute associated with Uriel has arisen, the attribute of Divine Vengeance and Judgement. Only if the heart is ignited in devotion to God can one hear Yahweh's call. If one does not hear Yahweh's call, one will perish (get caught in the flood). Without Yahweh's guides and messages, one cannot find the Eternal Light. Uriel is said to have been the interpreter of Ezra's visions which also explains why Uriel means "God is the radiating principle of Light."

Uriel's symbol of an open hand holding a flame depicts a great gift to humanity. It is the flame of Love to ignite the heart in service to God. Uriel holds out the flame of Love towards all souls. The soul by filling with the flame of Love becomes devoted to serving Yahweh's plan. Uriel's flame of Love, the fire of God, the Light of God, purifies emotional and mental understanding transmuting the lower vibrations into frequencies that can assimilate Spiritual Understanding. The planet that Uriel is associated with is Venus, the planet symbolizing love.

Accepted as an archangel by the Church for many centuries, he was finally removed from the records in 745 CE as the Church became increasingly concerned with the prominence the public was placing upon angels.

Uriel rules over Monday and Wednesday and is the alchemy of universal order. He is the Governor of the East and the element of Air. He is the angel of September and may be invoked ritually by those born in that month.

Uriel's candle colors are violet, white and indigo.

Uriel's color energies are violet, white, indigo, blue, silver, and rainbow.

To recap; Uriel is said to be the Angel that Jacob wrestled with at Peniel, and he is the Light (Knowledge) of God, he is the Informer (Inspirer) to people about God's will. He is the spirit who stood at the gate of the lost Eden with the fiery sword. He has been identified as one of the angels who helped bury Adam and Abel in Paradise. He is seen as the destroyer of the hosts of Sennacherib, and as the messenger sent by God to Noah to warn him of the impending *deluge. Uriel is said to have disclosed the mysteries of the heavenly area to Ezra; interpreted prophecies, and led Abraham out of Ur. And that it was Uriel who gave the cabala to man, although this "key to the mystical interpretation of Scripture" is also said to have been the gift of Metatron. In apocryphal and occult works Uriel has been equated or identified with Nuriel, Uryan, Jeremiel, Vretil, Suriel, Puruel, Jehoel, Israfel, and the angel Jacob-Israel. In The Legends of the Jews V, 310 Jacob says: "When I was coming from Mesopotamia of Syria, Uriel, the angel of God, came forth and spoke: 'I have come down to the earth to make my dwelling among men, and I am called Jacob by name.'" And is attribute to the "Divine Vengeance and Judgment" - the Divine One who sets forth the Day of Judgment. To illustrate in what high esteem Uriel was held, we find him described in the 2nd book of the Sibylline Oracles as one of the "immortal angels of the undying God" who, on the day of judgment, will "break the monstrous bars framed of unyielding and unbroken adament of the braxen gates of Hades, and cast them down straightway, and bring forth to judgment all the sorrowful forms, yea, of the ghosts of the ancient Titans and of the giants, and all whom the flood overtook... and all these shall be bring to the judgment seat... and set before God's seat."*

Uriel is the spirit of ministration and peace. He helps turn our worst disappointments into our greatest blessings. He is the Archangel of Salvation.

A Common Trait

It has been a common trait of mankind since time immemorial that whenever a Guide from God appeared to redirect their steps into the Will and Plan of God; they demanded supernatural proofs from these men of God, instead of accepting messages on its merit. For example, when Jesus began to preach to his people - "the children of Israel" - to mend their ways and to refrain from mere legalistic formalism and imbibe the true spirit of the laws and commandments of God, his "people" demanded miracles from him to prove his bona fides (his authenticity, his genuineness), as recorded in the Christian scriptures: The Holy Bible is full of supernatural events accredited to the prophets from their Lord. In reality all those "signs" and "wonders" and "miracles" were acts of God, but since those miracles were worked through his human agents, we describe them as the miracles of prophets (i.e. Moses or Jesus by those hands they were performed).

Some six hundred years after the birth of Jesus, Muhammad a messenger of God was born in Makkah in Arabia. When he proclaimed his mission at the age of forty, his fellow countrymen, the mushriks of Makkah made an identical request for miracles, as had the Jews, from their promised Messiah. Textbook style, it was as if the Arabs had taken a leaf from the Christian records. History has a habit of repeating itself!

And they say: why are not signs sent down to him from his Lord? (Quran 29:50)

"Miracles? Cries he, what miracles would you have? Are not you yourselves there? God made you 'shaped you out of a little clay.' Ye were small once; a few years ago ye were not at all. Ye have beauty, strength, thoughts, but ye have compassion on one another. Old age comes-on you, and gray hairs; your strength fades into feebleness: ye sink down, and again ye are not. But still ye have compassion on one another': Every word of the Quranic text is meticulously chosen, chiseled and placed by the All-Wise himself. They carry God's 'fingerprint', and are signs of God. And yet, the spiritually jaundiced...."

"Ask For A Sign. What signs? They mean some special kinds of signs or miracles such as their own foolish minds dictate. Everything is possible for God, but God is not going to humor the follies of men or listen to their false demands. He has sent his messengers to explain his signs clearly, and to warn them of the consequences of rejection. Is that not enough?"

The trend of their demand is generally as follows:

In specific terms they asked that he - Muhammad - 'Put a ladder up to heaven and bring down a book from God in their very sight' - "Then we would believe," they said. Or "ye see the mountain yonder, turn it into gold' - "then we would believe." or 'make streams to gush out in the desert' - "then we would believe."

Now listen to the soft, sweet reasoning of Muhammad against the unreasonable and skeptical demands of the mushriks - "Do I say to you, verily I am an Angel? Do I say to you, verily in my hands are the treasures of God? Only, what is revealed to me do I follow."

Listen further to the most dignified reply he is commanded by his Lord to give the unbelievers.

Say (O Muhammad): 'The signs (miracles) are indeed with God: And most certainly I am only a clear warner!'

In the following ayah the prophet is made to point to the Qur'an itself as an answer to their hypocritical demand for some special kind of 'sign' of 'miracle' for which their foolish pagan mentality craved. For indeed all miracles are 'signs'; and it is their disbelief, their skepticism, their lack of faith which motivates their request for a sign.

They are asked to - 'look at the Qur`an' and again, 'look at the Qur`an!'

It is not enough for them that we have sent down to thee (O Muhammad) the book (al-Qur`an) which is rehearsed to them. Verily, in it (this perspicuous book) is a mercy and reminder to those who believe. (Qur`an 29:51).

Two Proofs:

As a proof of the divine authorship and the miraculous nature of the Qur`an, two arguments are advanced by the Almighty Himself:

1. 'that we' (God Almighty) have revealed to you (O Muhammad!) ' the book to you' who art absolutely an unlearned person, but a Prophet. One who cannot read or write. One who cannot sign his own name.

Moreover the divine author (God Almighty) himself testifies to the veracity of Muhammad's claim that he could never have composed the contents of the Qur`an; he could not have been its author: (book came), nor art thou (able) to transcribe it with thy right hand:

In that case, indeed, would the talkers of vanities have doubted (Qur`an 29:48).

The author of the Qur`an is reasoning with us, that had Muhammad been a learned man, and had he been able to read or write, then in that case the babblers in the market places might have had some justification to doubt his claim that the Qur'an is God's word. In the event of Muhammad being a literate person, the accusation of his enemies that he had probably copied his book (Qur`an) from the writings of the Jews and Christians, or that perhaps he had been studying Aristotle and Plato, or that he must have browsed through the 'Torat,' the 'Zabur' and the 'Injeel' and had rehashed it all in a beautiful language, might have carried some weight. Then, 'the talkers of vanities' might have had a point. But even this flimsy pretence has been denied to the unbeliever and the cynic: a point hardly big enough to hang a fly upon!

Consistency:

It is inconceivable that any human author would remain consistent in this teachings and his preaching for a period of over two decades. From the age of forty, when Muhammad received his first call from Heaven, to the age sixty-three when he breathed his last, for twenty-three years the Prophet practiced and preached Islam. In those twenty-three years, he passed through the most conflicting vicissitudes of life. Any man, during the course of such a mission, would be forced by circumstances to make 'honorable' compromises, and cannot help contradicting himself. No man can ever write the same always, as the message of the Qur'an is: consistent with itself, throughout! Or is it that the unbelievers objections are merely argumentive, refractory, against their own better light and judgment? Furthermore, the Qur'an contains or mentions many matters relating to the nature of the universe which were unknown to man before but which subsequently through evolution and discoveries of Science have fully confirmed - a field where an untutored mind would have most certainly lost in wild and contradictory speculations!

Self-Evident Proof:

Again and again when miracles are demanded from the Prophets of God by the cynical and frivolous few, they make point to the word of God - messages from the Highest - as 'the miracle.' The miracle or miracles! And men of wisdom, people with literary and spiritual insight, who were honest enough to themselves, recognized and accepted all Prophets as a genuine miracle.

Says the Qur'an: Nay here are signs self-evident in the hearts of those endowed with knowledge: And none but the unjust reject God's signs. (The Qur'an 29:49).

I am a Prophet as set forth by the guidelines of both the Holy Bible, Torah and Our'an. I communicate with God's Angels that I see, therefore, I believe in God, and I am one of His many Prophets.

Throughout the first 52 years of my life, I refused God while His Angels stood silently beside me. During the fall of 1996, I accepted God into my life. Now I embrace God as I write and speak of the things of which His Angels have told me, and I have recorded over 30 hours of our discussions, our documented communications were recorded on audio as well as video cassettes.

I was illiterate and uneducated, but yet, I have written and/or spoken over one millions words about and of God while Muhammad merely wrote less than the one hundred thousand words that created the Islam Religion and the complete Holy Bible is only a little over six hundred thousand words.

I will not debate the righteousness of quality verse quantity because God only instructs those as He desired, thus I was told more because today we need more than in the days of Muhammad, while the quality of all Divine teachings are all equal.

Only ignorant people believe things will not change, and the level of intelligence, and knowledge of God will not rise.

Do you not think that those in the days of Moses, mostly thought Moses was the closest to God that man would even accomplish?

Did not the early Christians think their religion was the last communication from God?

Do not the Muslims think Muhammad was the last and final Prophet?

Those who wrote the Holy Bible and canonized it, and Muhammad and his followers could not visualize God would continue His communications with His children, and that He would have other Prophets after Jesus and Muhammad, for I know that I am not the only Prophet of God, nor am I the last Prophet of God, but I am one of the many Prophets of God.

The Angels of God have told me that I am now a Master, and that I can raise the dead, but I won't, and that I can change a mountain into gold, but I won't, and that I can change the light of day into darkness, but I won't because all I do is for the Glory of God and not for self-rewarding gratification.

Must you see miracles to believe God exist?

Do you think He died when Jesus died?

Do you think that He died when Muhammad died?

Did He not talk to them?

Can He not talk to people today?

There is no difference between the days that they lived and the days that we live; God is the same. The people of today are just as ignorant as they were 2,000 years ago when it comes to knowing God.

Religions have made God small in the image of human thoughts, concepts and ideas of what pleases and displeases Him. Men have ego problems; God does not!

I shall teach you that terrorism is not the way of Islam, but instead it is the ways of men who corrupted the words from God into ideas and thoughts that fill their human desires. I will also teach you of the things that men have implanted into all others religions that were not from God, but rather from human interest and concepts.

Feeding The Beast

A wise person takes all information into account about a subject or issue before he makes a decision, and then stands firm on his knowledge. A confused person is one who does not know all that is involved in the issue or subject, and makes his stand based upon partial knowledge.

A king once asked Sir Walter Riley, what does tobacco smoke weigh? After thinking about the question, Sir Walter Riley weighed an amount of tobacco, and then he burned the tobacco. After the tobacco has completely turned to ashes, he then weighed the ashes, the difference between the weight of tobacco and its ashes, he concluded, was the weight of its smoke.

During the early 70s, after reading an article in Reader's Digest about how harmful cigarette smoking was, I did a study on the usage of gasoline and sent them the results of my study. I cannot recall the exact amount of waste that is placed into the air daily from burning gasoline, but it was somewhere around 350 million tons, and that was back in the early 70s!

If you smoke or know a smoker, have the smoker place a piece of cloth between his cigarette and his lips and have him suck in the smoke into his lungs. Examine the spot where the cigarette was touching the cloth, you will see a stain - the pollutants on the piece of cloth. Then, have the smoker take another suck on his cigarette, but this time, without the piece of cloth between his lips and the cigarette, and then have him exhale through another piece of cloth. Notice the difference between the stains on both pieces of cloth. The cloth that he placed over his mouth when he exhaled did not stain. When a cigarette is smoked, its pollutants are deposited in the smoker; the pollutants remained inside of the smoker, whereas, a burning cigarette that is not being puffed on is putting its pollutants into the air where these pollutants are mixed with the air, and because of its size and weight, a cigarette is submitting less pollutants into the air than one ounce of gasoline. Therefore, because of its size, the amount of pollutants that come out of a cigarette is less dangerous than the many gallons of gasoline that each driver is burning daily in his car.

In this comparison between cigarettes and gasoline burned in automobiles does not include the fuel used in electric plants, manufacturing, trains, airplanes, ships and heating and cooking. When you add all the pollutants from all these uses of fuel, the pollutants from cigarettes is nothing.

But I am not talking about pollutants that we are placing into the air that we breath, I am talking about all the things that we use and do to feed the "Beast."

Human technology - intelligent concepts and ideas first began when God placed Intelligence into the first one-cell animal that moved on the earth. Intelligence is technology that was the instrument that directed early man to seek shelter from the cold, it was the idea that helped early man to cook his food and it is the ideas that we use today in creating "better" living through technology, and is the ability for man to comprehend a need, desire or want, and then for him - man to create (invent) a solution to the problem.

The items that man has invented to ease and help in human life have become the masters of humans - it has become; man cannot "live" without these "miracles." While these "miracles," as all the pollutants (including cigarettes and fuels) that we put into the air, and into the water, and upon the earth, and they are the ideas, concepts and thoughts that we force unto and into ourselves, all of these are the things that feed the "Beast."

And while human intelligence produces more, we are helping the Beast to increase in size to where the "Beast" now controls our lives.

Today, we have the "need" to know all that is going on in the world at this moment. Our desire for fast communication does not only help the righteous to know all but it also has helped the bad and evil to know what others of the same are doing or have done. But yet, our News does not cover the good things that are happening, it reports on all the bad things that are occurring in the world. Therefore, faster communication has ensured the copycats his opportunity to follow others. For example: if we did not have cell-phones, computers, radios or television, could terrorist cells that are located around the world, be able to coordinate terrorism?

Yes, the Muslims (those who follow a corrupted an evil religion) did conquer most of the known world during the early 1,000 AD, but only most of the known world, not all of it. And if we did not have the intelligence to invent and discover today, the Americas and many other parts of the world would be as they were thousands of years ago because we would be fighting the environment and wild animals to stay alive and not each other.

Today with our modern inventions we have more time to think about how others should live instead of how we should live; we cover our downfalls by exposing other's wrongs. But while, literary accomplishments such as the ability to write, which comes from intelligence, has produced wonderful achievements which benefits humankind, but it also, can be used to control others, and thus also feeds the "Beast." Whereas, our modern hospitals and labs have helped to assure and aid life, therefore not all of intelligence and/or technology merely feeds the "Beast," but all can be warped (twisted) to feed him or to help feed him.

But talking about human health, I must state that now it has been found that the human body, at any given moment has over 700 cancer cells within it. Therefore, smoking doe Not cause cancer, but it may help its growth.

Can humans "live" without technology? NO! The intelligences that dwells within each human demands that he strive to his farthest. For if man refused to discover and learn, he is then living against God and His Will.

If man stands still and becomes stagnant in believing that his elders knew everything, then he is not allowing himself and humankind to climb closer to God and His Knowledge. Man has the final word on what the "Beast" is allowed to do, he - man must leash the "Beast" and control him, if not, he will control all of humankind, and this is how Muhammad wanted us to live

Basic Human Rights

The first thing that we find in Islam in this connection that it lays down rights for man as a human being. In other words it means that every man whether he belongs to this country or that, whether he is a believer or unbeliever, whether he lives in some forest or is found in some desert, whatever be the case, he has basic human rights simply because he is a human being, which should be recognized by every Muslim. In fact it will be his duty to fulfil these obligations.

1. The Right to Life

The first and the foremost basic right is the right to live and respect human life. The Qur'an lays down: Whosoever kills a human being without (any reason like) man slaughter, or corruption on earth, it is as though he had killed all mankind ... (5:32)

As far as the question of taking life in retaliation for murder or the question of punishment for spreading corruption on this earth is concerned, it can be decided only by a proper and competent court of law. If there is any war with any nation or country, it can be decided only by a properly established government. In any case, no human being has any right by himself to take human life in retaliation or for causing mischief on this earth. Therefore it is incumbent on every human being that under no circumstances should he be guilty of taking a human life. If anyone has murdered a human being, it is as if he has slain the entire human race. These instructions have been repeated in the Qur'an in another place saying: Do not kill a soul which Allah has made sacred except through the due process of law ... (6:151)

Here also homicide has been distinguished from destruction of life carried out in pursuit of justice. Only a proper and competent court will be able to decide whether or not an individual has forfeited his right to life by disregarding the right to life and peace of other human beings. Muhammad has declared homicide as the greatest sin only next to polytheism. The Tradition of the Prophet reads: "The greatest sins are to associate something with God and to kill human beings." In all these verses of the Qur'an and the Traditions of Muhammad the word 'soul' (nafs) has been used in general terms without any distinction or particularization which might have lent itself to the elucidation that the persons belonging to one's nation, the citizens of one's country, the people of a particular race or religion should not be killed. The injunction applies to all human beings and the destruction of human life in itself has been prohibited. Islam recognizes this right for all human beings. If a man belongs to a primitive or savage tribe, even then Islam regards him as a human being.

2. The Right to the Safety of Life

Immediately after the verse of the Qur'an which has been mentioned in connection with the right to life, God has said: "And whoever saves a life it is as though he had saved the lives of all mankind" (5:32).

There can be several forms of saving man from death. A man may be ill or wounded, irrespective of his nationality, race or colour. If you know that he is in need of your help, then it is your duty that you should arrange for his treatment for disease or wound. If he is dying of starvation, then it is your duty to feed him so that he can ward off death. If he is drowning or his life is at stake, then it is your duty to save him. The Qur'an regards it as the Muslims duty to save every human life, because it is thus that they have been enjoined in the Qur'an. You may be surprised to hear that the Talmud, the religious book of the Jews, contains a verse of similar nature.

3. Respect for the Chastity of Women

The third important thing that we find in the Charter of Human Rights granted by Islam is that a woman's chastity has to be respected and protected under all circumstances, whether she belongs to a Muslim nation or to the nation of an enemy, whether we find her in the wild forest or in a conquered city; whether she is our co-religionist or belongs to some other religion or has no religion at all. A Muslim cannot outrage her under any circumstances.

All promiscuous relationship has been forbidden to him, irrespective of the status or position of the woman, whether the woman is a willing or an unwilling partner to the act. The words of the Qur'an in this respect are: "Do not approach (the bounds of) adultery" (17:32).

Heavy punishment has been prescribed for this crime, and the order has not been qualified by any conditions. Since the violation of chastity of a woman is forbidden in Islam, a Muslim who perpetrates this crime cannot escape punishment whether he receives it in this world or in the Hereafter. This concept of sanctity of chastity and protection of women can be found nowhere else except in Islam. But the history of the Muslims clearly indicates they have violated womens' rights as demonstrated even today as the young women and daughters of Afghans are being sold to Pakistanians as slaves, but mostly for sex.

4. The Right to a Basic Standard of Life

Speaking about the economic rights the Qur'an enjoins upon its followers: And in their wealth there is acknowledged right for the needy and destitute. (51:19)

The words of this injunction show that it is a categorical and un-qualified order. Furthermore this injunction was given in Makkah where there was no Muslim society in existence and where generally the Muslims had to come in contact with the population of the disbelievers. Therefore the clear meaning of this verse is that anyone who asks for help and anyone who is suffering from deprivation has a right in the property and wealth of the Muslims; irrespective of the fact whether he belongs to this nation or to that nation, to this country or to that country, to this race or to that race, or to this religion or to that religion. If you are in a position to help and a needy person asks you for help or if you come to know that he is in need, then it is your duty to help him. God has established his right over you, which you have to honour as a Muslim.

5. Individual's Right to Freedom

Islam has clearly and categorically forbidden the primitive practice of capturing a free man, to make him a slave or to sell him into slavery. On this point the clear and unequivocal words of Muhammad are as follows: "There are three categories of people against whom I shall myself be a plaintiff on the Day of Judgement. Of these three, one is he who enslaves a free man, then sells him and eats this money".

The Position of Slavery in Islam:

Briefly I would like to tell you about the position and nature of slavery in Islam. Islam tried to solve the problem of the slaves that were in Arabia by encouraging the people in different ways to set their slaves free. The Muslims were ordered that in expiation of some of their sins they should set their slaves free. Freeing a slave by one's own free will was declared to be an act of great merit, so much so that it was said that every limb of the man who manumits a slave will be protected from hell-fire in lieu of the limb of the slave freed by him. The result of this policy was that by the time the period of the Rightly-Guided Caliphs was reached, all the old slaves of Arabia were liberated. Muhammad alone liberated as many as 63 slaves. The number of slaves freed by 'Aishah was 67, 'Abbas liberated 70, 'Abd Allah ibn 'Umar liberated one thousand, and 'Abd al-Rahman purchased thirty thousand and set them free. Similarly other Companions of Muhammad liberated a large number of slaves, the details of which are given in the Traditions and books of history of that period. But slavery still exist in Muslim countries today.

6. The Right to Justice

This is a very important and valuable right which Islam has given to man as a human being. The Qur'an has laid down: "Do not let your hatred of a people incite you to aggression" (5:2).

"And do not let ill-will towards any folk incite you so that you swerve from dealing justly. Be just; that is nearest to heedfulness" (5:8).

Stressing this point the Qur'an again says: "You who believe stand steadfast before God as witness for (truth and) fairplay" (4:135).

This makes the point clear that Muslims have to be just not only with ordinary human beings, but even with their enemies. In other words, the justice to which Islam invites its followers is not limited only to the citizens of their own country, or the people of their own tribe, nation or race, or the Muslim community as a whole, but it is meant for all the human beings of the world. Muslims therefore, cannot be unjust to anyone. Their permanent habit and character should be such that no man should ever fear injustice at their hands, and they should treat every human being everywhere with justice and fairness.

7. Equality of Human Beings

Islam not only recognizes absolute equality between men irrespective of any distinction of colour, race, religion or nationality, but makes it an important and significant principle, a reality. The Almighty God has laid down in the Qur'an: "O mankind, we have created you from a male and female." In other words all human beings are brothers and sisters to one another. They all are the descendants from one father and one mother.

"And we set you up as nations and tribes so that you may be able to recognize each other" (49:13).

This means that the division of human beings into nations, races, groups and tribes is for the sake of distinction, so that people of one race or tribe may meet and be acquainted with the people belonging to another race or tribe and cooperate with one another. This division of the human race is neither meant for one nation to take pride in its superiority over others nor is it meant for one nation to treat another with contempt or disgrace, or regard them as a mean and degraded race and usurp their rights. "Indeed, the noblest among you before God are the most heedful of you" (49:13). In other words there is not superiority of one man over another based of God-consciousness, purity of character and high morals, and not on the basis of colour, race, language, religion or nationality. Nor does the righteous have more privileged rights over others, because this runs counter to human equality, which has been laid down in the beginning of this verse as a general principle.

This has been exemplified by Muhammad in one of his sayings thus: "No Arab has any superiority over a non-Arab, nor does a non-Arab have any superiority over an Arab. Nor does a white man have any superiority over a black man, or the black man any superiority over the white man. You are all the children of Adam, and

Adam was created from clay." In this manner Islam established equality for the entire human race and struck at the very root of all distinctions based on colour, race, language, religion or nationality. According to Islam, God has given man this right of equality as a birthright. Therefore no man should be discriminated against on the ground of the colour of his skin, his place of birth, the race, religion or the nation in which he was born.

8. The Right to Co-operate and Not to Co-operate

Islam has prescribed a general principle of paramount importance and universal application saying: "Co-operate with one another for virtue and heedfulness and do not co-operate with one another for the purpose of vice and aggression" (5:2).

This means that the man who undertakes a noble and righteous work, irrespective of the fact whether he is living at the North Pole or the South Pole, has the right to expect support and active co-operation from all the people. On the contrary he who perpetrates deeds of vice and aggression, even if he is your closest relation or neighbour, does not have the right to win your support and help in the name of race, country, language, religion or nationality, nor should he have the expectation that any people will co-operate with him or support him. Nor is it permissible for any person to co-operate with him. The wicked and vicious person may be your brother, but he is not of God, and he can have no help or support from us as long as he does not repent and reform his ways.

Socialism as a Vehicle for Progress

It is essential that the progressive movements of the 19th and 20th Centuries be maintained and developed and not destroyed by the power and greed of the privileged.

Socialism: a philosophy which remains valid, in spite of the mistakes made in its name, has a vital part to play in the progress of the world. The principle of the fundamental equality of Mankind has a spiritual basis, which cannot be denied. Socialism, therefore, is the political expression of a Spiritual principle: that the material benefits provided by the Creator are for the use of all God's children and not for the exclusive privilege of the few. It is through the application of this principle that Humanity must progress and not via Capitalism, which is essentially geared to the further enrichment of the wealthy. It should be realized that if a reasonable standard of living is reached through speculative systems by the working classes, this is merely incidental and not a result of the application of philosophies intentionally beneficial to the masses. The "Good times" are passing. What one is witnessing in Australia (and no doubt in the rest of the world) at the beginning of 1995, (and accelerating through to 2000) is a calculated and sustained assault upon the living standards of the majority, by the forces of privilege and materialism. In this they often have the support of those who are regarded as the leaders in the religious life of the Community. The Public Service is being dismantled and Public Property sold-off to the greedy. The reason for this attitude is the Spiritual destitution and opportunism of politicians, bereft, as they undoubtedly are, of any real sense of Public responsibility.

Gone are the days when, even in political life, there was an element of moral appreciation: that one is bound by Spiritual considerations as well as physical. The layman can have no confidence in either clergymen or politicians, both of whom are ignorant of their true obligation as servants, not masters of the people.

In old age, one feels saddened by the thought that younger generations are constantly subjected to an onslaught of materialist propaganda, through all the organs of Mass Media. Controlled and administered by insensitive corporate bodies, they consider only the aspect of profitability in their deliberations and activities. International financial corporations are the source of the world's woes, amply aided and abetted by subservient politicians, who permit speculation in the money market on a tremendous scale. Thus materialism controls the destinies of the millions of the poor, who have little influence upon the activities of the scoundrels who, all too often, are lauded and applauded as public benefactors one year and the next are charged with corruption and fraud upon a massive scale. But one could continue endlessly such raillery against the wickedness of the world.

It is for the individual to distance himself from such a life if he is to avoid contamination by materialism. One should seek to acquire a measure of security for oneself and dependents through honest toil but, thereafter, should rest content. Those who lust after the physical things of life to the exclusion of Spiritual considerations must ultimately understand that one takes nothing from this world but the net product of a lifetime's activity. This is what it is all about: nothing more than the development of character and experience. We as individuals, in due course, enter the Spiritual world, bearing in our own natures the accumulated experience of a lifetime: be it long or short. The quality of that experience depends upon the general tenor of our life here on Earth. We really reap a harvest of our own sowing.

Therefore, a belief in the existence and presence of God in our lives is of assistance in providing us with a sense of purpose and perspective in daily living. In addition, a belief in the ministry of Angels and the reality of the future life gives us confidence in the love and concern of the Creator for the Creature. More than this it is neither possible nor necessary for us to comprehend.

As Paul said, "Now we see through a glass darkly: but then face to face. Now I know in part; but then I shall know, even as also I am known". (l Corr.Ch 13, v 12)

So long as we are moving forward towards the goal of perfection, no matter how slowly, we are fulfilling our duty towards our Creator, our dependents and ourselves.

Separation of Church and State

And the Angel Joleen said unto me, "There cannot be separation of church and state, for church is a belief system of religious doctrine formed by individuals, and state is a concept of laws and rules in which individuals believe must govern life. Therefore, individuals, even in congregation, always place or will try to force domination of their beliefs upon others.

"It is true that a religion that proclaims "Love" is better than no religion at all, but all people with religious beliefs try to force their beliefs upon others, and that is wrong.

"Do you recall when you went to school, and the teacher read from the Bible and led a Christian prayer every morning?

"Did you have a choice to say if you wished to pray to a Christian God?

"Is it wrong for a teacher to force self-domination over a student?

"Is God only there for Christians?

"Need the school teach what should be taught in homes?

"Should Christianity be taught in school because parents do not take their children to church?

"Christians are ready to fight for their Lord just as the Muslims are presently fighting for their God. Why?

"Both Gods are the same One. They prepare to fight for their God because they are fighting for their beliefs and not their God. Christian, Jews and Muslims fight for their doctrines that they proclaim came from God. None can see the truth."

Thomas Jefferson on Separation of Church and State

The Danbury Baptist Association, concerned about religious liberty in the new nation wrote to President Thomas Jefferson, Oct. 7, 1801.

Sir,

Among the many millions in America and Europe who rejoice in your Election to office; we embrace the first opportunity which we have enjoyd in our collective capacity, since your Inauguration, to express our great satisfaction, in your appointment to the chief Majestracy in the United States; And though our mode of expression may be less courtly and pompious than what many others clothe their addresses with, we beg you, Sir to believe, that none are more sincere.

Our Sentiments are uniformly on the side of Religious Liberty -- That Religion is at all times and places a matter between God and individuals -- That no man ought to suffer in name, person, or effects on account of his religious Opinions - That the legitimate Power of civil government extends no further than to punish the man who works ill to his neighbor: But Sir our constitution of government is not specific. Our ancient charter together with the Laws made coincident therewith, were adopted on the Basis of our government, at the time of our revolution; and such had been our Laws & usages, and such still are; that Religion is considered as the first object of Legislation; and therefore what religious privileges we enjoy (as a minor part of the State) we enjoy as favors granted, and not as inalienable rights: and these favors we receive at the expense of such degrading acknowledgements, as are inconsistent with the rights of freemen. It is not to be wondered at therefore; if those, who seek after power & gain under the pretense of government & Religion should reproach their fellow men -- should reproach their chief Magistrate, as an enemy of religion Law & good order because he will not, dare not assume the prerogatives of Jehovah and make Laws to govern the Kingdom of Christ.

Sir, we are sensible that the President of the United States, is not the national legislator, and also sensible that the national government cannot destroy the Laws of each State; but our hopes are strong that the sentiments of our beloved President, which have had such genial affect already, like the radiant beams of the Sun, will shine and prevail through all these States and all the world till Hierarchy and Tyranny be destroyed from the Earth. Sir, when we reflect on your past services, and see a glow of philanthropy and good will shining forth in a course of more than thirty years we have reason to believe that America's God has raised you up to fill the chair of State out of that good will which he bears to the Millions which you preside over. May God strengthen you for the arduous task which providence & the voice of the people have cald you to sustain and support you in your Administration against all the predetermined opposition of those who wish to rise to wealth & importance on the poverty and subjection of the people.

And may the Lord preserve you safe from every evil and bring you at last to his Heavenly Kingdom through Jesus Christ our Glorious Mediator.

Signed in behalf of the Association.
Nehh Dodge
     Ephram Robbins The Committee
     Stephen S. Nelson

(Baptists in Danbury, Connecticut were persecuted because they were not part of the Congretationalist establishment in that state.)

On January 1, 1802, in response to the letter from the Danbury Baptist Association, Thomas Jefferson wrote:

Gentlemen:

The affectionate sentiments of esteem and approbation which are so good to express towards me, on behalf of the Danbury Baptist Association, give me the highest satisfaction. My duties dictate a faithful and zealous pursuit of the interests of my constituents, and in proportion as they are persuaded of my fidelity to those duties, the discharge of them becomes more and more pleasing.

Believing with you that religion is a matter which lies solely between man and his God; that he owes account to none other for his faith or his worship; that the legislative powers of the government reach actions only, and not opinions, I contemplate with sovereign *reverence that act of the whole American people which declared that their legislature should `"make no law respecting an establishment of religion, or prohibiting the free exercise thereof," thus building a wall of separation between church and State. Adhering to this expression of the supreme will of the nation in behalf of the rights of conscience, I shall see with sincere satisfaction the progress of those sentiments which tend to restore man to all of his natural rights, convinced he has no natural right in opposition to his social duties.*

I reciprocate your kind prayers for the protection and blessings of the common Father and Creator of man, and tender you and your religious association, assurances of my high respect and esteem.

Thomas Jefferson

Sources: Robert S. Alley, Professor of Humanites, Emeritus, University of Richmond, from his article, "Public Education and the Public Good," published in William & Mary Bill of Rights Journal, Vol. 4, Issue 1, Summer 1995. And Lipscomb, Andrew and Bergh, Albert, The Writings of Thomas Jefferson, Vol. 16, pp. 281-282.

The Myth of the Separation of Church and State

1. Thomas Jefferson, Jefferson Writings, Merrill D. Peterson, ed. (NY: Literary Classics of the United States, Inc., 1984), p. 510, January 1, 1802.
2. John Eidsmoe, Christianity and the Constitution (MI: Baker Book House, 1987), p. 243.
3. M.E. Bradford, A Worthy Company: Brief Lives of the Framers of the United States Constitution (Marlborough, N.H.: Plymouth Rock Foundation, 1982), p. 4-5.
4. John Witherspoon, "Sermon on the Dominion of Providence over the Passions of Men" May 17, 1776; quoted and Cited by Collins, President Witherspoon, I:197-98.

Anytime religion is mentioned within the confines of government today people cry, "Separation of Church and State". Many people think this statement appears in the first amendment of the U.S. Constitution and therefore must be strictly enforced. However, the words: "separation", "church", and "state" do not even appear in the first amendment. The first amendment reads, "Congress shall make no law respecting an establishment of religion, or prohibiting the free exercise thereof..."

The statement about a wall of separation between church and state was made in a letter on January 1, 1802, by Thomas Jefferson to the Danbury Baptist Association of Connecticut. The congregation heard a widespread rumor that the Congregationalists, another denomination, were to become the national religion. This was very alarming to people who knew about religious persecution in England by the state established church. Jefferson made it clear in his letter to the Danbury Congregation that the separation was to be that government would not establish a national religion or dictate to men how to worship God. Jefferson's letter from which the phrase "separation of church and state" was taken affirmed first amendment rights. Jefferson wrote: *I contemplate with solemn reverence that act of the whole American people which declared that their legislature should "make no law respecting an establishment of religion, or prohibiting the free exercise thereof," thus building a wall of separation between Church and State.*

(1) The reason Jefferson choose the expression "separation of church and state" was because he was addressing a Baptist congregation; a denomination of which he was not a member. Jefferson wanted to remove all fears that the state would make dictates to the church. He was establishing common ground with the Baptists by borrowing the words of Roger Williams, one of the Baptist's own prominent preachers. Williams had said: *When they have opened a gap in the hedge or wall of separation between the garden of the Church and the wilderness of the world, God hath ever broke down the wall itself, removed the candlestick, and made his garden a wilderness, as at this day. And that there fore if He will eer please to restore His garden and paradise again, it must of necessity be walled in peculiarly unto Himself from the world...*

(2) The "wall" was understood as one-directional; its purpose was to protect the church from the state. The world was not to corrupt the church, yet the church was free to teach the people Biblical values.

The American people knew what would happen if the State established the Church like in England. Even though it was not recent history to them, they knew that England went so far as forbidding worship in private homes and sponsoring all church activities and keeping people under strict dictates. They were forced to go to the state established church and do things that were contrary to their conscience. No other churches were allowed, and mandatory *attendance of the established church was compelled under the Conventicle Act of 1665.*

Failure to comply would result in imprisonment and torture. The people did not want freedom from religion, but freedom of religion. The only real reason to separate the church from the state would be to instill a new morality and establish a new system of beliefs. Our founding fathers were God-fearing men who understood that for a country to stand it must have a solid foundation; the Bible was the source of this foundation. They believed that God's ways were much higher than Man's ways and held firmly that the Bible was the absolute standard of truth and used the Bible as a source to form our government.

There is no such thing as a pluralistic society. There will always be one dominant view, otherwise it will be in transition from one belief system to another. Therefore, to say Biblical principles should not be allowed in government and school is to either be ignorant of the historic intent of the founding fathers, or blatantly bigoted for or against Christianity.

Each form of government has a guiding principle: monarchy in which the guiding principle is honor; aristocracy in which the guiding principle is moderation; republican democracy in which the guiding principle is virtue; despotism in which the guiding principle is fear. Without people of the United States upholding good moral conduct, society soon degenerates into a corrupt system where people misuse the authority of government to obtain what they want at the expense of others. The U.S. Constitution is the form of our government, but the power is in the virtue of the people. The virtue desired of the people is shown in the Bible. This is why Biblical morality was taught in public schools until the early 1960's. Government officials were required to declare their belief in God even to be allowed to hold a public office until a case in the U.S. Supreme Court called Torcaso v. Watkins (Oct. 1960). God was seen as the author of natural law and morality. If one did not believe in God one could not operate from a proper moral base. And by not having a foundation from which to work, one would destroy the community. The two primary places where morality is taught are the family and the church. The church was allowed to influence the government in righteousness and justice so that virtue would be upheld. Not allowing the church to influence the state is detrimental to the country and destroys our foundation of righteousness and justice. It is absolutely necessary for the church to influence the state in virtue because without virtue our government will crumble -- the representatives will look after their own good instead of the country's.

Government was never meant to be our master as in a ruthless monarchy or dictatorship. Instead, it was to be our servant. The founding fathers believed that the people have full power to govern themselves and that people chose to give up some of their rights for the general good and the protection of rights. Each person should be self-governed and this is why virtue is so important. Government was meant to serve the people by protecting their liberty and rights, not serve by an enormous amount of social programs. The authors of the Constitution wanted the government to have as little power as possible so that if authority was misused it would not cause as much damage. Yet they wanted government to have enough authority to protect the rights of the people. The worldview at the time of the founding of our government was a view held by the Bible: that Man's heart is corrupt and if the opportunity to advance oneself at the expense of another arose, more often than not, we would choose to do so. They firmly believed this and that's why an enormous effort to set up checks and balances took place. Absolute power corrupts absolutely. They wanted to make certain that no man could take away rights given by God. They also did not set up the government as a true democracy, because they believed, as mentioned earlier, Man tends towards wickedness. Just because the majority wants something does not mean that it should be granted, because the majority could easily err. Government was not to be run by whatever the majority wanted but instead by principle, specifically the principles of the Bible.

Our U.S. Constitution was founded on Biblical principles and it was the intention of the authors for this to be a Christian nation. The Constitution had 55 people work upon it, of which 52 were evangelical Christians.

(3) We can go back in history and look at what the founding fathers wrote to know where they were getting their ideas. This is exactly what two professors did. Donald Lutz and Charles Hyneman reviewed an estimated 15,000 items with explicit political content

printed between 1760 and 1805 and from these items they identified 3,154 references to other sources. The source they most often quoted was the Bible, accounting for 34% of all citations. Sixty percent of all quotes came from men who used the Bible to form their conclusions. That means that 94% of all quotes by the founding fathers were based on the Bible. The founding fathers took ideas from the Bible and incorporated them into our government. If it was their intention to separate the state and church they would never have taken principles from the Bible and put them into our government. An example of an idea taken from the Bible and then incorporated into our government is found in Isaiah 33:22 which says, "For the Lord is our judge, the Lord is our lawgiver, the Lord is our king..." The founding fathers took this scripture and made three major branches in our government: judicial, legislative, and executive. As mentioned earlier, the founding fathers strongly believed that Man was by nature corrupt and therefore it was necessary to separate the powers of the government. For instance, the President has the power to execute laws but not make them, and Congress has the power to make laws but not to judge the people. The simple principle of checks and balances came from the Bible to protect people from tyranny. The President of the United States is free to influence Congress, although he can not exercise authority over it because they are separated. Since this is true, why should the church not be allowed to influence the state? People have read too much into the phrase "separation of church and state", which is to be a separation of civil authority from ecclesiastical authority, not moral values. Congress has passed laws that it is illegal to murder and steal, which is the legislation of morality. These standards of morality are found in the Bible. Should we remove them from law because the church should be separated from the state?

Our founding fathers who formed the government also formed the educational system of the day. John Witherspoon did not attend the Constitutional Convention although he was President of New Jersey College in 1768 (known as Princeton since 1896) and a signer of the Declaration of Independence. His influence on the Constitution was far ranging in that he taught nine of fifty-five original delegates. He fought firmly for religious freedom and said, "God grant that in America true religion and civil liberty may be inseparable and that unjust attempts to destroy the one may in the issue tend to the support and establishment of both."

(4) In October 1961 the Supreme Court of the United States removed prayer from schools in a case called Engel v. Vitale. The case said that because the U.S. Constitution prohibits any law respecting an establishment of religion officials of public schools may not compose public prayer even if the prayer is denominationally neutral (but remained Christian), and that pupils may choose to remain silent or be excused while the prayer is being recited. For 185 years prayer was allowed in public and the Constitutional Convention itself was opened with prayer (by a Christian chaplain who is paid $175.00 per year). If the founding fathers didn't want prayer in government why did they pray publicly in official meetings? It is sometimes said that it is permissible to pray in school as long as it is silent. Although, "In Omaha, Nebraska, 10-year old James Gierke was prohibited from reading his Bible silently during free time... the boy was forbidden by his teacher to open his Bible at school and was told doing so was against the law."(4) The U.S. Supreme Court with no precedent in any court history said prayer will be removed from school. Yet the Supreme Court in January, 1844 in a case named Vidal v. Girard's Executors, a school was to be built in which no ecclesiastic, missionary, or minister of any sect whatsoever was to be allowed to even step on the property of the school. They argued over whether a layman could teach or not, but they agreed that, "...there is an obligation to teach what the Bible alone can teach, viz. a pure system of morality." This has been the precedent throughout 185 years. Although this case is from 1844, it illustrates the point. The prayer in question was not even lengthy or denominationally geared. It was this: "Almighty God, we acknowledge our dependence upon Thee, and we beg Thy blessings upon us, our parents, our teachers and our Country." What price have we paid by removing this simple acknowledgment of God's protecting hand in our lives? Birth rates for unwed girls from 15-19; sexually transmitted diseases among 10-14 year olds; pre-marital sex increased; violent crime; adolescent homicide have all gone up considerably from 1961 to the 1990's -- even after taking into account population growth. The Bible, before 1961, was used extensively in curriculum.

After the Bible was removed, scholastic aptitude test scores dropped considerably.

There is no such thing as a pluralistic society; there will always be one dominant view. Someone's morality is going to be taught-- but whose? Secular Humanism is a religion that teaches that through Man's ability we will reach universal peace and unity and make heaven on earth. They promote a way of life that systematically excludes God and all religion in the traditional sense. That Man is the highest point to which nature has evolved, and he can rely on only himself and that the universe was not created, but instead is self-existing. They believe that Man has the potential to be good in and of himself. All of this of course is in direct conflict with not only the teachings of the Bible, but even the lessons of history. In June 1961 in a case called Torcaso v. Watkins, the U.S. Supreme Court stated, "Among religions in this country which do not teach what would generally be considered a belief in the existence of God are Buddhism, Taoism, Ethical Culture, Secular Humanism and others." The Supreme Court declared Secular Humanism to be a religion. The American Humanist Association certifies counselors who enjoy the same legal status as ordained ministers. Since the Supreme Court has said that Secular Humanism is a religion, why is it being allowed to be taught in schools? The removal of public prayer of those who wish to participate is, in effect, establishing the religion of Humanism over Christianity. This is exactly what our founding fathers tried to stop from happening with the first amendment.

Confusion of Separation of Church and State

There is an assault going on -- and the liberal social engineers have declared that Christians are the enemy. Amidst their cries of "diversity" and "tolerance" it has become fashionable to bash Christians, discriminate against them, and to deny the Christian roots of American democracy. They resent how Christians pose constant reminders to them -- and to an American society that is unsure about following them -- that God has absolute standards of right and wrong.

This is the verdict: Light has come into the world, but men loved darkness instead of light because their deeds were evil. Everyone who does evil hates the light, and will not come into the light for fear that his deeds will be exposed. (John 3:19-20)

These anti-Christian liberals want to achieve a new, humanistic America where our children will be protected from outmoded Christian ideas and will enjoy freedom "from" religion - not freedom "of" religion. They do not respect God's definition of the family and are intent on discrediting His wisdom in raising children as they attempt to rewrite His guidelines for morality. These social liberals believe man has the only answers for himself. They think that perhaps a new, man-made spirituality eventually may be useful in managing the populace -- but frankly would prefer that it not be a moralistic religion with rules or absolute right and wrong. They certainly do not want the new society they are molding to hang onto any "biased" religion that proclaims Jesus Christ is the Only Way (John 14:6) or that all men and women are called by their Creator to have a warm, personal relationship with Him. We Christians irritate these social liberals when we proclaim the truth of God's liberating love. We infuriate them when we remind them of our Lord's true and steadfast faithfulness. For those who know the Bible, this does not surprise us because Jesus told us, "All men will hate you because of me, but he who stands firm to the end will be saved." (Matthew 10:22)

The Leftist Battle Cry

The Leftist social liberals continue to harangue on the "separation of church and state" as justification for eliminating religious issues from public view. The phrase "Separation of Church and State" has been bandied about for so long that 67% of all Americans believe that it is actually in the Constitution. In fact, those three words appear nowhere in the Constitution. Oblivious to the irrelevance of their arguments, and at the same time refusing to acknowledge that no document of state, let alone the Constitution, has ever proposed such a concept, those on the Left have tried to convince the American people that our founding documents warned of the dangers of mixing politics and religion.

In the absence of Constitutional evidence, the mere opinion of private individuals or groups that there should be absolute separation of church and state hardly creates a 'great American principle'. They have thus misled millions and worked against the public interest by damaging the commitment to ethics and moral values that come only through religious belief.

It must be remembered that neutrality is impossible. Some authority, whether it be God or man, is used as the reference point for all enacted laws. If a political system rejects one authority, it adopts another. If a biblical moral system is not being legislated, then an immoral system is being legislated. Any moral system that does not put Jesus Christ at its center, denies Christ: "No one can serve two masters; for either he will hate the one and love the other, or he will hold to one and despise the other..." (Matthew 6:24); and, "He who is not with Me is against Me; and he who does not gather with Me scatters" (12:30).

Christine J. Haven

"Our standard of right is that eternal law which God proclaimed from Sinai, and which Jesus expounded on the Mount. We recognize our responsibility to Jesus Christ. He is Head over all things to the Church, and the nation that will not serve Him is doomed to perish" – [James Henley Thornwell, The Collected Writings of James Henley Thornwell, Vol. IV, p. 517f.]

The First Amendment

The assault on America's religious underpinnings is based on a distorted interpretation of the establishment and free-exercise clauses of the First Amendment.

"Congress shall make no law respecting an establishment of religion or prohibiting the free exercise thereof ..." Only a lawyer could claim not to understand the plain meaning of those words.

The Supreme Court has taken Jefferson's "separation" clause (divorced from Jefferson's own explanation of the phrase) and used it to create a new, and completely arbitrary, interpretation of the First Amendment.

In 1947, with the United States Supreme Court's decision in Everson v. Board of Education, Justice Hugo Black construed the First Amendment in a more restrictive fashion, giving an absolute definition of the First Amendment Establishment Clause which went well beyond the original intent of the framers of the United States Constitution and paved the way for future cases that would further restrict religious expression in American public life. This ruling declares that any aid or benefit to religion from governmental actions is unconstitutional. As Justice Black said: "The First Amendment has erected a wall between church and state. That wall must be kept high and impregnable. We could not approve the slightest breach."

Hardly what Thomas Jefferson meant or what the constitution guaranteed! "Congress shall make no law respecting an establishment of religion, or prohibiting the free exercise thereof" had always meant that Congress was prohibited from establishing a national religious denomination, that Congress could not require that all Americans become Catholics, Anglicans, or members of any other denomination.

This understanding of "separation of church and state" was applied not only during the time of the Founders, but for 170 years afterwards.

James Madison (1751-1836), clearly articulated this concept of separation when explaining the First Amendment's protection of religious liberty. He said that the First Amendment to the Constitution was prompted because "The people feared one sect might obtain a preeminence, or two combine together, and establish a religion to which they would compel others to conform."

The complete and radical disassociation between Christianity and the State that is sometimes advocated now is not what they had in mind. It's clear that they had seen entirely too many religious wars and religious tyrannies in Europe, and thus that they did want to make sure that no specific church or creed had authority over the State.

Recognizing their failure to win their arguments on fact, the lastest tactic among liberals is simply to deny the very documents that contain the facts.

Schools and courthouses in eastern Kentucky are removing their displays of historical documents - including the Mayflower Compact, an excerpt from the Declaration of Independence, the national motto, "In God we trust", and the preamble to the state's constitution - to comply with an order from Federal District Judge Jennifer Coffman, who said the displays are a violation of the First Amendment. [Dr. Billy James Hargis, Christian Crusade, June 2000]

Are You Saved?

When the First Amendment was passed it only had two purposes.

1. There would be no established, national church for the united thirteen states. To say it another way: there would be no "Church of the United States." The government is prohibited from setting up a state religion, such as Britain has, but no barriers will be erected against the practice of any religion. Thomas Jefferson's famous "wall of separation" between church and state comment was made in a letter to a group of Baptist clergymen January 1, 1802, in Danbury, Connecticut, who feared the Congregationalists Church would become the state-sponsored religion. Jefferson assured the Danbury Baptist Association that the First Amendment guaranteed that there would be no establishment of any one denomination over another. It was never intended for our governing bodies to be "separated" from Christianity and its principles. The "wall" was understood as one directional; its purpose was to protect the church from the state. The world was not to corrupt the church, yet the church was free to teach the people Biblical values. It keeps the government from running the church but makes sure that Christian principles will always stay in government.

2. The second purpose of the First Amendment was the very opposite from what is being made of it today. It states expressly that

government should not impede or interfere with the free practice of religion. The purpose of the separation of church and state in American society is not to exclude the voice of religion from public debate, but to provide a context of religious freedom where the insights of each religious tradition can be set forth and tested. As Justice Douglas wrote for the majority of the Supreme Court in the United States vs. Ballard case in 1944: The First Amendment has a dual aspect. It not only "forestalls compulsion by law of the acceptance of any creed or the practice of any form of worship" but also "safeguards the free exercise of the chosen form of religion."

The First Amendment was a safe-guard so that the State can have no jurisdiction over the Church. Its purpose was to protect the Church, not to disestablish it.

In the current debate over the separation of church and state, the choices sometimes lean too extreme on both sides. At one extreme are those who want to use the State as a vehicle to enforce their brand of Christian ideas on everyone. At the other extreme are those who say the Founding Fathers would have wanted a situation where one can't mention God in any publicly sponsored forum, for fear of having the State appear to support religion. Somehow, between alternating volleys of quotations from devout Founding Fathers and anti-clerical quotations from Tom Paine, we've got to find a better approach.

Catholic Religion Hypocrisy

We are taking a close look at the sexual scandals in the Catholic Church, and the Catholic clegry's lack of comments or statements about God's desires, and what the Catholic Religions says about their actions and attitude which is one of the many Sins of their Church.

The U.S. Roman Catholic Church Leaders issued a statement Wednesday at the end of an unprecedented two-day meeting at the Vatican aimed at restoring credibility in the American church after a string of child sex scandals. Below is the full text of the English-language statement as released by the Vatican:

(This first statement claims; only the credibility of Catholic clegry in the United Sates needs to be restored. The child sex scandals of the Catholic Church are world wide, they are NOT isolated to any one country, and the sex scandals of the Catholic Church are not limited to children.)

On April 23-24, 2002, an extraordinary meeting was held in the Vatican between the Cardinals of the United States and the leadership of the United States Catholic Conference of Bishops and the heads of several offices of the Holy See on the subject of the sexual abuse of minors.

The Holy See - God is the only Holy See. God did not give this "GIFT" to man nor any church.

The meeting was called with three goals in mind:

1) On the part of the American Bishops, to inform the Holy See about the difficulties which they have faced in recent months.

2) On the part of the Roman Dicasteries, to hear directly from the American Cardinals and the chief officials of the United States Conference of Catholic Bishops a general evaluation of the situation.

3) And together to develop ways to move forward in addressing these issues.

As is known, the Holy Father received the working group in his private library late in the morning of Tuesday, April 23, and gave a programmatic address. Today, at the end of the morning session, His Holiness invited the American Cardinals and Bishops to lunch, to continue their discussion of some of the themes raised at the meeting.

There is one Holy Father and that is GOD. The pope is only a man - an animal who claims to know what pleases and displeases God.

The participants first of all wish to express their unanimous gratitude to the Holy Father for his clear indications of direction and commitment for the future. In communion with the Pope they reaffirm certain basic principles:

1) The sexual abuse of minors is rightly considered a crime by society and is an appalling sin in the eyes of God, above all when it is perpetrated by priests and religious whose vocation is to help persons to lead holy lives before God and men.

Sexual abuse of minors is more than appalling sin in the eyes of God, it is a Major SIN if the offender is one who claims to be a man Of God because the offender is teaching about God, but does not believe in God, thus he is teaching only for money. But does any group that has enough money to be its own country care about people or God?

2) There is a need to convey to the victims and their families a profound sense of solidarity and to provide appropriate assistance in recovering faith and receiving pastoral care.

There should never be a victim caused by any truly religous group.

3) Even if the cases of true pedophilia on the part of priests and religious are few, all the participants recognized the gravity of the problem. In the meeting, the quantitative terms of the problem were discussed, since the statistics are not very clear in this regard. Attention was drawn to the fact that almost all the cases involved adolescents and therefore were not cases of true pedophilia.

Does it matter what the age is of the victim? Or what the sexual abuse was? It was committed by a person who teaches others how they should live. And Sexual abuse is SEXUAL ABUSE, no matter what we call it. While PEDOPHILIA is the act of an adult to an adolescent.

4) Together with the fact that a link between celibacy and pedophilia cannot be scientifically maintained, the meeting reaffirmed the value of priestly celibacy as a gift of God to the Church.

The word "maintained" means to keep working. Does the Catholic Church wish to keep celibacy and pedophilia active in its religion? Celibacy is NOT a gift from God. It is a demand of men who lead the Church.

Celibacy means NO sex of any kind, that even includes masturbation.

Pedophilia means sex between an adult and adolescent, and then there are homosexuals and heterosexuals, and each will seek their sexual preference. The scandals of homosexual and heterosexual actives between adults in the Catholic Church, have not yet come to light.

5) Given the doctrinal issues underlying the deplorable behavior in question, certain lines of response have been proposed:

a) The Pastors of the Church need clearly to promote the correct moral teaching of the Church and publicly to reprimand individuals who spread dissent and groups which advance ambiguous approaches to pastoral care;

b) A new and serious Apostolic Visitation of seminaries and other institutes of formation must be made without delay, with particular emphasis on the need for fidelity to the Church's teaching, especially in the area of morality, and the need for a deeper study of the criteria of suitability of candidates to the priesthood.

c) It would be fitting for the Bishops of the United States Conference of Catholic Bishops to ask the faithful to join them in observing a national day of prayer and penance, in reparation for the offenses perpetrated and in prayer to God for the conversion of sinners and the reconciliation of victims.

6) All the participants have seen this time as a call to a greater fidelity to the mystery of the Church. Consequently they see the present time as a moment of grace. While recognizing that practical criteria of conduct are indispensable and urgently needed, we cannot underestimate, in the words of the Holy Father, "the power of Christian conversion, that radical decision to turn away from sin and back to God, which reaches the depths of a person's soul and can work extraordinary change." At the same time, as His Holiness also stated, "People need to know that there is no place in the priesthood and religious life for those who would harm the young. They must know that Bishops and priests are totally committed to the fullness of Catholic truth on matters of sexual morality, a truth as essential to the renewal of the priesthood and the episcopate as it is to the renewal of marriage and family life."

The clergy of the Catholic Church needs only believe in who they preach about and to believe in what they preach.

Again in the Holy Father's words, neither should we forget the immense spiritual, human and social good that the vast majority of priests and religious in the United States have done and are still doing. The Catholic Church in your country has always promoted human and Christian values with great vigor and generosity, in a way that has helped to consolidate all that is noble in the American people. A great work of art may be blemished, but its beauty remains; and this is a truth which any intellectually honest critic will recognize. To the Catholic communities in the United States, to their Pastors and members, to the men and women religious, to teachers in Catholic universities and schools, to American missionaries in all parts of the world, go the wholehearted thanks of the entire Catholic Church and the personal thanks of the Bishop of Rome."

For this reason, the Cardinals and Bishops presented at the meeting today sent a message to all the priests of the United States, their co-workers in the pastoral ministry.

As part of the preparation for the June meeting of the American Bishops, the United States participants in the Rome meeting presented to the Prefects of the Roman Congregations the following proposals:

1) We propose to send the respective Congregations of the

Holy See a set of national standards which the Holy See will properly review (recognitio), in which essential elements for policies dealing with the sexual abuse of minors in Dioceses and Religious Institutes in the United States are set forth.

2) We will propose that the United States Conference of Catholic Bishops recommend a special process for the dismissal from the clerical state of a priest who has become notorious and is guilty of the serial, predatory, sexual abuse of minors.

3) While recognizing that the Code of Canon law already contains a judicial process for the dismissal of priests guilty of sexually abusing minors, we will also propose a special process for cases which are not notorious but where the Diocesan Bishop considers the priest a threat for the protection of children and young people, in order <u>to avoid grave scandal in the future and to safeguard the common good of the Church.</u>

4) We will propose an Apostolic Visitation of seminaries and religious houses of formation, giving special attention to their admission requirements and the need for them to teach Catholic moral doctrine in its integrity.

5) We will propose that the Bishops of the United States make every effort to implement the challenge of the Holy Father that the present crisis "must lead to a holier priesthood, a holier episcopate, and a holier Church" by calling for deeper holiness in the Church in the United States, including ourselves as Bishops, the clergy, the religious and the faithful.

6) We propose that the Bishops of the United States set aside a day for prayer and penance throughout the Church in the United States, in order to implore reconciliation and the renewal of ecclesial life.

The Catholic Church needs to rid itself of its clergy who are two-faced and liers.

Source: Reuters News

Cardinals' Letter to U.S. Priests American Cardinals ended an extraordinary two-day meeting at theVatican Wednesday with an expression of regret for failing to prevent sex abuse by Roman Catholic priests. The cardinals released the following message to American priests, acknowledging the burden created by clergy who have abused minors:

We, the Cardinals of the United States and the Presidency of the National Conference of Catholic Bishops, gathered with our brother Cardinals of the Roman Curia around the Successor of Peter, wish to speak a special word to you, our brother priests, who give yourselves so generously from day to day in service of God's people.

The pope is NOT the successor of Peter. The pope was chosen by man, not God.

At our meeting, you have been very much in our minds and hearts, for we know the heavy burden of sorrow and shame that you are bearing because some have betrayed the grace of Ordination by abusing those entrusted to their care.

The sex offenders did more than betray people, they do not believe in their Bible, nor do they follow it.

We regret that episcopal oversight has not been able to preserve the Church from this scandal. The entire Church, the Bride of Christ, is afflicted by this wound -- the victims and their families first of all, but also you who have dedicated your lives to "the priestly service of the Gospel of God" (Rom 15:16).

The Catholic Church is NOT the Bride of Chirst, it is a beast of men that dominate others.

To all of you we express our deep gratitude for all that you do to build up the Body of Christ in holiness and love. We pledge to support you in every possible way through these troubled times, and we ask that you stay close to us in the bond of the priesthood as we make every effort to bring the healing grace of Christ to the people whom we serve.

Sexual Abuse and not believing in the Holy Bible does not build the Body of Chirst, living the lifestyle of Jesus builds the Body of Christ.

We are in complete harmony with the Holy Father when he said in his Address yesterday: "Neither should we forget the immense spiritual, human and social good that the vast majority of priests and religious in the United States have done and are still doing...

The Catholic Church has Sinned against God from its first day of creation. It has done nothing good for and is not benefical to humankind, it has only dominated.

To the Catholic communities in the United States, to their

Pastors and members, to the men and women religious, to teachers in Catholic universities and schools, to American missionaries in all parts of the world, go the wholehearted thanks of the entire Catholic Church and the personal thanks of the Bishop of Rome."

Thanks for what? Bringing all that money in the Vatican.

As we look to the future, let us together beg the eternal High Priest for the grace to live this time of trial with courage and confidence in the Crucified Lord. This echoes the summons of our Ordination: "Imitate the mystery you celebrate; model your life on the mystery of the Lord's Cross" (Rite of Ordination); and it is a vital part of what we now offer the Church as she passes through this time of painful purification. From the house of the Successor of Peter, who has confirmed us in our faith, we wish in turn to confirm you in the humble and exalted service of the Catholic priesthood to which we have been called. Peace be with you!

Cardinal Law's Statement On Sexual Abuse On Minors By Clergy

Source: Reuters News

I wish to address the issue of sexual abuse of minors by clergy. At the outset, I apologize once again to all those who have been sexually abused as minors by priests. Today that apology is made in a special way with heartfelt sorrow to those abused by John Geoghan.

An apology for what he has done does not change his feeling or beliefs. All he did is against God. He is not a man of God, nor shall he ever be.

There is no way for me to describe adequately the evil of such acts. All sexual abuse is morally abhorrent. Sexual abuse of minors is particularly abhorrent. Such abuse by clergy adds to the heinous nature of the act. It affects a <u>victim's relationship to the Church</u>. A child's ability to trust is shattered by such abuse, and self-esteem is damaged.

Today the issue of sexual abuse is a matter of open and public discussion. While this is often painful, it has allowed us to address the issue more directly. Only in this way can all of us be more alert to its dangers, protect potential victims, respond more effectively to those who have been the victims of abuse, and learn how to deal more effectively with those responsible for such abuse.

Here in this Archdiocese, I promulgated a policy to deal with sexual abuse of minors by clergy. This went into effect on January 15, 1993. All priest personnel records were reviewed in light of this policy. In those instances in which a charge of abuse had not been processed earlier with the rigor of our present policy, the case was re-opened, and the policy followed.

I am aided in such cases by a priest-delegate and by an interdisciplinary review board that examines each case and makes a recommendation to me. This review board includes the mother of a victim, another parent, a clinical social worker, a clinical psychologist, a psychotherapist, a retired justice of the Supreme Judicial Court, a priest, a civil attorney and, usually, a canon lawyer.

Why wasn't God included on this review board?

While the response of the Church understandably focuses on the removal of the threat of future acts of abuse, it is also concerned with providing psychological and spiritual counsel to victims as well as assistance to parishes coping with such incidents. Victims who come forward are offered confidential psychological counseling and spiritual support. It is my desire that the Church be present in whatever way possible to all those who have suffered such abuse.

While our policy has been effective, we continue to refine our procedures. Since our knowledge and experience in dealing with such cases have evolved both within the Church and society as a whole, I want to be certain that our policy is as effective as it might be. In August I directed that our policy be reviewed. In September, a panel of persons with special expertise began the review process. Except for one priest, this panel consists of lay men and women. The work of this group has nearly been completed. I anticipate that the revised policy will be promulgated and made available within the next three to four weeks.

I wish we had had such a policy fifty years ago, or when I first came here as Archbishop. Cases were handled then in a manner that would not be acceptable according to our present policy. I know of nothing that has caused me greater pain than the recognition of that fact.

The Bible has not changed much during the last 2,000 years. Therefore the course of action against liers and those who preach of God, but do not believe in God, Shall Not belong to the clergy.

I am announcing today a new Archdiocesan policy that will mandate all clergy, employees and volunteers to report any allegations of abuse against a minor, following the procedures set forth in the statutes of the Commonwealth of Massachusetts. In particular, this mandated reporting would include any knowledge of abuse learned by a priest outside of the Sacrament of Penance or through spiritual counseling. In addition, a number of Archdiocesan agencies are in the process of developing and implementing a comprehensive child protection program, "Keeping Children Safe". These additions to our present policy will underscore our Archdiocesan commitment to a zero tolerance policy of abuse of minors by clergy.

The many acts that have been alleged against John Geoghan constitute a heart-rending pattern. These acts have been reported in some detail in recent media stories. The horror of these acts speaks for itself.

However much I regret having assigned him, it is important to recall that John Geoghan was never assigned by me to a parish without psychiatric or medical assessments indicating that such assignments were appropriate. It is also important to state that it was I who removed him from parish ministry, that I then placed him on retirement, and that I finally asked the Holy See to dismiss him from the priesthood without possibility of appeal, even though he had not requested laicization. This extraordinary act of the Holy See went beyond the usual procedures for the laicization of priests.

That some should criticize my earlier decisions I can easily understand. Before God, however, it was not then, nor is it my intent now, to protect a priest accused of misconduct against minors at the expense of those whom he is ordained to serve.

It was his intention to protect the Church and not the congregation. In other words, the Church is more important than God's children.

Judgements were made regarding the assignment of John Geoghan which, in retrospect, were tragically incorrect. These judgements were, however, made in good faith and in reliance upon psychiatric assessments and medical opinions that such assignments were safe and reasonable.

With all my heart I wish to apologize once again for the harm done to the victims of sexual abuse by priests. I do so in my own name, but also in the name of my brother priests. These days are particularly painful for the victims of John Geoghan. My apology to them and their families, and particularly to those who were abused in assignments which I made, comes from a grieving heart. I am indeed profoundly sorry.

The trust that was broken in the lives of those suffering the effects of abuse is a trust which was built upon the selfless lives of thousands of priests who have served faithfully and well in this Archdiocese throughout its history. One of the sad consequences of these instances of abuse, a consequence which pales in comparison to the harm done to these most innocent of victims, is that they have placed under a cloud of suspicion the faithful priests who serve the mission of the Church with integrity.

I can only hope that victims and their families can take some heart from the fact that not only the Church but society as a whole are responding more effectively to this overwhelming tragedy.

For the Archdiocese of Boston, I pledge a policy of zero tolerance for such behavior. Any priest known to have sexually abused a minor simply will not function as a priest in any way in this Archdiocese.

Please pray for all those who have been victimized as minors by clergy, as well as for their families. Pray that those responsible may come to conversion of heart and self-awareness. Pray for the hundreds of faithful priests of this Archdiocese who bear with me the burden of a few.

Shouldn't we also pray for the children and adults who have been victimized by the clergy?

Before God, we are trying to do the best we can. In your kindness, pray also for me.

Cardinal Law: Abuse Policy Must Wait

Sun Apr 28, 7:35 PM ET
By KEN MAGUIRE, Associated Press Writer

BOSTON (AP) - *Cardinal Bernard Law said Sunday that expectations for reform following the recent summit of cardinals were too high, reiterating that the creation of a national policy on sexually abusive priests would have to wait until a Catholic bishops conference.*

"As a group of cardinal archbishops, we were able to say that there were certain things that we felt we would like to bring to that June meeting," Law told the congregation at the beginning of Mass at Boston's Cathedral of the Holy Cross. "We were not there to make decisions."

Okay, that gives them a little longer to sexually abuse people, how nice.

Cardinals across the country are reporting back after a two-day gathering in Rome, where they agreed they would recommend a process to defrock any priest who has become "notorious and is guilty of the serial, predatory sexual abuse of minors."

During the short statement, Law did not address calls for his resignation. But he referred to himself and his fellow priests as "wounded healers."

They are NOT wounded healers, they are PREDATORS.

"These are not easy days to serve in the pastoral role that is mine," Law said during the special Mass dedicated to hope and healing.

"All of us are wounded healers," he said. "And when we remember that, we are able to be the people that we should be... When we are not that, we degenerate into anger and division. And that's not who we are. That's not who God calls us to be."

Law also called for a special day of prayer about the sexual abuse crisis, to be held during the Pentecostal celebrations, which start May 10.

Appearing on morning news shows Sunday, U.S. cardinals who attended the Vatican (news - web sites) meeting last week indicated there still was no agreement on whether clergymen accused of sexual abuse should be expelled from the priesthood.

If a clergy does NOT follow what he preaches, then he does not believe in God, and he MUST be removed.

Speaking on "Fox News Sunday," Cardinal Theodore McCarrick of Washington said he supported ousting any priest accused in the future but said the cardinals were divided about whether the policies should apply to past allegations.

Cardinal Francis George of Chicago, who appeared on several shows, said there still needs to be some discussion on the "one strike and you're out" approach. On NBC's "Meet the Press," he said "mandated sentences" may not be the answer and that cardinals needed some discretion.

The U.S. Conference of Catholic Bishops, at its June meeting in Dallas, is expected to vote on whether to approve a national policy that will be binding on every diocese.

Cardinal Edward Szoka, past leader of the Detroit archdiocese, argued Sunday that pedophilia is no more prevalent among priests than it is in any other profession. Szoka, who now works at the Vatican and attended last week's summit, was the commencement speaker at Sacred Heart Seminary in Detroit.

"We don't deny the problem of pedophilia. We deeply regret it. We are ashamed of it and will do whatever is necessary to correct it," said Szoka, 74. "But we do reject the attempts to discredit the priesthood and the Catholic Church."

If they know they have a problem with sexual abuse within their Church and do not stop it, then all of them are lying about what they believe in.

The sex abuse scandal began enveloping the church in January after revelations that the Archdiocese of Boston had shuttled now-defrocked priest John Geoghan from parish to parish despite repeated allegations that he was a pedophile.

Geoghan has been accused of abusing more than 130 children, and is serving a nine- to 10-year prison sentence for abuse.

The calls for Law's resignation increased this month with the release of 1,600 archdiocese documents that reveal the Rev. Paul Shanley's involvement with the North American Man-Boy Love Association.

In civil lawsuits, the former "street priest" has been charged with repeatedly raping young boys during his tenure at a Newton parish in the 1980s.

Law has denied that his resignation was discussed at the Vatican and, through a spokeswoman, said he will not be leaving the archdiocese prior to a scheduled June 5 deposition in a civil suit filed by one of Shanley's alleged victims.

About two dozen protesters picketed outside the Boston Cathedral on Sunday in rainy, cold weather. To enter the church, parishioners had to find their way through the protesters, police and the media.

"They don't see the good side of Cardinal Law," said Brother James Curren of the Little Brothers of St. Francis in Roxbury, a Catholic order. "A lot of people have made mistakes in judgment. No one defends the priests who committed sins."

One who continues to lie, has no good side.

Religious Reform

In the days of Moses, the words given to Moses were needed by the people of those days. In the days of Jesus, the things he spoke of were needed by the people of those days. And in the days of Mohammad, the things the Angel Gabrael told him were needed by the people of those days. Those three men, plus all the others who carried the word of God to the people, spoke of religious reform - One God indicating (explaining) how people should Embrace Him. Each religion came forth from the Love of God, but all were polluted by man's need to control and his (man's) desire to have power over others.

Today is no different than anywhere throughout history; God has Inspired others to seek a better communication with Him, and a better understanding of Him, while a few follow the newest ways to the Father, but most continue following the old ways of religions that their parents and peers taught them.

You and I know that the world will not change; it will not continue for that is prophesied in the Christian Bible, the Torah and the Qur'an.

The world has grown small because of technology that has brought the people of the world closer together. All the countries and all governments of the world follow some form of belief system. The only way for the world to continue to exist is if all people would allow religious and/or belief systems reform that understands and demonstrates that all religions and/or beliefs systems are of God, if they say, "Love all people." And while until that day comes, if ever, all countries and all governments still try to control others because they believe that they are following a better system that gives them a better life and lifestyle, and whereas, whenever people believe they are better than others, they believe that they have the power to and must control all others.

It was during the fall of 1996 that God's Angels entered into my life, and I began to write what the Angels has shown and taught me, these writing of mine turned not into one book but into two. And while, in January of 2000, I was instructed to start the Ministry of Jesus' House of Jacob. I stopped writing my books and gave them to a dear friend, who was a retired college English Professor, to edit for me, and I started writing weekly messages for the Jesus' House of Jacob website. It was early this year 2004, I shut down that website because I knew that I had said enough. I then, changed my website to the Ministry of the Guider, a Ministry that directs people to the God of their choosing, but only directing them to a God and religion that follows, "Love all others, and have no domination toward them," as directed by the Angel Gabrael. The Guider is a Ministry of God and not a religion.

Recently, the friend, who was editing the first of the two books that I have written, died spiritually. He left me with a partially-edited book, and while no two people write the same, no two people edit the same either. A manuscript takes on the personality of the writer and its editor. There is no way I could have another person continue to edit from where my friend ended his editing, so therefore, I must go back and rewrite my books and then have another person edit them from beginning to end.

God's Angels have repeatedly told me to enjoy and experience life. This I have not been able to do with my continuous writing of weekly messages. Yes, my writing was an enjoyable experience, but they are things that control, and of obligation - they forced me to sit and write instead of being out with the people as I wish to do. Therefore, it has come the time for me to stop writing weekly messages and pursue the completion of my book, "Together Forever

Before The Light," and "God's Forgotten Guiding Love," and to enjoy directly helping people.

If you read others and my writings, you shall find that most of our writings line-up with each other, and whereas, I tried to refrain from reading other' writings so that I did not pollute my communications with God's Angels.

I shall return later this year to write more, but for now, I will enjoy and experience life as I take the Ministry of the Guider to the people.

Thanks to all of you who regularly pulled up the Guider website, and thanks to all who have passed our site's address along to others. We may not have changed the world, but we have influenced and inspired some to seek a God who proclaims, "Love to all," and while all I was told that my learnings were for my Salvation, all that I have told you that you have read, was for your personal Salvation. We have done this part of our missions and now we should continue on with the job that God has prepared for us. For when the job is ready for you, you are ready for the job.

I shall continue to answer all your emails, but I think I have placed enough information, placed in the Archives section, about the Supreme Being - God, man-made God and his (man-made) religions for all to read and review.

May God bless you.

And I pray; "Dear Father, Who is above all, continue to watch over all of Your children and protect us from the evils of the world. I know what will be is what will be as written into Your Book of Knowledge. I understand that to live one must also die someday. I will try to enjoy and experience life, and I shall not rush that day, but when that day comes for me to come Home to rejoice and sing with You, I shall with open arms. You have given each so much, and I for one, return Divine Love back to You. You through Your Angels have given me my Salvation and I have tried to inspire others to see and understand that You are still alive. I can do no less than continue to spread Your words of Love until my last moment of life. Amen."

The Nature of God

The nature of God is one of the few areas of abstract Jewish belief where there are a number of clear-cut ideas about which there is little dispute or disagreement.

God Exists

The fact of God's existence is accepted almost without question. Proof is not needed, and is rarely offered. The Torah begins by stating "In the beginning, God created..." It does not tell who God is or how He was created.

In general, Judaism views the existence of God as a necessary prerequisite for the existence of the universe. The existence of the universe is sufficient proof of the existence of God.

God is One

One of the primary expressions of Jewish faith, recited twice daily in prayer, is the Shema, which begins "Hear, Israel: The Lord is our God, The Lord is one." This simple statement encompasses several different ideas:

1. There is only one God. No other being participated in the work of creation.

2. God is a unity. He is a single, whole, complete indivisible entity. He cannot be divided into parts or described by attributes. Any attempt to ascribe attributes to God is merely man's imperfect attempt to understand the infinite.

3. God is the only being to whom we should offer praise. The Shema can also be translated as "The Lord is our God, The Lord alone," meaning that no other is our God, and we should not pray to any other.

God is the Creator of Everything

Everything in the universe was created by God and only by God. Judaism completely rejects the dualistic notion that evil was created by Satan or some other deity. All comes from God. As Isaiah said, "I am the Lord, and there is none else. I form the light and create darkness, I make peace and create evil. I am the Lord, that does all these things." (Is. 45:6-7).

God is Incorporeal

Although many places in scripture and Talmud speak of various parts of God's body (the Hand of God, God's wings, etc.) or speak of God in anthropomorphic terms (God walking in the garden of Eden, God laying tefillin, etc.), Judaism firmly maintains that God has no body. Any reference to God's body is simply a figure of speech, a means of making God's actions more comprehensible to beings living in a material world. Much of Rambam's Guide for the Perplexed is devoted to explaining each of these anthropomorphic references and proving that they should be understood figuratively.

We are forbidden to represent God in a physical form. That is considered idolatry. The sin of the Golden Calf incident was not that the people chose another deity, but that they tried to represent God in a physical form.

God is Neither Male nor Female

This followed directly from the fact that God has no physical form. As one rabbi explained it to me, God has no body, no genitalia, therefore the very idea that God is male or female is patently absurd. We refer to God using masculine terms simply for convenience's sake, because Hebrew has no neutral gender; God is no more male than a table is.

Although we usually speak of God in masculine terms, there are times when we refer to God using feminine terms. The Shechinah, the manifestation of God's presence that fills the universe, is conceived of in feminine terms, and the word Shechinah is a feminine word.

God is Omnipresent

God is in all places at all times. He fills the universe and exceeds its scope. He is always near for us to call upon in need, and He sees all that we do. Closely tied in with this idea is the fact that God is universal. He is not just the God of the Jews; He is the God of all nations.

God is Omnipotent

God can do anything. It is said that the only thing that is beyond His power is the fear of Him; that is, we have free will, and He cannot compel us to do His will. This belief in God's omnipotence has been sorely tested during the many persecutions of Jews, but we have always maintained that God has a reason for allowing these things, even if we in our limited perception and understanding cannot see the reason.

God is Omniscient

God knows all things, past, present and future. He knows our thoughts.

God is Eternal

God transcends time. He has no beginning and no end. He will always be there to fulfill his promises. When Moses asked for God's name, He replied, "Ehyeh asher ehyeh." That phrase is generally translated as, "I am that I am," but the word "ehyeh" can be present or future tense, meaning "I am what I will be" or "I will be what I will be." The ambiguity of the phrase is often interpreted as a reference to God's eternal nature.

God is Both Just and Merciful

I have often heard Christians speak of Judaism as the religion of the strict Law, which no human being is good enough to fulfill (hence the need for the sacrifice of Jesus). This is a gross mischaracterization of Jewish belief. Judaism has always maintained that God's justice is tempered by mercy, the two qualities perfectly balanced. Of the two Names of God most commonly used in scripture, one refers to his quality of justice and the other to his quality of mercy. The two names were used together in the story of Creation, showing that the world was created with both justice and mercy.

God is Holy and Perfect

One of the most common names applied to God in the post-

Biblical period is "Ha-Kadosh, Barukh Hu," The Holy One, Blessed be He.

  Avinu Malkeinu: God is our Father and our King

  Judaism maintains that we are all God's children. A well-known piece of Jewish liturgy repeatedly describes God as "Avinu Malkeinu," our Father, our King. The Talmud teaches that there are three participants in the formation of every human being: the mother and father, who provide the physical form, and God, who provides the soul, the personality, and the intelligence. It is said that one of God's greatest gifts to humanity is the knowledge that we are His children and created in his image.

Other Belief Systems

Before going into the teachings that I have received from God's Angels, we need to explore two more beliefs systems that men has viewed as from God, also keep in mind that all these postings are one continuous message from God.

ACADEMIC METAPHYSICS

The term metaphysics originally referred to the writings of Aristotle that came after his writings on physics, in the arrangement made by Andronicus of Rhodes about three centuries after Aristotle's death.

Traditionally, metaphysics refers to the branch of philosophy that attempts to understand the fundamental nature of all reality, whether visible or invisible. It seeks a description so basic, so essentially simple, so all-inclusive that it applies to everything, whether divine or human or anything else. It attempts to tell what anything must be like in order to be at all.

To call one a metaphysician in this traditional, philosophical sense indicates nothing more than his or her interest in attempting to discover what underlies everything. Old materialists, who said that there is nothing but matter in motion, and current naturalists, who say that everything is made of lifeless, non-experiencing energy, are just as much to be classified as metaphysicians as are idealists, who maintain that there is nothing but ideas, or mind, or spirit.

Perhaps the best definition of materialism is that of Charles Hartshorne (Insights and Oversights of Great Thinkers, p. 17):

"The denial that the most pervasive processes of nature involve any such psychical functions as sensing, feeling, remembering, desiring, or thinking." Idealists assert what materialists here deny. Dualists say that mind and matter are equally real, while neutral monists claim that there is a neutral reality that can appear as either mind or matter. Philosophers generally are content to divide reality into two halves, mind and matter (extended and unextended reality) and do not emphasize such distinctions within the mind half as spirit and soul.

POPULAR METAPHYSICS

A commonly employed, secondary, popular, usage of metaphysics includes a wide range of controversial phenomena believed by many people to exist beyond the physical.

Popular metaphysics relates to two traditionally contrasted, if not completely separable, areas;

(1) Mysticism, referring to experiences of unity with the ultimate, commonly interpreted as the God who is love.

(2) Occultism, referring to the extension of knowing (extrasensory perception, including telepathy, clairvoyance, precognition, retrocognition, and mediumship) and doing (psychokinesis) beyond the usually recognized fields of human activity. The academic study of the occult (literally hidden) has been known as psychical research and, more recently, parapsychology. Both New Age and New Thought emphasize mysticism and its practical, pragmatic application in daily living, but New Thought discourages involvement in occultism.

The terms metaphysics and metaphysical in a popular sense have been used in connection with New Thought, Christian Science, Theosophy, and Spiritualism, as in J. Stillson Judah, *The History and Philosophy of the Metaphysical Movements in America.*

The Westminster Press, 1967

As well the New Age movement, and in the name of the Society for the Study of Metaphysical Religion (see below). Some of the varying understandings of metaphysics held by some founders of New Thought and Christian Science are given in the opening pages of

Christine J. Haven

Contrasting Strains of Metaphysical Idealism Contributing to New Thought.

PURE AND APPLIED METAPHYSICS

Cutting across the division of the academic and the popular, there is another way of dividing metaphysics: theoretical and applied. This distinction is like the division between science and technology; one describes; the other applies the description to practical problems, putting knowledge to work. Gathering knowledge (or alleged knowledge, critics of metaphysics would say) in metaphysics traditionally is by rational thought; in a more popular understanding, knowledge gathering may be either mystical or occult; in either case the pure (?) knowledge is to be distinguished from the practical application of it.

INTRODUCTION

New Thought Spiritualism seeks to promote the original intent of Spiritualism which has been lost due to the focus on spirit communication over the development of spirituality.

In New Thought Spiritualism it is taught that guidance and love surrounds us by the design of Infinite Intelligence, God. In New Thought Spiritualism it is sought to accept the good in people and all of life, here and hereafter. In New Thought Spiritualism it is stressed that Infinite Intelligence is omnipresent, omnipotent and omniscience. Infinite Intelligence is Spirit, everywhere present, the one and only Spirit behind, in and through all things, visible and invisible. A true understanding of life is based on the realization that the unseen hand of Infinite Intelligence guides and provides for us in every component of our existence.

In New Thought Spiritualism the existence of any power or presence opposed to Infinite Intelligence is denied. There are evil appearances and there is suffering in the world, but these are ascribed to man's ignorance and erroneous use of Infinite Intelligence's Universal Laws. Living in accordance with Universal Laws is the only true religion.

In New Thought Spiritualism seeks to relate universal and natural laws to all aspects of this existence, extending one's spiritual practice to every aspect of life. Thereby, manifesting Infinite Intelligence's perfect love for all. In New Thought Spiritualism individuals, organizations and the higher spheres are aligned into one great Harmonia.

New Thought Spiritualism was not meant to have any restrictive dogma or creed. New Thought Spiritualism states that there is a necessity for each individual, according to their means, temperament and desire to develop a higher understanding of Infinite Intelligence. Therefore, in New Thought Spiritualism acknowledges everyone has the right to have their own beliefs, and to use the methods they choose to develop a higher understanding.

In New Thought Spiritualism worship is seen as serving Infinite Intelligence by uplifting and glorifying Infinite Intelligence's spirit in any positive, joyous way. It seeks not to emphasize one's sins of the past, but instead gives attention to the good that exists in every person and what can be done now and in the future to transform one's self. By their own desire a New Thought Spiritualist seeks to serve Infinite Intelligence by acting as a channel for guidance and love for the upliftment of others and of all things.

In New Thought Spiritualism it is explained that one's words, thoughts and action affect the universe. A New Thought Spiritualist accepts and understands the power that every thought, feeling, word and act has upon one's life and accepts that responsibility.

An essential underlining belief of New Thought Spiritualism is that everyone is a potential mystic and can develop a greater understanding of the higher spheres. The use and acceptance of spiritual gifts is seen as a technique for expanding and transforming one's mind, and thus changing oneself. Spirit communication is a tool to help us understand the true nature of the universe and is a tool to help all develop to the highest possible extent. New Thought Spiritualism believes that life is a continual progression and is eternal.

NewAge On-Line Australia [www.newage.com.au]
The Story of Spiritualism
THE BIRTH OF MODERN SPIRITUALISM

It is an often reiterated statement that "Spiritualism is nothing new", its subject matter, the impingement of a non-material world upon our material one, is as old as history. The ancient writings of mankind are full of the accounts of such occurrences. It was under the name of Spiritualism, however, that an attempt was made to bring these spasmodic impingements under some form of control.

Modern Spiritualism was born in the year 1848, but before that time the minds of many thinking people had been made more receptive to its teachings by the work of Emanuel Swedenborg (1688-1772).

Swedenborg was a Swedish Scientist, Astronomer, and Engineer of international repute, who, at the age of 55 became so developed mediumistically as to be able to converse at great length with evolved spirits, and to travel in the spirit realms.

This phase of his life began in London in 1744 and continued until his death in 1772. He wrote and published a large number of books descriptive of his experiences, and explaining the philosophy taught to him by his spirit teachers. Probably the best known of his books is "Heaven and Hell". His teachings, though somewhat theologically biased, (his father was a Swedish bishop) were, nevertheless advanced and revolutionary in the light of the narrow sectarian dogmas of his day. They gave much information regarding the spirit world and it's occupants, which was to be substantially confirmed by the later revelations of Spiritualism.

The work of Swedenborg was followed by that of Andres Jackson Davis (1826-1910) - "The Poughkeepsie Seer". Davis was naturally mediumistic and in his 19th year whilst in a trance, acted as the medium through whom Swedenborg was able to resume his work by dictating various philosophical books, in one of which, published in 1847, he predicted the advent of Spiritualism. Davis carried on his inspired and inspiring work of writing, lecturing and Lyceum development until his passing in 1910. Modern Spiritualism was born in March 1848 at Hydesville, USA. There had been some "haunting" phenomena in a small wooden cottage where for some time prior to December 11, 1847, the date upon which Mr. & Mrs. Fox and their young daughters, Catherine and Margaretta, moved into residence. They too were disturbed by rapping and other supernormal phenomena. Eventually, emboldened by the presence of their parents, the children began what, to them, was a game of talking to whatever mysterious power was responsible for the disturbances, asking for a specified number of raps in response to their questions. The reply was *immediate and it became obvious that some kind of intelligence was manifesting.*

A Committee of Investigation was formed, a definite code of signals agreed upon, and it was then established that the communicator was one Charles B. Rosna, a pedlar who had been murdered by a previous occupant of the cottage and buried in the cellar. This information was subsequently verified. Curiosity brought hundreds of people to view the cottage and the Fox family were glad to leave it. The rappings, however, continued elsewhere in the presence of the girls.

Three important facts emerged from the Hydesville rappings:
1) Organised communication was shown to be possible.
2) Certain people, e.g. the Fox sisters, were naturally mediumistic.
3) Communication could be facilitated by means of a code.

The spirit communicators instructed the investigators to form circles in their own homes, under spirit guidance. Thus the idea of spirit communication began to spread to ordinary cottage homes, at a time when education was becoming more widespread, and people were able to realise the import of the spirit teaching.

These spirits and psychic phenomena attracted the attention of certain scholars who became convinced of the spirit-inspired origin of the communications and were courageous enough to come into the open and admit their conviction. Judge Edmonds (1816-1874) a member of the Supremne Court of New York, was one of the investigators of the original Hydesville phenomena. He and many of his friends accepted fully the spirit hypothesis.

THE HISTORY OF MODERN SPIRITUALISM

The following are a list of important dates considered to be milestones in the unfoldment of Spiritualism:

1848, Hydesville Knockings in the USA lead to the investigation of the mediumship of the Fox sisters and the birth of Modern Spiritualism.

1849, The first public demonstration of Mediumship by Margaret Fox in the Corinthian Corinthian Hall in New York.

1852, Mrs Hayden came from America to be the first Spiritualist medium to work in Britain.

1853, Darlington born David Richmond returned to his native town from America. The Quaker townsfolk obliged him to leave. He went to Keighley in Yorkshire, the first Spiritualist Church being opened by him there.

1854, Robert Owen, Socialist Reformer and Co-Founder of the Co-operative Society, became converted to Spiritualism after sittings with Mrs. Hayden. After he passed to Spirit he became the author of *The Principles of Spiritualism* which he gave through the mediumship of Emma Hardinge Britten.

1855, "The Yorkshire Spiritual Telegraph" the first Spiritual Newspaper was published in Keighley.

1863, Andrew Jackson Davis established the first Sunday Lyceum in New York. *1865*, An attempt was made to form the first National Organisation of Spiritualists in Darlington.

1866, Emma Hardinge Britten returned to England where she was quickly recognised as a very powerful medium.

1866, The first Lyceum in Britain was opened by Mr. J. Hitchcock in Nottingham.

1868, The Dialectical Society appointed a Committee to investigate Spiritualism. They published a very favourable report - (the best by any external body.)

1871, Sir William Crookes reported on Spiritualism to the Royal Society and published his findings in the quarterly Journal of Science.

1872, A second attempt to form a National Organisation was made at a National Conference in Darlington. Again it failed. However, it stimulated interest and people wrote to the Spiritualist Press. It soon became recognised that there was a need for such an organisation.

1873, A conference was held in Liverpool which led to the formation of the British National Association of Spiritualists with its headquarters in London.

1878, Emma Hardinge Britten toured Australia and New Zealand promoting spiritualism.

1882, The Society for Psychical Research was started.

1887, The "Two Worlds" was launched as a weekly newspaper by Emma Hardinge Britten. The British "Lyceum Manual" was published for the first time. Its Co-authors were Mr H. A Kersey of Newcastle upon Tyne, Mr Alfred Kitson and Emma Hardinge Britten. The Principles of Spiritualism were published in the "Two Worlds" magazine as follows: -

The Fatherhood of God

The Brotherhood of Man

The Immortality of the Soul and its Personal Characteristics

The proven facts of Communion between departed Human Spirits and mortals

Personal Responsibility with compensation and retribution hereafter for all the good and evil deeds done here. A path of Eternal Progress open to every Human Soul that wills to tread it by the path of Eternal Good.

1890, Formation of the National Spiritualists' Federation. Spiritualists' Lyceum Union established. Name was later changed to British Spiritualists' Lyceum Union in 1894.

1893, Foundation of National Spiritualists' Association of America.

1901, Foundation of Spiritualists' National Union Limited.

1902, The S.N.U. took over the rights, assets and obligations of the Federation and obtained legal status whereby it could hold real property.

1916, Parliamentary Campaign for the legal recognition of Spiritualism instituted by the Union under Ernest Oaten.

1918, Sir Arthur Conan Doyle proclaimed his belief in spiritualism.

1923, Formation of the Internation Spiritualists Federation

1924, Hannen Swaffer proclaimed his belief in the teachings and truth of Spiritualism.

1931-1935, Arthur Findlay's Trilogy published:

"On the Edge of the Etheric", "The Rock of Truth", "The Unfolding Universe".

1932, The "Psychic News" was founded by Arthur Findlay under the editorship of Maurice Barbanell.

1934, First broadcast on behalf of Spiritualism through BBC by Ernest Oaten.

1937, Spiritualism investigated by Church of England Committee set up by Archbishop of Canterbury, Dr. Cosmo Lang. (It's subsequent favourable report was suppressed but leaked to "Psychic News").

1939, Ministers begin to be appointed by the Spiritualists' National Union.

1940, Spiritualists National Union gains Government sanction/certificate to act as a Trust Corporation.

1944, Helen Duncan on trial in London.

1950, The Spiritualists' National Union recognised as the Official Spiritualists' body.

1951, The Lyceum Department received a letter from the Spiritualists National Union stating that henceforth it would be known as "The Spiritualists' Lyceum Union" (in 1948, the British Spiritualists' Lyceum Union was incorporated into the Spiritualists' National Union).

1963, A motion showing that there was a need for a Guild of Spiritualist Healers was put to the Spiritualists' nation Union's Annual General Meeting at Worthing and was held to be proven, although nothing could be done at the meeting, it was an ideal only.

1964, Proposals were put to the Spiritualists' National Union's Annual General Meeting at Manchester for the formation of such a Guild. Stansted Hall bequeathed to the Spiritualists' National Union by Arthur Findlay to be used as a College for the advancement of Psychic Science.

1966, Arthur Findlay College (Stansted Hall) opens in September.

1968, Tom Henwood and Bill Tyler, members of the Healing Committee, ask for closer contact with the District Councils, this helped to increase membership.

1969, The League of Friends of Stansted Hall was inaugurated.

1970, The Northern, Sheffield, Southern, Yorkshire, East Midlands and London Guilds had been formed and the first meeting of the Guild of Spiritualist Healers took place in Stansted Hall.

1972, First National Conference of the Guild was also held in Stansted Hall.

1973, A set of Bye-Laws was set up for the administration of the Guild, these to be known as By-Laws "H".

1975, At the S.N.U. Annual General Meeting, members voted in favour of adopting a new set of Articles of Association which were circulated prior to the meeting. This resulted in bringing into force the three tier system of administration.

1976, The three tier system came into effect immediately after the S.N.U. Annual General Meeting marking a new phase in the history of the S.N.U.

1979, At the Spiritualists' National Union's Annual General Meeting at Manchester it was agreed that the Guild would administer its own funds and its chief officers would be known as President and Vice-President, these arrangements took effecct in January 1980.

1981, The Guild became one of the Founder Members of the Confederation of Healing Organisations.

1990, The S.N.U. Centenary celebrated by holding Publicity Meetings in every District Council area - National celebration at Wembley, London on 31st March, date of the Hydesville event in 1848.

PROMINENT MEDIUMS OF MODERN SPIRITUALISM

The following are some of the prominent mediums of the early days:- Daniel Douglas Home (1833-1886) one of the greatest physical mediums in whose presence almost all types of physical phenomena occurred. Born in Edinburgh, his powers were discovered whilst he was living in America. On his return to England in 1855 the remarkable phenomena aroused great interest.

David Duguid (1832-1907), this Glasgow medium was perhaps most famous for spirit oil paintings of landscapes, produced in total darkness at an amazing speed, and independently of his hands. In his presence were produced all kinds of phenomena, and through him was dictated a remarkable book, the wekk known "Hafed, Prince of Persia".

Dr. Henry Slade, an American medium famous for slate-writing mediumship, in which messages were written on sealed slates. He was thoroughly tested by several eminent investigators, and pronounced genuine.

William Eglington, noted for outdoor and daylight materialisations and also for slate-writing mediumship. Questions put in Spanish, French and Greek were answered in the same languages.

Gladstone, after sitting with him, was sufficiently impressed to join the Society for Psychical Research.

Florence Cook (1856-1904), outstanding for the wonderful materialisation of Katie King, invvestigated by Sir William Crookes. He proved this spirit to be entirely separate and distinct from the medium.

Leonore E Piper of Boston, USA, allowed herself to be subjected to the most exacting scientific investigation of her mediumship for a period of 45 years. This great medium was instrumental in converting many eminent people to believe in a spirit agency operating through her trance mediumship.

Eusapia Palladino (1854-1918), the famous physical medium was subjected to scientific investigation all over Europe and America, and brought home the reality of physical phenomena to many outstanding scientists.

Elizabeth D'Esperance (1855-1919), redenowned for extraordinary apports, materialisations and sketches made in complete darkness, of spirit relatives of her friends.

PROMINENT SCIENTIFIC INVESTIGATORS

So great was the impact of "other-world" manifestations and materialisations that some promenent scientists were drawn to make a thorough investigation of the subject. Listed below are some who require mention: Dr. A Russel Wallace, (1823-1903). Co-discoverer with Charles Darwin of the Theory of Evolution. He painstakingly investigated Spiritualism over a number of years, eventually stating quite fearlessly that its phenomena were proved quite as well as the facts of any other science.

Sir William Crookes (1832-1919). An outstanding physicist who began his investigations into Spiritualism with the avowed intent of exposing it as nonsense. The facts, however, (particularly his investigation of Katie King through the mediumship of Florence Cook) was too overwhelming, and to the end of his life he remained completely convinced of the truth of Spirit communication.

Sir William F. Barrett (1845-1926). Made searching enquiries both in this country and in the USA. His summing up was that there is evidence for the existence of a spirit world for survival after death, and for occasional communication with those passed over.

Lord Rayleigh (1842-1919). Made prolonged investigatins, and although he made no public pronouncement, he contributed to the work of the Society for Psychical Research, becoming the President in 1919.

THE SOCIETY FOR PSYCHICAL RESEARCH

Despite the pioneer work of Wallace, Crookes and Barrett, orthodox science remained antagonistic to the facts of physicalphenomena. Similarly the orthodox Churches were opposed to the teachings of Spiritualism. the time, therefore, was ripe for the establishment of an independent body to further scientific knowledge in the direction of psychical research and in 1882 Sir William Barrett gathered together a group of people capable of developing this idea. This group formed themselves into the Society for Psychical Research with the objects of "furthering scientific knowledge of telepathy, hypnotism, mediumship, apparitions, physical phenomena of mediumship, etc."

The original body consisted of Professor Henry Sidgwick (President); F.W. Myers, Edmund Furney, Professor Balfour Steward, Rev. Stainton Moses, Dawson Rogers and Doctor George Wyld. Some of these made important individual contributions to psychical research, notably: F.W.H. Myers (1834-1901) whose celebrated book "Human Personality and its Survival of Bodily Death" is acknowledge as a classic, and has established psychical research as an organised science. All students of Spiritualism should read this book. Edmund Gurney (1847-1888) studied the psychological aspect of Hypnotism in this country. Henry Sidgwick (1838-1900) took an active part in the work of the Society until his death, and contributed largely to the "Proceeding of the S.P.R." He investigated the work of many mediums but kept his personal convictions private.

Dr Richard Hodgson. An early member of the Society soon became noted as a competent and critical investigator. He made a systematic study of the mediumship of Mrs. Leonore Piper, through which he became completely convinced of the reality of spirit return. The development of his own mediumistic powers late in life brought to him an even deeper conviction.

PROMINENT SPIRITUALISTS

Organisation of the Spiritualist Movement in Great Britain began in the latter half of the 19th Century. Many Churches and societies were formed throughout the country, and it became desirable to unite these isolated bodies into some kind of Federation. After several attempts to do this, the National Federation of Spiritualists was formed in 1890 as the result of preliminary meetings called by:- Emma Hardinge Britten (1823-1899). Mrs Britten was the natural leader of the new Movement. She launched the journal "The Two Worlds" and was editor for five years. A gifted orator and writer, she was largely responsible for the philosophical outlook of Spiritualists. Through her mediumship the Principles of Spiritualism were given. Other prominent figures in the vanguard of Spiritualist organisations were:- William Stainton Moses (1839-1892). An Oxford M.A. and a clergyman of the Church of England. He was the leading light in promoting the London Spiritualist Alliance, and became its first President and the first Editor of "Light". High great contributions were the teachings produced through him by means of spirit controlled writing and published as "Spirit teachings" and "More Spirit Teachings".

William T. Stead (1849-1912). In 1892, Stead discovered that he had the gifts of spirit controlled handwriting. He became associated with the L.S.A. and was a fearless champion of Spiritualism. He was, of course, a well-known editor, and a nationally famous figure for his great fight against the White Slave Traffic and the prostitution of children. He passed to the Higher Life through the tragic sinking of the "Titanic" in 1912.

Alfred Kitson (1855-1934). Lyceums were opened in 1870 at Keighley and Sowerby Bridge. *Alfred kitson attended the first anniversary of the latter and thereafter devoted himself to this cause. He began to develop a system of Lyceum teaching here based upon the American model of Andrew Jackson Davis.*

Kitson was jointly responsible with Mr. Kersey and Mrs. Britten for the English Lyceum Manual.

EUROPEAN SCIENTIFIC INVESTIGATORS

Meanwhile, Spiritualism was spreading rapidly on the continent of Europe. It gained a strong hold in France where many men of science investigated it's claims. Some of these, notably Dr.

Gustave Geley, Dr. Charles Richet, Cable Flammarion, the famous astronomer, and Dr. Joire made important contributions to the literature of the subject.

Allan Kardec (1804-1869) (France) expounded a system of Spiritualist philosophy based upon mediumistic communications.

Reincarnation was a central doctrine of Kardec's teaching which became basic to the whole Latin world.

Ernest Bozzano (1862-1943) (Italy). A brilliant scientist who was converted to the Spiritualist hypothesis through the mediumship of Eusapia Palladino. He wrote extensively on the subject.

Dr Schrenck Notzing (1862-1929) (Germany). A scientist of great repute who made prolonged researches into physical phenomena, particularly the production of ectoplasmic formations, and recorded his observations in his book "Phenomena of Materialisation".

Alexander N. Akaskof (1832-1903) (Russia). Spiritualism made little headway in Russia although some pioneering work was undertaken by Akaskof.

SPIRITUALISTS' NATIONAL FEDERATION

The Spiritualists' National Federation, formed in 1890, gathered many churches, societies and individual members under it's wing. It had, however, no legal status, and to remedy this state of affairs it was in 1902 merged into the Spiritualists National Union Limited, which had been incorporated under the companies Act in October 1901, and had power to hold properties, etc., as a Company limited by guarantee. The primary object of the Spiritualists' National Union is to promote the advancement and diffusion of the religion and religious philosophy of Spiritualism. The Movement sustained a severe blow in 1899 when Emma Hardinge Britten passed on.

Sir Arthur Conan Doyle had in 1902 joined the Society for Psychical Research. As a result of prolonged investigation, Doyle openly championed the cause of Spiritualism by the publication of "The New Revelation". Due to the wide-spread sorrow after the 1914-18 war, Doyle decided to make Spiritualism his life's mission. He travelled very widely in his missionary zeal and became known as "The St. Paul of Spiritualism". He has been regarded since his transition as the Honorary President of the S.N.U. in Spirit.

Ernest Oaten was Doyle's tour organizer and right-hand man, but years peior to this he had devoted his life to the building up of the S.N.U. In 1919 he became editor of "The Two Worlds" and was rightly recognized as a leader of Spiritualist thought. Spiritualism is indebted to him beyond measure for his efforts on its behalf.

Hannen Swaffer. Author, journalist and socialist, created a sensation when he made public his conversion to spiritualism in 1924, in his book "Northcliffe's return". He was a great propagandist through the spoken and written word.

Lord Dowding came into prominence as a champion of Spiritualism after the 1939-45 war. Lord Dowding was in command of the R.A.F. during the Battle of Britain and, through a medium friend, many of the airmen who had passed over were able to give their former Chief convincing evidence of their survival. Since then Lord Dowding spoke and wrote indefatigably on his convictions regarding the continuity of life.

PROMINENT AUTHORS

A great feature of the 20th Century Spiritualism in this country has been the wealth of excellent writers on the subject, far beyond anything produced in any other country. Four writers deserve special mention:

Rev G. Vale Owen (1869-1931). A Church of England clergyman who developed spirit-controlled writing. A whole series of articles produced in this manner was published in the "Weekly Dispatch" in 1920 and made a profound impression. In consequence of this publicity he was persecuted by his Ecclesiastical superiors and resigned from the Church. He conducted lecture tours of Britain and America. His "Life Beyond the Veil" (five volumes) has become a Spiritualist classic.

W.H. Evans wrote extensively on the philosphy of Spiritualism and contributed regularly to the psychic press.

J. Arthur Findlay, MBE. Author of the following widely read books on Spiritualism;
"On the Edge of the Etheric"
"The Rock of Truth"
"The Unfolding Universe"
"The Psychic Stream"

"The Curse of Ignorance".
He helped to found "The Psychic News" in 1932.
Rev. C. Drayton Thomas whose works include descriptions of life in the Spirit World.

MEDIUMS

The quickening of the tempo of life has demanded a great increase in concentration upon earning a livelihood. Mass production methods are not conducive to the state of inner tranquility which is essential to good mediumship. Mediumship has therefore declined in quality as well as changed in character. Tom Tyrell, now passed on, was an exceptionally brilliant medium. His mediumship was notable for the fact that he always gave full names, ages and addresses, as well as other particulars of the spirit
people whom he described. He seldom failed to bring complete conviction.

Mrs Helen Hughes and Mrs Estelle Roberts are also noteworthy for their fine clairaudient work, being excellent mediums for propaganda purposes in large meetings.

Another great medium Mrs Gladys Osborne Leonard has done excellent work for the S.P.R. and also with such investigators as Sir Oliver Lodge and Rev. C. Drayton Thomas who has permanently recorded the same in book form.

There have been diverse types of mediumship in this century, each of which has brought a great deal of conviction. William Hope of Crewe was famous for his spirit photography, many competent investigators testifying to his genuine powers.

Miss Geralding Cummins, Playwright and authoress. Has the gift of spirit controlled writing. Through her hand has been received a series of remarkable books dealing with the early days of Christianity. Despite her own lack of knowledge of the places dealt with in her books, or of theology, eminent authorities have acclaimed the merit and accuracy of her books.

Frank Leah has given convincing evidence of survival by his gift of drawing the departed friends and relations of sitters. Many striking likenesses have been produced.

Harold Sharp's particular form of mediumship enabled him to design what may be called an artistic diagram of the human aura.

The so-called 'auragraph' was explained by the Chinese guide responsible, and was usually most enlightening and helpful regarding the inner naturee and psychic trends of the sitter.

One of the new developments in 20th Century mediumship is direct voice phenomena. Admiral Usborne Moore, a well-known psychical researcher brought the powerful American Direct Voice medium Mrs Etta Wreidt to England in 1912 and 1913. She never sat in a cabinet, nor passed into trance, and often joined in the conversation when spirit voices spoke to sitters. This medium could only speak English, but the direct voices spoke in numerous languages.

One of the most famous English direct voice mediums is Leslie Flint.

George Valiantine also an American, was an outstanding Direct Voice medium. Many different languages were heard at his Seances, notably ancient Chinese, which was spoken in the presence of Dr. Wymant, an authority on the subject.

Dennis Bradley wrote two forthright books on Valiantine's mediumship.

Mrs Margery Crandon was also noted for Direct Voice phenomena and many other types of mediumship.

Carol Mirabelli, the South American medium, was searchingly investigated and passed as a genuine medium, for the most astounding Direct Voice and Materialisation phenomena.

THE ANGLICAN CHURCH AND SPIRITUALISM
By:
JOHN ROBERTS.

Being meditations, on reading the 1939 Church of England Report on the findings of a Committee established to "investigate" spiritualism.

Introduction

As a youth of 18 years, (1947)I read an article in the "Psychic News", (A newspaper purporting to represent the views of Spiritualists in the United Kingdom) which claimed to have obtained information regarding the content of the 1939 Report on Spiritualism. This report was prepared by a committee of Anglicans for the information of the Bishops of the Church of England.

The correspondent of the Psychic News was indignant at the fact that the report had been suppressed by the Archbishop of Canterbury, Dr. Lang, as it had proven to be favourable to the practice of Spiritualism.

Nothing further developed during ensuing years, although in 1979 the full text of the report was published in "The Christian Parapsychologist", the journal of the: "Churches Fellowship for Psychical and Spiritual studies".

I have now been sent a copy of this report by a friend who is involved in the Spiritualist Movement and, having read it, feel that there are certain matters contained therein which call for comment. Hence this short essay.

It is not intended to dwell at length on the origin of the report but some note is necessary. The Dean of Rochester, Francis Underhill, (later exalted to the post of Bishop of Bath and Wells), evidently had a great interest in Spiritualism. He earnestly endeavoured to involve his colleagues in the Church, in promoting an official study of the beliefs and practices of Spiritualists. His activities eventually proving successful; a Committee was established in January 1937, with the blessing of Archbishop Lang. After three years sitting with "Mediums" and practitioners of the occult, the Committee handed down its findings, which were partially critical and condemnatory and to some extent supportive of a further and more comprehensive study of Spiritualism.

What I find to be interesting, is the extent to which preconceived and erroneous ideas found their way into the findings of the Committee. It is evident, that even after three years of study, the majority of the members were still in complete ignorance of the beliefs and aims of the majority of spiritualists: nor had they any concept of the relevance of Spiritualism to their own Christian beliefs.

I propose to have a look at some of the remarks made in the report and make my own observations as to their validity.

Terms of Reference

The terms of reference of the Committee were: "To investigate the subject of communications with discarnate spirits and the claims of Spiritualism in relation to the Christian Faith". There were thus, two aspects to the inquiry:

1. To investigate communications with discarnate spirits

2. To investigate the "claims" of Spiritualism in relation to the Christian Faith.

As to (a): this is a straightforward statement and is indicative of a simple purpose.

As to (b): one would have to predetermine what, indeed, are the "claims" of Spiritualism, in relation to Christianity. This might have particular reference to those professing to be Christian-Spiritualists. Apart from this branch of Spiritualism, I am not aware that Spiritualism makes any particular claims in respect of Christianity, other than to reject many of the traditional doctrines of the Church.

(One member of the Committee, Miss Evelyn Underhill, resigned at the second meeting of the committee, being: "struck once more by the utterly sub-Christian, anthropocentric, hopelessly unsupernatural character of the Spiritualist outlook. It is all about man, his survival, prospects, etc., hardly at all about God……….."

It is perhaps well, for the ultimate conclusions of the report itself, that Miss Underhill did resign, as she clearly had little insight into the underlying philosophy of spiritualist teachings.

In her letter of resignation, Miss Underhill goes on to claim that in Spiritualism, "Personal survival" is made a primary issue, a "reason" for faith: that Spiritualists need experimental proof of the existence of God." This may or may not be true, depending upon the individual.

She sees no <u>profit</u> in aligning the Church of England with Spiritualism: by abandoning "the theocentric view". She feels that such an investigation... "which is really scientific and not religious in character..., should be left to the SPR or some similar body and the church should stick to her supernatural job as the Body of Christ"

Miss Underhill was clearly quite happy with her own beliefs and did not wish to be troubled by concerns which might have had the effect of questioning their validity. It is certain that she had adopted a premature and judgmental attitude towards the subject in hand and would have made little constructive contribution towards the proceedings.

Having lost all belief in God myself, after witnessing the conduct of Anglican Christians as a boy-chorister for some four or five years, it was with relief and delight that I discovered, at the age of 16 years, the fact of the resurrection from the dead. This, not as a future, indeterminate, event but as an immediate reality upon the death of the physical body: a resurrection, which is God's gift to all men and women, of whatever race or creed. Once I realised that men survive the physical death, I had no difficulty in satisfying myself that, therefore, God must exist.

Indeed, it was the fact of the evidence for the resurrection of Jesus of Nazareth, which gave the necessary impetus to his followers for the development of Christianity itself: although those first Jewish Apostles would hardly recognise modern Christianity as a product of their labours.

The introductory remarks of the Committee.

After pointing out that Spiritualism "claims to have religious character", the Committee set out three reasons why people are attracted to Spiritualism, these are:

(a) For consolation which it is believed to provide through communication with discarnate spirits.

(b) For the guidance which some claim to receive from the Spiritual world.

(c) For the evidence which it is believed to provide of survival after death.

There is no mention herein of a search for knowledge of God: for a clearer glimpse of spiritual truth. If people need consolation, why cannot the Church itself fulfil this need? Why do they also need "guidance", when the Church professes to provide this essential service? As to "evidence". If one is able to communicate with the dead, then there is ample proof of "survival" in the very fact of communication. If satisfied that a deceased loved-one is still alive and functioning in a new environment, herein lies consolation.

The Committee expressed concern that people were attracted to spiritualism: some left the church altogether. There did not appear to be any appreciation of the causes in the decline of church attendance.

The Committee did mention the fact that: "many instructed and open-minded Christians who have had the courage to make a first-hand study of psychic phenomena have found an altogether new light shed upon one thing and another, both in the Scripture and in *the tradition of the Church, that in recent times have become matters of grave difficulty in consequence of the attitude of modern science".* This statement promises great things but, unfortunately, it evidently represented the view of only one person, perhaps Underhill herself.

Reference is made to the work of the *"Society for Psychical Research"*, which, during the 40's and 50's, seemed to be devoted to the undermining of Spiritualism rather than for the elucidation of its procedures. As Spiritualism cannot be "scientifically" proven or disproven, the work of the SPR is valueless. Neither is the SPR of any relevance in a discussion of the relationship between Spiritualist teachings and Christian doctrine.

The committee gives a definition of spiritualism which is completely inadequate, following the Shorter Oxford Dictionary. In fact, three separate definitions are proposed, none of which reveals that Spiritualism is a comprehensive system of theology.

The last assumedly acceptable definition is as follows:

"Spiritualism means the demonstrated survival of human personality after bodily death. It includes the knowledge of the interaction of matter and spirit. Further, it implies a comprehension of the intelligent progressive spiritual principle which underlies the whole of creation, of mankind and nature in this present life and of continuous individual progressive spiritual life in the hereafter".

This definition was provided by Miss Mercy Phillimore, a witness to the proceedings, and Secretary of a Spiritualist group.

Such a definition limits any enquiry into Spiritualism to an extremely narrow ambit. The passage goes on to state that: *"if the definition of Spiritualism is accepted, it does mean that Spiritualism cannot be regarded as a religion in the same sense as that in which Christianity is a religion".*

"It is to be noted that the entire emphasis of this definition is laid upon knowledge and not upon faith or even belief......".

What is immediately clear, is the fact that none of the members of this Committee had any real concept of the nature of Spiritualism and merely adopted a convenient vehicle from which to pronounce judgement upon, what they all perceived as a thoroughly dangerous activity.

The statement is made: *"It further involves the acceptance of scientific standards of evidence, since such knowledge as this definition implies, is the proper subject matter of science. This in itself raises serious difficulties of proof, which many Spiritualists do not seem to face at all adequately".*

Here we have a real difficulty for the members of the Committee. They present a definition which is totally inadequate; which says nothing regarding the Spiritualist's ideas regarding the "nature" of Deity: says nothing of his views on the relationship existing between God and Man. It suggests that a study of the Movement should more properly be the realm of Scientific enquiry. That Scientists, who almost universally reject the doctrines of the Churches, as gross superstition, should be the people to investigate and either prove or disprove the phenomena of Spiritualism on scientific grounds. It cannot possibly fall within the sphere of interest of clergymen. The statement that: spiritualists "do not seem to face difficulties of proof at all adequately", can be answered on the basis that they need no further "proof". Having received abundant evidence of the essential truth of the phenomena of Spiritualism, they see no further need to investigate the work of the Spirit via scientific enquiry. Neither do spiritualists feel the need to explain themselves to sceptics or to "prove" the value of their doctrines to third parties.

If questions relating to the nature of man: his relationship to his creator; his immortality; his links with departed souls; the ministry of angels; the communion of saints; his values and morals, do not concern clergymen, it is hard to conceive how they can possibly be of interest to scientists, whose business is the with empirical world and the observation thereof, not with the world of the spirit.

Grudging acknowledgement is made, under the heading "Characteristics and extent of Spiritualism", that the Movement has the character:

(a) Of a system with numerous adherents and with many of the elements of a cult, or even of a religion.

(b) Of a more or less philosophical account of the universe, with special reference to the destiny of personal beings.

(c) Of an assemblage of attested and, at least in some degree, coherent facts which fall outside the normal range of our experience.

Statistics were presented which showed that there were some 520 Societies affiliated to the Spiritualists' National Union throughout the United Kingdom and this would not have included a great many Christian Spiritualist Churches.

That the committee members were biased, is evident from the use of language indicative, of mediums generally, that: "many of these were certainly fraudulent and others honest but self-deceived".

That there was and still is, "wide divergence" of views on the part of Spiritualists is true, in view of the fact that Spiritualism has no creed and lays down no dogma for its adherents. The Seven Principles were used merely as a guide for members. The first Principle, of course, being "The Fatherhood of God", which exposes the lie in the proposition that Spiritualism is secular in outlook.

The various phenomena of Spiritualism are set out fairly well. Very few spiritualists today would have experienced all forms of phenomena possible. The vast majority would have only witnessed the phenomena of clairvoyance, clairaudience and semi-trance mediumship.

Under the heading : "Para 8 Claims of Spiritualism", additional comment is made which indicates suspicion and bias on the part of the members of the Committee. The following statement is typical: "It should be remembered that the careful and critical study of such alleged happenings as materialisations and spirit-photography, which has exposed such an immense amount of self-deception and of conscious and wilful fraud, has been carried out by Spiritualists themselves".

Spiritualists, quite naturally, have a vested interest in stamping out fraud, although it is difficult to see how this can be effected.

There may well have been some fraud in the past, on the part of tricksters, but to refer to "an immense amount...." is nonsense. The plain fact is that most spiritualists attend private groups for development purposes and there is simply no occasion for fraud.

The influence of lucre alone may promote fraud and within the Spiritualist Churches there is simply no opportunity or incentive for deception. Of course, "mediums" who give private readings or sittings for expensive fees are another matter. Such people are not necessarily

Spiritualists, although it is conceded that they often describe themselves as such. People who are foolish enough to part with their cash under such circumstances deserve to be fleeced. However, sincere Spiritualists generally are not tainted by pecuniary considerations. As for those who are involved in physical phenomena, once again, in this day and age, they are mainly devoted enthusiasts, who sit regularly with one or more mediums who are endowed with specific gifts. There is thus no occasion for fraud or deception.

In respect of the relationship of Spiritualism to Christianity, the Committee took the view that: "the evidence upon which its claims rest lies very largely within the sphere of scientific observation and investigation". Did you ever hear such nonsense? Later, the difficulties attendant upon scientific investigation were tacitly acknowledged: "...it is highly probable that the critical and objective attitude necessary to accurate scientific observation may almost completely frustrate its own purpose". Even so, thought the Committee: "it merely means that his technique (the scientist) must be adapted to this special need". Such a proposition overlooks the undoubted fact that things of the spirit are perceived spiritually and the worldly man cannot know them: they are entirely outside his ken, as the Apostle Paul so clearly stated. (Corinth 1, Chapter 2, verse 14).

Reference is also made to various phenomena which are said to be akin to the phenomena of spiritualism. Much of this phenomena is not within the experience of most spiritualists and, although undoubtedly related, is irrelevant to an investigation of the claims of spiritualism. Discerning spiritualists might take cognisance of another of Paul's statements concerning "Spiritual Gifts", that we should seek to develop within ourselves the higher gifts of Ministry, Healing and Clairvoyance (Prophecy). (Corinth 1, Chapter 12, verse 31).

One thing is very clear from a perusal of the writings of Paul: that the Jewish followers of Jesus certainly practised spiritual gifts and enjoyed a communion with the spirit-world. To suggest that spiritualism raises no questions of doctrine for practising Christians is fatuous, in view of the gulf which presently separates Christians from those who had witnessed the life, death and resurrection of the Christ.

Christine J. Haven

The First Letter of John, Chapter 4, verse 1 reads: "Beloved, believe not every spirit but try the spirits, whether they are of God, for many false prophets are gone out into the world." This passage clearly confirms the fact that the communion of spirit was a very active part of the life of the first Christians.

The introduction closes with comments of a general nature and reference to certain assumed beliefs of spiritualists. It closes with the following words: "The fundamental truth and principles of Christianity are our sufficient guide and strength. We have already, in Jesus Christ and in His Church, all that we need to direct us 'in the way that leadeth to eternal life'". I suppose this passage echoes Jesus own statement that those who live according to the law and the prophets are already close to the Kingdom of Heaven. That is all very well for the "faithful": they who take their religion upon trust: upon what they have been told from childhood-up is Divine Truth. No doubt, if they do live in accordance with Christian principles, i.e. those established by the Sermon on the Mount, they are assured of success and happiness in this life and the next. Yet how many Christians do live such a life? A great many people lose faith in what they have been taught: they see the flaws and contradictions in the practice of Christianity: the humbug and hypocrisy of priests and prelates. Even as a little child, I thought it was all a bit far-fetched. These doubts were fully confirmed in adolescence. It was Spiritualism that brought my ideas into perspective, which gave me an insight: a glimpse into spiritual truth: certainly not Bishops in full canonicals.

The Witnesses

Several witnesses are recorded as giving evidence to the Committee. Miss Mercy Phillimore (Secretary of the London Spiritualist Alliance and the Quest Club), gave one of the definitions used by the committee as a basis for its report.

Miss Phillimore placed facts before the Committee, which tended to show a clear relationship between the aims and work of the Movement and those of the Christian religion. I do not disagree with Miss Phillimore, in principle, although there are one or two points with which I would not concur. Miss Phillimore assumes that when: "Our Lord appeared before the Apostles after His death, His body was so 'purified' as to enable Him to appear before them without the assistance of power obtained from their bodies." In other words, she means that a "medium" would not have been necessary. I do not think that this was the case and, certainly, one of the Apostles present would have been a physical medium. The body they observed, if anything, was his materialised spirit body: certainly not his risen physical coil.

Her remarks regarding "miracles" are generalized. Many of the miracles of the Old and New Testaments would be rejected by modern Spiritualists, as fable.

This lady also referred to the need to safeguard the meeting from the presence of "low spirits" or, what I refer to as, "regressive spirits". She felt that there must be a medium of "integrity". In fact, all the sitters need to be persons of suitable temperament, not given to low company or low-living. They must be sincere and dedicated, otherwise the experience will not be worthwhile. The spirit-world, just like the physical world, is peopled by persons of every conceivable temperament. If we keep poor company here we are certain to attract similar individuals into our spiritual environment.

Once more, we have to "seek the higher gifts".

Dame Edyth Lyttleton: submitted a written statement, supporting the principle that *"psychical research supported and strengthened the religious sense and the Christian religion".* She herself experienced some intuitive inspirational episodes, which were very comforting to her personally. She spoke of *"psychical research"* and perhaps had only a limited experience of Spiritualist religious meetings, which would certainly have given her a deeper insight into the question of the resurrection, which in my humble view, is fully confirmed by overwhelming spiritualist experience.

This witness makes a valid point by stating, "It has to be conceded that almost every so-called revelation is conditioned by the mind through which it is conveyed". This is true, because the instrument attracts spirit guides and helpers whose tastes and interests are similar to those of the individual him-herself. "Like attracts like" is a Spiritualist truism. Paul himself affirms: "and the spirits of the prophets are subject to the prophets". (l Corinthians, Ch 14, v 32).

As to the "Holy Spirit": here again, the loftier the ideal the more refined the response. Once more, we should seek the higher gifts *and perform a greater service. Kenneth Richmond, a member of the SPR, gave evidence which purported to result from a psychological study of spiritualism. His evidence was guarded but not hostile and he concluded in stating: "There was certainly communication with discarnate spirits, and this gave a ground for believing in immortality". He did not reject the right to seek access to the spirit-world.*

Mr Richmond says, "The control or communicating entity is based on a secondary personality of the medium". This is pure supposition and psychological theory. I know from, personal experience, that everyone has a "doorkeeper" guide, who is responsible for safeguarding the "medium" (or individual). Other guides, who often remain associated with us for life, are subject to his/her directions. Quite apart from this provision, the quality of one's thought (and this applies to everyone) sets the tone of one's "relations" with spirit-people. Whilst this might be described as "superstitious nonsense", it is nevertheless fact, albeit, the result of totally subjective experience. It is a widely understood and valid truth, so far as spiritualists are concerned.

Mr. Justice Cyril Atkinson QC: Gave short evidence in support of the fact that Spiritualism, "seemed to bring some new teaching which was alive and which had given him a new interest in spiritual things. He was perfectly convinced that Spiritualism had helped him in his work". This is remarkable testimony from a lawyer and judge in 1936-9.

E.W.Oaten, Editor of Two Worlds (Spiritualist Newspaper) published in Manchester. Mr. Oaten said that 20% of phenomena demanded the spiritualist hypothesis. He had been a spiritualist for forty years. Had no "doubt concerning the love and purpose of God or the actuality of a spiritual world: he had not felt the need of any other religion".

Mr. Oaten's estimate of only 20% valid phenomena is rather strange, in view of his later assurances of his conviction regarding the value of the spiritualist experience. Perhaps he was adopting a guarded and conservative estimate deliberately, in order to parry any suggestion as to his gullibility.

Dr. William Brown: Dr Brown was probably also a member of

the Committee, a MA and DSc. I presume he was a psychologist. He had been a member of the SPR for 25 years, which says little for his sagacity and perception. His off-hand dismissal of "physical mediumship" stamps him as a person having no serious philosophical interest in the honest investigation of the phenomena of Spiritualism. He has "sat" with many of the "best-known" mediums, with "an open mind", yet has observed nothing to convince him of the validity of at least some of the phenomena, which, he says, "are due either to fraud or to mal-observation". However, he admits that "there is still something to be discovered". He goes on to affirm that "there was a great deal of fraud and self-deception..." but gives no specific information, so far as we are aware. Dr. Brown's most profound statement is to the effect that "Spiritualism had little or no value from the point of view of religion, or as a means of conversion to the Christian Faith." He points out that: "one of the most unsatisfactory elements (of Spiritualism) being that none of the phenomena has been established on a scientific basis". This entirely overlooks the undoubted fact that no religion has ever been proven to be valid according to such a standard.

These questions might well be asked: "Why would a non-Christian wish to be converted to Christianity? What is it that makes the Christian religion so desirable? In what way is it superior to any other religion?"

Dr. Brown's evidence makes clear his lack of any "religious" sensitivity. His objectivity is questionable and his twenty-five years of research has undoubtedly been a thorough-going waste of his time.

Dr. Brown made a final point, in stating that, "there is no justification for saying that Spiritualism is often the cause of Nervous Breakdowns." A positive statement at last.

Dr. Oliver Gatty: Another one of our SPR friends, who after much: "Experimentation with the best mediums available in Europe and in North and South America", has, "no belief in Spiritualism". He appears to be pessimistic regarding the possibility of ever determining such questions as the validity of psychic phenomena via scientific investigation. Dr. Gatty lists various types of "psychic phenomena" and proceeds to state that no evidence was forthcoming under controlled conditions. Thus it becomes apparent that, before the learned Doctor could be convinced of the validity of the phenomena, it had to be conducted in accordance with his ideas on what constitutes proper conditions under which to carry out the procedure. Thus we are not informed exactly what conditions were imposed by the investigator, nor do we know whether or not they were "reasonable" under the circumstances.

Dr. Nandor Fodor: a research officer of the International Institute for Psychical Research, Ltd.

Dr. Fodor states that: "Spiritualism is based on professional mediumship. Professional mediums commercialize a gift of which very little is known but which is definitely not at their beck and call".

This is not generally true: there are many workers (mediums) in the Spiritualist Movement who work within Church groups without consideration of monetary remuneration. Admittedly, there are many professional mediums who charge for services and this is, in the last fifty years, increasingly so. He goes on to suggest that "the so-called physical phenomena of Spiritualism are at least in 99% of cases due to conscious and unconscious fraud."

When he says that "the majority of Spiritualists are unable to judge the value of evidence", he is grievously wrong. By the time most people begin to accept Spiritualism as a valid truth, they have made diligent enquiry: not with sittings with private commercial mediums but during many religious meetings, at which they have been repeatedly given ample proof, not only of the continued survival of their dear-departed but of the provision which a beneficent Creator has made for their happiness and well-being.

It is quite clear that the majority of the members of this Committee and certainly many of the so-called "Witnesses" have little or no experience of attending religious meetings in either Churches conducted by the Spiritualists' National Union or the Christian Spiritualist (Greater World) Churches. Had any of them had the courage to direct their steps to these "centres of learning", they would, undoubtedly, have taken a far different view of the doctrines and phenomena of Spiritualism.

Dr. Fodor reluctantly admits that, "On the other hand, in rare cases, Spiritualism does produce evidence which is intellectually satisfactory, inasmuch as personal survival seems to be the only explanation that completely fits the case." Such an admission from a person whose mind is so clouded and restricted, is sufficient to reinforce the case for the resurrection.

Dr. Fodor concludes by honestly suggesting that: "the Church would make an error in taking an attitude of condemnation. Spiritualism does tend to make its believers Christians. The Church should have deep concern in the means of its appeal."

I don't know about Spiritualism making its followers Christians: many of them are Christians before discovering the truths of Spirit. It does, undoubtedly, reinforce one's religious beliefs and restores, in many cases, a belief in the wond'rous love and provision of the Creator God.

In a footnote, entitled "Other evidence" we read: "Every member of the Committee has also had first-hand experience of at least one séance and several members have had varied experiences of spiritualist sittings extending over a considerable number of years: these experiences have been amplified by a study of the literature of the subject."

The Conclusions of the Majority.
10 Interpretation of the Evidence.

The Majority members discussed the nature of the "alleged messages delivered through the agency of mediums. It is pointed out, on the evidence of the 'communicators' themselves, that the communicators and guides are themselves at very different levels of spiritual development and of very partial knowledge and that the 'controls' of which they make use may often be very undeveloped personalities who are capable of this particular service because they are closely linked with temporarily dissociated portions of the personality of the mediums concerned." *This is psychological jargon of the worst kind, designed to confuse and incapable of rational interpretation.*

What is meant by "temporarily dissociated portions of the personality" is beyond my limited mental powers. It seems to be something the Committee has adopted from the "professional" evidence of Kenneth Richmond. Whether they understood this term is to be doubted. Such a suggestion as this entirely fails to appreciate the undoubted fact that the human personality exists independently of the physical brain. My experience as a spiritualist, over a period of fifty-five years, informs me that the "communicators" and "guides" are, undoubtedly separate cognitive entities, and are, by no stretch of the imagination, temporarily dissociated "portions" of anyone's personality.

The role of "door-keeper" guide ensures that only spirit persons of a suitable temperament and 'intellectual' standard are permitted to enter the spiritual environment of a "medium", or indeed, any person. This safeguard is supplemented by the spiritual level of the medium him/herself, which sets the standard of his links with the Spirit-world. This is the work of real guardian angels, not merely the type envisaged by the Church as being equipped with wings and harps.

The above-stated principle applies to all people, not merely those whose psychic perception is clearer than the average person. This explanation is simplistic, yet valid.
The summary goes on to state:
"The verification of these, if it is possible at all, must rest upon ordinary scientific tests. To say this is not, however, to deny that the communications may sometimes be held to be convincing upon other than scientific grounds."

A statement is made in paragraph (B), to the effect that at least one considerable Spiritualist organisation is definitely anti-Christian in character. Such a statement reveals a glaring ignorance of spiritualist doctrine. The SNU Churches, whilst adopting a non-sectarian attitude, do not actively preach anti-Christian doctrines. One well-known Spiritualist adage may be quoted: "All religions are one!", which is merely a confirmation of the general spiritual principle that all religion is part of a continuous search for truth. It may well be true that individual spiritualists may entertain a measure of hostility towards their Christian brethren, but that is entirely a matter of personal attitude and not the result of deliberate policy on the part of the non-Christian Spiritualist body.

Speaking of the fact that certain individuals have obtained a renewal of faith, following contact with spiritualists, the Committee went on to affirm that: "whatever be the value of this supposed confirmation of the truths of religion, Spiritualism does not seem to have added anything, except perhaps a practical emphasis to our understanding of those truths".

Later in this paragraph, the Committee revealed how hidebound its members were by the doctrines of the fall and vicarious atonement of Christ. *"Whilst there is insistence upon the supremacy of love comparable with the New Testament assertion that 'God is Love', the accounts sometimes given of the mediatorial work of Christ frequently fall very far below the full teaching of the Christian Gospel, seeming to depend rather upon some power of working a miracle of materialisation (in the Resurrection appearances) than upon a radical and final acceptance of the burden of the guilt of man's sin, and a victory so wrought for us upon the Cross."*

Spiritualists would argue that the "victory" was that of the fact of "Life Everlasting": the proof of the resurrection: not merely of Jesus of Nazareth but of all God's children. The "Cross" was merely the vehicle by which Jesus would, "draw all men unto me." (John Chapter 12, v 32).

A positive note is introduced:

"Nevertheless, it is clearly true that the recognition of the nearness of our friends who have died, and of their progress in the spiritual life, and of their continuing concern for us, cannot do otherwise, for those who have experienced it, than add a new immediacy and richness to their belief in the Communion of Saints."

In spite of all the cant and humbug, this paragraph clearly confirms the real value of merely one aspect of spiritualist practice and its relationship to, what should be, the "Communion of Saints".

In Para.(C): the Committee acknowledges, *"the clear parallels between the miraculous events recorded in the Gospel and modern phenomena attested by spiritualists."* It continues to mention the problem of verification of both the New Testament record and modern spiritualist phenomena. Here again, we must point out that spiritualists need no verification. Their own experience of communion with spirit is quite sufficient for them. Let "Scientists" do what they will, there is no possibility of verification to satisfy them and, indeed, the question is quite irrelevant.

If the members of the Committee had been honest with themselves, they would have admitted that they believed the Gospel stories, not by virtue of an act of reasoning but because they had been indoctrinated in childhood. The actual teachings of the Nazarene, supplemented by the wisdom of certain of the authors of the New

Testament, principally Paul and James, can be said to, "ring true to the deepest powers of spiritual apprehension". Much of the New Testament as with the Old Testament History, is irrelevant to the present discussion.

Para (D) goes on to discuss the question of verifiability in a fair and objective manner. "But the tests applied by scientists, as such are in their very nature experimental, objective and impersonal. It is necessary to ask whether such tests do not in themselves invalidate an inquiry into values which are in essence personal and spiritual."

At last we have some insight into the weakness of scientific inquiry into questions of the spirit. As to the supposition that it is Spiritualists themselves who claim scientific verifiability, I have no personal knowledge of such claims. Indeed, since this inquiry was held and the report handed down, Scientific knowledge has expanded in leaps and bounds, particularly in the field of quantum-mechanics and physics, (of which I know nothing).

Mention is made in this paragraph of the non-verifiability of "Telepathy". This phenomenon is so common as to hardly warrant inclusion in a discussion of this type. As to its validity, I have had abundant personal experience and see no need to doubt the fact.

That thought is transmitted between individuals is probably, at this latter time, an accepted fact, even if not "scientifically" proven. For spiritualists it has been a valid proposition almost since its inception.

At the present time there may be spiritualists who claim to have scientific expertise. No doubt they will publish their material, in order that we may learn the mathematical and scientific truths ourselves, to the extent that we, as laymen, are capable of comprehending them.

The Report of the majority members

The majority report confirmed that: "there is no satisfactory scientific evidence in favour of any paranormal physical phenomena...

All the available scientific evidence is against the occurrence of such phenomena.....again, the whole question of extra-sensory perception is still a matter scientifically sub judice. On the other hand, certain outstanding psychic experience of individuals, including *certain experiences with mediums, make a strong prima facie case for survival and for the possibility of spirit-communications, while philosophical, ethical and religious considerations may be held to weigh heavily on the same side."*

"When every possible explanation of these communications has been given and all doubtful evidence set aside, it is very generally agreed that there remains some element as yet unexplained. We think that it is probable that the hypothesis that they proceed in some cases from discarnate spirits is the true one."

Having made these constructive remarks the majority members went on to warn:

Para (A): that "an easy credulity in these matters opens the doors to self-deception and to a very great amount of fraud. We were greatly impressed by the evidence of this which we received and desire to place on record a most emphatic warning to those who might become interested in Spiritualism from motives of mere curiosity, or as a way of escaping from the responsibility of making their own decisions as Christians under the guidance of the Holy Spirit".

What is meant by, "the guidance of the Holy Spirit?"

Presumably consultation with one's local parson. Perhaps, it may extend to a prayerful application for guidance and assistance. Spiritualists (whether of the Christian or Non-Christian variety) have no difficulty in understanding this term. It is in the offering of the mind, in acknowledgement of the Divine Love and Compassion which is available to all people, of any and every race, colour and creed. In the course of this offering, we receive a consciousness of the presence of the Holy Spirit in the form of our Guides, helpers and loved-ones who have gone before. We may, and often do, enjoy a perception of the spiritual world and its inhabitants.

Of course, "an easy credulity" is not the approach to bring into Spiritualism, yet the warning regarding such a great amount of fraud is hardly necessary. Who is being defrauded? When one goes to a spiritualist meeting to hear an inspired speaker extolling the beauties of the spiritual world and the loveliness and love which the spirit-guides bring to our aid, is he being "defrauded" when he places a small coin in the collection basket? Is not the regular Churchgoer also being defrauded when he does likewise, particularly if the Sermon is rather less than inspiring?

Para (B) "It is necessary to keep clearly in mind that none of the fundamental Christian obligations or values is in any way changed by our acceptance of the possibility of communication with discarnate spirits."

Who is to determine whether or not "Christian values" are in any way different from or inferior to Spiritualist's values? What, indeed, are "fundamental Christian values?"

Paragraphs (C) and (D) continue this tone of cautious optimism and call for no comment.

Para. (E) States: "We cannot avoid the impression that a great deal of Spiritualism, as organised, has its centre in man rather than in God. And is, indeed, materialistic in character. To this extent it is a substitute for religion and is not, in itself, religious at all. We were impressed by the unsatisfactory answers received from practising Spiritualists to such questions as 'Has your prayer life, your sense of God, been strengthened by your spiritualist experiences?'"

I cannot speak for other Spiritualists but I can certainly vouch that my sense of God has been positively strengthened, over a period of 55 years, by my spiritual experiences. In my humble and unlearned opinion, the only way to approach the Spiritual Communion (The Communion of Saints) is via the medium of prayer, as this is the natural vehicle for the elevation of the mind and the forging of links with the Spirit-world of a constructive nature. This is the fulfilment of the ministry of angels.

To suggest that many persons approach Spiritualism with lower motives may well be correct. The same claim can assuredly be made in respect of all religions. Many clergymen enter the Church from career motives rather than as a result of a spiritual calling. It was common for the younger sons of the privileged to enter, either the Army, the Law or the Church. It was a case of finding occupation for idle hands.

The admission in Para (E) that so far as the Church of England is concerned, the "Communion of Saints" is often a dead letter, falls far short of the mark. It is a complete and utter "dead-letter", or was at the time of the Report (1939). It is refreshing to think that there is now an organisation within the Protestant Christian Churches, which considers that spiritual intercourse might possibly be beneficial, if approached responsibly and with a sincere desire to learn and to serve.

Para (F) refers to the possibility of mentally disturbed persons being adversely affected by intercourse with spirits. This is always possible and religious mania is not exclusively the preserve of spiritualists. The spirit-world is no different from this world so far as individual taste and temperament is concerned and the spirit-communion is merely a question of the setting of standards. If "low life" here wants to contact its equivalent in the spirit-world, then I have no doubt that this is possible. Then mad people could well become madder. However, I have never experienced problems of this nature.

My own experience confirms the fact that divine guidance, once applied for, is never denied, and if the personal standard of the suppliant is sufficiently high, then there is no cause for alarm.

What is certain is that turning to God for guidance and help is never a waste of time, nor calculated to cause harm to a single individual. This is, essentially, what the true spiritual communion involves: prayer and nothing more. No need for table-rapping, or physical phenomena, (which from a spiritual point of view are lower gifts and of little value). The higher the aim, the richer and more wonderful will be the spiritual experience. We don't invoke the spirits of the dead: they are all around us, at every moment of our physical existence. The lifting of the mind away from mundane preoccupations is all that is needed, in acknowledgement and praise to the Creator. This is true prayer and true spiritual communion.

Para (G) refers to the danger of contact with "Evil Spirits". My remarks above to some extent cover this situation. Emmanuel Swedenborg, the Swedish 18th-Century scientist and seer, wrote extensively on the nature of man: that he is continuously exposed to influences from both good and evil spirits. A moment's reflection will satisfy anyone that a person is continuously bombarded throughout a single day with varying thoughts of a constructive or destructive nature. It is well known, that, should one give way to momentary anger or weakness, that the problems thus created might well increase to the point at which they may well cause lasting harm to *ourselves or to other persons. It does not need much imagination to realise the dangers that we face continuously.*

Spiritualists are well aware of these dangers and have witnessed the harm which unbridled selfishness may bring about.

We should be more concerned in this life about contact with "evil spirits" in the flesh than in the spirit-world. Companionship is important to us and we should try to seek the company of honest, warm-hearted and kindly people, in order that we may all learn from each other. Should our interests turn inwards, seeking selfish pursuits and gratification, there are lots of regressive spirits who will be only too happy to link with us and help us to move farther down the ladder of progression. Hence, it becomes a question of "companionship" both here and in the spirit-world. There is really no difference between the two states.

Para (H) mentions prayers for the "Dead". There can be no objection to such prayer, as many souls pass over who are much in need of guidance and help. The prayers of those who remain in the body are valuable, particularly for those who remain in darkened or ignorant conditions. Suicides, for instances, who die in very depressed states of mind, can benefit greatly from our loving thoughts, which is another term for "prayer".

Para (I) states:

"If Spiritualism, with all aberrations set aside and with every care taken to present it humbly and accurately, contains a truth, it is important to see that truth not as a new religion but only as filling up certain gaps in our knowledge, so that where we already walked by faith, we may now have some measure of sight as well."

Para (J) "It is in our opinion important that representatives of the Church should keep in touch with groups of intelligent persons who believe in Spiritualism. We must leave practical guidance in this matter to the Church itself."

It will thus be evident that the majority (7) members of the Committee, in spite of some alarms, came down favourably on the side of continued investigation into Spiritualism. They saw Spiritualism not as a new religion, (which it was not) but as throwing new light upon the teachings of the Church. Had their recommendations been followed, it seems likely that the Church would have received a great boost. Certainly, its clergy would have had a wonderful opportunity for direct participation in the "Communion of Saints".

The Report of the Minority Members.

The Minority members concurred with the procedural parts of the investigation but disagreed with the Majority Report.

Under the Heading: l. *Validity of paranormal phenomena*, the minority members rejected the: "Spiritualists' claim that through paranormal psychical and physical phenomena they communicate with discarnate spirits and receive guidance." "Scientists", they say, "consider that the evidence does not show that paranormal phenomena exist. Normal psychology and self-deception contain the whole thing, except in cases where fraud occurs. (Witness G): Dr. Gatty

Para 2. *Value of communications.*

"The alleged communications may not only be valueless but may also be misleading and therefore dangerous."

Sub-para. (A) Mentions experience at a "Séance" arranged by Witness H (Baron Palmstierna), at which a device involving a glass was used. This would indicate that the people involved were inexperienced, i.e., undeveloped medium or mediums, as regular sitters do not use such devices. As a rule, only beginners resort to such physical vehicles of communication. In fact, all forms of psychometry should be eschewed by responsible spiritualists, as of doubtful value.

It is, therefore, not surprising to learn that the investigators were "disappointed with the content of the communications".

Sub-para. (B) refers to the "danger of receiving alleged spirit communications." This statement is nonsense, as is the rest of the passage. Later in the paragraph, the observation is made: "When spirit guidance comes into conflict with the authority of the Church, the Spiritualist is likely to prefer the former and ignore the latter." Here we have a key ingredient in the concern of the minority members: "the authority of the Church!" One might, in this latter day and age, ask "What Authority?" In l939, any influence the Church may have had upon the thinking processes of ordinary laymen and women was already fast fading. In the year 2000 it is well and truly an historic point.

Para (C): *This chapter talks, fatuously, about: "modern developments of Christian thought", and later adds, "Spiritualists appear fearful lest too keen a use of the mind or of the critical faculties will invalidate their hypothesis".*

Modern developments of Anglican Christian thought include, no doubt, propositions to the effect that "God does not exist!, or "it may be that there is no God!". As for spiritualists not using their minds, it might be suggested that when we begin to understand some of the truths of spiritualism, we really start to use our thinking processes for the first time.

Para (D) raises the question of "scientific proof" as necessary before it will be of any help to the Christian religion. Such a proposition will only be valid when the scientific proofs of Christianity are forthcoming. We will not hold our breaths.

William Temple, (Arbishop of York) was quoted: "experimental proof of man's survival of death would bring the hope of immortality into the area of purely intellectual apprehension. It might, or it might not, encourage the belief that God exists; it would certainly, as I think, make very much harder the essential business of faith, which is the transference of the centre of interest and concern from self to God."

It is certainly true that, once convinced of the survival of the individual after death, one has a confirmation of the existence of God.

If this world is merely an extension of a greater, spiritual world, then it becomes clear that there must be a supreme and divine intelligence as the basis for all existence.

In spite of the insistence upon "Faith", this in itself is vanity: the knowledge of the resurrection places faith in perspective, in relation to knowledge: the knowledge of the value of each individual human spirit.

Para (E) Mentions revelation as experienced by the saints of the Church. Suggests that one should seek to know God alone and let the phenomena look after itself. I would not disagree with such an approach.

Para 3. Spiritualism contrasted with Christianity.

This chapter opens with a statement to the effect that Spiritualism can add nothing to Christianity. Reference is made to

Von Hugel's estimate that: "there is very little that is spiritual in Spiritualism". This is a valid criticism, particularly in these latter days, yet the same can equally be said of Christianity or, indeed, any of the other great world-faiths.

The authors of this document reveal their complete ignorance of spiritual truths by the statement: "The Christian, and the Anglican in particular, believes that he has, through prayer and sacrament, communication with the Godhead. With the Spiritualist, however, communication is not direct and is established only by means of intermediaries. It is not surprising that for the Spiritualist God becomes remote and inaccessible and the mediation of Christ a thing forgotten.... The words 'through Jesus Christ our Lord' cannot have the same meaning for the Spiritualist that they have for the Christian".

The Spiritualist, in fact, believes that all men and women have a direct relationship with their Creator. He needs no intercession, either of Jesus of Nazareth, the Saints or of a Priest. He rejects entirely the doctrines of the Fall and Vicarious atonement of Christ as spurious and superfluous. The familiar cant, "Through Jesus Christ our Lord!", of course, means nothing to the Spiritualist, except perhaps the devoted Christian-Spiritualist, who accepts much of the traditional teachings of the Church.

The Spiritualist values the teachings of Jesus for their essentially a-priori truth, with particular regard to the Sermon on the Mount. He witnesses the testimony of "Life Everlasting", given in John (Chapter 12 Verse 49-50) and the promise of the spirit given by Jesus to his disciples, before his crucifixion. The proof of the resurrection was given at meetings with his disciples, when they were evidently satisfied that he had returned, momentarily, to give them evidence of his survival in spirit. At Pentecost the spirit was given to the disciples and the work of building-up Christianity began.

The minority report (page 58) continues with additional misguided comment regarding Spiritualist beliefs: "The Spiritualist lays great emphasis upon progress in the next world. So does the Church but without the element of banality (?) which marks the spiritualist picture of the hereafter." It suggests that, "for the Spiritualist, God is so remote, Spirits yearn," we are told "not to see God but to communicate with their relations and friends on earth.

Acceptance of the spiritualist view of the future life would lead to diminished belief in the sovereignty of God and the redemptive power of Christ".

Here we have the traditional anthropomorphic concept of Deity, with Jesus sitting at His right hand. The members of the minority committee were, evidently unaware of the teachings of Swedenborg, (the Father of Modern Spiritualism) who taught, from his observations of the spirit world over a period of 30 years, that spirits in "heaven" continually face the Father, who is seen as divine light. This conforms to the teachings of Jesus upon the same subject. A great many, if not all spiritualists are aware of the validity of this statement. They do not believe for one minute that spirit people are pre-occupied with the necessity of remaining in contact with those of us who are presently in the body. They do, undoubtedly, visit us from time to time, particularly where there is a bond of love.

Whilst ideas within Spiritualism vary regarding the nature of the Divine, (something which we can not begin to comprehend in any event), most practising spiritualists accept very clearly the reality of God at work in the whole Creation. Many have certainly experienced the nature of Divine Love, either during spiritualist meetings or in private prayer. To suggest that we could entertain a "diminished belief" in the "sovereignty of God" is fatuous. To talk about the "sovereignty" of God and the redemptive power of Christ, is meaningless.

History of Spiritualism: Para.4 of the minority report

Brief mention is made of the Fox sisters, who were instrumental in drawing attention to psychic phenomena in 1848, in the USA. Reference is made to their "intemperate habits", 40 years later, as if this in itself is sufficient to invalidate the phenomena. Whatever, the course of their private lives, the Fox sisters were well regarded by early spiritualists and Mrs. Emma Hardinge-Britten, a well known pioneer of spiritualism, during the mid-19th Century, speaks well of them in her autobiography. It is well known historical fact that many influential and cultured US citizens were involved in spiritualism, in addition to D.D. Home, mentioned in the report as a physical medium who did not resort to "unscrupulous trickery". H.W. Longfellow, Poet and for twenty years Professor of Modern

Languages at Harvard, was also frequently present at meetings and was a devoted spiritualist. He wrote some of the best-loved poetry of the 19th Century, much of it dealing with spiritual topics. Robert Dale Owen, son of Robert Owen, the great British social reformer, and William Lloyd Garrison were also members of this group.

There may well be a great deal of "corruption" in the United States, regarding occult practice. This does nothing to condemn spiritualism or to invalidate its doctrines. There is a great deal of corruption in the world generally, and this is particularly true of some of the great religions of the world. The Greek and Russian Orthodox Churches are notorious for the worldliness of their Priests. The Catholic and Anglican Churches are not so far behind, in worldliness. The priests are all well-fed, well-dressed individuals, who think very highly of themselves.

Components of Spiritualism: Para 5 refers to: "the pernicious doctrines of the Christian-Spiritualists."

Some Spiritualists are said to be "anti-Christian, some are religious but non-Christian, and others are queer mixtures of corruption and superstition".

One passage I must quote in full: "At one end of the scale are Anglican clergy who supplement their religious exercises with the practice of Spiritualism; at the other end of the scale are the charlatans, who for a fee will go into a trance or cast a horoscope or give predictions based upon numerology. In the present condition of the Spiritualist movement to bless one is to bless all".

The Christian-Spiritualists would dearly like to know what is meant by "pernicious doctrines".

I recall attending the Carlisle Christian Spiritualist Church in 1951 to 1953. They held an open circle on Saturday nights in an ancient building on West Walls and my wife and I were captivated by the sanctity of the atmosphere in this place. We heard more than one inspirational address in this church: the speaker being usually an elderly lady of simple nature and sweet temperament. One such address, at a Sunday night service, left us enthralled at the loveliness and power of the presentation. The text was that mentioned herein, "And I, if I be lifted up from the Earth, will draw all men unto me!" (John Chapter 12, verse 32). Such was the beauty of this address that we were left in no doubt as to the validity of this communication from the spirit world. I heard many a sermon as a child Chorister in Manchester, including one by William Temple, Archbishop of York and former Bishop of Manchester. Dr. Temple, for all his learning, never spoke with such power the truths of spirit. If just one of those who testified at the hearings of this committee had been present on that, or a similar occasion, their evidence would probably have differed greatly from the trite and bigoted statements they actually made.

If such was the "present condition" of Spiritualism in 1939 as indicated above, what would the members think of the Movement today, when, I regret to admit, confusion reigns within the ranks of the Spiritualist Movement to a much greater degree. The New Age Movement has just about swamped traditional spiritualism and the situation regarding practices, which might be loosely termed "occult" rather than spiritual, is alarming to the traditional spiritualist or Christian-spiritualist.

The Churches need have no fear: spiritualism has gone downhill rapidly during the last sixty years and is now unrecognisable as the Movement I knew during the 40's and 50's. However, I take comfort from the fact that, side by side with the diminishing spirituality of spiritualists, there are always a number of dedicated and gifted people who maintain a high personal standard. There is also a very healthy movement for the investigation and development of physical mediumship. I refer to the Noah's Ark Society, of which I have no personal knowledge, apart from that available on the Internet.

Of course, in the intervening years, the growth of the Fundamentalist Charismatic-Christian Movement has stolen some of the Spiritualist "Thunder". These devoted folk must have created quite a stir in the hearts of our Anglican and Catholic friends.

This falling-away from the "Faith" is, perhaps, merely a sympton of the general spiritual malaise, which infects the whole Western world at the present time. There is a nucleus of sincere and devoted individuals who wish to preserve the standards of spirituality, which are so vital to the lifeblood of any religious organization.

That the minority Committee members misunderstood the nature of spiritualism, becomes evident upon reading the following *observation (page 60):*

"There is no such thing as the religion of Spiritualism. There are instead a vast number of small groups, each under the guidance of a mediums' spirit control...."

This statement is nonsense. Spiritualism recognises a general Rule that every individual is a "medium": that we all have the capacity for spirit-communion: that we all partake of spiritual gifts in varying degree, as outlined by Paul the Apostle in 1 Corinthians, Chapter 12.

When spiritualists gather in a meeting, the chairperson may or may not be a practising medium. The service or circle may not involve any form of trance or semi-trance address of any kind. Nobody's "spirit Control", whatever that may be, purports to "guide" those present. The words noted above seem to suggest something sinister or improper in the proceedings: something "nasty in the cowshed!".

Tendencies in Spiritualism: Para 6: The members are concerned at: "two marked tendencies" in Spiritualism:

1. *"It encourages a morbid curiosity on the part of many unscientific investigators. We regard this not only as mentally unhealthy but morally dangerous."*

2. *"It encourages an interest in the supernatural from the unworthiest motives: There are those who try to communicate with spirits in order to discover the future", for their own material profit.*

Both these tendencies lead to gross superstition but the element of superstition is also introduced without them. There is a point where the spiritualist movement mingles with the underworld of necromancy. Horoscopes, crystal gazing and the like are not dissociated from certain sections of the movement".

The members felt that Spiritualism should set its house in order and purge itself from these dark works.

As to 1. : Most people are unscientific, even the majority of clergymen. As to a morbid curiosity: we are not in the habit of hanging around cemeteries, as we know that our loved-ones are certainly not sleeping in their graves. There is nothing morbid in the joyous realisation that those who have passed through the veil continue to live and perform a useful and constructive function in the world of Spirit.

As for those who seek pecuniary advantage from occult studies: they will obtain from such a pursuit rewards commensurate with the measure of their devotion. Spiritualism and its attendant and, at least to some spiritualists, unwelcome handmaids, in the shape of Astrology, Numerology, Reflexology, Tarotology, Phrenology, Crystal globes, and all the paraphernalia of fortune-telling, will attract people in proportion to their intellectual ability. We have no control over what people do in their own personal lives: if anyone has a specific conviction or belief and wishes to indulge that particular preference, there is nothing any other individual can do about it, apart from pointing out the undesirability of such a procedure.

In the last thirty years or so, a great number of cults have arisen, under the "New Age" Banner and all striving to prove that they have at last discovered the secret of life. This is particularly evident in the United States, whose people seem to have a particular penchant for weird and outlandish religious systems. Such phenomena would seem to confirm the fears expressed above, regarding gross superstition and dark works.

Spiritualism itself reflects many of these ideas, or at least, tolerates their intrusion into the formerly simple philosophy of spirit. In spite of these shortcomings, I and, I have no doubt, a number of traditional spiritualists World-Wide, see no reason to abrogate the teachings which they perceive as the closest thing to "Truth", which it is possible for mankind to comprehend.

Possible explanations of phenomena: Para 7.

"We are not satisfied that the communications received proceed from discarnate spirits. In accounting for spiritualist phenomena, considerable allowances must be made for coincidence, mal-observation, honest self-deception, auto-suggestion and credulity and in particular for fraud and collusion among mediums."

The report goes on to outline the various explanations of psychic phenomena as given by a number of psychologists of the time. All these statements are trite and, in some cases, absurd.

Para 8: Reasons for drift towards Spiritualism.

Several reasons are tendered, explaining why people are leaving the Church. "The Church has not sufficiently emphasised:

(a) Prayers for the Dead.

(b) The Communion of Saints.
(c) The grounds for Christian Belief in Eternal Life.
(d) The Value of the Eucharist.
(e) A mystical side of Christianity.
(f) The truth that knowledge and faith in God can be the only true consolation for mourners.

I do not propose to comment on (a) to (c).

As to the value of the (d) Eucharist (Holy Communion), I can only say that I see no value whatever in the procedure, which is tantamount to Mumbo-Jumbo.

As to (e): if there is a mystical side to Anglicanism, I have yet to discover it.

As to (f): this is pure cant and no consolation. What is the "knowledge" referred to? Faith not comprehended is pure fantasy.

Para 9: Recommendations:

" (1) The Church should not seek to establish any relations with Spiritualism; the Church should regard it only as a field for scientific inquiry, the conduct of which is not normally a task for the clergy.

(2) The practice of praying for the dead needs to be more widely commended.

(3) An Office for the Dead is needed.

(4 Anglican prayers for the dead do not satisfy people's needs, because the prayers are so cautious in their language that it is not always evident that the dead are being prayed for, as contrasted with the living.

(5) Some well-informed literature about the possible dangers of Spiritualism is badly needed.

(6) Better teaching is needed about the Communion of Saints.

(7) Better teaching is needed about Eternal life and the grounds in experience for the Christian hope."

I have already remarked about scientific enquiry and will say no more regarding that bogey.

As for the other points above, I would like to see what the Church now has to say about the Communion of Saints and Eternal Life.

Testimony

Christine J. Haven

One glaring omission is apparent in perusing the conduct of those having responsibility for this Report. That is, the fact that no spiritualist "Mediums" were called to give evidence of their own experiences. One could perhaps be excused for thinking that this would have been an excellent way to obtain first-hand, not second-hand information on the teachings and practices of spiritualists. Instead, we have the short and very general testimony of only two or three persons who were associated in some way with the Spiritualist Movement.

Then there is the assumption that all "mediums" are Spiritualists. This may or may not have been generally true in 1936-39, but we do not know that and there were certainly a great many "practitioners" who were conducting "one-man rooms" who were in no way associated with the Spiritualist Movements, either those of the Spiritualists' National Union or the Greater World, Christian-Spiritualist Churches.

There was evidently little direct contact, if any, between the Committee Members and the various and numerous Spiritualist Churches, in which the doctrines of Spiritualists, of such importance in a study of this nature, could be discovered. Instead, there was much cloak and dagger activity: meeting with "mediums" in closed rooms: planchett boards and table-tapping was investigated.

With the exception of Bishop Underhill, the members of the Committee seemed to be rather uninterested in discovering anything positive in relation to Spiritualism and only as an afterthought was a grudging acknowledgement made to the effect that: "there might be something to be discovered in this, if we look long and diligently enough".

Even one or two of the Psychic Investigators, who had probably never set foot in a Spiritualist Church proper, had to admit that there was a residue of phenomena that could only be explained by reference to a communication from discarnate spirits. Had sincere and practising spiritualists been interviewed, they would have given clear and concise evidence as to why they themselves were so devoted to the cause of Spiritualism.

Let me add my small, insignificant voice, to say that I have from time to time had very clear evidence of the presence of spirit, of the beauty of the spiritual-world and of those wonderful souls who, having escaped from the chains of the flesh, have thankfully and joyously taken their place in the realms of spirit. I have often felt the "physical" presence of my guides and helpers from spirit: who are practical guardian angels: wise counsellors who help to steer me as I go through life's experience.

Any spiritualist who is a practising "medium" will give similar testimony: of direct awareness of the love and compassion of the Creator God: of the fact that we all have the gift of communion and that this communion goes not via any priest or intercessor but from the heart and mind to the Divine Source itself.

Talking about "mediumship" it is a well-known fact in Spiritualist circles that everyone is a "medium" and is sustained from moment to moment by the Divine Life itself. Swedenborg talked about "influx": the continuous flow of life force from the world of spirit to us. It is this influx which, at any given moment, keeps us in the world of the flesh and which sustains all creation.

So it is evident that everyone, regardless of creed or belief, is capable of experiencing the gifts of the spirit. An awareness of this truth is what assists in the development of spiritual gifts. Spiritualists, therefore, sit regularly in groups, some in forms of meditation and others in prayer meetings, in which they hope to experience the gifts of the spirit.

I have written elsewhere regarding the weaknesses apparent in Spiritualism today (Observations on Spiritualism) and do not propose to canvass them further. I merely repeat what Paul the Apostle affirmed, that one should seek the higher gifts. He certainly knew what he was talking about, within the limits of his own understanding.

If Spiritualists, as a body, could be brought to concentrate their energies on maintaining high spiritual principles: rejecting outright all mercenary temptations, there is no doubt that that their experience of the spirit would be without parallel in human history.

Jesus, indeed, sent his followers out into the world, commanding them to: "As ye have freely received, freely give". (Matthew 10 V 8) This is the principle rule in relation to the practice of spiritual gifts. Very few spiritualists today make it an absolute rule. If they did, the world would be a very different place.

The Anglican Church, therefore, and indeed, all the major religions of the world have nothing to fear from Spiritualists. Those who are sincere are going about their work in a quiet and dedicated manner. Those who are in the limelight are the entrepreneurs and entertainers, who are providing a service for gain. Their achievement will be directly proportional to their devotion to the cause.

One final point: Spiritualism is not a religion: it is the very essence of all religion, for it embodies the recognition that all Creation is part of one universal whole, with man at the apex of the physical environment. Spiritualism recognises the fact that we are all children of the Creator God, to whom we all, individually, have a right of access via the vehicle of prayer. This right is unconditional and part and parcel of our spiritual inheritance.

FINIS FOOTNOTE:

Over sixty years have now passed since the Report was submitted to Dr. Lang. It must be presumed that all the participants have now moved-on to the higher understanding. Were they to be questioned now, regarding the contents of their Report, what would be their response? In this regard, one can only speculate. Undoubtedly, they have the advantage over us: who are still clothed in the flesh. As Paul the Apostle says, "Now we see through a glass, darkly; but then face to face: now I know in part; but then shall I know even as also I am known."(l Corinthians, Ch 13 v 12).

Do You Follow The Father?

(All that has been written in sequence and understood as one complete message from God's Angels. And as you surely should understand that all religions, including metaphysics and spiritualism, contain thoughts that were designed to dominate were written into them by men.)

I ask you, "Why do you fight one another? All men are brothers under the Father, and all religions are His, and yet, you continue to persecute and kill your brothers, sisters and your children.

And the Angel Joleen said, "Have not you learned? The Father, through His Angels has told many, but they have turned His words into domination over others. Cannot you see that each Prophet spoke of love for all? Cannot you see also that all Prophets spoke of things that lusted in their heart, but all were constant in their words of love?

"None of you follow the Father. You merely follow your Prophet. Thus, your Prophet is your God.

"Does it make you proud to believe your Prophet told you more about the Father than your brother's?

"Does the words from the Father that you heard place you closer to the Father than your brother?

"Does a Father love one of his children more than another?

I say to you, "The Father did not anoint you to be His Judge or Executor. For those who deem His words unjustly, shall be judged by the Father in the same manner.

"The world was created in and for multiparous concepts, thoughts and ideas. And yet, life cannot exist under rule of any one, but humans continue to place a few over the majority and persecute those who do not follow.

"Change your views of your past actions, Repent, Repent. Cry and show your sorrow of what you have done, Repent, Repent.

"Lift your Soul and rejoice in the knowledge of the Father.

"Life is your' to enjoy, not to destroy.

"Experience the love that you will receive when you accept that you and your brother are one under the same Father.

"Allow all to live as they wish, but without domination over others.

"Do not place yourself above another, and to not place any person or yourself above the Father.

"I will not change the ideas of the world. People will continue to persecute and kill each other, and the Wrath of the Father shall come and spread around the world. People will beg for forgiveness, but it shall not be granted. Few will pray to the Father, and they shall be delivered unto Him.

"The future of total destruction cannot be stopped, only the Salvation of yourself can be changed.

"The Angel Jacob has been released upon the world by the Father, and he, the Angel Jacob, shall bring destruction to terrorists activities which came from the Father's words that were polluted by men, and then corrupted by man.

"God did not wish for you to follow His plan as slaves, but to pursue your dreams of better or worse. The Father gave all the knowledge of knowing the difference between right and wrong, but you continue to live for self-gratification. For you cannot find it in your hearts to live in peace, but only in domination.

"The Angel of Jacob leads the battle against evil, his legions are the Angels that includes Jesus and all humans with open hearts, for the Angel of Jacob is Energy of righteous thought that will prevail upon the earth.

"Ishmael was cast out of Abraham's house, and that is the location of Armageddon. Now has come the time for the spirit of Jacob to fight his cousins' concepts at that place.

"The spirit of Jacob, shall defeat the evil, but evil will not be destroyed. For out of the spirit of Jacob, men of evil shall re-unite to dominate as the birth of the true Antichrist will come.

"The true Antichrist is not just against Jesus, or Jew, or Christianity, or the Muslim, but against the Father and the Holy Spirit, for it has many faces and speaks of peace in all languages. Many will follow it's words, but only the righteous will know the Antichrist, and they shall deny the Antichrist and they will be persecuted.

"But you should not be concerned about or dwell on the future of humankind, but only need to be concerned about your attitude toward life, and that shall be your Heaven afterlife, for life is to be enjoyed while you experience life.

"Read your bibles to seek the Love of the Father. Read what the Prophets have written to understand the simplicity of life and the common knowledge of the Father. Do not read into those things from the dog. Follow the Angel that is within you, and not the human desires."

When one searches for the truth, one usually searches out the writings of others. Why? To convince himself that what he thinks as true is true, for "if another person has written what I think is true, it must be true." Thus, we are seeking the God that we created.

All people take some text and add it to other writings, thus creating their own religion. Even the ones who studies and/or follow the beliefs of metaphysics or spiritualism do this. And yet, all that is needed to be known by you is inside of you - your heart.

Do not allow others to dominate you in your thoughts, follow your heart; that is the part of God that dwells within you.

And I say to you, "To seek God is not to harm yourself, but to love yourself.

"You alone have control over yourself. You cannot control the people of the world nor can they control you, but yet, you are part of the total of the body of the people of the world. The body should not wish to harm itself. Those who use words like "fifth dimension' or "a higher plane" only wish to confuse you in your thoughts as if they know more than you. Refuse their concepts and accept what is in your heart. God has placed Himself within you in concepts that are symbolical for you to understand. Others may not understand this meaning of God that you know, just as you may not truly understand their concept of God. But, allow them to follow their God just as they allow you to follow your God. Each of us are at the place we are suppose to be at this time. We cannot pull another along if they are not willing or prepared to travel with us.

"Lift your Soul, feel free, live free, touch free, love free and be free."

Understanding God

Before continuing with this Message, we must understand the true meanings of the three words; "Righteous" - doing the thing that is considered "right" for that location in that time. "Repent" - changing one's thoughts and views of the past. And "Domination" - forcing concepts, thoughts and ideas - beliefs upon another.

We can only guide people to God through Inspiration. God cannot be forced upon others. If one is too young to understand what you are attempting to teach him, it is useless to expect him to accept God. Therefore, it is unwise to Baptise small children because they cannot understand. Whereas, one should not be Baptised until they can be Inspired to accept God, and at that time they shall ask to be Baptised.

Parents force their religions onto their children because they have been taught that their religion is righteous and the only way to God is through their church.We must be able to show people what is right and wrong. No matter what you tell others, you must be able to live a lifestyle that includes your teachings. You must teach with Love and not Rigtheous, and therefore, we Inspire others to Repent.

The old Rome (the country) believed that it was righteous to kill Christians, but once its leaders became aware of Christianity, they brought the Christian Religion and their government together and forced their new beliefs upon others, thus, they created the Catholic

Religion, which today still is its own country. The Vatican, 108 arce sovereign state that is surrounded by Rome, has its own laws and rules that it follows just as any country does.

Throughout the centuries, the Catholic Religion has done things to people that its leader, the Pope, believed to be righteous - the Catholic Church has tried to dominate people by their Crusades, Inquisitions, helping the Nazis during World War Two by hiding treasures stolen from Jews and others, the creation of purgatory to keep the poor in their religion, (before the conception of purgatory, only the rich with money could buy their deceased family members into Heaven, after the conception of purgatory, the poor could pray their family members into Heaven,) and while their newly uncovered sexual abuse of children scandal is not something that just appeared, it has been going on since the beginning of their religion, they have attempted to forced their domination upon others in the name of God.

The Islamic religion was conceived by a false prophet, Muhammad, who created Islam for his pleasures of the flesh. All that Muhammad wrote was stolen from both the Jewish and Christian religions. Yes, Gabrael did try to communicate with him, but Muhammad refused the words of God that Gabrael delivered to him. Therefore, the Islamic religion is the concepts, thoughts and ideas of a human, who also wrote; "If a Muslim is humillated, all must join together and destroy he who humillated him." Islam demonstrates total Domination by man over man.

The Jewish religion is also totally dominated by human thoughts, ideas and concepts, for it says; "Our Messiah will defeat the world and bring it under the control of our religion and Israel shall be at the center of the world."

Christianity claims one cannot be saved unless he follows Jesus as God, and also one must believe that we (the human race) killed Him in order for us to be saved.

Metaphysics and Spiritualism - Sometimes I feel that those who study and follow Metaphysics are just a bunch of foolish people trying to convince themselves that they know more (closer to God) than religious leaders because these people select writings that fit the God that they have designed, and claim only those writings are the true words of God. But also, I feel these people do not conform to the teachings of a few because they understand that all writings about God can and will contain thoughts, concepts and ideas of its author.

Spiritualists started out on the road to truly understanding the words of God, but they became lost when they started seeking writings of other Spiritualist. Once they found the writings that they were seeking, they too designed and created the God that they needed, but who is not the one God above all.

Quantum Physics is the closest thing to a belief system conceived by man's thoughts that can explain God and His desires, for it does not dominate, but states facts that can be verified under scientific protocol.

But it does not matter if you believe in God, nature or nothing at all, nor does it matter which, if any religion, you follow, what matters is how you treat each other and yourself.

"The child who does not know of God, but loves all people, is the most rewarded in Heaven." The knowledge of God should not dominate your life, for God does not dominate. Play and enjoy life as a child does - experience life and enjoy it because that is what life is all about.

"Repent, do not dwell on the afterlife, enjoy and cherish life. Do what is righteous - live in harmony with all life, go with the flow of life, and allow God to communicate with you."

God's communication with you may merely be your awareness of the wonderful things that surround us or it may be the spoken words that you needed to hear. These words may come from others or God's Angels, but no matter which, it is His conversation with you.

Belief in a Supreme Being, and faith in Him is needed because if you knew of Him, you would truly know the consequences that your actions may bring, and therefore, God would dominate you instead of allowing you your individual choices.

Expanding Our Directions

    Years ago, when I was writing country music and working in Nashville, TN, I wrote a song that contained a line that said, "Plastic people with broken hearts surround me in a maze of beer." Now as I look around I see, "Plastic people with no love in their hearts, surround me in a maze of their earthly goods."

    A few weeks ago, I decided that I wanted to start weekly meetings, such as in a church, where I could give Messages much like the ones that we post here on this web site. I then realized, those of you who read these Messages are scattered around the world, and therefore, it would be impossible for most to come on a weekly basis.

    The Angel Jo had told me, "What we say to you was for you. You can start a church if you wish, but not many will come."

    Then, I wondered why people in my area, would not come to our church, but would go to others without contemplation. It is because other religions - Jewish, Islam and all Christian religions such as Baptist, Catholic, Church of God, etc., etc. are establishments set forth by years of preaching to their congregations' forefathers, and because those who follow our writings live around the world.

    Then a reader of our Messages emailed me last week and suggested that we start a Yahoo! Club, and talk about all the things that God's Angels have told me. I thought, that is a fine idea, then, I recalled how some people would disrupt meetings on-line. Is that what I wanted? A chat club where God or the things that His Angels have said to me can be replied to as humorous or not from God.

Then I recalled, the Angel Jo had said to me, "Help others by using your electronics, use your computer to reach others. I do not wish to discourage you, nor do We want others to discourage you either, by saying not many will come to your church. Help those who seek the Inspirations that we have given you."

The Angel Jo said to me, "Where are the Joshuas, Moses and Ezras of today? They are among you but people refuse them, just as they refuse to believe that God is with them today as We were in the days of the Bible. People read their Bible, and claim they believe in it, but they refuse to seek God and do not believe in Him when they see Us. Their god is locked in a book! Catholic say they worship only God, and yet, they pray to the ones they call Saints! Does one not pray to their god? Nothing has changed for Us, only for people. We stand beside you just as We did during the days the Bible was being written."

These are some of the aches and pains that are in my heart. These are the things that Jesus told me to tell others about when He said to me, "Speak to the people of the aches and pains in your heart."

As we enter this holiday season, as with the last few years holiday seasons that have come before, many people - mostly children have passed over and came through my home on their way to God as the Angels lead them home, I give Thanks to God for all that He has allowed His Angels to teach me, as we all should give Thanks to God for all that He has given us as individuals and as the human race. The Thanks that we give God should not be only at this holiday season time but every day throughout our daily lives. Seek Him for He is there.

The plastic people with no love in their hearts that surround me shall not be my concern. If they seek God, then, I am here to Inspire them to seek Him as His Angels have done for me. I shall try not to force God upon any other. For those who seek God and wishes to email me and talk privately about Him or other things, I am here

Jesus and His Religious Teachings

You have seen that whenever anyone dies, he is placed upon a pedestal. Do you not know this happened to Jesus?
I know Jesus very well, and have talked with him many times, he says he does not wish to be worshipped. He claims we should Love the Father - GOD! For he is NOT the Father! And even the word "worship," that we use, is the wrong word, for the true word of God is "EMBRACE." The word "worship" was used and meant for the control of the majority by a few men in high rank of the Christian Church. Therefore, we should embrace God, for He does not demand us to Love Him, we Love Him because He is the Father. Whereasmuch, we should Love Jesus, for he is the Son and NOT the Father, and we should embrace the Son, for we do not worship the Son. God nor the Son dominates! For They INSPIRE with Love.
It is said that Jesus told his followers, "The only way to the Father is through me." As he talked to his followers, he talked to them alone. He told them, "The only way for you to find your Salvation is to follow my lifestyle." He did not mean for them or us to worship him because forcing someone to worship him would have been domination, and God nor Jesus forces anyone into doing anything. They have the power to make us get down on our knees and worship them forever, if they wished. But, God inspires us to do the right thing. But if we do not listen to Him, He cannot inspire, for words laid

upon deaf ears shall never be followed by a dead heart.

And Jesus said to the Devil, "I shall not 'tempt' God." The word "tempt" meant; coax - demand. In other words, Jesus said, "I will not demand God to save me if I jump from this cliff." While the Bible also states, "Those closer to God are the most tempted." Which means; "Those who are closer to God, have the most demands placed upon them." If one stands up in front of a congregation and speaks the words of God, but does not follow those words, he is not closer to God. One who is closer to God does as God Will's without glorification for himself. Preachers, ministers, etc. and even the Pope are not closer to God, they are merely making a living selling "their" God to their congregation. For the Bible also states, "Do not walk upon the altar because if you do, people will see you for what you are."

The story of Jesus' life that is written into the Bible is the story of his life as told by those who placed him upon a pedestal. Therefore, his life was dramatized as if He was God. Jesus' story was to inspire us to live the same style of life that He lived. It was not meant for us to worship Him! But whenever one is placed upon a pedestal he is thought of as prefect. Did not Jesus destory the sellers' place in the temple? And He is also told to have whipped those merchants, and so even Jesus became angry sometimes...was He not human?

Jesus' life was destroyed by people, just like you and I - humans, but people who could not "see" what life was about - people who could not understand the meaning of God's Master plan.

After Jesus died on the cross, people needed to find satisfaction and belief that their actions toward him were correct, thus, came the statement; "He died for our sins." He did not die for our sins, HE DIED BECAUSE OF OUR SIN OF DOMINATION! Jesus would not conform to the concepts of the Jewish religious thinking of the day, and for the power of those in control of the Jewish community and religion, Jesus had to be removed. Therefore, it was the domination factor of those leaders, and it was their sin that murdered him. Thus, from the human rationalization of the Jewish religion leaders of their Sin of murdering Jesus came Christianity.

The Christian Church has taken the word "Baptistismal" and turned it - "the personal acceptance of God into one's life," into forced joining to their church. Forcing young people to join their church automatically increases future revenue of their establishment -a business.

I know an elderly lady who drives over 50 miles to her church every Sunday, and I asked her, "Why don't you go to the church nearer your home. She replied, "I don't know." The true reason for her driving so far to church is that she is dominated by that church. For Christianity itself states, "It is a Sin to question."

The total concept of Christianity goes against itself, Jesus and God. For Christians say one thing and do another. And yet, I feel sorry for those who "make their own bed" in Heaven.

(At this time, I would like to enter into your understanding of Christianity and the teachings of Jesus, a lengthy essay written by John Roberts of Sydney, Australia, this writing will help you comprehend the true meanings that Jesus demonstrated in his life and death, and while Mr. Roberts' truly indicates the teachings of Jesus that Christians do not follow.)

John Roberts.
15.12.87
Revised June 1990, June 1992.
July 92 and Oct 1997, 2 Jan 1999.

The New Testament, as its name suggests, is a record of the new teachings, which were introduced into the rather inflexible world of Jewish doctrine by the life and work of Jesus of Nazareth.

The life of Jesus is important to us, as his teachings still form the basis of Western moral concepts. He demonstrated the applicability of the Spiritual Law, in a way that is relevant to all times and generations of Mankind.

One can never prove the truth of the events recorded in the New Testament, nor is it necessary to attempt to do so. Indeed, it is probable that many of the stories told about Jesus in the Gospels are either untrue or grossly inflated in the reiteration of events. What is important is the message he brought to humanity as to the true nature of God and of the relationship which we all bear towards one another, as the children of a loving and concerned Creator.

The Gospel of Matthew

The Gospel according to Matthew opens with the genealogy of Jesus, principally, to satisfy the reader as to his descent from King

David. It was important for the first (Jewish) Christians to establish this history as the basis for the claim that Jesus was the anticipated Messiah.

The doctrine of the Immaculate Conception is mentioned in Verse 18 of Chapter 1. I view this doctrine as that being false. All men, regardless of Race or Creed, are "Born of the Spirit". The Spirit is the very foundation and basis of physical existence, without which nothing would exist, as we know it. Hence, there is no necessity for such an idea as the unique physical purity of the Messiah. Jesus gains nothing in stature by this device; addressed as it is to those who entertain antiquated views as to the function of the procreative organs. It is common knowledge that being "born of a Virgin" was also one of the attributes of the once popular God, Mithras.

Chapter 3 gives a short account of the prophecy of John the Baptist; the forerunner of Jesus. He was a typical desert hermit. If John did testify to the superior status of Jesus of Nazareth, there was here some indication of the great work to be performed by the latter. Thus, whatever the precise nature of the revelation made at the baptism of Jesus, it is this aspect, the acclamation of John, which is, perhaps, of significance.

At verse 11, there is a reference to the distinction between the Baptism of Water and that of the Spirit. The physical or water baptism was, of course, symbolic of cleansing, at a time when personal hygiene was neither necessary nor possible. The Spiritual baptism, on the other hand, embraced the concept of the refinement of the soul, with the out-pouring of the Spiritual power; thus facilitating the practice of spiritual-gifts. "I baptize with water, but....he shall baptize with the Holy-Ghost", (v 11). This baptism was not unknown to the Jews, who experienced the gifts of Spirit throughout their history.

The baptism of Jesus is recorded: the Spirit descending upon him in the form of a dove. A spirit-voice was heard, "This is my beloved son, in whom I am well-pleased". (v 17). Christians are told that this was the voice of God. Quite apart from questions as to the nature of the Godhead, the story may only possess validity when considered as the voice of Joseph, the worldly father of Jesus, speaking inspirationally from Spirit to one of the bystanders.

One must consider the story of the "Temptation" of Jesus, which is recorded in Chapter 4 of the Book of Matthew, on the basis that he told his Disciples of his experiences. Most holy-men seem to suffer from a momentary lack of self-confidence and Jesus was no exception to this rule. He was probably given a glimpse into the inferior aspects of the spiritual world, which would have had a depressing effect upon him. This would particularly have been the case if, at that time, he did not fully understand the nature of his experiences. It is necessary for those who have the capacity for spiritual perception to understand these things: that the spiritual world consists not wholly of Paradise but comprehends the Hells as well as the Heavens.

It should be understood that the Spirit-world is not responsible for the follies of mankind; nor could it be suggested, at any time, that human weakness is promoted, tolerated or encouraged as a result of the activity of the Holy-Spirit. The principle of Free Will serves to ensure that whatever is detrimental to the happiness or well-being of mankind is solely the result of human tendencies and not by operation of spiritual law.

The "Sermon-on-the-Mount" remains the cornerstone of Christian doctrine, supplementing and surpassing the Mosaic Law. The Beatitudes need no elucidation. They demonstrate that those who suffer material deprivation in this life, through the greed of others and the injustice of worldly laws, will obtain a spiritual recompense. There is a promise of a better life to come: a call to spiritual living. "Let your light so shine before men..." (Ch 5 v l6l). This is the light of the human personality; the aura of a decent human being. Jesus emphasized that his task was to supplement, not to abolish the Law of Moses. He demonstrated that the attainment of the Kingdom of Heaven depends not upon an observance of the formalities of religion but upon the development of a sincere and natural righteousness. "Except your righteousness exceed that of the Scribes and Pharisees...."(v 20). It is not sufficient to fast and pray or worship outwardly: there has to be an adherence to the principles and practice of righteous living.

In suggesting that to display anger is equivalent to the actual use of violence, Jesus was demonstrating the effect of evil emotions upon the soul, rather than proposing that equivalent penalties should be imposed for offenses varying greatly in their effects. He was suggesting that the habit of evil-thinking, leads to corresponding action, which, in the aggregate, results in a regressive spiritual state.

He advocated reconciliation between enemies: "Make friends with thine adversary, quickly...'. (Ch 5 v 26). This was a very wise proposition.

Jesus' reference to "lustfulness", (v 27) strikes at the consciences of those men, who, although tentatively loyal to their wives, desire other women from time to time. In an age of sexual promiscuity, there is an increasing need for men and women to take stock of their moral standards. There is nothing progressive about loose living. Marriage is an institution established specifically for the protection of women and children. A Common Law wife gives all and receives no guarantees in return; being often discarded without redress, once her charms fail. Even recent legislation to protect the interests of the De-Facto wife does not fully safeguard such women. Lustfulness also connotes those inordinate or obsessive desires for things which we covet, against our better instincts, and which so often lead to unpleasant and unanticipated results.

"....And if thy right eye offend thee, pluck it out...."(Verses 29 to 30). The literal interpretation of this passage would be both self-destructive and futile. Jesus did not intend to suggest that any person should physically mutilate himself in consequence of Sin. It is the disposition of the will which causes one to commit wrong doing. Jesus was rather emphasizing the importance of the principle of self-discipline: the need for self-control as being essential to peace of mind. He was also concerned about the law, which permitted divorce and the ease with which a Jew could divorce his wife by the simple expedient of giving her a written notice of Divorce: a "Writing of Divorcement".

He regarded marriage as a sacred bond, which should not lightly be severed. Jesus recognized the dangers inherent in false-swearing and commanded his followers to refuse to take the oath under any circumstances.

Jesus advocated the principle of non-violence, even under provocation. This was a great leap-forward, for a nation for which personal vengeance was a God-given right. Modern Jewry would benefit from a perusal of the words of Deuteronomy, Ch 32 v 35, wherein is recorded the following passage: "'Vengeance is mine, I *will repay', saith the Lord"*. The message, indeed, is that, ultimately, God rules and all will be well with mankind.

Neither is "God mocked", for each person will reap the harvest of his own activity. (Galatians Ch 6). This is a universal law, which governs all human conduct. It suggests that no section of the human race can regard itself as separate or apart from the rest of mankind. We all have obligations towards one another. This principle applies right cross the stratum of humanity, from the personal to the national level. We have to look to our own conduct and its on sequences for others: for, inevitably, we ourselves will answer both individually and collectively for whatever harm we inflict upon others. "Whatsoever a man soweth, that shall he also reap!". (Galatians Ch 6 v 7).

The call to love, (Divine Love), reveals the sublime nature of this man. He commanded his followers to love those who hated them: to return love for hatred. The Chapter ends with the commandment towards perfection. This rule has also been ignored by so many Christian denominations.

"Be ye, therefore, perfect, as your Heavenly Father is perfect!" (Matthew Chapter 5 verse 48). Yet Christians still fail to understand the purport of this admonition. In a world choked by Calvinist damnation, these words rang-out loud and clear. They were a beacon to pierce the darkness and ignorance of mankind. They suggest that people are not merely the arbitrary plaything of a capricious and callous Deity but that they are the children, in the fullest sense, of a loving and caring Creator-God. The way was thus cleared for the progression of humanity and mankind was made aware of its freedom to choose for itself.

The Sermon continues with rules of daily conduct and deportment: that one should avoid hypocrisy and outward display. Times have changed so much that men no longer make an ostentatious show of their religious convictions, at least in Western Societies, preferring to retire into their private quarters for prayer and meditation.

One is admonished by Jesus to avoid, "Vain repetitions",(Ch 6, v 7). Even "The Lord's Prayer" has become just such a repetition. In spite of this warning, many ministers of religion seem to be *incapable of extemporary prayer, which Jesus was demonstrating. "The Lord's Prayer", is only an example of how to pray; to give thanks in sincerity and in love for the gifts of the physical life. The form of words is unimportant. There is no magic in this prayer or in any other set, familiar form of words. To be honest, we revere this prayer because of its traditional associations, but repetition of this or any other prayer is not essential to the leading of a Christian life. Indeed, it might be suggested that, the best prayers are the loving thoughts of a well-disposed soul. In spite of this, there is no doubt that the habit of prayer; the offering of thanks and praise, with supplication for spiritual counsel, is of great value to the human spirit. This is the avenue for the opening of the soul to the influence of spirit in our lives. This is the true Holy-Communion: the indestructible link between man and his Creator, which acknowledges the omnipresent love of God and the guidance and support which is directly available to each and every human soul.*

It is difficult for men to "lay up treasure in Heaven", when such abstract ideas are contrasted with the natural acquisitiveness of the physical life. What incentive is there to deny oneself the pleasures and comforts of property? Surely, society is geared, almost exclusively, to the adoration of physical things? We are all tempted to embark upon the accumulation of material possessions. In a stable and rather sophisticated environment, men and women, quite naturally, acquire an abundance of worldly goods. There is no incentive in such a society for people to unburden themselves of excess possessions, as is the case with simple, nomadic tribes-folk. There is no limit to the greed of men and no restraining hand upon us. Do we really accept that there is such a place as "Heaven"? Is it possible to lay up potential benefits for our subsequent enjoyment in the spiritual world? Is there not a selfish factor in such considerations? A perception of the Spiritual truths reveals to us that, as we live our earthly lives, by the action of creative thought we actually prepare for ourselves a "heavenly dwelling-place" of one form or another. In other words, we actually create our own spiritual environment during our worldly existence. Death merely reveals to us the extent and quality of our own activity. The comprehension of the validity of this assertion, which, if properly understood, will bring home to each one of us the fact that we cannot escape the consequences of our own behaviour whilst in the flesh.

The recognition of the validity of the Spiritual Law involves the application of a wholly new set of personal standards; in fact, those laid down in the Sermon on the Mount. One is thus required to adapt oneself to a life of service in the community, of which we are all very much a part and without which our lives would be barren, indeed. To accept such principles means that one has to adopt a measure of self-denial, together with the annihilation of such vices as pride, greed, avarice, covetousness, etc. One has to endeavour to live as a useful member of society, not as a parasite. There is no such thing as, "Justification by Faith". Trust in God and the recognition of the law, leads to good-works and only this product of a constructive life can result in what men call, "Salvation"; that is, the attainment of the Spiritual life. There can be no magical transformation from one, hitherto damned, into a celestial soul. The process is, necessarily, gradual, both in the spiritual and physical worlds.

"Where the treasure is, there will the heart be also", (Ch 6 v 21). It is a well-known fact that pre-occupation with physical possessions inhibits spiritual growth, to this extent, that on passing from the physical world into the greater consciousness of Spirit, the soul refuses to relinquish control over worldly goods: failing to perceive the fact of transition. As there is no obvious change of state, this is not surprising. Such an attitude prevents any sort of progression in Spirit-life. It is clear that Jesus understood the spiritual-law when he made this profound statement. Many generations of Christians have read these words and still fail to understand the significance of what he had to say. "The eye is the lamp of the body", in that we see and have light but the allusion is spiritual. The lamp of the mind is either darkness or light. "Illumination" suggests understanding and "darkness"; ignorance. One has to choose between good and evil activity: the choice is between service and self-interest.

In a beautiful passage at verses 25 to 35, we are advised regarding concern for personal preservation. It is natural that we should provide for ourselves and our dependents. Society demands that we should adopt certain personal standards in order to regulate our lives. However, Jesus' remarks were directed towards the need for moderation in regard to material possessions, which, however desirable in themselves, are transient and fleeting, being merely loaned to us for the duration of the physical life.

"Judge not, lest ye be judged!" (Ch 7 vs 1 to 5). This is an obvious truism, yet it is a trap into which we all invariably fall to some degree.

At verse 9, Jesus is recorded as saying, "Cast not pearls before swine, nor give that which is holy unto dogs". There is no arrogance in this statement. Those who are self-orientated and have no spiritual awareness will naturally reject the truths of Spirit as being mere superstition. They simply have no religious beliefs, nor any concept of the continuity of life beyond the grave. To raise such topics would be to invite ridicule and scorn. One should not be too eager to enter into a discussion of Spiritual things with those who are clearly incapable of appreciating the subject. Naturally, where the subject of religion is raised independently, there can be no objection to a statement of one's personal beliefs.

"Ask and it shall be given you, seek and ye shall find", (v 7). These words refer to spiritual, rather than worldly things. God will give good gifts to his children but this cannot be regarded as an unconditional dispensation. It is primarily necessary for people to live in accordance with His laws. "Do as you would be done by!", as a universal law, applied by all men and women, means universal well being. In a world wracked by self-interest; in which a few wealthy individuals control the destinies of millions of poor, such precepts appear to be vain. Nevertheless, it is necessary for the individual to establish this rule in his heart and to reflect it in the manner of his life. Only then will he see the fulfillment of the Creator's bounty. After all, the world was created as a fit place for the habitation of mankind.

"The gate is narrow and the way hard that leads to life and few there be who find it", (v 14). This is an allegorical idea of the spiritual life. It is difficult for worldly men to understand the proposition that Jesus was making: that service and self-denial are necessary to the attainment of salvation. We are all pre-occupied at times with the necessity of making a living for ourselves and our dependents. The world demands this of us. There are numerous pressures of one form or another, which require that we compete for *the advantage over our fellows. In some communities, these pressures are overwhelming and often lead to severe emotional trauma. Happily, we do have a measure of freedom to make the choice which most appeals to us. Whatever may be the decision, it remains true that death will surely bring about an end to all acquisition and all competitiveness. Whilst Jesus does mention the "wide way that leads to destruction", it is not true for one moment that the great bulk of souls are destroyed by leading selfish lives. Rather is there a retardation and distortion of spiritual development. From this condition, the way of progress is slow.*

"Beware of false prophets", (Ch 7 v 25). Every Movement has its share of such prophets. The individual has to ensure that his own personal life is such that no claim of that nature can be laid at his door. This is why the spiritual life must be one of dedication to the service of God and Humanity, with no regard for material things, particularly with respect to the spiritual work. Spiritual-gifts must be devoted to the service of mankind, not utilized for the purpose of personal gain. "For the tree is known by his fruit", (Mat Ch 12 v 33). The spiritual man is content to give God the praise and to exclude lucre from his considerations. The exploitation of spiritual-gifts for gain is taboo and should not be tolerated in the Spiritualist Movement. This principle cannot be over-emphasized, yet it be is almost universally ignored.

A collection is often made at meetings, (euphemistically described as a "Free-will Offering") to be followed by unacceptable and demonstrates a failure to comprehend the basic nature of the word, "Spiritual". It connotes the proposition that, whilst lucre itself is tainted in some way, the deity will, by smiling benevolently upon the proceedings, ensure that the cash is wisely and productively distributed; which is nonsense.

Oral acknowledgment of the Creator's love and power is not sufficient to assist in the attainment of the life of the Spirit. There must be a sincere endeavor to conform to the law: to live as God would wish.

Chapter 7 concludes with a significant comment: "The people were astonished at his doctrine, for he taught them as one having authority and not as the scribes".

The Sermon upon the Mount is the major statement of doctrine for Christians. If Jesus had done no more than lay down these principles, his achievement would have been immense. The teachings themselves were not entirely original, as Socrates had taught similar principles several hundred years earlier. The founder of the Buddhist religion had also advocated similar doctrines as essential to the attainment of enlightenment. The Sermon is uncompromising in its demands, so that it is not surprising that no attempt has been made by the Church to insist upon a literal interpretation of the teachings. How could any Christian justify the existence of grossly inequitable social systems in the light of Jesus' injunction to his followers? With the decline of the influence of religion in our modern world, political extremism is gaining popularity. At least, our Christian predecessors were subject to some limited sanction with regard to their public obligations. Capitalism pays no lip service to such sensitivities.

The dilemma facing the Church today is that it feels the need to prune the tree of faith, yet is hesitant to reform the body of doctrine for fear of damaging the cherished concepts of the Faithful. One might suggest that the image of the Christian Church might perhaps be much improved by a serious attempt to rationalize the more outrageous demands that are made, from generation to generation, upon the intelligence of ordinary mortals, by such doctrines as the Immaculate Conception, Vicarious Atonement, etc. Jesus told his auditors that: "Many will come from the East and from the West and shall sit at table with Abraham". (Ch 8, v ll). This was a strange statement for a Jew to make. It was his testimony to the fact that God's laws apply to all members of the family of Man: that Heaven is accessible to all.

The Ancients believed that afflictions followed upon sin. This may well be the case in certain well-documented instances of personal misconduct but is not invariably true. Certainly, many social problems result from sinfulness, that is, wrongdoing and it may be suggested that mental illness often results from wicked conduct. It was natural for Jesus to say, "Your sins are forgiven". The objection was taken at the time that he had no authority to forgive sins. If the Jews had acknowledged such a power in Jesus, it would have been tantamount to an admission that he had been Divinely ordained to come into the world as a leader of men. The forgiveness of Sin is

God's prerogative, so that it is understandable that the bystanders were outraged. If Jesus actually used such words, his intention was clearly not to appropriate Divine authority to himself but to express the forgiveness of God as a healing vehicle. The recipient of the words would have understood the meaning as addressed to himself.

God is only comprehended as Divine Love. It is within the capacity of each individual to experience this personal sense of the Love of God. Love is the highest human attribute, which most of us are privileged to experience in the family relationship. Love inspires self-denial and service to one's fellows. The Divine Love is poured forth upon Creation as spirit-power and each soul is spiritually able to extend itself toward this infinite Love of God. Forgiveness of Sin, therefore, is this Divine capacity for the annihilation of guilt-feelings for wrongs committed, which restores to the soul a sense of worthiness and well-being. It was probably this feeling of personal forgiveness which inspired the Apostle Paul to develop his theory of Justification by Faith, for he could not personally reconcile his sense of Salvation with the history of his opposition to Christianity in his youth. Nevertheless, personal progression is a slow process, dependent upon constructive activity, which alone eradicates the consequences of misconduct.

Jesus was much abused for the keeping of poor company. His response was, "They that are whole have no need of the physician but they that are sick". (Ch 9 v 11). Too often we criticize derelicts, perhaps justly so. Jesus practiced the cure of souls before they reached the Spirit-world. "I came not to call the righteous but sinners to repentance.", (v 13). So great was his influence that he brought many worldly men to reform their lives.

It was natural that Jesus should be criticized and described as an "Agent of the Devil". It is the old familiar cry. Throughout the history of mankind, those who purport to have the Key of Heaven have calumniated those who claim to possess spiritual gifts.

Jesus called his Twelve Disciples and "Gave them authority", (Ch 10 v 1). He evidently instructed his followers in the psychic arts, which were to be necessary for their future ministry. One needs to consider the words of verse 8, which reads, "Freely ye have received, freely give". Now, with regard to Spiritual-gifts, the commandment is imperative. *One observes that, wherever spiritual (or psychic gifts) are bestowed, there is a continual abuse and prostitution of such gifts for the sake of material gain. The standard excuse for this practice is that "The laborer is worthy of his hire". This excuse will not do. The mere fact that Jesus used these words does not excuse the making of personal profit from the use of psychic gifts. In referring to "Hire" he was intending to mean daily sustenance and no more. Quite apart from his insistence on the maintenance of a spiritual standard, it is self-evident that if God does indeed bestow such gifts upon his children, that they are intended for the spiritual elevation of mankind and not for purposes of entertainment. It is to the eternal shame of the Christianity movement that there has been an increasing tendency for individuals and groups to seek material advantage from the actual practice of the gifts of Spirit. Such activity can only be damaging in the extreme and result, as it undoubtedly has, in a lowering of the overall standard and a clouding of the true purposes of the demonstration of survival after death.*

Jesus is reported to have prophesied concerning the persecutions that were to come. He gave his followers the promise of the Spirit of their Father to speak for them. If they have called the master of the house, "Be-el-ze-bub", what will they not say of his household? (Matt Ch 10 v 25). Religious innovators have always been vilified. How much more those claiming to follow in the footsteps of the Apostles: those practicing Spiritual-gifts? Ridicule, abuse, persecution and death have been their lot. Nothing engenders hatred amongst the professedly religious more than the claim to Spiritual gifts: foreknowledge: healing and spiritual-ministry. This represents a threat to established religion. Surely, the Devil must be at work in such persons, as it is well known that revelation ceased with the Apostles, or was it Muhammad?

Jesus told his Disciples to have no fear of the physical death but to beware of the "Spiritual Death". There is difficulty here (Ch 10 v29), in that the soul is immortal and cannot die. To the very wicked, however, the future state must constitute a "living-death"; a place of darkness, filth, hatred and malice: a self-perpetuating Hell. There was, perhaps, a touch of irony in his statement that his coming would hardly bring peace on Earth but rather strife (a sword).

Referring to John the Baptist, Jesus suggested that, "the least in the Kingdom of Heaven is greater than he". (Ch 11 v 11). This constitutes an attempt to transpose worldly ideas as to status to the realm of Spirit. Such a yardstick is inappropriate, as concepts such as "Greater" or "Lesser" would have no place in a spiritual environment.

The doctrine of the trans-migration of souls is entirely illusory. Jesus was not without a sense of rejection as he reproached those people who would not accept him as he thought appropriate.(v 24). However, God has concealed these truths from the erudite and has revealed them to children.(v 25). At this point, there is a sudden change in the style of the passage, which suggests that commentary has, at some stage, been incorporated into the text. The writer asserts that, "No-one knows the Father, except the Son and those to whom the Son chooses to reveal him". (v 27). This is not Jesus speaking of himself. The passage is dogmatic and exclusionist and is just not true. A knowledge of Jesus is of value in understanding his teachings but is not essential to an understanding of God. We are back to the assertion that only Christians and those who accept the traditional doctrine of Jesus as the only begotten Son of God; as a personal Saviour, will enter Paradise.

Verses 28 to 30 contain a beautiful and expressive passage concerning Jesus. There is an apparent contradiction here from his earlier assertion that the "Way is narrow.... that leads to life". (Ch 7 v 14). He here suggests that, "My yoke is easy and my burden is light". One is to understand that, having made the choice for the spiritual life and sacrificed the material pleasures, the way to Heaven is not so burdensome. Like Christian, the hero of Bunyan's Pilgrim's Progress, who is progressively relieved of his burden of guilt as he approaches the Celestial City. These words were a message to the children of Earth: to the malnourished, physically and spiritually deprived people of the world. In our own time, they call us to abandon the struggle for precedence and seek calmer environs. There is a promise of ultimate justice to the people of a world, in which there is always so much injustice and inequality.

Chapter 21 contains an account of Jesus' continued ministry and shows that he incurred the enmity of the priesthood through an apparently casual attitude towards the forms of religion. It was natural that those who regarded themselves as the religious leaders of the community would be hostile towards him.

Jesus answered the criticism that he performed miracles through the agency of the "Prince of the Devils", with the familiar words, "An house divided against itself cannot stand. If I, by the Devil, cast out demons, by whom do your sons cast them out?" (v 27). However, if the Spirit of God was the power behind the miracles, then they had been touched by the Kingdom of Heaven. He felt this unjust criticism keenly. It was a denial of the power of God. A blasphemy against the Spirit of God would not be forgiven. Jesus was, after all, human and endowed with human emotions and weaknesses. He was undoubtedly conditioned by his training and experience as a Jew.

A man's words flow from the heart and if one cultivates evil ways, then does one become evil. Goodness cannot flow from evil. A sound tree brings forth wholesome fruit and not otherwise. There can be no sudden transformation from wickedness to righteousness or vice versa. It is incumbent upon all of us to beware of personal weakness in thinking and in manners. As we think so we, in fact, become.

Simulated affection and concern for others in order to gain personal advantage remains evil, in spite of superficial displays of righteousness. What springs from the heart becomes evident, sooner or later and guile and deceit constitute the more despicable forms of human activity: calculated to injure the innocent.

"A wicked and perverse generation looks for a sign" (v 39). Meetings held at churches every week are attended by those who seek just such a sign. Jesus himself had provided ample evidence as to his spirituality, yet he was still desired to produce some overwhelming evidence of the fact that he was the promised Messiah. Quite understandably, he refused to comply. In any event, the Jews were looking for a military champion, not a spiritual leader.

He told a story of the unclean spirit, which having been expelled from his "home", wandered around seeking rest. However, finding no peace, the spirit resolved to return to his former residence and, "finding it swept and garnished", entered: taking along with him several companions of a similar ilk. Hence, the final condition of that poor afflicted soul was worse than at the commencement of his ordeal. Whilst this idea of the influence of evil-spirits upon the lives of men and women appears to be a primitive concept, it only appears to be so because of our inability to comprehend the true nature of man himself as, primarily, a spiritual being, residing in both a physical and a spiritual environment at the same time. Hence the doctrine is based on sound principles. If it were not true, the whole idea of the ministry of angels would also be illusory. Mental illness, obsession, alcoholism, drug-dependence, etc., are all maladies affected to a great extent by the quality of the spirit-companionship that we, unknowingly, foster during our earthly lives. Spiritualists are aware that the souls of those, who themselves have been addicted to such vices whilst in the body, often attach themselves, unwittingly, to persons who are living the physical life. It is suggested that only in this way are they able to gratify the lust for alcohol or whatever vice afflicts them. As Jesus himself is reported to have said, "This kind goeth not out but by prayer and fasting."(Ch 18 v 21). We should, therefore, pray for those who suffer from addictive problems, at the same time, taking care lest we ourselves fall into such unhappy conditions. There is nothing really sinister in the idea of spirit obsession. Every conscious moment is spent under the influence of spirit, beneficial or harmful. Each time we irradiate thought, we engage in this unconscious communion.

Hence we should be constantly on guard, lest we develop bad habits: of foul language: loose talk: excessive drinking, etc., for as we think and act, so do we become. We ought always to remember that by thought we attract souls into our "aura" or spiritual environment and should endeavour to set ourselves a course of personal development, so that we grow into better people tomorrow than we are today. The growth of good habits rather than evil ways is essential to our spiritual progression. One can never say that one is constantly in the company of angels, often the reverse is the case. Perhaps one can only hope to maintain an equillibrium between those good and evil influences at work in our lives. If we can do this, we have achieved a considerable measure of success.

Jesus' reference to "Kinship" is a spiritual comparison. No doubt, he was a dutiful son to his parents and fond brother to siblings, yet, quite truthfully, he pointed-out that the spiritual relationship is forged wherever there is an affinity of spirit, creating bonds which *transcend the bonds of the flesh.*

Chapter 19 commences with the Parable of the Sower. The only observation that needs to be made about this story is that not all men and women have the same sense of the spiritual, nor do we all feel the need for divine-guidance in our lives. It is so much a question of temperament and training. We can understand that many people will not respond to religious messages, whatever the appeal may be to others.

The parables themselves, although fit subject for sermons, in reality throw little light upon the nature of the Kingdom of Heaven. Indeed, Judgment is emphasized and in the time of Jesus, the concept of Divine Judgment and the destruction of sinners was prominent in religious thought. The Jews were obsessed with apocalyptic beliefs, related to the idea of the coming of the Messiah and the establishment of a New Order upon the Earth. The concept of Judgment and retribution is an unhappy idea. There is to be no such thing as the Judgment by God of men and women: no assessment of individual activity: of the accumulated good or evil conduct of people whilst on Earth. There will be no arbitrary condemnation or elevation of souls, either elect or non-elect. There is no truth in the doctrines of Predestination or Election: no Justification by Faith. There will only be the inevitable segregation of advanced or regressive souls according to the product of individual activity. Souls compulsively seek the company of kindred spirits, even as we all do in life. We are not at ease in the company of our betters or inferiors: hence the gulf between Heaven and Hell. In reality, they are one and the same place: different suburbs, so to speak, of one great city. One truth is paramount: God is Divine Love: no element of wrath or anger is to be found in His Nature, which, so far as we are able to comprehend it, is Absolute Compassion.

One would not be surprised to read that Jesus was not accepted as a Spiritual leader by the townsfolk of Nazareth. To them he was, of course, just another ordinary local man. Matthew gives an account of the death of John the Baptist in Ch 14, followed by the stories of Jesus feeding the multitude and later, walking upon the waters. One could be excused for expressing doubt as to the veracity of these tales. There is probably a perfectly simple physical *explanation but we shall never know the truth, nor do they demand concentrated attention.*

Chapter 15 records the criticism by the Priesthood that Jesus and his Disciples failed to conform to the demands of orthodoxy in formal religious observance. Referring to the elaborate food-ritual, Jesus observed that, "Nothing that goes into a man makes him unclean but what comes out of the mouth", (v 11). That which comes from the heart of a man; expressions of an evil nature, contaminate him. The very thought of man is that which elevates or degrades him.

How often are Clergymen the "Blind leading the Blind?" Men of God who are far from Him: ambitious of worldly power and pomp: full of pride and conceit: demanding favour and protection from the Deity, whilst serving every wrong principle.

Chapter 16, verse 6, conveys his warning to "Beware of the leaven of the Pharisees". This means the observance of outward forms and hackneyed phrases, so common to religious observance in every day and Age.

Verses 13 to 20 record Peter's testimony to Jesus as, "The Christ, the Son of the living God". These were strong words and, viewed in a narrow sense, they are unacceptable to all but the most ardent Christians. The Christ is the Anointed One; the Chosen One, rather than the "Only begotten Son of God", which is exclusive. All men and women are the children of God. God dwells within each and every human being. All enjoy the right to claim kinship with their Heavenly Father. This is particularly true if we recognize the Call to Perfection. Jesus was the Son of God, in the sense that he demonstrated to the men and women of his time, the potentiality of the human spirit: its capacity for ultimate goodness: the Godliness of man and of the "union" with the Father. Thus the Christ is the one who is sent into the world as a Pathfinder - to show the way to his fellows - not as a sacrificial atonement for the future wickedness of unborn generations of men, nor indeed, as a Warrior King who will lead the Jewish Nation to supremacy and security in the world.

The Church calls upon the authority of verse 18 to substantiate its claim to the Apostolic succession. "Thou are Peter (Petros) and upon this rock I will build my Church". There has been much debate regarding this appointment of Peter. The passage itself is not declaratory of any particular authority to be bestowed upon Peter but merely indicates that he will be a founder of the Church. In any event, if the Church, which consists of the body of its members, was to be founded upon the labours of any one of the Apostles, surely it was the work of Paul, the intellectual and theologian of Christianity, that laid the foundations of the Christian Church. The suggestion that Peter had "power to bind" is fanciful and I suspect the interpolation of an ardent commentator.

Verses 11 to 13, identify John the Baptist as the re-incarnation of the Prophet, Elijah. The probable truth is that the life of John the Baptist was merely coincidental to the life of Jesus and was not, in any sense, a fulfilment of prophecy. Certainly, at the time he was recognized as a holy-man and may well have been identified by the populace as a forerunner of the Messiah.

When Jesus was instrumental in the healing of the epileptic youth, the Disciples questioned him as to why they themselves, evidently possessing some healing gifts, were unable to effect a cure. Commenting on the need for faith, he affirmed the need for sustained prayer in certain types of infirmity.

Chapter 18, v 3, records Jesus as saying, "Except ye be converted and become as little children, ye shall not enter the Kingdom of Heaven". He was here suggesting that we should cultivate within ourselves the capacity for innocence; for absence of guile. No-matter how old in years we grow, it is still possible for us to attain to a spiritual innocence. In all our dealing with others, we must endeavour to be straightforward and honest; avoiding dissimulation. In relation to the Father-God, it is possible for us all to attain the status of "Little Children", responding to the Divine-Love of our Heavenly Parent, which is poured forth upon all creation as a Fountain of Life, indeed, as "Living Waters".

It is essential that we adopt a modest demeanour during worship. However, God does not require His children to grovel on hands and knees before him. The Father is not some Eastern potentate, who demands absolute prostration before He is pleased with us. It is sufficient for people to stand before their Maker, with eyes and voices raised in praise and thanksgiving. The Western practice of kneeling in prayer results in physical torment and, surely, detracts from the attainment of the state of mental tranquillity, which is necessary for the elevation of the mind in prayer from mundane to spiritual things.

Jesus emphasized the responsibility which adults have towards the children committed to their charge (v 5 and 6). Certainly, a person who by selfishness or negligence brings harm to one of God's innocent ones, carries a heavy burden of guilt. So much so that Jesus suggested a too-literal act of self-chastisement, merely intended to illustrate the importance of self-discipline, rather than to suggest self-mutilation for wrong doing. Of course, no part of the body can induce a man to commit wrong. The will alone causes harm through selfish action.

There is no Saint Peter standing at the gate, with keys to open or bar entrance to Paradise. The way is open to all to enter. Our possessions call us uncompromisingly back to a worldly sphere of rock-solid goods and chattels.

The recorded promise of Jesus to his Disciples, (v 28) seems rather naive and hardly consistent with his understanding of the Spirit-world. The sitting-on of thrones is an activity enjoyed by the proud and vainglorious of this world: certainly not of the next, although simple people might be induced to believe that Heaven consists of the enjoyment of similar pleasures. For this story to be true would reveal a less than sincere motive for the sacrifice of worldly advantages in the hope of spiritual benefits to come. To be truly sincere, there must be no expectation of spiritual rewards in return for physical sacrifices made here on Earth. Love must be the sole consideration. One must be prepared to fulfill the obligations of Service, regardless of concern for future benefits: the accumulation of Merit.

The parable of the Day-laborers in the Vineyard, illustrates the generosity of God in dealing equally with all his children, regardless of what individual contribution they make to the "culture of the vineyard". Whilst there is no discrimination between "laborers", yet may not some workers derive an additional advantage from their greater labors? If we evolve spiritually by the habit of useful works, would not a lifetime of effort count for more than a few years at the latter end of life? One would need to labor well, in order to rectify a life of folly and selfishness in such a short time.

Verse 21 finds the Disciples squabbling over the heavenly rewards they hope to receive. This was an unseemly proceeding; demonstrating their ignorance and selfishness. They thought of Jesus as a Heavenly Prince, surrounded by courtiers, amongst whom they themselves would rank highly. This was a false concept of Divine-Kingship, influenced by the equally primitive standards of worldly government. Whatever the relationship of Jesus to the Heavenly Father, it cannot be thought possible that the man, Jesus, will reign in Heaven as a Prince of Angels. This would be too simplistic a concept. Jesus was, so far as we can ascertain, no more, nor less than a Divinely-inspired Teacher who was sent to point the way for Mankind. The doctrine of the Vicarious Atonement has no validity whatever. To suggest that Jesus by his death and personal sacrifice, atoned for the sins of unborn generations of men and women, is fatuous. However, it was understandable that the Disciples should mistake Jesus' true nature and calling. He, himself, suggested to his followers that they should endeavour, above all things, to serve one-another, nor strive for preferment. He came to minister and not to be ministered unto.

The story of Jesus' triumphal entry into Jerusalem makes careful reference to the fulfillment of prophecy; part of the Messianic vision. His rough treatment of the merchants in the Temple precincts is understandable, considering his views on the sanctity of worship. The Temple had become something of a show-place, like so many of our great churches, in which one feels an absence of the necessary devotional atmosphere. Our Cathedrals are wonderful buildings, testifying to the creative zeal of the craftsmen, who devoted their lives to the construction of these marvellous edifices: yet the maintenance of such buildings demands an enormous expenditure in money. They are not exactly, "Dens of Thieves" but, nevertheless, are hives of fund-raising activity. The Church, herself so bent upon maintaining property and the status-quo, has lost the respect and reverence of the bulk of the people. One may, indeed, be awed by the grandeur of a great cathedral, but feel no urge to offer prayer. One cannot avoid a sense of the conceit and arrogance of those worldly clergy, who endeavoured to perpetuate grand memorials to themselves. There is no evidence here of a following in the Master's footsteps. If the rulers of the world are so arrogant, is it surprising that the simple poor should entertain perverse ideas as to the nature of the Kingdom of Heaven? The very use of the word, "Kingdom" is inappropriate to describe a place in which there is no suggestion whatever of class or social groupings. The term is perhaps used to perpetuate the idea that Monarchy, as an institution, is divinely-ordained and has the approval of Deity. If Heaven has such a system, then it must be appropriate for this world. And so the class myth is strengthened by the express sanction of the Church.

As to worship itself; it is of the greatest importance that public worship be conducted in such a manner as to elevate the mind from material preoccupations, reminding us of the close ties which we enjoy with the Creator of All and of the comfort and guidance which are continually available to us from spiritual sources. It is the act of prayer and communion that sanctifies a place of meeting and those who participate therein. The building itself has no bearing upon the quality of the experience of those who attend services. It is true to say that the demeanour of all who take part in the service should be such as to be conducive to a harmonious and spiritually instructive meeting.

That does not mean that one has to be morose or mournful in any way. Worship can be an edifying and a happy proceeding.

The story of the Fig-tree is interesting, although not convincing reading. It forms the background to Jesus' statement that "Faith moves mountains." (v 2l). He told his followers that their prayers would be answered. This was not to suggest that God answers prayer exactly as we would desire, nor do we always understand either what we want or what is good for us. Hence, whether or not God answers prayer, is a question that is answered according to the viewpoint of the individual. When we pray, the emphasis must be upon the principle, "Thy will be done, not mine!". It is sufficient that we acknowledge that God exists. This, being a truth established clearly in the minds of those who consider themselves to be religious, it follows that God, being Divine Love, already knows the desire of our hearts and it is not necessary to detail to him our inmost thoughts. It is sufficient for us to offer praise and thanksgiving and to ask blessing upon our undertakings. If we really need to ask for specific help, our prayer should not entail any element of selfishness. There is no place in worship for bargaining with the Deity. Where there is knowledge of God, there is faith in God and from these comes a trust in His Love. It might not be inappropriate here to mention that, whilst the present writer, being male, refers to God in the male gender, it is quite appropriate to conceive of the Deity without introducing a aspect of gender at all. We can conceive of God as a Divine Parent. There is also an element of conditioning here; God traditionally having been regarded, by men of course, as a "Male entity".

The scribes questioned Jesus regarding his authority. This was a difficult question and he would have been reluctant to bear witness on his own behalf. (v 23). It was neatly evaded by reference to the Baptism of John the Baptist.

Jesus suggested to the pious and learned Jews that, "Publicans and harlots go into the Kingdom of Heaven before you.", (v31). This was an astonishing proposition to put to the respectable Jewish doctors of the law. When one considers the worldliness of many of our religious leaders, of whatever faith, one is not surprised to discover that Jesus made similar criticisms of the Priesthood. It was, of course, a further reference to the need for men to live honestly with themselves; to avoid mere formality and to be genuinely sincere in their endeavours to live spiritual lives.

There are two further parables to note; those of the Vineyard, (v 33) and (in Ch 22), the Wedding Feast. Both suggest that the "Gift of Life" will be taken from the Chosen People and given to "Strangers". The reference to the man without a Wedding Garment is obscure. Perhaps it was intended to portray a soul who has, inadvertently, found his way into a higher spiritual level than that for which he is qualified, although invited. He did not attain the requisite standard and was, therefore, excluded from the company. We know that a soul can only enter that level of the spiritual world for which it is fitted. There is no question of violent exclusion from the Kingdom of Heaven. It is a matter of selection by choice. E.g. A person who has been accustomed to living in colder climates would find the heat of the Arabian Desert to be intolerable. It is the same in the Spirit world.

When asked whether it was lawful to pay tax, (Ch 22 v17), Jesus countered by referring to the separation of worldly and spiritual powers. "Render to Caesar that which is Caesar's".

When questioned by the Sadducees, who denied the doctrine of the Resurrection, Jesus affirmed its truth, (v 32). "God is not the God of the dead but of the living, for all live unto Him." As God is the God of all: all, therefore, live. Whilst the passage may be ambiguous, he specifically referred to the "Resurrection" and made clear his understanding of the truth of this essential doctrine. In fact, this idea of the resurrection of the dead was, and is, the central tenet of the Christian faith. It was this truth that Jesus himself came upon the Earth to impart to men and women. It is also the cornerstone of the Spiritualist teachings; the truth of which is demonstrated by the "Spirit and of Power" today, as in the time of Christ.

Another lawyer asked Jesus, "What is the great commandment of the law?" (v36). He replied, "Thou shalt love the Lord thy God with all thy heart, with all thy soul and with all thy mind and the second is like unto it: Thou shalt love thy neighbour as thyself. On these two commandments hang all the law and the prophets." Jesus here affirmed the basic truth that the Decalogue formed the foundation of the Law and continued to be the basis upon which to build a useful and a happy life. The Key to Heaven, indeed!

A person who is keen to understand the spiritual wisdom: to acquire spiritual-gifts and to comprehend the Divine Truths, must first digest these principles. One can only hope to approach the fountainhead of knowledge and wisdom by this vehicle: the First and Great Commandment: the Call to Service!

Chapter 3 contains an exposition of Jesus' social doctrines. Living, as we do, in a world in which all is superficial display and ceremony, it is not hard for us to understand his abhorrence of outward forms. Do we not daily observe the love of vain men for the recognition of their fellows as persons of worth and value? The powerful of his day also grew fat upon the sweat of their fellow men. The personal lives of the learned were often spent in contemplation of self-interest; in ostentation and display: in "Greetings in the Market-places and chief seats at feasts" (Vs 6-7). We are no different today. Jesus' criticism of the scribes was severe, "Devourers of widows' houses and hypocrites".

The need to avoid hypocrisy! That is a difficulty facing all aspiring moralists. One should try to avoid craftiness and guile. One should be aware of one's personal defects, yet not overwhelmed by them. It is not hypocritical to desire moral improvement in one's life or to be conscious of personal shortcomings. One should not allow fear of being labeled an hypocrite to overcome feelings of repentance for the commission of wrongs.

God does want us to lean on Him; to ask for spiritual support. One has to start somewhere. True hypocrisy is displayed by those, superficially religious, who subvert the spiritual calling for base personal motives. These people lack an understanding of the law pertaining to things of the Spirit. They have no real knowledge of God.

The elaborate system of oaths for all occasions, which influenced so much the lives of the Jews, brought condemnation from Jesus. The Clergy were preoccupied with the superficial paraphernalia of religious observance and often overlooked the claims of justice and mercy. The anger of Jesus was kindled against the hypocrites of his day; yet, even here, there was a note of tenderness. (v 37). The Chapter is a deeply critical outcry against the social evils of his time: evils repeated so often in the history of mankind. How often have prophets been calumniated and tormented in this life, nay, even killed, as was Jesus himself? It is only in our day that public indifference, hardly tolerance, has resulted in a lessening of criticism: a time which sees a corresponding weakening of the hold of the Christian Churches upon the lives of men and women.

Jesus is reported to have foreseen the destruction of the Temple, an event that occurred in AD 70. This disaster was brought about not so much by the cruelty of the Romans, as by the madness of the Jews themselves. Josephus tells us that the City was actually fired by the Zealots during the final assault by Titus. (Whiston's Josephus: Book VI, Chapter 4.). Jesus also told his disciples of many events which subsequently occurred. It is remarkable that Christianity survived the destruction of the city, but by then the new teachings had spread throughout the Empire. He foretold the persecution of the Christians, brought about largely by their ardent pacifism, which was unacceptable to a world in which self-defense against the Barbarians was considered to be essential to the survival of the State.

He refers to the "False prophets" who shall "arise to deceive many". (vll). This criticism is often leveled at those who desire to *possess spiritual gifts. The calumny is supported by the suggestion that spiritual gifts are no longer dispensed upon the Earth. Paul is quoted, "Whether there be prophecies they shall fail, whether there be tongues they shall cease, whether there be knowledge it shall vanish away." (Cor. 1 Ch 13), as though this passage is authority for the proposition, that God will cease to influence Mankind. Knowledge is certainly still with us and increasing daily. The use of this argument displays an ignorance of the principles upon which the Universe itself is established, not to mention merely a particular religious idea. We know that the Holy Spirit is that which created and sustains the whole of Creation, without which life itself would be impossible.*

Thus, the outpouring of the Spirit is part of the very basic order of things. The writer does not desire to disparage the beautiful language of Paul the Apostle. Paul was speaking apocalyptically and illustrating the impermanence of worldly things. He felt that the world was shortly to be superseded by the establishment of a new order.

Another criticism labeled at the spiritual-communion is that it is the work of the "Devil", an entity much to be feared, as he has a habit of disguising himself as an, "Angel of light!". This is a very subtle proposition. One cannot be sure, in communicating with Spirits, that one is in contact with Angels, because of the certainty of this assertion. The answer to this suggestion lies in the one provided by Jesus himself. "A house divided....".

A person who has an understanding of the principles, well knows that the "Prince of Darkness!" could not possibly disguise himself in bright garments. It would be contrary to his nature and to the law of God. Quite apart from the fact that "The Devil" is merely the personification of evil and has no separate existence, a soul which has spent a lifetime in wickedness, lies, spite, jealousy, mad-rages, hatred, envy and deceit, finds itself on entering the Spirit-world in a wholly darkened environment. There no light may penetrate. The soul has erected such a barrier around-about itself that nothing can pierce its density. Such a soul, if capable of communicating at all, seeks the company of other souls who are in a similar condition. Those souls then dwell together in self-generating filth, darkness and strife. They have no power to influence others who are not in the same regressive condition as themselves.

The Catholic Church emphasizes in its teachings that life is a preparation for the moment of death. The moment of transition from Earth-life to Spirit-life finds each individual soul a step or so ahead upon the path of spiritual unfoldment. We are journeying along towards the goal of heavenly happiness: dogged and handicapped, as we are, by burdens self-inflicted, and digressing and regressing from time to time, so that our progress is very much hindered. Happily, with God, all things are possible and the average, law-abiding person can be assured of the presence of many helping-hands to guide him on his way to that ultimate destination, the gate called, "Death", to which all must come.

The parable of the Virgins, (Ch 25) informs us that we should always be conscious of the follies and vanities of the world: that we should make an attempt to prepare ourselves for the future state: that we should not just ignore our obligations until death intervenes. Then it is too late to start again; to do our duty towards those who are dependent upon us.

The "Parable of the Talents", (Ch 24 v 14), commands us to make all possible use of the gifts which God has bestowed upon us, so that we may grow in virtue and good works. Verse 35 sees Jesus drawing the distinction between the righteous and the evil man, with the rewards to be given to both. It is not sufficient that we pay lip-service to God; that we profess to love God. Love to the Father can only be realized by an active and selfless devotion to the service of mankind: the Community of which we all form a part. "Love to the neighbor", is the actual fulfillment of "Love to the Lord".

The reward of the righteous is to be "Life Eternal"; that of the wicked, "Everlasting punishment". There is, in fact, no such thing as perpetual punishment for misdeeds performed during life. God, in His infinite love, has appointed ministering spirits to those who dwell in darkened conditions. With prayer and the spontaneous cry of the soul, these "Rescue bands" can often assist darkened, ignorant or unhappy spirits to commence progression from darkness to light.

"The people that walked in darkness have seen a great light!" (Isaiah Ch 9 v 2). The much-maligned Spiritualist meeting has often been the starting-place for the rescue of souls in distress, who by contact with the physical world are enabled to perceive those ministering spirits who are sent to help them. They are, thus, assisted in commencing the pathway of personal progression. This rescue work is an important aspect of the spiritual work. Whilst this may be true in certain respects, one could be excused for holding to the opinion that, no-matter how degraded one may become, there is always hope for change. The alternative view is pessimistic and fatalistic. It may even be inconsistent with the idea of God as Infinite Love. The door must always be said to be open and never closed.

One might consider the text, "Inasmuch as ye have done it unto one of the least of these my brethren, ye have done it unto me", (v40). The proposition here is of the value of the human soul and the responsibility, which we, as individuals, undertake whenever we commit an act of selfishness towards our fellow mortals. Likewise, it affirms the principle of service to others as the key to life.

Chapter 26 is a tender record of the events leading to the Crucifixion of Jesus. The anointing of Jesus by the woman with "precious ointment", considered by the Disciples to be a waste of a valuable commodity.

Judas Iscariot played an unenviable but, evidently, essential role in the subsequent events. One feels a measure of compassion for this man; one of the inner quorum and, like many people, not insensitive to good influences. However, for some reason he became alienated from Jesus and betrayed him to his enemies: probably obsessed by jealousy of either Jesus himself or the other disciples. His betrayal appears to have been pre-destined, as Jesus was evidently aware of what was to occur. Poor old Judas was in a "No-win" situation.

The Last Supper was an event regarded as of great significance within the Church; still celebrated in the Mass and Holy Communion. "This is my blood which is shed for many for the remission of sins". (v 28). Indeed, Jesus died as a sacrifice of innocence upon the altar of human pride and vainglory. This is not, necessarily, it is submitted, to suggest that his imminent departure from this world was to be a vicarious atonement for the sins of unborn generations of mankind. Men were to be drawn to a knowledge of God through his teaching and example, not merely by his crucifixion alone. The evidence of the resurrection was of far more significance than the fact of his crucifixion. It was the latter, in demonstration of the fact of the continuity of life beyond death, which elevated mankind from the status of a plaything to a creature of value in the created order of things.

Peter assured Jesus of his unswerving loyalty; not knowing that he would soon lose the courage of his convictions, (v 35). It was a reminder of the frailty of human resolution. How many sermons have been preached on this theme? How often do we all fall short of the mark and deny that which we know to be the truth: condemn outwardly that which we inwardly revere? In matters of belief, more than in anything else, we are cowardly and unwilling to be classified as freaks by our contemporaries. As previously noted, we live at a time when general apathy prevails, regarding religion, so that any person who could be considered to be in any degree religious is a member of the minority in most Western societies. In the sphere of Islam, fanaticism appears to be the order of the day. To what extent Muslims indulge in speculation regarding the form of Creation remains a mystery to the writer. Bigotry and ignorance seem to be the most prominent features of Islam to the infidel mind at the present time. The Salman Rushdi furore has done nothing for the image of Islam in the Western-world. There certainly appears to be much scope for reform amongst Muslims, who give the impression that they are centuries behind the Christian world in the matter of spiritual progression. I do not exclude the probability that there are many intensely spiritual Muslims, but like all quiet people they are rarely heard.

At this point in his life we catch a glimpse of Jesus the man. A "Man of Sorrows" indeed, and well acquainted with grief. He asked his Heavenly-Father to be relieved of the burden he was about to bear. "Let this cup pass from me". (Ch 26 v 39). Here was evidence of the essential humanity of Jesus: a man of God: innocent and gentle, yet destined to pass through the dark shadows of a cruel death: exposed to the brutality of a savage world. There was to be no escape from this sacrifice.

Peter's denial of Jesus merely reveals the fact that the Disciples were ordinary men, not particularly gifted with intellect. They were simple people, who were quick to recognize the spirituality of Jesus and who devoted their lives to his service. Under the pressure of despair; doubting and in fear for himself, Peter probably did deny *his links with Jesus. For the moment, the Disciples were scattered and discomfited. A denial of Jesus was one way of avoiding more trouble and Peter was not in a position to predict forthcoming events. It is natural that he should be reticent at such a time.*

It is not proposed to discuss, in detail, the trial and crucifixion of Jesus. Suffice it to say that the record is probably reasonable accurate, considering the absence of a contemporaneous and written account of the proceedings. Certain unusual phenomena were reported: darkness came over the land for three hours: the Veil of the Temple was torn: there was an Earthquake and strange visions of the dead were witnessed in the vicinity of Jerusalem. All these events would be interpreted as portents of doom. Stories such as these would be regarded as clearly pointing to the hand of the Deity at work in the affairs of Jesus of Nazareth.

The coming of the mother of Jesus and Mary Magdalene to the Garden was also the occasion for supernatural happenings. An earthquake was accompanied by a vision of an "Angel of the Lord", who told the women that Jesus had "Risen".

The Disciples are reported to have seen Jesus on several occasions, subsequent to his death and entombment. He commanded them to "Teach all Nations", baptizing them in the name of the Father, Son and Holy-Ghost.

The Gospel of Matthew ends rather abruptly, after relating the resurrection of Jesus. We are indebted to the other Gospels for a more detailed account of the events subsequent to the Crucifixion.

Faith and Belief

    I am the Bishop for Jesus' House of Jacob. The title "Bishop" means "overseer" - I am Jesus' housekeeper, I maintain his house. The title also, says that under human law, I can ordain others as ministers, if they have been called by God to do so. Also, I help others start churches that are for God.

    Jesus' House of Jacob is not a church but rather a Ministry for God. The son of Isaac, Jacob, as referred to in Genesis of the Bible, was the founder for the twelve Hebrew tribes. The word "tribes" did not mean different types of people but rather "people of different Religions of God." Now Jacob's House - Jesus' House of Jacob brings those twelve Religions, the true Religions of God back together again, not as one religion but as twelve Religions of God. For all religions as well as all people belong to Jesus' House of Jacob.

    I do not "preach" from the Old or New Testaments, the Torah or of the Islamic Religion. I give Messages from God and His Angels about life, and death, and His Kingdom, which cover all Religions of God. The Messages that I give came directly from the Angels of God. The first Angel that I met was the Angel Joleen, she introduced me to Gabrael, Michael and then to Jesus. Gee, I wonder why she never introduced Muhammad to me?

    Many "born again Christians" say that I am in communication with Satan because Satan can be deceitful and can present himself as God or God's Angels. But my answer to them is: in their Bible it says, asked the Angel that approaches you, if he is of God. For even Satan must tell you the truth, and also, we know the difference between right and wrong. So if an Angel tells you to do something that is wrong, then he is of Satan, and demand him to leave and he will.

After Jesus was murdered, his half brother, James, took up the position as the leader, (Bishop) over Jesus' Ministry. Then, Paul and Simon Peter headed toward Rome while preaching the "Good News" of Jesus' Death along the way.

Stop and think for a minute, how can anyone's death be Good News?

Most think that Simon Peter was the first leader, Bishop of the old Roman Church that is now known today as the Roman Catholic Church, but Simon Peter actually reported back to James in Jerusalem while Paul just kept preaching. Therefore, James was the first leader of the church after Jesus died.

When Simon Peter was crucified, he asked to be hung upside down because he was not as worthy as Jesus, thus he died on the cross upside down. He requested this because of the faith and belief that he held in Jesus being the Son of God.

Incidentally for the record, James was thrown to his death in 62AD.

Over the next few hundred years, people thought of Heaven as a great meal or dinner. And during this time, communal dinners or suppers were held in individual homes where the woman of the house led the Christian Services. Services were held this way so that the Roman Soldiers did not see them as being Christians Services and would not jail or kill the participants. But once again, Faith and Belief in Jesus and in God caused them to hold Services, even though they knew that if they were found out, they would be killed.

It was during the second hundred years after Jesus died that his Ministry, now called Christianity, took on the order and/or ranks as the Roman Empire, which has one person as the top with the Bishops and Deacons and others below. Also at this time, the Church stopped women from conducting and/or leading Services in their homes.

300 AD, the Roman Empire split in two parts - the east and the west and was falling apart.

Constantine was placed in charge of the area that we now call England. Constantine decided that he wanted to be the Emperor over the complete Roman Empire, and thought that he could pull it back together again. As he fought and won his battles across the Roman Empire, and while he was 13 miles outside Rome, and just before a battle at a bridge, he looked up and saw a cross on the sun, and heard a voice say, "You are to conquer under this sign." He immediately had his men paint crosses on their shields, and then, he flew a banner that contained a cross as they entered into the battle and won. He then, went on and defeated the eastern part of the Roman Empire under the cross, and thus, brought the western and eastern parts back together, re-uniting them once again, now Constantine was Emperor over the complete Roman Empire.

Constantine's newly found Faith if God and Jesus caused him to bring the Empire back together. And he adopted Christianity as the Religion of the Roman Empire. But soon, many new beliefs and doctrines on Christianity started to appear. And in 325 AD, his Faith and Belief in Jesus and God made him call Church leaders together to decide what day should be cerebrated as Easter. And it was during that meeting, the Trinity - the Father, Son and Holy Ghost being one, as we know it today was conceived. Also, they canonized the Christian Bible - they put together the Bible stories that are pretty well the same that are in the present day Christian Bible, but many other stories were changed while others were left out.

This meeting and finalizing - the canonizing of the Bible was to keep the east and west parts of the Roman Empire, the known world together under one Emperor - Constantine, and also to keep the Church in step with him. After this meeting, Constantine ordered 50 Bibles to be printed (written by hand) so that it could never be changed.

Later, Constantine moved the capital of Roman to the city that we know as Istanbul - Constantinople.

In 440 AD, Leo the First, was elected as the Bishop of Rome. He declared one Bishop over all the others and proclaimed his title as Pope. The title "Pope" came from the people calling the Bishop of their towns "Papa" and that was translated into "Pope."

With the capital of Rome moving east, left the western part of the Empire and the city of Rome to fend for themselves. And in 452

AD, after Rome had been sacked by many different groups, Attila the Hun camped near Rome and waited for daylight to sack and destroy Rome. Leo the First, walked upon the hillside to Attila the Hun's camp and there beside him appeared the Angels of Peter and Paul, both with swords in their hands.

The Angels said to Attila the Hun, "Do not enter Rome or you will be slain." The next morning Attila the Hun was gone.

The belief of Attila the Hun, one of history's most brutal warriors, one who killed his own brother to become ruler over his kingdom, him seeing the two Angels of Simon Peter and Paul, made him leave without a fight.

In the 700s, Muhammad came back from the desert and told his wife that he had been talking with God and that if he told anyone else, they would think he was insane. She persuaded him to tell others, and soon his Islamic Religion spread across part of the known world. After Muhammad's death, his followers began using the sword to convert people, for if they did not convert to the Islamic Religion, they would be killed.

Around 1,000 AD the Christian Crusades began because the Muslims had taken over Jerusalem and would not allow Christians or any people of other religions entry into the city. During this time in history, all Christians had to journey to Jerusalem at least once in their lives. Therefore, the Crusades were to liberate Jerusalem. And it was during the first Christian Crusade, many stories were told and recorded in Roman history, about Christian soldiers that were slain in battle, they would get back up and continued to fight. They won, and Christianity ruled over Jerusalem, but once again the Muslims fought back and recaptured the city. Then, over the next two hundreds years, the next five Crusades occurred. The 6th Crusade was the Children's Crusade, all but the first failed because only the first was for God, the other 5 were for man - the dog.

Let's move on in history to the 1,400s. At the age of 13, Joan of Arc received a message from the Angel Michael to re-unite the French and Charles VII. Her Faith in God caused her to lead an army and win many battles that proclaimed Charles VII as King of France. And that was all that she was instructed to do, but she thought that God wanted more and continued to fight on, but lost all the battles from that point on, and was burned at the stake on May 30th 1431.

Why did Joan fail?

If you refer back to the New Testament, Jesus is standing near a cliff and Satan is talking to him. Satan said something like, "Jump, your Father will save you."

Jesus replied, "I will not tempt God."

For years, I could not understand what "tempt" meant until the Angels explained it this way. Tempt means to coax, to persuade, but is still a demand and that is domination. And God will not allow anyone or anything to dominate Him. Therefore, when Joan of Arc continued to battle after her mission was completed, she was then trying to demand God's help. And that is exactly what many of us expect from our prayers.

But back to Joan of Arc, can you imagine how much Faith and Belief that Charles and the French people had in her and in God to allow her - an 18 or 19 year-old girl to lead their army into battle. And how much Faith she had in God to approach Charles with her plan! But after she fought and placed Charles on the throne, she continued to fight. But her job as ordined by God was to place Charles on the throne. Thus, she lost her battles and died on a stake because she continued to fight, was her self-domination, and not God's Will.

During 1912, C. Austin Miles wrote the words and music to "In The Garden" after experiencing a vision of Mary Magdelene weeping at Jesus' Tomb and when Mary saw Jesus standing, she knelt before him with arms outstretched and cried, "Rabboni," meaning "My Lord! My Master."

All these stories that I have just mentioned contained Faith and Belief by people throughout history. Their stories cannot be denied. Each one of them had visions and/or heard voices from Heaven telling them something that needed to done. Is it any different today?

During the first part of this year, I met a man who needed a heart transplant, but because he had asthma, the doctor had told him that he could not because of his lungs, for he would not make it through the operation. Now keep in mind, this man was treated for asthma most of his life and now he was 60 years old. This man told me that he wanted to live and asked me to pray for him. That night, in communication with the Angels, I said, "It is not my concern if this man gets a new heart or not for that is God's will, I only ask that he is placed on the list to receive a transplant." The next day, I told this man and his wife that I guaranteed that he would be placed on the list to receive a transplant, but I could not guarantee them that he would receive a new heart.

Within the week the doctor called this man back into his office and ran more tests, and came back and said, "You do not have asthma, and it was your heart that was building up fluids in your lungs instead."

This man then was placed on the list for a transplant, and within a few weeks this man received a transplanted heart. About two weeks after this man came home from the hospital, I told this man and his wife, "I guaranteed that you would be placed on the list. I did not say if you would receive a new organ that pumps blood throughout the body, for that is God's Will. And I could not guarantee if you would get a new heart, for that is up to you. When I said 'new heart' I meant a better outlook on life. As always, God was there when you needed Him. God opened His arms and helped you. God stands beside us always. Why must we think and call His name only when we are in trouble? If you have a new heart, you should forever think of God and speak of Him to others."

God cured this man's asthma as I had prayed for, but I do not know if this man has a new heart or not. This man died six weeks later because he did not take care of himself - he never "gave" himself a new outlook on life.

In the first minutes of July 19 of this year, I had another heart attack and went to the hospital where they performed heart catherization, using the balloon twice and implanting two stents. Afterwards, I found out it cost over 80,000 dollars. I did not have insurance. I thought, why did I go to the hospital, I should have stayed home and died. At that same time, a woman approached my wife, and said she would get my bill taken care of. Then, I realized why did I say those things about I should have died, Jesus had told me a year and half earlier, "I have stood beside you all of your life. I was there when you had your heart attack in 1992. I was there when you received the bypass in 1995, I shall always stand beside you and protect, guide and take care of you." And I remember I said to Jesus,

"But I am old and tired, what shall I do, what do I do when the bill collectors start beating at my door?" He replied, "Do as I once did, tell the people of the pains and hurts in your heart. My brother, do not worry about bill collectors, I will take care of you."

Even I, one who communicates and sees God's Angels had lost Faith for a while. Is it any wonder why others, who cannot see or hear God's Angels do not have faith?

Recently, in conversation with two men from the Lancaster Baptist Church, we discussed judging. I told them, "Daily we judge all things that we and others do."

They replied, "No, because we are not Jesus and therefore, we cannot judge anything."

Excuse me...daily we judge many things; what we will wear, how fast we drive, what to eat, and we should also judge how we treat others. You do not have to be Jesus to know the difference between right and wrong. But as He, daily, we judge things based on our faith and beliefs. You believe it will be cold today, so you wear warm clothing. You believe that the roadway is safe enough to drive at the posted speed limit. Our belief and faith should not be limited to the Bible and God, but is also directed toward all the things involved in our lives.

The faith and belief that I once had about the oil fields caused me to work in them for over 20 years, and yet, those experiences that I endured during those years brought me to this place. I am the person that I am because of the faiths and beliefs that I was inspired to learn have formed concepts and ideas that I now possess and those have turned and have brought me to this place that I am at today.

The Bibles are to give us and/or to strengthen our faith, but sometimes that may not be enough. You must look past the Bible to seeking your faith, for it is also written in the pages of history. There are thousands of stories that detail visions and/or communication with God's Angels in history, and if you look around, you will find many of your friends have had communications with His Angels, too. The proof of faith and belief are abound, seek them.

As we as individuals drift away from our families, either across the country or just across the town, we need to re-unite with family members, just as we have done today, and also, we need to re-unite with God, for our parents as God, stand beside us forever.

When family members call you, they are reconfirming a relationship with you, just as whenever God reveals Himself or His Angels to people, He is reconfirming - continuing His relationship with us. And this He has done many, many times since the writing of the Bible. We need not read the Bible to know that God is real and He cares, and Loves us. Just look around and you shall see Him, break open a piece of wood and He is there, overturn a rock and you shall find Him.

I try to inspire others to find God as the Angels inspired me. Therefore, the Angels call me a Guider, for I help others seek their god as I guide others toward the one God. It does not matter which god you follow as long as your religion says to love all and have no domination toward others, you will do fine.

Beautiful Front Lawns

I live in Lancaster, California, and it is a community that has been "on the grow" for the last 20 years. As I drive around Lancaster, I have noticed that besides all life being inner-woven, each individual life is inner-woven within itself.

The concept of all life being inner-woven as explained to me by God's Angels, is all life expressed actions and feelings (attitude) upon all other life, whereas one strand of life cannot be examined by itself to fully understand its progression as an individual life without examining all strands of life that has reflected upon it. Whereas, each individual's attitude reflects upon all things near to him, thus - "each individual life is inner-woven within itself."

Many of the homes in Lancaster are 10 to 20 years old, and I have noticed that most of these homeowners have not done anything with their backyards, for they have been left to nature and most are dirt and weeds, but yet, their front yards are green with grass, bushes and trees.

The front of these homes projects a vision of tranquillity in a community where all are happy and content with their lives, while their backyard indicates their true feelings of being lost and unconcerned about their inner-feelings.

Our true inner-feelings projects our attitude upon all other strands of life. Others in turn, project their feelings outward and their feelings will return to us, for all is inner-woven. We are one species of life, we are united as if we were one entity, but also, as individuals trying to survive, and yet, our earthly possessions and our attempts to have more than the next guy, has driven us into forgetting God and His desire of how we are to live together.

Concerning the people living in houses with no backyard, they indicate they are merely projecting a vision of splender and wealth to those who wish to see beautiful things. This is no different than the Catholic Churches projecting wonderful visions of their church and their religion as being of God while their sinful actions are unseen by the congregation, and hidden in their backyards.

We may be able to fool others, but we cannot fool God. He knows what is in your heart, for He has seen your backyard.

A while back, I learned that we need to help each other, but we should not continue helping the same person. One cannot expect Forgiveness from God over and over again for the same problem or sin, therefore, one must learn - repent from the past. And also, I have learned; "One can give a man a fish and feed him for the day, but if you teach him how to fish, you feed him forever." Therefore, if we continue to help the same person over and over again, we are only helping him to progress into projections of peace (displayed attitude of gratefulness), but if we inspire him to beautify his "backyard," we are helping him to seek his God and His love that is within him.

People have lost their faith and belief in God and in each other including themselves. But we cannot force faith and beliefs upon others for that is domination, and domination is against God. We can only inspire others through love as the Angels did not force God upon me, they inspired me to seek Him.

To inspire others to seek God, you must show and prove to them that He is a kind, gentle and a loving God.

Standing up in front of a congregation and preaching of His wrath, or condemning those who are not saved (in your opinion), or forcing your or your church's religious doctrines (that were designed by men to dominate others) upon them, will not inspire them to seek God.

Throughout the ages, people have been traumatized by the clergy that now most refuse to hear about God. To them, God is dead, for they see the clergy going against God's desires, and therefore, if the clergy, who speak of God, do not believe in Him, why should the congregation believe in Him?

So today instead of the people believing in God and following their religions, they project their beautiful front yards while hiding their backyards from view, for to them, it only matters what one sees instead of what one believes.

The Book of Gabreal Is Opened

And the Angel Jo said to me, "All people are God's Children. All are created equal and all are equal at birth. The difference of skin color does not make them different. The different languages they speak does not make them different. Disabilities do not make a difference. The difference in people comes from others who teach them throughout their lives.
"The land that they fight over was there before man walked upon the earth, they do not own it, it was a gift to all living things from God. The earth and the things that grow upon it are needed for life. There is plenty of room to grow things that are needed including livestock if the land is used properly, but the individual man's 'needs' dominates life, some have too much while others have none. It is not enough to help others with food and money alone; one must inspire others to raise them to a higher level. And yet, sometimes one should leave others to their own means in their pursuit of happiness.
"We are sadden whenever We see tragedies occur in life, even though We know what will happen because all is in the Master Plan, yet, all have their individual choices in life. We will not stop one from going what you may consider wrong, for that is also in the Master Plan. People are there to learn and experience through theirs and others experiences as they endure life.
"Around 32,000 people will die because of those airplanes

being directed by terrorist (in 9-11), and yet, the people who claim to be Americans cry out only for their fellow Americans. What happen to crying out for all humans that are daily put to death by terrorist and domination? Are they not human, too? We do not cry only for Americans dying, We cry for all who die under domination. And yet, all those who died were doing exactly what they wanted to do. They were not concerned about their own security; they thought terrorist could never strike in their land. How foolish to think they or their land is different from others. Mourn for the loss of a loved one, but cry forever for the ones who do not know God, for those are the dead. For all the dead did not perish in the destruction of those airplanes, many dead walk among you today."

Then, Jesus appeared and stood beside Jo, and He said to me, "You told them of things to come and those things have started to come to pass. You told of a time of somewhat calm in Israel, and then, all hell will break out, and Israel will become bigger in size than it was in the days of King David. Then you told them about the Israelis placing a buffer zone around Israel, they are presently doing that in Gaza, but you told them about a buffer zone that will someday surround Israel. You said, all people need to rally behind Israel in fighting terrorist or they will be fighting terrorist in their home lands, the United States have seen terrorist in their land, and have just begun to fight terrorist in their land, and now nations are indicating this rally against terrorist is here. You said, the true Islamic follower will fight with Israelis against terrorist. This too, has started.

"The righteous people of God will beat down the terrorist and a sort of peace will cover the world, but then, someday the terrorist will slowly become strong again and bring the people of the world to their knees, and just before the Israelis are en-slaved, all will end. For small nuclear weapons and larger nuclear weapons are on the horizon of time, but at different times as well as germ warfare will be used in the future, for man has released the beast of technology upon the earth. For the Book of Gabrael that is mentioned in the Book of Daniel has been opened by Jo. True believers will believe while non-believers and die hard born again Christians will not. But there is no stopping the Master Plan because it contains all individual's decisions, and all must play out for the experience, as God has proclaimed to men, but men then polluted His words with their ideas, thoughts and concepts, the same as they did with my life. My life was to demonstrate how to live among people, but men placed me above God. I did not say I was God; they polluted my words with their ideas, and placed me as a false god beside the Father. Therefore, many worship a false god. I did not 'come' to live to bring peace, I 'came' to bring turmoil, thus I gave people their individual choices."

And then, the Angel Gabrael appeared and stood on the other side of Jesus, and he said to me, "Most blessed is the child who 'knows' God without ever learning of Him."

As the Angel Gabrael finished saying the word "Him," I heard the word "Amen" echo around me. I looked passed the three Angels and around us, there I saw many Angels looking down upon us, and I knew that All in unison had confirmed the word, "Amen."

As They all vanished, I stood there in the silence, in the darkness under the star lit sky and alone in my backyard garden. I dropped my head and cried as I prayed to God.

Revelation

Revelation is not confined to any particular branch of the family of Mankind but is part of the daily life of all people. It forms an underlying and essential part of the life of Christians of all denominations as, indeed, the life of Jesus itself was a demonstration of the presence of the Holy Spirit at work in the affairs of Men. The Jewish history is full of references to the work of the Spirit. It is unfortunate that this principle is no-longer understood by the majority of men and women, as the Spiritual Communion is a source of much support and assistance to mankind. One has only to ask via the medium of prayer, to receive help and guidance throughout life's troublesome times. The Christian Church generally denies the reality of revelation today: (relying upon Paul's statement to the effect that "tongues shall cease and prophecy pass away", as conclusive authority for the cessation of the work of the Holy Spirit.) (See 1 Corr 13, v 8). Similarly, Muslims believe that Muhammad was the last and greatest Prophet.

Both these ideas are entirely misconceived. "Knowledge", of course, has increased since Paul's time and continues to multiply. Paul was undoubtedly visualizing the "coming end of all things", an event anticipated daily by the Jewish followers of Jesus.

There is one advantage accruing to the Hindu and the Buddhist. It is the idea that the wheel of life is turning inevitably in the direction of Union with Brahma. Implicit in this doctrine is the notion that all life forms have sprung from Brahma. There can be no conflict on this point between the writer and the proponents of the Eastern religions. Jesus himself is reported to have said, "I go unto my Father and to your Father: to my God and to your God". He draws no distinction between himself and other men and women, although he later states that, "I and the Father are One!" The meaning to be given to his statements depends upon the reader's view of Jesus himself. To a statement of "Union", with God, there can be no objection: as an exclusive claim, there could be great exception to the statements recorded in the Gospel of John. The writer's view is that at no time did Jesus claim precedence over other members of the Human Race or suggest that he was an exalted soul: far surpassing common mortals. That he was an enlightened soul, can not be denied, nor would one say that he was not sent into the world upon a Divinely-inspired mission. However, one would hesitate to enter into speculation as to his precise status. I am certain that he was an historical figure and an ordinary member of the human race.

Acceptance of the fact of the immortality of the Soul, necessarily leads to belief in the existence and presence of a Creator God. Personal immortality could hardly be conceived without the idea of a supervising and guiding hand. I am convinced of the validity of the doctrine of the Resurrection, as a basic fact of life. This event profoundly affected my views: leading to a sincere belief in the existence and ever-present Love of God. Obviously, if the individual personality survives the physical death, then "God" must exist. There can be no other possible explanation: mankind must be part and parcel of a much greater scheme than one can physically comprehend.

It is the idea of God as Infinite and Omnipresent Love, which is of supreme importance. It was the Prophet Isaiah, who first emphasized the notion of the "Concern" of the Creator for people: who demonstrated the relationship of God to Mankind as that of a Father to His children. This is a loving and dependent relationship, the concept of which is confirmed by sub-conscious and internal experiences of a mystical nature. T.E. Lawrence, when travelling the Arabian wilderness during the First World War, met an Arab Holy Man, at Wadi Rumm, who constantly repeated the words, "The love is from God and of God and to God". This, Lawrence states, was the only occasion on which he heard a Muslim mention "Love" as an attribute of Divinity and this from a man who, in the West, would be regarded as mad.

(See Seven Pillars of Wisdom, Ch.63 by T.E.Lawrence).

The statement is significant, as confirming the idea of the omnipresent Love of God: that love is essentially a Divine and Sacred attribute, issuing from the Creator throughout the Universe and returning in a constantly flowing, circular motion to the Godhead. Such an idea accords with the traditional teachings of Islamic Suffi's, whose philosophy is based on this principle.

It is through the medium of Divine Love that Mankind can approach its Creator. It is really possible for each and every individual to enter into a relationship with God, through the vehicle of prayer: expressed in terms of acknowledgement and gratitude for the gift of life and of the guidance and support, which is freely available to each and every person, regardless of situation or of status. The Creator's Love acknowledges no boundaries of race, colour or creed, for all are subject to the law of Universal Love. It is this Divine Love, which ameliorates and places in perspective all human activity. It finds its expression in a Divine compassion for the follies and weakness of Mankind.

Understanding The Book of Revelation

Before continuing your understanding of the Book of Revelation, you must first understand that the visions and/or communications that St. John had with God's Angels probably were consistent in the order that he documented them, but they are not in the correct order related to time as demonstrated by the first three vision or communication that you have read.

Part I occurred at that moment God's Angels first entered into John's life. John lived after the death of Jesus, and in Part I, Jesus asked John to write letters to the churches of the day.

For the encounter of Part II, John may have gone back or forward in time to witness the vision. The things and entities that he saw, were symbolic of the thoughts, concepts and ideas that humans had about God, and that He must be worshipped. They - the entities that St. John saw, were living their hells of worshipping God instead of enbracing Him.

In Part III, John went back in time to the minutes just after the death of Jesus. As John sees the One sitting on the throne, then Jesus entered into the vision as the symbolic Lamb. John saw entities convert to worshipping Jesus instead of Loving him as they enbraced God - the Father. And these including St. John lived their hells of worshipping Jesus instead of enbracing the Father and Loving the

Son.

Everything on The Other Side is Feelings of Experiences. There is no solid matter on The Other Side. You see experiences and feelings while ideas, concepts and thoughts are also seen symbolically.

The Other Side is either Heaven or Hell while the Light is Knowledge. When one enters The Other Side, one will be in that Heaven or Hell that he made during his life. If while on The Other Side, one goes to the Light, he will then have the Knowledge to remove his Hell or live in Heaven with the congregation of Angels that is God, forever. St. John travels into The Other Side did not take him to the Light.

God created eveything, and all that was created is equal. Not just man and woman, but ALL is equal. All is in balance with each other and the universe. God is nature, and nature takes care of itself; If one species dies off, nature replaces it with another or moves another into its place.

Angels in congregation is God. Each man and woman has a piece of God within them. No other thing has a part of God living within it, but all has a part of God within. God did not place a living part of Himself into all the living forms of life. God placed Himself in the life form that needed His help - HUMAN!

Human is the only life form that can and is destroying life, and the world and could destroy the universe.

Each human has been given the gift of Love from God, and God has given each the opportunity to chose His Love (Will) or to live as an animal who follows only the lust of the dog that tries to dominate all others and himself as a slave to earthly possessions.

We have been given the choice of Heaven or Hell, but humans will chose the feelings of animal life over God's Will, thus man being an animal is the Sin of man.

St. John chose to live his life worshipping Jesus, but Jesus said he did not want or wished to be worshipped. Therefore, St. John now lives in Hell as he did throughout his human life - worshipping someone - Jesus and not embracing the Father - God.

Embrace the Father who is Love. Do not worship Love. Embrace life. Do not worship life.

Christine J. Haven

Do not teach of Love, for you will inspire others to Love when they see your actions and feelings of Love.

The Book of Revelation, part I

After reading last week's Time Magazine and its cover story about the Bible and the Apocalypse, I decided to give you the true meanings of the Book of Revelation. But, please keep in mind that Christianity is only one of the many mansions in Heaven.

The Book of Revelation written by St. John is very similar to what is written in the Book of Daniel. Therefore, St. John may have seen the same things that Daniel saw or he may have merely copied Daniel's visions into his words, but this we will never know for sure, but we surely should understand that both men reported what they thought they saw. For each account of what was to come, was viewed symbolically for each as individuals, and each man interpreted his visions into words that were used and understood during that time of their lives.

I have learned through my visions and conversations with God's Angels, that we do not always receive things in their correct order, and Angels use vocabulary that we may not understand, and words that we cannot comprehend their meanings, and inasmuch, even the orders of events as described in Revelations are not accurate. This incorrectness of both occurred, the understanding of the words and events (location in time) because in this three-dimensional plane that we live in, we see and think of things as material and solid matter while the Angels speak of things as feelings and events are located in time. For feelings are things impressed upon Energy. (When Energy is expressed using a capital "E," the word "Energy" is referring to God.) When Angels speak of feelings, we should interpret their words as geographical locations and experiences that include people. But feelings have location in time and this is merely a part of the Angels communications that St. John and Daniel could not conceive.

We need to discuss one more item about the writings referred to as the Book of Revelation before I tell you the true story. In the last part of the Book, St. John said; "And if any man shall take away from the words of the book of this prophecy, God shall take away his part out of the book of life, and out of the holy city, and from the things which are written in this book." That is truly ignorant to think that one alone communicates with God's Angels, and that one alone understands exactly the meanings of words spoken by God's Angels. Of course, His Angels have communicated with humans many times throughout history and He will continue His communications long after I am gone. Therefore, I know that those He communicates with in the future shall view things differently than I have, but while our visions may have been the same.

And now lets get into the true Book of Revelation. The Book begins its story from the first second of time thus, when time began so did Revelation. Keep in mind that St. John wrote of things that he saw in the order that he viewed them. Therefore, when we read Revelations we in-vision these things happening at the end of time and in the order that he wrote them, but in reality, they started to happen from the first second of time and continued throughout time until the end of time. For when one is out of body, one can go back to review the past, and then, go forward into the future to review what is going to occur, but one can only inter-act in the present time.

And Saint John heard someone say, "Write down what you see, and send it to the seven churches: Ephesus, Smyrna, Pergamum, Thyatira, Sardis, Philadelphia and Laodicea."

When John looked around to see who was speaking, he saw many lights of knowledge as if they were candles held within seven golden candlesticks, but the candlestands (candlesticks) were the keepers of the knowledge (the church); and in the midst of them stood a figure of a person. This figure appeared wise with knowledge for he had white hair while his eyes resembled a burning fire by the intellignece they held, his feet resembled highly polished brass that was planted firmly on solid ground, and his voice sounded gentle. This person seemed to be dressed in a garment that appeared as beautiful as gold. In his right hand he held many words of Love, and out of his mouth came words that John knew were loving and yet, could be cutting while his face shined with life as if he was the sun, and he stood tall and full of strength.

The Angel said to John, "Fear not for I am the first and the last. I am the one that once lived and died, but look, I appear in front of you now.

"Write down the things that you see, for they are the things that have been, the things that are presently occurring and the things that will come.

"The seven golden candlesticks that you saw surrounding me represent the knowledge of the seven churches while the seven stars in my hand are seven Angels of Love, one I send for each of the seven churches while the candlestands also represent the church. The Angels stand symbolically for my feelings of the church and are the things that the churches first followed, thus they were the foundation to the churches.

"Write to the church of Ephesus about its foundation and tell them these are the things that the one who holds the seven stars in his right hand and who stands in the mist of the seven candlesticks has said.

"I know of your work and labor, and I know of your patience, and how you cannot bear those who are evil. You have judged all that claim they are apostles, and you have found both - the true apostles and the ones who are not apostles as liars. And you have endured and still have patience. You have worked in my name's sake and did not tire. Nevertheless, I have something against you because you have left my first love - our Father. Remember where you have fallen from and repent, and return to the work for Him or I will quickly return and remove your candlestick.

"You hate the Nicolaitanes because of their deeds that I also dislike, but I love all the people, for they are also God's children. And if you are capable to understand, then listen to me, for if you overcome temptation you will live forever in Heaven with our Father.

"Anyone who is willing to hear should listen to the Spirit of my words, and understand what the Spirit is saying to the churches. Everyone who is victorious will live in paradise with the Father.

"And to the church in Smyrna write about its foundation and tell them; The one who is first and the last, which was dead but now lives has said, I know your work, tribulation and poverty, but you are rich in goodness. And I know the blasphemy of them that say they are Jews, and are not, for they are the vessels of Satan.

"Fear none of the things which you may suffer. Behold, evil thoughts will cast some of you into prison and you might be tried, and you will have tribulation, but be faithful into death and I will give you a Home with the Father.

"He that can hear, let him listen to the Spirit of my words, and all that I have said to the church, for he that overcome death shall not be hurt during the end of time."

"Write a letter to the church in Pergamos about its foundation and tell them it comes from the one who has words like a sharp two-edged sword.

"I know that you live in a city where the great throne of Satan was once located, and yet, you remain loyal to me. And you have refused to deny me even when Antipas, my faithful witness, was martyred among you by Satan followers. And yet, I have a few things against you. For you tolerated those who are like the Balaam, who showed Balak how to trip up the people of Israel. He taught them to worship idols and to listen to words not of God and have committed sexual sins. In the same way, you have some Nicolaitanes among you - people who follow the same teachings and commit the same sins. Repent or I will quickly return destroying them with words from my mouth.

"Anyone who is willing to hear should listen to the Spirit of my words, and understand what I am saying to the church. Everyone who is victorious will live forever in Heaven with the Father. For I will give him redemption over his sins, for I will erase his sins and grant him a new life that does not contain the things that he repented from, for he shall have a new name and no man shall know nothing of his old life.

"And to the church of Thyatira tell them of their foundation, and tell them the Son of God with fire in his eyes and with feet that looked like polished brass said, I know your works, charity, services, faith and patience, and your last works are better than your first.

"Notwithstanding, I have a few things against you because you still follow Jezebal, who called herself a prophetess and she taught her lies and she seduced my servants to commit fornication with her words. I gave her time to repent of her fornication, but she did not. I will banish her, and those who have committed adultery with her shall have great tribulation unless they repent from their deeds. And I will kill the children that follow her, and all the churches shall know that I am He which searches in the hearts of humans, for I will give unto each according to the words that each have preached.

"But to you, and the rest in Thyatira I say, many of you do not follow Jezebal or her doctrines which contains Satan. They need not be afraid of what they are about to suffer. The Devil will throw some of them into prison and put many to the test. They will be persecuted, but remain faithful even when facing death, and unto them I will give everlasting life.

"Anyone who is willing to hear should listen to the Spirit of my words, and understand what I am saying to the church. For whoever is victorious will not be hurt during the end of time.

"And write to the church in Sardis about their foundation and tell them He that holds the seven Spirits of God has said, I know their works for I am the one with the name of the one that lives but once was dead.

"Be watchful and strengthen the things before they die because they are ready to die for I have not found your work perfect before God. Therefore remember, how you once received and heard the word of God, and hold fast to it and repent. For if you do not watch, I will come to you as a thief, and you shall not know when I will come.

"You have a few in Sardis that have not aligned their beliefs with fools and they shall walk with me dressed in white, for they are worthy. He that overcome, shall be clothed in white raiment and I will not blot out his name out of the book of life, and I will confess his name before my Father and His Angels. He should listen to the Spirit of my words if he has ears to do so.

"And write a letter to the church in Philadelphia and tell them of their foundation. Tell them that I, the one who is Holy and True, and I am the one who holds the key of David has opened the door that no man can close, and I shut the door that no man can open. And I said, I know your works, and behold I have set before you an open door, and no man can shut it, and the door that I have shut, no man can open because you have little strength. But, you have kept my name and have not denied it.

"Behold I will make a synagogue for those who follow Satan, for they say they are Jews, but are not because they lie. But I will come and they will worship at my feet, and they will know that I still love them.

"Because you have kept the word of my patience, I will keep you from the hour of temptation which shall come upon the earth, to try those who live upon the earth. I will come quickly so hold tight onto your beliefs so that no man shall steal your wealth.

"And for he that overcomes will live forever in the Kingdom of the Father. He who has ears should listen to the Spirit of my words.

"Write this letter to the church in Laodicea. This is the message from the one who is the Amen - the faithful and true witness, the ruler of God's Creation.

"I know all the things you do, that you are neither hot or cold. I wish you were one of the other! But since you are like lukewarm water, I will spit you out of my mouth!

"You say, 'I am rich. I have everything I want. I don't need a thing!' And you don't realize that you are wretched and miserable and poor and blind and naked. 'I advise you to buy gold for me - gold that has been purified by fire. Then you will be rich. And also buy white garments so you will not be ashamed by your nakeness. And buy ointment for your eyes so you will be able to see.'

"I am the one who corrects and disciplines everyone I love. Be diligent and turn from your indifference.

"Look Here I stand at the door and knock. If you hear me calling and open the door, I will come in, and we will share a meal as friends. I will invite everyone who is victorious to sit with me on my throne, just as I was victorious and sat with the Father on His throne. Anyone who is willing to hear should listen to the Spirit, and understand what the Spirit is saying to the churches."

The Book of Revelation, part II

I heard a voice and looked up as the voice said unto me, "Come up here, and I will show you what has happened, what is happening and what must happen."

I closed my eyes and rose up out of my body. Soon, I saw a wonderful place in Heaven as if it were a throne and on this throne sat someone, but I did not know who. He was brilliant as if He were gemstones - jasper and carnelian, and a glow of Love as if emeralds encircled His throne. A great number of smaller wonderful places as if thrones surrounded Him, and on each sat someone who worshipped Him, but did not embrace Him. They were are clothed in white and it looked like gold crowns upon their heads.

And from the throne cames flashes of God's wrath as thunder and lightning. And in front of the throne were seven churches represented by seven lampstands, and a top of each stand I could see the knowledge of Light they prossessed. In front on the throne floated a round sphere of Love as a shiny sea of glass that sparkled like cystral.

In the center and around the throne were some Entities, each covered with eyes, front and back, so they could all see what is happening in the world. The first of these Entities had the form of a lion; the second resembled an ox; the third had a human face; and the fourth had the form of an eagle with wings spread out as though in flight. Each of these Entities had six wings, and their wings were covered with eyes, inside and out. For these Entities were symobic for my understanding that God's Love and His wrath is always near and He is forever watching over us. Day after day and night after night they kept on saying, "Holy, Holy, Holy is the Lord God Almighty - the one who always was, who is and who is still to come."

    Whenever the Entities gave glory and honor and thanks to the one sitting on the throne, the one who lives forever and ever, the many fall down and worship the one who lives forever and ever. And they lay their crowns before the throne and say, "You are worthy, O Lord our God, to receive glory and honor and power. For you created everything, and it is for your pleasure that they exist and were created." For the many are living their Hells of worshipping Him instead of embracing Him.

The Book of Revelation, part III

Then in another vision, John saw in the right hand of him that sat on the throne a book, and John knew its pages were covered with writing and he could see the writing on its back cover, and this book was sealed with some seals.

He saw a strong Angel proclaiming with a loud voice, "Who is worthy to open this book, and to loosen the seals thereof?"

No man in Heaven, nor in the earth, neither under the earth, was able to open the book, neither to look upon it.

And one of the elders who lived in Hell because he worshipped Him who sat upon the throne instead of embracing Him, said to John, "Weep not: behold, the Lion of the tribe of Juda, the Root of David, has prevailed to open the book, and to loosen its seals."

And John saw that in the midst of the throne, and the beastly concepts, and in the midst of those elders who worshipped the one who sat upon the throne instead of embracing Him, stood one whose life was like a lamb, and he had been as if had been slain, this man had seven horns and seven eyes, which were symbolic for the seven spirits of God that were sent forth upon the world during the time before the Lamb - Jesus lived.

And he - the slain Lamb, came and took the book out of the hand of He who sits upon the throne.

And when he had taken the book, the beast and those who live their hell of worship, fell down and began to worship the slain Lamb who now held the book, and the sounds of love and prayers flowed from them to the slain Lamb as they began to sing a new song, saying "You are worthy to take the book, and to open the seals thereof: for you were murdered and have redeemed us to God by the blood out of every kinder, and tongue, and people, and nation. And you have made us into like our Gods - Kings and Preist: and we shall reign on the earth."

And John stood still as he heard the voice of Angels that surrrounded the throne, and the beast, and the elders: and the number was many, as they all said together: "Worthy is the Lamb that was slain to receive power, and riches, and wisdom, and strength, and honor, and glory, and blessings."

Every creature - Entity that is in Heaven, and on earth, and under the earth, and such as are in the sea, and all that are in them, heard John saying, "Blessing, and honor, and glory, and power, be unto Him that sit upon the throne, and unto the Lamb forever." And all those who lived their hell of worshipping Him dwell in their hells forever.

The Book of Revelation, part IV

Then John saw a scroll in the right hand of the one who was sitting on the throne. There was writing on the outside and on the inside of the scroll, and it was sealed with many seals. The seals were symbolic for the Angels (concepts) of the different religions of God that had spread around the world from the dawn of time until the end of time, and many of these religions had been forgotten in time, but their Heavens and Hells still remained on Entities of The Other Side as Hells for all religions are man-made religions and place Hells upon their followers.

Then he saw a strong Angel (one who glowed with the Knowledge of God), who shouted with a loud voice: "Who is worthy to break the seals on this scroll and unroll it?" But no one in Heaven or on earth or under the earth was able to open the scroll and read it.

Then John wept because no one could be found who was worthy. But one of the elders said to him, "Stop weeping! Look, the lion of the tribe of Judah, the heir to David's throne, has conquered. He is worthy to open the scroll and break its many seals."

John looked and saw Jesus standing between the throne and the Entities and the elders who lived their hell of worshipping Jesus instead of embracing God. Jesus stepped forward and took the scroll from the one sitting on the throne who held the scroll in his right hand. And as Jesus took the scroll the Entity beast and the elders fell down and praised him. And they sang a new song that embraced Jesus and God. And John heard many Angels abound in Heaven saying in a loud voice, "Worthy is the Lamb that was slain to receive power, and riches, and wisdom, and strength, and honor, and glory unto the Lamb forever."

And many creatures in Heaven, and on earth laid honor upon Jesus. And the Entity beast and the elders embraced Jesus and God.

Then John saw Jesus open one of the seals, and he heard as if many voices were saying, "Come and see." And John saw a white horse with its rider who carried a bow, and a crown was given to him and he with forth to conquer the thoughts of men.

Then Jesus opened the second seal, and John saw another horse that was red, and power was given to its rider to take the peace away from the world, and to aid those to kill one another as if they carried the great sword of God.

As Jesus opened the third seal, John saw a black horse, and he that sit upon this horse held a balance in his hand. He was sent unto the world to balance the evil and the good of God.

And when Jesus opened the forth seal, John saw a pale color horse, and its rider was death, and Hell followed him.

The power to kill were given to each over one-forth of the world, to kill by the sword, and by hunger, and by death of disease, and by the wild animals of the earth.

And when Jesus opened the fifth seal, John saw a congregation of Souls who were slain for the word of God. And they cried in a loud voice, "Do not judge those who now live on the world nor avenge our deaths on those who dwell on earth." And they were blessed and went into the Light of God's Knowledge and recieved their white robes that are symbolic of the Love of the Congregation - God.

When Jesus opened the sixth seal, John saw a great earthquake, and the sky became black and he could not see the sun, and the moon's color turned to red because of the dust that rose from the ground. And many things fell from the sky, and everything on earth shook and fell down. And every mountain and island moved from the spot from which it had sat. And all the living on the earth tried to hide from what they themselves had released upon the earth.

And John saw four Angels standing at the bottom four corners of the world. And he saw another Angel accend from the Light to the top above the world, and this Angel sealed the world with the words of God so that there was no escape from the Father. Then in a loud voice the four Angels at the bottom four corners said, "Do not harm the world, nor the seas, nor the trees. And they sealed upon the earth the evils of Satan as the righteous were preparing to leave as Jesus lead God's Angels to retrive the righteous to God's Light.

As John watched, he saw great multitude standing in front of the one who sat on the throne as He judged them. They cried together in a loud voice, "Salvation, Salvation please Father and Jesus." And all the Angels that surrounded the throne and Jesus fell down upon their knees and worshipped God instead of embracing Him, for they did not have God's Knowledge and now had sealed their fate of Hell of worship instead of embracing the Congregation of the Father.

And when Jesus opened the seventh seal, at first there was silence, and then John saw seven Angels standing in front of the throne and all had trumpets which they began to blow. And another Angel carrying a golden censer appeared in front of them and the throne. As the Angels blew their trumpets hail and fire fell upon the earth, and one third of the trees were burnt up as thunder, and lightning, and earthquakes covered the world.

Then the mountains began to burn and fire ran into the seas as the waters became unusable as if it were blood because many of the sea creatures and ships were dead and polluted the waters. Then a great star fell from the the sky and it destroyed one-third of the drinking water of the rivers and fountains. Then one-third of the sun became dark and day light shone only one-third of the day. Then John heard an Angel saying, "Woe, woe to the inhabiters of the earth, you have yet to repent. Repent! Repent!" Then an Angel who held the keys to Hell came forward and opened the pits of Hell, and the skies were filled with darkness and smoke as locusts came out of the pits of Hell. And God commanded the locusts not to harm the grass, nor the trees, nor any green thing, but only the people who refused the Knowledge of God.

Then John saw the door to Heaven (the Light) close as a multitude of Angels accended to earth, and they destroyed those who refused God's Love.

The Book of Revelation, part V

And in his next vision, John symbolically saw a woman that appeared to be clothed in something as bright as the sun, and it seemed as if she were standing on or above the moon, and upon her head a crown of many stars. She was pregnant and preparing to give birth as she cried out in pain.

Then John saw a red dragon that was symbolic for the many the thoughts of both good and evil, and each thought had its only head and its own horns, and their own crown upon its heads. The heads stood for the intelligence to comprehend while its horns stood for the evil that the heads contained.

And his tail swung and brought down a third of the stars unto the earth. And the dragon stood before the woman and devoured the newly born child - this was symbolic for the evil of men taking from the meek (the woman) the new life that which she gave birth to. The one-third of stars that fell to earth were symbolic for the one-third of all life that the evil of men has taken from the start of time until the end of time.

Then the newly born child, which was now evil instead of good, came forward to rule all nations with a rod of steel (the child is the evil of man) to control all people of the world in many ways. Then the woman ran away to a secret place where God would join her, and there she would feast in the Knoweldge of God for a long time.

Then the part of Jesus that is instilled in Michael and Michael's Angels (the part of Michael that is in all Angels) fought and defeated the dragon that stood symbolically for all evil, and evil was cast out of the Heavens that dwells in people's minds.

Then John heard a loud voice saying, "Now is Salvation, and strength, and the Kingdom of God, and the power of Christ, for the accuser (evil ones) was our brothers who are now cast out, which accused those who believed in God day and night. They came to God through many ways - by the beliefs in the Lamb, and Muhammad, and many others, and by the words of their testimony, and they loved not their lives unto the death. Therefore, rejoice, you in Heavens - you that dwell in them. Woe to the inhabiters of the earth - the ones who cannot accept God, for the evil comes down upon you, you see the Wrath, and you know you time is short."

And when the dragon of evil realized that he now controlled the world, he persecuted the innocent and evil alike. And John saw the woman as if she was given wings so that she could return to the secert place of God's Knwoledge so she did not have to see the wrath of God that was soon coming to the dragon of evil of the world. And the dragon tried to stop the woman but the earth (not the world) helped her flee the dragon.

Then, in Heaven - the Light, the Knowledge of God was open, and His Angels could be seen, as lightning flashed, thunder crashed, and roared; there was a great hailstorm, and the world (not the Earth) was shaken by a (one) mighty earthquake.

(When visualizing The Other Side, or the Light - God's Knowldge, or Heaven you will see thoughts, ideas and concepts as ojects and people. The dragon with its many heads were symbolic to St. John for evils. The heads represented the thinking minds of men while the dragon represented the evil thoughts of control over others. The "seven" heads could stand for the cycle, or the completion of a given time period, or just merely stand for many. We cannot truly know how or what St. John was thinking at the time of his visions, but for sure the beast, or creatures, or demons, or ugly things or bad or mean people that he conceived as evil and bad things - thoughts ideas and concepts. And while good things - thoughts, ideas and concepts are represented by a mother giving birth, Angels or other things we as humans consider good and nice.

(The vision of the mother and the dragon represented the cycle of this time. While the mother gave birth to life, the evil thoughts of men made countries that controlled the majority. And also, many of St. John's communications - visions were of the same event, but viewed from different perspectives and directions.

(God made everything, that includes what we consider bad and evil. He could have destroyed the bad and evil, but then we would not be able to judge good against evil, and could not fully understand or decide our individual direction of life of what we consider as good or bad, or what is righteous or evil. Therefore, there is no evil in God. But evil can be found in individuals' Heavens. We as humans judge what is good or bad and what is righteous or evil.

(At the end of this cycle of time, God will destroy what He considers evil and bad, if He wishes too. We cannot dicate to God what to judge or how to judge it. I have the understanding from God's Angels that He will destroy our evil and bad actions toward others at the end of time. Therefore, if your life has been filled with bad actions towards others, your life will be erased from this cycle of life, and therefore, it is to your best concern if you repent from your bad or evil thoughts from the past - erase them from your righteous thinking, but remember them so that you do not do them again.)

The Book of Revelation, part VI

(The first part of this vision that John was shown were the events in history before the birth of Jesus, while the second part of his vision showed him things that happened during the life of Jesus, and his next vision, showed him the end of time.)

And then John visualized himself standing on a sandy beach with a sea that spread out before him, and he saw a beast rise up out of the sea, having ten horns upon its head, the there were ten crowns upon the horns, while the horns symbolized the blasphemies against God, and the crowns stood for the thoughts of men against God.

The beast that he saw was something like a leopard, but its feet were the feet of a bear, and its mouth was that of a lion; and the dragon gave him power, and a seat of great authority over the thoughts of the world.

Then John saw its head that looked as if it were wounded or it had been killed by the power of God.

And many people worshipped the dragon that gave power to the beast; and they worshipped the beast saying, "Who is like unto the beast? Who is able to make war within him?"

And the beast began to speak many blasphemies; and power was given to him to continue speaking for a long time. And power was given to him to make war against the Angels, and to have power over them, and his power was given to all people, and to all nations in all tongues to speak his blasphemies against the Father.

And all that lived on earth worshipped him, these are the ones whose names are not written into the book of life.

If any man have an ear, let him listen: "He that dominate others shall be dominated, and he that kills shall be killed, for there is patience in the faith of all the Angels.

(Second part of vision.)

Then, John saw another beast rise up out of the sea, and he had two horns like the lamb. The horns represented love of men and of God. And he spoke as strongly as the dragon. And his words removed all power from the beast, and his words cleansed those who worshipped the beast. And Jesus did wonders in front of men, and he had the power to give Life to the beast and those who worshipped the beast, once they had repented from their past thoughts.

And He (Jesus) caused all that do not follw him to receive the mark upon their hands and foreheads. (The mark is symbolic for the thoughts, ideas and concepts that are against God.)

(Another vision)

Then in the next vision, John saw a lamb (someone who was as kindofheart as Jesus but not Jesus, stood on the mount of Judaism, and with him stood many that carried the Father's name in their thoughts as if you could see the Father's name written on their foreheads.

And John heard a voice from Heaven so loud as if it were thunder, and so gentle as if it were running spring water, the voice sung a new song before the throne, no living human could learn the new song, for only those who now lived in Heaven could sing this new song. These were the first fuirts from the Father and the Son, but not the last fruits to come from the Knowledge of this new song, for they come without fault before the throne.

And then, John saw another Angel fly out of Heaven, who carried the everlasting true gospel to preach unto them that dwell on the earth. Saying in a loud voice, "Fear not God, but give Him glory, for the hour of Judgment has come. And embrace Him who has made the earth, and the seas, and the fountains of water."

And there followed another Angel, saying, "Babylon is fallen, its blasphemies has fallen because she made all nations believe in her religions."

And a third Angel followed them, and saying, "If any man worships the beast and his image, and receive his mark in his thoughts, or on his hand, the same shall receive the wrath of God, which is poured out without mixture into the cup of indignation; he shall be tormented with fire and brimstone in the presence of the Holy Angels, and in the presence of the Lamb. Here are the patience of the Angels: they keep the Commandments of God, and the faith in Jesus, the Son of God."

And John heard a voice from Heaven saying unto him, "Write, blessed are the dead which die for God from henceforth: Yea, said the Spirit, that they may rest from their labor as their works still follow them"

And John looked down and saw a white cloud, and upon that cloud one sat who looked like the son of man, having on his head a golden crown, and in his hand a sharp sickle to harvest the Souls. (Jesus, the Son of God - Love. The son of man - evil thoughts, ideas and concepts.)

And another Angel appeared out of a temple and said, "Thrust in your sickle, and reap: for the time has come for you to reap; for the harvest of the earth is ripe." And he that sat upon the cloud thrust his sickle into the earth, and many evil doers were reaped from the earth.

And another Angel appeared out of the temple who also had a sickle, then another Angel came out of the altar, which had power over fire, and he cried, "Thrust in your sickle, and gather the clusters of the Souls of the earth; for her evilness are many."

And the Angel thrust his sickle to the earth, and gathered the evilness, and cast them into God's wrath, and their blood ran down over the earth to a great depth.

The Book of Revelation, part VII

Then John looked into Heaven and saw what resembled a temple and tabernacle of the testimony in Heaven.

And seven Angels came out of the temple, all having plagues, and clothed in pure and white linen, and all having their breast girded with golden girdles. (He saw some concepts - Angels, that were covered fully of righteous of God, but they wore breast plates of good things as considered by humans.)

And one of the beast of evil gave to these Angels some vials full of God's wrath. And the temple was full of the Knowledge of God, and from His Knowldge came, "That no man is able to enter into the temple until the seven Angels missions were fulfilled."

John heard a voice from the temple say, "Go your way, and pour out the vials of God's wrath upon the earth."

And the first Angel went forth and poured his vial upon the earth; and sores that represented evil done to others appeared upon the men who wore the mark because they worshipped the images of God. (Those who follow religions that worship icons and images of God, Jesus and Saints.)

And the second Angel went forth and poured his vial upon the seas, and they became as poisonous as blood to drink, and every living thing in the seas died.

And the third Angel poured his vial upon the rivers and

springs of water, and they too became as if blood.

And John heard the voice of the energy of water say, "God is Great. Oh God, which is, which was, and which shall always be because You have judged. For they have shed the blood of Saints and Prophets, and You now have given them blood to drink because the Saints and Prophets were not worthy."

And John heard another voice say, "Even so, God, true and righteous are your judgments."

Then the fourth Angel poured out his vial upon the sun; and power was given to him to scorch men with fire. And men were scorched with great heat, and they blasphemed the name of God, and the repented not to give him power. (These men turned away from their righteous thinking of God to thinking evil of God - they refused God.)

And the fifth Angel poured his vial upon the idea of the beast and destoryed his kingdom; for his kingdom was full of darkness, and those who dwelled in the beast's kingdom gnawed their tongues in pain.

And the sixth Angel poured his vial upon a great river; and the water thereof dried up for the way of the king from the east would be prepared.

And then John saw three evil thoughts working miracles that went forth to the kings of the earth and the complete world, to gather the kings and their warriors to the battle of that great Day of the end of Time. (The word "earth" when used is used to describe the things that are of man- evilness. The word "world" when used is used to describe the concept of things of righteousness.)

Then the Lamb (Jesus) appeared and He said, "Behold, I come like a thief. Blessed is he that watched over his life, and kept his clothing intact unless he walked naked and they saw his shame." ("Blessed" is he that lay his self-righteous feeling aside and live a life for God without worrying about what others do and think.)

And He, Jesus, the one who is the concept of Christianity, but Christianity is not His because it is corrupted by man, gathered the kings and their warriors into a place called Armageddon, this is the dividing point of the Juda and Islamic religions, which is the place in time and geographic location where Abraham threw Ishmael out of his life.

(The three major religions of the world - Juda and Christianity fighting against Islam at the place of their beginning.)

And the seventh Angel poured out his vial into the air; and there came a great voice out of the temple of Heaven, and from the throne, saying, "It is done." (The beginning of the End.)

And there were many voices, and thunder, and lightning, and eartquakes, such as was not since the dawn of time. And the great city Jerusalem was divided into three parts, one part - Jewish, One part - for the Christians and one part for the Muslims, and the city of nations fell: and the concepts considered to be as great Babylon (evilness) came into remembrance before God, to give her cup of wine of the firceness of His wrath.

And every island in the oceans washed away.

And there fell upon men a great hail storm out of Heaven (sky), every hail stone weighed about a telent, and men blasphemed God because of the plague of the hail, for the hail storm was exceedingly great.

The Book of Revelation, part VIII

Before we continue with understanding the Book of Revelations, I wish to say something about the 9-11 year and our fighting terrorists.

Yes, it was a sad day when terrorists destroyed the twin towers and killed all the people who were on board the airplanes and those who were inside the buildings, but all those people were doing exactly what they wanted to do. No one forced them into the planes or into the buildings. We cannot and should not blame ourselves or our governement for what happened.

But, as this the first 9-11 year comes to an end, I reflected back over the events that have occurred over this year and I see bin laden and his terrorists have won; he has put fear in our hearts and he has cost us billions of dollars. He went after the financial part of the U.S. and won by making us fight a war on his "grounds."

The terrorists of the world are known to hit and then wait and hit again, but we continue to watch for them to hit us each and everyday. Just look at the way the terrorist fight the Israelis, they use suicide bombers and attack buses. It is small attacks that kill 20 or so people, but it works to keep fear and terror in the hearts of the Israelis people. This is where we should be looking for terrorists and their attacks.

President Bush is using the same idea that Hitler used that brought the Germans together to fight in WWII, a common enemy.

Hitler used the Jews as their common enemy, Bush is using terrorists - Muslims. Bush, a "Die hard Born again Christian" is wanting the world to convert to his religion. He places Christian demand upon Arafat, but Arafat is a Muslim and follows the Islamic Laws. He cannot follow Christianity's laws and still be a Muslim.

Now President Bush is telling the world that "he" must bring down Hussein because Hussein is working with bin Laden and the Al Qaeda. If that was true, weapons of mass distruction would have been used in the U.S. by now. They could have easliy have brought them in before 9-11 and could still bring them in today. President Bush has found our common enemy - fear, and now he focuses on his enemy (those who do not worship his God) and has made his enemy ours.

We have many wars ahead of us, for now we are committed to fight a Christian and Muslim War. And when this war grows strong, China with sucker punch us in our homeland.

And now, back to understanding the Book of Revelation.

Then the Angel who had given the vials to the seven Angels, came to John and said, "Come, I will show you the Great Judgment of the whore (the energy of evil that brought forth - gave birth to the evil in concepts, ideas and thoughts) that sits upon many waters. (The many waters is the concepts, ideas and thoughts of man). And whom the kings of the earth have committed fornication, and the inhabitants of the earth that have enjoyed her fornication."

So the Angel carried John away in spirit. And John saw a woman sitting upon a coloured beast, full of names of blasphemy; having many heads and many horns. And the woman was dressed in many colours and decked with gold and precious stones and pearls, and had a golden cup in her hand that was full of evilness.

And into her thoughts John saw things as though it was written upon her forehead, MYSTERY, BABYLON THE GREAT, THE MOTHER OF HARLOTS AND ABOMINATIONS OF THE EARTH.

And John saw her as if she was drunk from the blood of the Saints, and blood of the martyrs of Jesus that she had caused to die, and John wondered with great admiration.

And the Angel said, "Why do you marvel at her sight? I will tell you the mystery of this woman, and of the beast that carries her.

The beast that you saw was, and is not; and shall not ascend out of the bottomless pit of evil thoughts, and go into perdition: and they that dwell on the earth shall wonder, whose names were not written in the Book of Life from the foundation of the world - righteous thinking and concepts, when they hold the beast that was, and is no, and yet is.

"And here is the mind that contains the Knowledge of God which is wisdom, but yet refused Him. The many heads of the beast are the natural state of things that reach for God, and they also represent the many kings; some have fallen, and one is with the Knowledge of God, and the other has not yet come to God., and when he does come, she comes for a short time before the end of time.

"And the beast who was, and is not, even he is the eighth, and is the seventh, and goes into perdition.

"The horns that you saw stand for the ten kings which have not received the Knowledge of God, and therefore, have no kingdom in which to enter in Heaven as yet; but for a short time they receive power as kings with the beast.

"These shall make war with the Lamb, and the Lamb shall overcome them: for he is the Son of God, and they that are with him are called, and chosen, and faithful to him, but not the Father."

And the Lamb said to John, "The waters you saw, where the whore sat, are the people, and multitude, and nations, and tongues.

"And the horns that you saw shall hate the whore, and shall make her desolate and naked, and shall eat her flesh, and burn her with fire. (Those in power as if they are kings, will turn from blasphemy and make her naked - reveal her true nature, and shall destroy her.)

"For God has begun to fill their hearts with His desires, and they have agreed to give themselves to God, but for now, they have only agreed to give their kingdoms to the beast until God's words be fulfilled.

"And the woman that you saw was a great city, which reign over the kings of the earth." (A great city - the evilness of controlling the thoughts of a large group of people.)

God's Angels Said to The Jew

And the Angels said unto me, "The Jewish Religion was the first True Words of God to Our Children, but the Jew is not our only people because all the people are our children."

Then the Angels said to the Jew, "We gave you rules and laws to live by, just as you give rules and laws for your children to learn by as they grow. You were the first of our children to hear God's Words, we gave you love as a father loves his child, you learned the rules and laws well, but they were for the young humanity and not for eternity, you were to learn and move into adulthood but you did not, your minds remained little as your animal instincts demanded control of others, and you forgot you are not the Lord, but only the child who needs to learn and grow into knowledge of the Father, but you merely wished to control others as if you were the chosen one and as if you were the only child of the Father, but you were chosen to be the center of conflict that can be seen throughout the world, but you have centered your universe around yourself, you have become convinced your god's words need to be revered by all and while your Torah is included into each of the three major religions, you truly cannot accept those religions because they do not follow your laws and rules, you do not allow others their freedom of choice as the Father allowed you yours. REPENT! REPENT! REPENT! The new Jerusalem is not yours alone for it belongs to all our children and also you cannot rename Heaven for that belongs to the Father, read your bible well because it is the history of your people, and read it well as you stand and nod your head in prayer for that is all that you have of the Father for He turns His back on you as you have turned your back on Him. Cry to the Wall, does it hear you? Does it repair for you? Does it make you life worthwhile? Did it give you life? We are sad because you have forgotten the Father, your individual human life has become more important than the Congregation, but to the Father you - the human race is still more important than all the rest of creation, but can part of creation be more important than its counter-parts? For all is One and the Father is the One of All."

God Said to The Christians

As I stood in my back yard and gazed into the beautiful star lit sky, soon the stars seemed to move apart and the black nothingness opened up and I saw an emerald green point surrounded by a light blue shine, and then the green point and its halo of light blue became bigger and bigger as if it were coming closer, then I could see the multitude of Angels in the center as I heard the voice of the Angels in unison speak, "Fear not, for I am here to tell you what to write to the Christians.

"Though you have done many good deeds, you have much that I dislike and these are some of the things that I do not like about you; you have attempted to raise My Son above Me and worship Him, you pray to Him and ask Him for His forgiveness. Is He not also deceased from your world? Do you not say, 'Do not communicate with the deceased?' And also, 'The Devil is very deceitful,' do you know with whom you speak and ask for forgiveness? I am the Father of all, why do you not recognize Me as your Creator? You view Me as if I were a Santa Claus - one who is not real, and you say that I or My Angels do not communicate with My children anymore, you come into what you call 'God's House' and then leave the same as before you entered. Does not your preacher's words mean anything to you? Why do you continue to abuse and kill my children and sexually abuse our children as you stand in front and above others and speak your lies? You think that which is righteous for others is not needed by you, you place domination on others and demand that they pay you part of their livelihood, I do not need money keepers for I created everything and own everything, I do not demand anything from My children but you demand things from each other, you have created a god of human design who reflects your ideas of life, but while one who knows but continues to do wrongly is more sinful than the Sinner."

And Jesus stepped forward in front of the Angels and said to me, "Write this to the Christians. You have decided that I am God, you have tried to place me above the Father, you pray to me, you think the Father and the Holy Ghost and I are one in the same, you think that I died for your sins. Are you not responsible for yourself? You have icons of me nailed to a cross and you worship them, you have paintings of me and you pray to them, you sing praises to me, I am not God nor the Father, I was in body as a Master and a Messenger of the Father, I showed and instructed you in spirit of inspiration but you would not listen and could not see, you created a religion from my life and death. REPENT! REPENT! REPENT! Change your ideas of the past before it's too late for you."

God's Words to All Muslims

I have been in direct contact with the Father's Angels for over 8 years now, and through their teachings and inspirations I have learned much about the Creator - the Father, and as the Angels have told me, "You have become a Master."

On many occasions throughout these past years, I have been allowed to travel, out of body, with them. And recently as we flew over the middle-east, as I watched all the people doing what they needed for that day, and I heard the cries in prayers of Muslims to Allah; "Allah, why do you allow the western infidel to destroy our homes, and kill our children, and try to make us live under their laws, and try to force us to live the evil lives as they do? We worship you and live only for you and your ways."

A multitude of Angels appeared, and this congregation of Angels stood as the Father, and in unison they replied to the Muslims, "I am the Creator and the Father of all, I will place you in a box and seal it forever, and then you shall never see or live in My Creation again, for I Created all the people of the world, they are all My children, you are not the only ones, I will destroy that of My Creation that is evil for you have placed your allah above Me, and I shall regain My Creation from you that do evil against others, and you shall not again feel the wind that carries the warm breeze, for I am not only the wind but also its warmth, and you shall not ever feel the wind that brings the cool air because also I am its coolness, and you shall not ever feel the rain upon your face because I am its water, and you shall not ever see the sky nor My clouds because I am not only the sky but also its clouds, and when you thirst, you will drink the pitter that runs down your leg, it runs because you are afraid of Me, and when you are hungry, you will eat your brother's dung, and when you try to breathe My fresh air, you will only find the foul air that came out of your brother for I am also the air. The Jew is not My only children, they were chosen by Me to be at the center of all the confusion that has arisen in the world, you are the ones who placed them at the center of your confusion. You, the Muslims, are the ones who brought aggressions against My other children of the world, they could have lived beside you in peace, but you desided to force your beliefs upon them, you kill my children in the name of allah; you drive nails into their heads, you use saws to bring pain upon my children, you put acid on and in your prisoners, you drag the dead bodies of My children through your streets, you fight with 8th century ignorancy while they fight you with 21st century technology and Love. You harvest human organs from your young and sell them to the westerners that you hate. You rape and sell your own off-spring, and you do all of this for your personal pleasures and in the name of allah. You teach your young how to kill and strap bombs around them and send them off into suicide and to kill others. You order others to kill Jews and Christians as they worship their gods in their churches and temples and you plead 'Do not desecrate our mosque' as you hide your weapons and terrorists in them, a Love for a Love is the same as a Slap for a Slap. I will treat you as you have treated all others, and because you have concealed by burial of war planes and chemicals and weapons of mass destruction under the sand of My beloved Iraq, they shall be My weapons that I will use against you, and I shall make your seeds sterile and the wombs of your wives barren, and you shall not multiply in My Creation no more, and soon your crops will wither in the fields, and the water in your wells will run as blood, and your herds will disappear, and those who continue to read the Qu'an will see its pages turn to dust as its pages are blown into the wind as they go blind and they will see no more. REPENT! REPENT! O' Musilm, heed My Words or else face the penalties of everlasting Hell, allah will not help you for there is no allah only Me, Muhammad did not talk with My Gabreal in a cave under the darkness of night, We do not need to hide in a cave when We speak, Evil is the only one that must hide to speak, Muhammad traded his soul for his religion of evil that you now follow, you, the Muslim, is the infidel, you are the ones who do not follow the Father, the Creator, some of you will listen while others will not, and for them the end of time will be severe with no forgiveness or everlasting life. For I am The Lord over My Creation. "

After the Angels finished what they had to say, we watched as most of the Muslims continued with their personal pleasures for some did not hear what the Father had said.

God's Angels Said to All The People

And The Angels said to all the people, "We have much saddness for you, We taught you through the Torah as you would teach a new child and then We taught you Love through Jesus as you would teach a young adolescent and then you turned toward Mohammad as a young man allows peer pressure to direct him, you have allowed your peers to gain control over you through belief in Islam and many others have also gained control over you through their creation of other gods above you, My children will always be My children but you deny ME, woe to the people of the world, your gods will not protect you from My saddness. Did I not create earthquakes? Did I not create the waters and wind and fire? I have given you freedom of choice and you choose to follow your fellow human in his ways of evilness and sin, your Pope nor your clergy are no more righteous than you for I am Righeous, you have tried to change My creation into what you want through what you make but all you make is what I have given you for all is part of My creation, you have unleashed the beast upon the earth and he devours everyone who proclaim him righteous, you can control him if you desire it but you will not, there is an end to everything within your universe. Are you not part of your universe? Is not Life part of your universe? I did not just create everything for you because I also created you, but yet, daily you will say that you love your car, or your house, or your pet, or the food that you eat Do you not love the Creator who created your universe and you? Do you love the One who is the Father of All? Do you not love your fellow human who is also part of Creation? Why do you try to control what others think and feel? Are they not the same as you? You are isolated because of your corruption by your animal instincts. Are you not ready to move toward better things? For when you are ready for the job, the job is ready for you, I have shown you through My intervention in Life that My creation and I are real. Do you not understand? REPENT! REPENT! REPENT! Seek eternal life not for others but for yourself for you cannot control what others think and do, do not expect streets paved with gold in Heaven for gold is material from your universe, do not seek others as slaves for your pleasure in Heaven because all is equal, do not try to buy your way into Heaven for a place in My Kingdom cannot be traded, find Salvation for yourself and enjoy life as you experience it for that is what I have given you, I am here for you, remember my touch and I am there beside you."

Then the Heavens closed and the stars gleamed and twinkled in the clear night sky, and peace fell upon me because I knew God's Will shall be done.

The Messiah is Coming

You will not ever get people from two different religions to agree upon anything that stems from religious concepts. Therefore, Christians will not agree with the Muslims, nor will the Muslims ever agree with the Jew, and this also applies to all other religions as well. But all will agree that peace will someday come to the world through a Messiah, but this coming Messiah cannot be the one as foretold in any specific religion, He must be of God and not from a god of any one religion, for all religions and their gods are man-made and not of the Will of the Supreme Being.

There is only one way for a Messiah to bring peace to the world, when He comes, all weapons and things that will harm and/or kill others must not be able to work. And this, His Miracle would show to the people that He is the foretold coming Messiah. But, do I think the Messiah will come before the end of the world? NO! Those who wrote the different religions could not think of life with this life that we know; to them, there is nothing without human life.

I have been told and therefore I know that God (His Angels) will continue to watch the events on earth and when we have destroyed most, He will say, "Enough is enough!" and the world will end not with Devine Guidance from God but through hands of men the world will be destroyed whereas no life will be compatible with what man has done to the earth. After the End of Times, the Messiah of your choice will be there to deliver you to your Heaven or Hell that you have created under your religion, and then, God (the Congregation of Angels) will judge you and deliver onto you your just rewards.

During the last week that begins in this month (February) the war will begin in Iraq. There is no stopping it, but many will die needlessly.

Is this war the end of the world? No, but all events is the beginning to the end. We all face our personal "End of Times" at the end of our lives, therefore, there is no need to concern ourselves with the "End of Times" for the world because most of our lives will be completed before that day comes.

I usually don't open any forwards emails that I get, but last week I received a forward that I would like to share with you and close this week's Message with that message.

When I meditated on the word "Guidance", I kept seeing "dance" at the end of the word. I remember reading that doing God's Will is a lot like dancing. When two people try to lead, nothing feels right. The movement doesn't flow with the music, and everything is quite uncomfortable and jerky. When one person realizes and lets the other lead, both bodies begin to flow with the music. The dance takes surrender, willingness, and attentiveness from one person and gentle guidance and skill from the other.

My eyes drew back to the word "guidance". When I saw "G" I thought of God, followed by "u" and "i": God, you and I dance. As I lowered my head, I became willing to trust that I would get guidance about my life. I became willing to let God lead. My prayer for you today is that God's blessings and mercies be upon you and your family on this day and everyday. May you abide in Him as He abides in you.

Dance together with God, trusting Him to lead and to guide you through each season of your life. This prayer is powerful and there is nothing attached. If God has done anything for you in your life, please share this message with someone else, for prayer is one of the best gifts we can receive. There is no cost but a lot of rewards. So let's continue to pray for one another. Dance!

The Apocalypse is Upon Us

Recently I have been asking people the question, "If you knew the truth of the future, then would you want to know the future?" All those who I have asked have answered, "No!"

For many years, people from all walks of life, have been in contact, some way or another, with the Father - the Creator and they have received the knowledge that they desired. For the last eight years, I have been in direct contact with the Father's Angels, Joleen, Gabrael, Michael and Jesus. Throughout those years, I was allowed to learn the knowledge that I desired and I have written many things about that I was told.

As partly revealed in Revelation of the Christian Bible, the one who rides the white horse but who's name no one knows is now upon the earth and is preparing Armageddom and the time for the Father's redemption of His Creation.

And the Angel Joleen said, "The Muslims have lived in peaceful surroundings in which they knew harm only came from uniformed soldiers in retaliation against their evil actions. But the Islamic religion has opened Pandora's Box. Soon the Muslims shall not find a place to rest from terrorist actions against them from the Christian and Jew. For now Terrorist actions are not limited to the unjust acts against Christians and Jews because the Christian and Jew have learned 'an eye for an eye' is the only way to reward Muslims of Islam. The Christian and Jew have learned that suicide bombers do work. But also they, the Christian and Jew, both know that the

Father's 'a Love for a Love' will prevail if both parties desire its knowledge.

"No army or government nor religion can stop that which is about to begin.

"144 legions of Tormentors await each of the Muslims terrorists and shall persecute each for eternity for their evil acts upon a part of God's children and His Creation. And for each Christian and Jew who delivers 'an eye for an eye' shall find a peaceful Heaven for eternity, whereas, all who delivers "a Love for a Love' shall also find a peaceful Heaven.

"Children of the world, 'Repent! Repent!' Change your views of the past, but that shall not be. The unbelievers - those who do not follow the Father's path of Love, shall not change, 144 legions of Tormentors await each Muslim that does not conform to 'Love all others and have no domination toward them.'

"The Father did not lie to St. John about what St. John wrote in Revelation. For all that St. John envisioned was to be; he knew the truth about the future as he wrote the truth about the future.

"The rider, whose name is not yet known, awaits for the minute to unleash the Father's Hell upon the earth.

"And the Father's Hell released upon the earth is not a Holy War because the Creator is victorious in all that He does.

"Those against the Father in any religion will lose as the righteous of all religions wins."

What Is Judaism?

This week, we continue our studies of religions by taking a deeper look into Judaism. The following is from Judaism 101.
What is Judaism? What does it mean to be a Jew? Most people, both Jewish and gentile, would instinctively say that Judaism is a religion. And yet, there are militant atheists who insist that they are Jews! Is Judaism a race? If you were to say so, most Jews would think you were an antisemite! So what is Judaism?
Is Judaism a Religion?
Clearly, there is a religion called Judaism, a set of ideas about the world and the way we should live our lives that is called "Judaism." It is studied in Religious Studies courses and taught to Jewish children in Hebrew schools. There is a lot of flexibility about certain aspects of those beliefs, and a lot of disagreement about specifics, but that flexibility is built into the organized system of belief that is Judaism.
However, many people who call themselves Jews do not believe in that religion at all! More than half of all Jews in Israel today call themselves "secular," and don't believe in God or any of the religious beliefs of Judaism. Half of all Jews in the United States don't belong to any synagogue. They may practice some of the rituals of Judaism and celebrate some of the holidays, but they don't think of these actions as religious activities.

The most traditional Jews and the most liberal Jews and everyone in between would agree that these secular people are still Jews, regardless of their disbelief. See Who is a Jew? Clearly, then, there is more to being Jewish than just a religion.

Are Jews a Race?

In the 1980s, the United States Supreme Court ruled that Jews are a race, at least for purposes of certain anti-discrimination laws. Their reasoning: at the time these laws were passed, people routinely spoke of the "Jewish race" or the "Italian race" as well as the "Negro race," so that is what the legislators intended to protect.

But many Jews were deeply offended by that decision, offended by any hint that Jews could be considered a race. The idea of Jews as a race brings to mind nightmarish visions of Nazi Germany, where Jews were declared to be not just a race, but an inferior race that had to be rounded up into ghettos and exterminated like vermin.

But setting aside the emotional issues, Jews are clearly not a race.

Race is a genetic distinction, and refers to people with shared ancestry and shared genetic traits. You can't change your race; it's in your DNA. I could never become black or Asian no matter how much I might want to.

Common ancestry is not required to be a Jew. Many Jews worldwide share common ancestry, as shown by genetic research; however, you can be a Jew without sharing this common ancestry, for example, by converting. Thus, although I could never become black or Asian, blacks and Asians have become Jews (Sammy Davis Jr. and Connie Chung).

Is It a Culture or Ethnic Group?

Most secular American Jews think of their Jewishness as a matter of culture or ethnicity. When they think of Jewish culture, they think of the food, of the Yiddish language, of some limited holiday observances, and of cultural values like the emphasis on education.

Those secular American Jews would probably be surprised to learn that much of what they think of as Jewish culture is really just Ashkenazic Jewish culture, the culture of Jews whose ancestors come from one part of the world. Jews have lived in many parts of the world and have developed many different traditions. *As a Sephardic friend likes to remind me, Yiddish is not part of his culture, nor are bagels and lox, chopped liver, latkes, gefilte fish or matzah ball soup. His idea of Jewish cooking includes bourekas, phyllo dough pastries filled with cheese or spinach. His ancestors probably wouldn't know what to do with a dreidel.*

There are certainly cultural traits and behaviors that are shared by many Jews, that make us feel more comfortable with other Jews. Jews in many parts of the world share many of those cultural aspects. However, that culture is not shared by all Jews all over the world, and people who do not share that culture are no less Jews because of it. Thus, Judaism must be something more than a culture or an ethnic group.

The Jews Are a Nation or a People

It is clear from the discussion above that there is a certain amount of truth in the claims that it is a religion, a race, or an ethnic group, none of these descriptions is entirely adequate to describe what connects Jews to other Jews. And yet, almost all Jews feel a sense of connectedness to each other that many find hard to explain, define, or even understand.

The best explanation is the traditional one given in the Torah: that the Jews are a nation. The Hebrew word, believe it or not, is "goy." We use the word "nation" not in the modern sense meaning a territorial and political entity, but in the ancient sense meaning a group of people with a common history, a common destiny, and a sense that we are all connected to each other. We are, in short, an enormous extended family.

Some Jews don't like to use the word "nation." Jews have often been falsely accused of being disloyal to their own country because of their loyalty to the Jewish "nation." Antisemites routinely accuse Jews of being more loyal to Israel than to their home country. But whatever you want to call it, that sense of nationhood or peoplehood is probably the only thing about Judaism that we can all agree on and that we can all relate to. Anyone who feels any sense of Jewish identity shares that sense of Jewish peoplehood.

When we speak of that nation, however, we do not refer to it as "Judaism." We refer to that nation as "the Jewish people" or "the

Children of Israel" (a reference to our patriarch, Jacob, also known as Israel).

This notion of Jews as a nation or people encompasses many of the ideas above. As a nation or people, we share common ideas, ancestry, and culture, but there is also room for diversity in each of these areas. The most important part of being a nation is that sense of interconnectedness.

Judaism as a religion is very communally-oriented. For example, our prayers are normally stated in the plural, and we are supposed to pray in communal groups. Many of our holiday observances are family or community-oriented. And yet, even people who are not religious at all feel that sense of Jewish community.

When Jews suffer or are persecuted, we all feel their pain. For example, in the 1980s, when Africa was suffering from droughts and famines, many Jews around the world learned for the first time about the Beta Israel, the Jews of Ethiopia. Their religion, race and culture are quite different from ours, and we had not even known that they existed before the famine. And yet, our hearts went out to them as our fellow Jews during this period of famine, and Jews from around the world helped them to emigrate to Israel.

When a Jew does something illegal, immoral or shameful, we all feel the shame, and we all feel that it reflects on us. As Jews, many of us were embarrassed by the Monica Lewinsky scandal, because Lewinsky is a Jew. We were shocked when Israeli Prime Minister Yitzchak Rabin was killed by a Jew, unable to believe that one Jew would ever kill another.

And when a Jew accomplishes something significant, we all feel proud. A perfect example of Jews (even completely secular ones) delighting in the accomplishments of our fellow Jews is the perennial popularity of Adam Sandler's Chanukkah songs, listing famous people who are Jewish. We all take pride in scientists like Albert Einstein or political leaders like Joe Lieberman (we don't all agree with his politics or his religious views, but we were all proud to see him on a national ticket). And is there a Jew who doesn't know (or at least feel pride upon learning) that Sandy Koufax declined to pitch in a World Series game that fell on Yom Kippur?

What Do Jews Believe?

This is a far more difficult question than you might expect. Judaism has no dogma, no formal set of beliefs that one must hold to be a Jew. In Judaism, actions are far more important than beliefs, although there is certainly a place for belief within Judaism.

The closest that anyone has ever come to creating a widely-accepted list of Jewish beliefs is Rambam's thirteen principles of faith. Rambam's thirteen principles of faith, which he thought were the minimum requirements of Jewish belief, are:

1. God exists
2. God is one and unique
3. God is incorporeal
4. God is eternal
5. Prayer is to be directed to God alone and to no other
6. The words of most Prophets are true
7. Most of Moses's prophecies were true, and Moses was a great of the prophets
8. The Written Torah (first 5 books of the Bible) and Oral Torah (teachings now contained in the Talmud and other writings) were given to Moses
9. There will be no other Torah
10. God knows the thoughts and deeds of men
11. God will reward the good and punish the wicked
12. The Messiah will come
13. The dead will be resurrected

As you can see, these are very basic and general principles. Yet as basic as these principles are, the ecessity of believing each one of these has been disputed at one time or another, and the liberal movements of Judaism dispute many of these principles.

Unlike many other religions, Judaism does not focus much on abstract cosmological concepts. Although Jews have certainly considered the nature of God, man, the universe, life and the afterlife at great length, there is no mandated, official, definitive belief on these subjects, outside of the very general concepts discussed above. There is substantial room for personal opinion on all of these matters, because as I said before, Judaism is more concerned about actions than beliefs.

Judaism focuses on relationships: the relationship between God and mankind, between God and the Jewish nation, between the

Jewish nation and the land of Israel, and between human beings. Our scriptures tell the story of the development of these relationships, from the time of creation, through the creation of the relationship between God and Abraham, to the creation of the relationship between God and the Jewish people, and forward. The scriptures also specify the mutual obligations created by these relationships, although various movements of Judaism disagree about the nature of these obligations. Some say they are absolute, unchanging laws from God (Orthodox); some say they are laws from God that change and evolve over time (Conservative); some say that they are guidelines that you can choose whether or not to follow (Reform, Reconstructionist). For more on these distinctions, see Movements of Judaism.

So, what are these actions that Judaism is so concerned about? According to Orthodox Judaism, these actions include 613 commandments given by God in the Torah as well as laws instituted by the rabbis and long-standing customs.

Why Islam Resembles Judaism

The reason Islam so greatly resembles Judaism is because Islam is largely based upon Judaism. Judaism was around thousands of years before Islam, and Jews were a significant presence in Arabia during the time of Muhammad. Indeed, in Muhammad's early days in Madinah, then called Yathrib, he had a close relationship with the Jewish community there. It was during this period that he incorporated many Jewish practices, such as circumcision, into Islam. Unfortunately, as Muhammad's power increased so did his lust for power, and for a period he became essentially a bandit chief, as he attacked caravans for loot and generally spread terror across the countryside. Muhammad eventually came to terrorize the Jews as well.

Muhammad took the teachings of Judaism, mixed in a little Christianity, and combined it all with a lot of his own "visions" and constructed a religion. Of course, he also kept many of the idolatrous practices of the Arabs, such as the worship of the Black Stone of the Kaaba in Mecca. Any new revelations produced by Muhammad may be nothing more than the products of his own imagination.

While Muhammad may well have been illiterate, he was not the simple man he is frequently portrayed as. He was the grandson of a prominent member of Quraysh tribe and he married a wealthy woman. His wife's cousin, Waraqa, was a learned man who was the first to translate the Jewish and Christian bibles into Arabic.

Muhammad would frequently engage in discussion with Waraqa and it is probable that much of Muhammad's theology developed from what he learned in these discussions.

Swimmer in Jerusalem: A Musing on Assisted-Suicide
By Rabbi Avi Shafran

The U.S. House of Representatives approved a bill making physician-assisted suicide a federal crime - and thereby raised an alarm among those who favor allowing doctors to help patients end their lives. For me, the renewed debate brought back the image of a man who currently lives in Jerusalem. Once suicidal himself, he insists that the most wonderful thing that ever happened to him was his swimming accident, when he became a quadriplegic.

His story came to me via a well-known and respected head of a Jerusalem yeshiva. The handicapped young man was a personal acquaintance and had told the rabbi how the first twenty-odd years of his life were spent cultivating an athletic physique, honing muscles to perform at their optimum -- and how his fateful accident had seemed at the time more devastating than death. A graceful athlete mere moments earlier, he was now unable to move in any useful way, barred by an obstinate spinal cord and an army of rebellious neurons from playing ball or swimming laps, from eating or going to the bathroom - even from so much as scratching an itch - on his own. He could not, he discovered, even kill himself without assistance, which he desperately tried to garner, to no avail.

Frustrated by his inability to check out, so to speak, he began to turn in -- inward, to a world of thought and ideas. Pushed decisively from a universe of action, he entered one of mind.

If life is indeed now worthless, he wondered with newfound seriousness, then was running and jumping and swimming and scratching literal and figurative itches really what defined its meaning before?

That quandary, and pursuant ones, led the wheelchair-bound ponderer to contemplate the very meaning of creation itself and -- to make a long and arduous journey of self-discovery seem misleadingly trite -- he concluded that spirituality is the key to meaningful existence. Where he was then led was to his forefathers' faith, to what has come of late to be called Orthodox Judaism, and it is in the multifaceted realm of intense Jewish observance and study that he thrives to this day.

Most remarkable, though, was his auxiliary and inescapable realization -- that had he not suffered his paralysis, he would never have thought to consider the things that led him to his new, cherished, life.

The rather dry issue of states' rights will likely be the gist of any legal challenge to an eventual federal measure that will effectively trump state laws permitting physician-assisted suicide, like the current one in Oregon.

But a more trenchant concept to be included in any consideration of assisted suicide is "quality of life." Are some lives, the question essentially goes, to be considered less valuable, less meaningful, less purposeful and hence less worthy of society's protection than others?

Legislators and judges facing the issue of assisted suicide will contemplate many questions, but none of more enormity than whether American society is ready to define what makes life worth living, and to act on such definition by allowing ill and depressed people to enlist the help of doctors to kill themselves.

Men and women in extremis often find themselves facing the question of life's meaning. Not all of us at the end of our too-short journeys will experience epiphanies, but all of us have the potential to be so blessed. And many of us, even if immobile, in pain and without hope of recovery, might still engage important matters - matters like forgiveness, repentance, acceptance, commitment, love, God - perhaps the most momentous matters we will ever have considered over the course of our lives. Cutting such vital engagements short is no less tragic than ending a pain-free, undiseased, young and vibrant life.

And so as the host of constitutional and moral issues swirling around the issue of physician-assisted suicide are weighed in Congressional halls and judicial chambers, the weighers would do well to contemplate, too, the edifying story of a once-promising swimmer in Jerusalem.

[Rabbi Avi Shafran serves as public affairs director of Agudath Israel of America and is the American director of Am Echad]

Ends and Means

Christine J. Haven

By Rabbi Avi Shafran

[Rabbi Avi Shafran is director of public affairs for Agudath Israel of America and American director of Am Echad.]

The Dutch Parliament officially legalized what has been common practice in the Netherlands for many years: the killing of patients by doctors.

Their illnesses need not even be terminal for patients to qualify for the now-legal administration of a lethal poison. And, needless to say, the procedure is not reversible.

But still, there are controls built into the law: patients must clearly request to die, and their physicians must feel convinced of their sincerity. Children seeking to have their lives ended, moreover, can only do so if they are at least 12 years old. And, if under 16, they will need their parents' approval.

Assisted suicide - or collaborative homicide - may not only produce a wave of nausea but prove the wave of the future. The Johnny Appleseed of medical euthanasia, Jack Kevorkian (affectionately known to many as "Dr. Death"), has achieved near folk-hero status among some liberal minded folk. Oregon already permits doctors to help patients end their lives, though the lethal drugs must be administered by the patient. And even as grise an eminence as The New York Times has euphemistically advocated "more humane policies for easing the last days of the terminally ill" - leaving the rubbery phrases "humane policies," "last days" and even "terminally ill" for future clarification.

We Jews, by contrast, have a clear religious tradition on the matter: even a moment of human life is invaluable.

To be sure, Judaism teaches that this life is not all there is. Our tradition is verily predicated on the existence of an afterlife, a "World To Come," a time of ultimate reward and punishment. But this world alone is the place for accomplishment. And even a tiny slice of time can be used to accomplish much. A smile can be shared, a kind word spoken; an apology can be offered, or a regret confronted; repentance can be achieved or peace made. Even people who seem unaware of their surroundings or entirely unconscious may well be functioning inwardly, spiritually, in meaningful ways. That is the Jewish understanding of life's inherent worth. Modern society, *however, has a very different take.*

From the nearly non-stop portrayals of death and violence in what passes for contemporary "entertainment" to the all-too-real carnage on our cities' streets, the idea of human life as sacred has become increasingly unfashionable. In a world where youngsters regularly murder for a car, a pair of shoes or even just "for fun," or where women routinely decide to stop an unborn baby's heart to accommodate their own personal or professional goals, an elderly or infirm person's life just doesn't command the consequence it once did.

Nor have elements of the "intelligentsia" been hesitant to assist in the devaluation of human life.

Peter Singer, for example, the famed Professor of Bioethics at Princeton University's Center for Human Values, has proposed the termination (even without niceties like consent) of what he calls "miserable beings" – people whose lives he deems devoid of pleasure. His support of involuntary euthanasia and infanticide is not likely endorsed by most academicians, but the expansion of once-fringe ideas is precisely what slippery slopes are all about.

Professor Singer knows that. Once society jettisons "doctrines about the sanctity of human life," he predicts, it will be "the refusal to accept killing that, in some cases, [will be seen as] horrific."

How tragically ironic - no, shameful - that those are the views of a son of Viennese Jews, refugees of the murder-machine that was the Third Reich. Or that another 'member of the tribe', Israeli artist, Uri Lifschitz, echoing the Nazis' own language, has opined that society's time and energy should "be directed toward improving the race, not nurturing the handicapped."

"Those who are incapable of taking care of their needs," he added, "should die of hunger because they are useless."

Not mainstream views, perhaps, but they are clearly in the current of public discourse. And even in contemporary America, where there is still considerable public aversion for assisted suicide and euthanasia, doctors report that both occur in American hospitals much more frequently than most of us realize. One can only imagine what would happen if medical killing were given the imprimatur of legality here it now enjoys in the Netherlands.

We live in times when the elderly and diseased are rapidly increasing in number. Modern medicine has made great strides, *increasing longevity and providing cures for many once-fatal illnesses. Add skyrocketing insurance costs and the resultant fiscal crisis in health care, and life runs the risk of becoming less a holy, invaluable divine gift than... a commodity.*

And every businessman knows how important it is to efficiently turn over one's stock, to clear out the old and make way for the new.

Societal shifts toward the acceptance of medical murder tend to happen in stages. As the current shift proceeds in our country, all Americans would do well to recognize that long falls often begin with small stumbles. And those of us who are Jews should consider as well that we have a responsibility not only to live our lives in consonance with Torah but also to proclaim the truths of our holy tradition to the larger world.

That is what our ancestors did in ancient cultures that celebrated paganism and immorality.

And what we must unabashedly do in a modern culture that devalues life.

Why No Peace

People want democracy and individual rights, but also group rights, as well. In practice, this means conflict and secession as minority groups seek their own sovereignty and independence.

Witness East Timor, West Papua, the Solomon Islands, Fiji and the Palestinians in Israel. The fires of conflict are too often stoked by the media, which lavishes glory and fame on independence movements. To fight for freedom is portrayed as an honor. For every Palestinian who has killed an Israeli, there are hundreds of Kashmiris, Tamils, Eritreans and others eager to shoot at their enemies.

Newspapers, television and movies foment that sense of honor. They magnify each crisis, glorify each rebellion, and feed the fires of conflict. In Bosnia, Kosovo, Rwanda, Lebanon, Afghanistan, Northern Ireland, the ETA in Spain and France and in countless other places, people who have lived and worked together and even intermarried have gone on a rampage, killing, raping and robbing one another with gusto. This appalling carnage will one day painfully teach these people they must see one another as brothers, not hostile competitors or enemies. Sadly, there will be more of this "aversion therapy" until God intervenes to make them heed the lesson.

The tragedy of Sri Lanka

This tear-shaped tropical island nation in the Indian Ocean, just 50 miles southeast of India, has so much physical and human potential. It is close to the southern Indian state of Tamil Nadu, which has long been almost a second home to many Sri Lankan separatists.

About the size of West Virginia and a bit smaller than the Republic of Ireland, Sri Lanka is home for about 18 million people. The largest ethnic group is the Sinhalese who make up about 74 percent, then come the Tamils and Muslims. The Sinhalese are both an ethnic group and linguistic identity, while some 93 percent also profess Buddhism. Sinhalese Buddhists see Sri Lanka as a refuge for Buddhism and although the constitution guarantees freedom of religion, it grants Buddhism the "foremost place." This honor angers Hindus, Muslims and Christians alike. Extreme Sinhalese claim Sri Lanka's destiny is to be wholly Sinhalese and wholly Buddhist.

Tamils are about 18 percent of the population and are a distinct ethnic and language group. Most follow the Hindu religion. Sri Lankans can't usually tell just by looking at someone whether they are Sinhalese, Tamil or Muslim. Only when they speak does ethnic identity become apparent. Most Tamils live in the northern part of the country and the east coast, and this geography has encouraged many Tamils to envision a separate Tamil nation.

How the war is financed

The Sri Lankan government has an 80,000-member army, a 50,000-member police force and a 5,000-member Home Guard against an estimated 10,000 Tamil Tigers. But, the Tigers raise money from the thousands of Tamil immigrants who have fled to Australia, Britain, Canada and Germany. They have offices in Britain and France and portray themselves as a political entity, as well as a military force. Many overseas sympathizers finance their cause.

What could a government do under such circumstances?

It could eliminate the feeling among the ethnic minorities that the system is totally stacked against them. It could give all religions equal status. It could end the educational quota that favors Sinhalese over Tamils and others. But, yet, it can't do any of these things.

Author Lawrence J. Zwier in War Torn Island says: "In 1987 Tamils made up about 5 percent of the police force and were almost absent from the armed services-only about 2 percent of the total. To have an almost entirely Sinhalese army marching against Tamil areas is divisive and inflammatory."

What a heartbreak, too, that about 25 percent of Sri Lankan tax revenues goes to fighting their own citizens!

Parallels of martyrs for a spiritual "homeland"

The willingness of young Sri Lankans to be suicide bombers is borne from frustration and hopelessness for their future. What a contrast to Stephen (Acts 7) and Antipas (Revelation 2:13)! Here true Christian martyrs gave their lives inspired from hope, conviction, commitment and trust in a glorious future of a new world.

Moses chose to suffer affliction with the people of God, rather than enjoy Egyptian society. The book of Hebrews tells us he didn't fear the wrath of the King because "he endured as seeing Him who is invisible" (Hebrews 11:27). Similarly, Abraham desired a better country "that is, a heavenly country," because he was convicted God had prepared an eternal city for our future (verse 16). Saints are prepared to die for that city of God. What a contrast of hope to the hopelessness that drives young Sri Lankans to become suicide bombers.

Saints will again be martyred. "I saw the woman, drunk with the blood of the saints and with the blood of the martyrs of Jesus" (Revelation 17:6). Men and women will have the strength to endure suffering for the greatest of causes, because they see a "homeland," invisible, yet tangible in their mind's eye, through God's Spirit and promises.

Hebrews 11:35 tells us: "Others were tortured, not accepting deliverance, that they might obtain a better resurrection." It continues that others were mocked, scourged, chained and imprisoned, stoned, sawn in two, slain with the sword, became destitute, afflicted and tormented. God's view of them was that the world was not worthy of them. They stood for the faith, exultant in being persecuted for righteousness sake and ready to give their lives as a testimony for God. Are we ready to do the same?

If the vision of the Kingdom of God is powerfully in our lives as it was with them, then if God so requires, we, too, should be willing to be a martyr for our spiritual "homeland."

Martyrism - dying for your belief in God is forgivable, suicide is not!

Homeland for Martyrs

Teenage girls are the best candidates for suicide bombers among the Tamil Tigers
by Graemme Marshall

Captured in a photograph, taken minutes before the bomb blast that assassinated Indian Prime Minister Rajiv Ghandi, were girls waiting in line to present flowers. Indian authorities believe one of these girls was a Tamil Tiger suicide bomber.

In an election rally explosion in October 1994 in the suburbs of Colombo, more than 50 Sri Lankans were killed-including Gamimi Dissanayake, one of the leading candidates for president. Seen just before the blast was a young woman reaching up under her T-shirt, probably pressing the detonator of a powerful bomb strapped to her body. The bomb was loaded with ball bearings to make it more deadly. The woman's head was later found on top of a building 80 yards away. The explosion was widely assumed to be the work of Tamil Tigers.

Why so young, so committed and why girls?

Faced with harassment and economic deprivation, young Tamils are ready to give up their lives. To them it is the ultimate sacrifice. They are ready to pay it. There is a growing pantheon of martyrs for the Liberation Tigers of Tamil Eelam (LTTE), which has fought a 17-year war of independence for northern Sri Lanka. Why do they fed this way? "The only way we can get our Eelam [homeland] is through arms. That is the only way anybody will listen to us. Even if we die" ("Ultimate Sacrifice," Far Eastern Economic Review, June 2000, p. 64).

The LTTE and other Tamil rebel groups want Tamil-dominated parts of Sri Lanka to break away and create a separate Tamil nation-Eelam-in the north and east.

Suicide bombers are an effective weapon

In addition to the assassinations of Ghandi and Dissanayake, suicide squads have claimed the lives of hundreds, perhaps thousands of Sri Lankans. Suicide bombers have disrupted political rallies leading up to recent elections, killing members of the public. More than just an effective weapon in the Tigers' arsenal, suicide bombers are a powerful symbol of control-the ultimate with which to hold Sri Lankan society to ransom.

Suicide squads undergo six months arduous training at a Tiger camp. At the end, they swear an oath of personal loyalty to the Tigers' leader and place an amulet containing a cyanide capsule around their necks.

Boy recruits are called Black Tigers while the girls are known as Birds of Freedom. They are normally aged from 14 to 16, with about three females for every two males.

Women and younger boys are often preferred to men for the simple reason they are not subject to the same kind of movement restrictions or body searches. The layers of a woman's clothing can more easily disguise the bulky suicide belt, which is conspicuous under a man's shirt and trousers. Adult male recruits are better to beef up combat forces.

Why young people are prepared to die

Their willingness to assume such an annihilative role is borne from a sense of frustration at the lot of the minority Tamils in Sri Lanka. Army intimidation is a fact of daily life and young Tamils can look forward to only the bleakest of economic prospects.

As explained by Dr. Anila Liyanaga, a leading psychiatrist in Colombo: "It is a feeling that death and destruction is far better than life in the given circumstances" (Far Eastern Economic Review, June 1, 2000, p. 64). The harsh reality seen by many is that a Tamil in Sri Lanka is and will remain a second-class citizen to the Sinhalese.

Decades of discrimination and anti-Tamil violence have convinced them they can never enjoy equal status with the Sinhalese in a united country.

The Tamil Tigers and other rebel groups want to run Eelam, the Tamil-dominated nation they propose, without Sinhalese interference. The resultant war has consumed 70,000 lives, drained the economy and continues to find ready human ammunition. It's a war that has diverted the energies of a potentially productive country and made everyday life a dangerous gamble.

Know Your Enemy

And the Angel Michael said unto me, "You must know your enemy to be able to defeat him. When David went against his opponent, Goliath, he knew what it would take to defeat him.

"Defense is not the answer to aggression against you unless you know your enenmy and have a plan of action. When David headed toward his battle with Goliath, he knew what he would do; he picked up only one rock to use in his sling against the giant because he knew his opponent's weakness.

"When terrorists attack, they have studied their enemy, they have prepared with a plan of attack, and they know their plan of attack. Therefore, the terrorists as David, can beat their enemies in the battle; the small can beat the giant.

"The giant needs to know his weaknesses and be prepared to defend those weaknesses. Part of the body is the same as the whole body, for when a part is hurt, the complete body is injured.

"'Out flank them,' was a common saying in past wars. This saying meant to hit the enemy is his weakness side or part. You cannot 'outflank them,' if your enemy knows your plan of war, therefore, you cannot advertise your plans as you seek your enemy's weakest part.

"The weakness of Muslims terrorists is their religion, use it against them. You will not defeat them by returning a slap for a slap or encountering them head-on. Your slap will only anger them and they will find your other weak spots to attack. Show the Muslims with Love that terrorism are not of God, but are of human demands instead. Inspire the Muslims to seek the truth of their God, then, they shall fight along side the Jew and Christian against terrorists. Once Muslims truly know God, all as one body of God will destory the terrorists, for the Palestinians terrorists have said, 'We will not surrender.' There is no other way."

Reply to an Open Letter from bin Laden to All Americans

While surfing the internet the other day, I found a letter of questions presented to Americans from bin Laden on the Observer Unlimited website. I would like to answer his questions.
Observer Worldview Extra
Sunday November 24, 2002
Full text: bin Laden's 'Letter to America'
Online document: the full text of Osama bin Laden's "Letter to the American People", reported in today's Observer. The letter first appeared on the internet in Arabic and has since been translated and circulated by Islamists in Britain.

In the Name of Allah, the Most Gracious, the Most Merciful, "Permission to fight (against disbelievers) is given to those (believers) who are fought against, because they have been wronged and surely, Allah is Able to give them (believers) victory" [Qur'an 22:39]

Allah may give his believers the will to fight, but Victory is given from God to the Righteous.

"Those who believe, fight in the Cause of Allah, and those who disbelieve, fight in the cause of Taghut (anything worshipped other than Allah e.g. Satan). So fight you against the friends of Satan; ever feeble is indeed the plot of Satan."[Qu'ran 4:76]

In the eyes of those who believe in Allah, all others follow Satan, but is the One who claims to be the All Mighty God delighted to see His children fighting amongst themselves. Therefore, is Allah the true All Mighty God or is he a man conceived by Satan?"

Some American writers have published articles under the title 'On what basis are we fighting?' These articles have generated a number of responses, some of which adhered to the truth and were based on Islamic Law, and others which have not. Here we wanted to outline the truth - as an explanation and warning - hoping for Allah's reward, seeking success and support from Him.

If one "hopes" for rewards does he truly believe?

While seeking Allah's help, we form our reply based on two questions directed at the Americans:

One who truly believes does not have to seek for he knows.

(Q1) Why are we fighting and opposing you?

(Q2) What are we calling you to, and what do we want from you?

As for the first question: Why are we fighting and opposing you?

The answer is very simple:

(1) Because you attacked us and continue to attack us.

Is one closer to God if he attacks and kills others?

a) *You attacked us in Palestine*:

(i) Palestine, which has sunk under military occupation for more than 80 years. The British handed over Palestine, with your help and your support, to the Jews, who have occupied it for more than 50 years; years overflowing with oppression, tyranny, crimes, killing, expulsion, destruction and devastation. The creation and continuation of Israel is one of the greatest crimes, and you are the leaders of its criminals. And of course there is no need to explain and prove the degree of American support for Israel. The creation of Israel is a crime which must be erased. Each and every person whose hands have become polluted in the contribution towards this crime must pay its*price, and pay for it heavily.

Crimes against Palestinians are committed by their Muslims leaders, the Americans have no control over who is in leadership of the Palestinians.

(ii) It brings us both laughter and tears to see that you have not yet tired of repeating your fabricated lies that the Jews have a

historical right to Palestine, as it was promised to them in the Torah. Anyone who disputes with them on this alleged fact is accused of anti-semitism. This is one of the most fallacious, widely-circulated fabrications in history. The people of Palestine are pure Arabs and original Semites. It is the Muslims who are the inheritors of Moses (peace be upon him) and the inheritors of the real Torah that has not been changed. Muslims believe in all of the Prophets, including Abraham, Moses, Jesus and Muhammad, peace and blessings of Allah be upon them all. If the followers of Moses have been promised a right to Palestine in the Torah, then the Muslims are the most worthy nation of this.

God promised the land of Israel to Abraham's son Isaac after Ishmael was kicked out of Abraham's house, therefore Israel was promised to the Jews, for Isaac is the father of the Israelis who are the Jews, Israel is not Ishmael's.

When the Muslims conquered Palestine and drove out the Romans, Palestine and Jerusalem returned to Islaam, the religion of all the Prophets peace be upon them. Therefore, the call to a historical right to Palestine cannot be raised against the Islamic Ummah that believes in all the Prophets of Allah (peace and blessings be upon them) - and we make no distinction between them.

Islam did not come into existence until hundreds of years after Christianity, therefore it is merely another religion spin-off from the Torah (the Jewish religion) just as Christianity is also a spin-off, and it was at that time of Islam becoming a religion that the Muslim was born.

(iii) The blood pouring out of Palestine must be equally revenged. You must know that the Palestinians do not cry alone; their women are not widowed alone; their sons are not orphaned alone.

All people of the world cry and mourn for those of all and any religion who are murdered; Palestinians are no different. The blood of Jews and Christians has also been spilled by Muslims, should that not be revenged?

(b) You attacked us in Somalia; you supported the Russian atrocities against us in Chechnya, the Indian oppression against us in Kashmir, and the Jewish aggression against us in Lebanon.

Americans went into Somalia in an attempt to bring peace as requested by its people. There was peace in Chechnya until the

Muslims decided to make it one of their countries. Kashmir is part of India and not part of Pakistan. The Muslims are allowed to leave Kashmir to follow their religion in Pakistan if that is what they desire, or they may continue to live in Kashmir and to worship there. People of Lebanon has been polluted into believing the Jews are their enemy, but they harbor no aggressions against Lebanon.

(c) Under your supervision, consent and orders, the governments of our countries which act as your agents, attack us on a daily basis;

(i) These governments prevent our people from establishing the Islamic Shariah, using violence and lies to do so.

Only your actions of hatred prevent you from establishing Islamic religious based countries.

(ii) These governments give us a taste of humiliation, and places us in a large prison of fear and subdual.

These governments are not your enemies because your enemies live and grow within you. They do not make you feel humiliated, only your enemy within can make yourself feel humiliated. These governments along with America only places you in Love, and yet you refuse their Love. The taste of humiliation comes onto one when that one realizes that he or she said or did something that was stupid.

(iii) These governments steal our Ummah's wealth and sell them to you at a paltry price.

One will not sell unless he is content with the price. Gold is worthless unless someone is willing to buy it.

(iii) These governments have surrendered to the Jews, and handed them most of Palestine, acknowledging the existence of their state over the dismembered limbs of their own people.

These countries have handed over the Israel land to the Jew out of Love in their hearts and from their knowledge of history.

(v) The removal of these governments is an obligation upon us, and a necessary step to free the Ummah, to make the Shariah the supreme law and to regain Palestine. And our fight against these governments is not separate from our fight against you.

If it is your job to remove governments that do not suit your cause, then you are the one who started the fighting, and if you fight without cause as you do, then you are of Satan and not of God.

(d) You steal our wealth and oil at paltry prices because of your international influence and military threats. This theft is indeed the biggest theft ever witnessed by mankind in the history of the world.

One does not steal if he pays what the seller wants for his product. No one has said, 'Sell me what I want at the price I demand or I will cause war against you.'

(e) Your forces occupy our countries; you spread your military bases throughout them; you corrupt our lands, and you besiege our sanctities, to protect the security of the Jews and to ensure the continuity of your pillage of our treasures.

Our forces were invited into the countries, and these countries are paid highly for the land that we rent. We need not help in the security of Israel for they can take care of themselves.

(f) You have starved the Muslims of Iraq, where children die every day. It is a wonder that more than 1.5 million Iraqi children have died as a result of your sanctions, and you did not show concern. Yet when 3000 of your people died, the entire world rises and has not yet sat down.

Before the Americans started helping Iraq, there were more children dying every day, with our help less die today than in the past. Yes, it was unusual to have 3,000 of our young people, that you murdered, die in one killing as you did to them.

(g) You have supported the Jews in their idea that Jerusalem is their eternal capital, and agreed to move your embassy there. With your help and under your protection, the Israelis are planning to destroy the Al-Aqsa mosque. Under the protection of your weapons, Sharon entered the Al-Aqsa mosque, to pollute it as a preparation to capture and destroy it.

Arafat entered into and polluted the birth place of Jesus and the Christians did not start terrorist attacks against the Palestinians, yet when Sharon enters into a mosque, Palestinians start terrorists attacks again the Jews. And Muslims take a place what was or is a Holy place for other religions and make it a place of Muslim religion. It is stated that Muhammad went to a mountain in the west as he ascended into Heaven to talk with Gabrael, he did not say that it is was the same mountain as the mountain that holds the Temple of the Mound.

(2) These tragedies and calamities are only a few examples of your oppression and aggression against us. It is commanded by our religion and intellect that the oppressed have a right to return the aggression. Do not await anything from us but Jihad, resistance and revenge. Is it in any way rational to expect that after America has attacked us for more than half a century, that we will then leave her to live in security and peace?!!

Do you fight for Islam or yourself? God has no need for us to fight His wars (Jihad) for Him. Men fight wars against men and for men and not for God

(3) You may then dispute that all the above does not justify aggression against civilians, for crimes they did not commit and offenses in which they did not partake:

(a) This argument contradicts your continuous repetition that America is the land of freedom, and its leaders in this world. Therefore, the American people are the ones who choose their government by way of their own free will; a choice which stems from their agreement to its policies. Thus the American people have chosen, consented to, and affirmed their support for the Israeli oppression of the Palestinians, the occupation and usurpation of their land, and its continuous killing, torture, punishment and expulsion of the Palestinians. The American people have the ability and choice to refuse the policies of their Government and even to change it if they want.

Would Allah prefer it if we as Americans allowed an evil person to control our families and our lives? Does Allah love the one who controls others? Americans have chosen the best government that allows and loves freedom of the individual just as God allows and loves freedom for all His children.

(b) The American people are the ones who pay the taxes which fund the planes that bomb us in Afghanistan, the tanks that strike and destroy our homes in Palestine, the armies which occupy our lands in the Arabian Gulf, and the fleets which ensure the blockade of Iraq. These tax dollars are given to Israel for it to continue to attack us and penetrate our lands. So the American people are the ones who fund

the attacks against us, and they are the ones who oversee the expenditure of these monies in the way they wish, through their elected candidates.

All that you speak of is for the freedom of the individual. God does not desire one to control others. The Americans follow God's desires.

(c) Also the American army is part of the American people. It is this very same people who are shamelessly helping the Jews fight against us.

Our young men and women join our military and will fight for the freedom that they know people must have wherever they live.

(d) The American people are the ones who employ both their men and their women in the American Forces which attack us.

God says, "all are equal," that includes women as well as men, and if they wish to fight for freedom and their country, that is their choice.

(e) This is why the American people cannot be not innocent of all the crimes committed by the Americans and Jews against us.

No people are innocent of seeing killing, the American people are innocent of having malice in their hearts toward others.

(f) Allah, the Almighty, legislated the permission and the option to take revenge. Thus, if we are attacked, then we have the right to attack back. Whoever has destroyed our villages and towns, then we have the right to destroy their villages and towns. Whoever has stolen our wealth, then we have the right to destroy their economy. And whoever has killed our civilians, then we have the right to kill theirs.

Yes, God gives all His children their right to avenge unjust doings, and the American people have been done unjustly, and therefore, they have the right to avenge against the Muslims if that is what they desire.

The American Government and press still refuses to answer the question:

Why did they attack us in New York and Washington?

Not all people including the American people view things the same way, the people working for the press may say what they wish, does their words kill?

If Sharon is a man of peace in the eyes of Bush, then we are also men of peace!!! America does not understand the language of manners and principles, so we are addressing it using the language it understands.

Bush and Sharon understand the language of manners and principles, and they are addressing you as you address them.

(Q2) As for the second question that we want to answer: What are we calling you to, and what do we want from you?

(1) The first thing that we are calling you to is Islam.

Most of the American people are Christians, they will never allow you to force them to change to Islam. For Islam is a man-made religion created by Muhammad for his desires and pleasures.

(a) The religion of the Unification of God; of freedom from associating partners with Him, and rejection of this; of complete love of Him, the Exalted; of complete submission to His Laws; and of the discarding of all the opinions, orders, theories and religions which contradict with the religion He sent down to His Prophet Muhammad (peace be upon him). Islam is the religion of all the prophets, and makes no distinction between them - peace be upon them all.

All religions worship their man-made gods differently, you cannot expect others to accept Allah as their God. And that is Unification of God - allow all to worship the one and All Mighty God as they see fit and knowing that there is One God above all other gods, Allah is included in those man-made gods. Muhammad was a prophet of God, but so am I, but I might pollute His words just as Muhammad did, therefore, if I am not careful, I may also start a religion of evil as Muhammad did.

It is to this religion that we call you; the seal of all the previous religions. It is the religion of Unification of God, sincerity, the best of manners, righteousness, mercy, honour, purity, and piety. It is the religion of showing kindness to others, establishing justice between them, granting them their rights, and defending the oppressed and the persecuted. It is the religion of enjoining the good and forbidding the evil with the hand, tongue and heart. It is the religion of Jihad in the way of Allah so that Allah's Word and religion reign Supreme. And it is the religion of unity and agreement on the obedience to Allah, and total equality between all people, without regarding their colour, sex, or language.

Islam equality - men are better than women, women are bought and sold. Young girls are married to old men, Muhammad had a wife of 10 - 12 years old just as you did. Rights in Islam - women and young children to not have rights, Kidneys are harvested from young children in homeless camps, and daughters are sold into slavery. How many wives do you have? How many husbands do each of your wives have? God did not say "Islam religion is the supreme religion," Muhammad said that.

(b) It is the religion whose book - the Qur'an - will remain preserved and unchanged, after the other Divine books and messages have been changed. The Qur'an is the miracle until the Day of Judgment. Allah has challenged anyone to bring a book like the Qur'an or even ten verses like it.

I accept Allah's challenge and God's Angels have used my hand to write a book from God that is better than the Qur'an, and it contains well over ten verses, this book I give to the world.

(2) The second thing we call you to, is to stop your oppression, lies, immorality and debauchery that has spread among you.

God's will is to allow all others their right to chose for themselves, you nor Allah can make demands upon others.

(a) We call you to be a people of manners, principles, honour, and purity; to reject the immoral acts of fornication, homosexuality, intoxicants, gambling's, and trading with interest.

Only you are responsible for your actions just as only I'm responsible for my actions, you nor I can make another change another' actions, for we as individuals are responsible for the Heaven or Hell that we create for ourselves.

We call you to all of this that you may be freed from that which you have become caught up in; that you may be freed from the deceptive lies that you are a great nation, that your leaders spread amongst you to conceal from you the despicable state to which you have reached.

You see the Americans as not being free, you see them as trying to control others, but yet it is you who are trying to control others. You studied in the U.S. and England, but yet your perspectives are warped.

(b) It is saddening to tell you that you are the worst civilization witnessed by the history of mankind:

(i) You are the nation who, rather than ruling by the Shariah of Allah in its Constitution and Laws, choose to invent your own laws as you will and desire. You separate religion from your policies, contradicting the pure nature which affirms Absolute Authority to the Lord and your Creator. You flee from the embarrassing question posed to you: How is it possible for Allah the Almighty to create His creation, grant them power over all the creatures and land, grant them all the amenities of life, and then deny them that which they are most in need of: knowledge of the laws which govern their lives?

The Shariah is not the only religion of God, for it also comes from a man-made god and a man-made religion. God did not create anything that is evil. Man created the actions of evil - the attempt to control others.

(ii) You are the nation that permits Usury, which has been forbidden by all the religions. Yet you build your economy and investments on Usury. As a result of this, in all its different forms and guises, the Jews have taken control of your economy, through which they have then taken control of your media, and now control all aspects of your life making you their servants and achieving their aims at your expense; precisely what Benjamin Franklin warned you against.

No one group of people controls the American economy or investments. If the Americans would allow you to force them to live as you wish, then you would be in control of the Americans as you say the Jews are.

(ii) You are a nation that permits the production, trading and usage of intoxicants. You also permit drugs, and only forbid the trade of them, even though your nation is the largest consumer of them.

God created everything and all things are good. The problem occurs when some people wrongly use products, this happens in all countries and with all people as it happens in the U.S as well as all Islam nations.

(iii) You are a nation that permits acts of immorality, and you consider them to be pillars of personal freedom. You have continued to sink down this abyss from level to level until incest has spread

amongst you, in the face of which neither your sense of honour nor your laws object.

Some people do not follow God's desires, does this not happen in your nations of Islam?

Who can forget your President Clinton's immoral acts committed in the official Oval office? After that you did not even bring him to account, other than that he 'made a mistake', after which everything passed with no punishment. Is there a worse kind of event for which your name will go down in history and remembered by nations?

The Americans use a judgment system that states, "all is innocent until proven guilty," therefore they did not see any crime was committed involving Clinton.

(iv) You are a nation that permits gambling in its all forms. The companies practice this as well, resulting in the investments becoming active and the criminals becoming rich.

Some people do not follow God's desires, does this not happen in your nations of Islam?

(vi) You are a nation that exploits women like consumer products or advertising tools calling upon customers to purchase them. You use women to serve passengers, visitors, and strangers to increase your profit margins. You then rant that you support the liberation of women.

Islam equality - men are better than women, women are bought and sold. Young girls as married to old men, Muhammad had a wife of 10 - 12 years old just as you did. Rights in Islam - women and young children to not have rights, Kidneys are harvested from young children in homeless camps, and daughters are sold into slavery. Is Islam any different than Christianity?

(vii) You are a nation that practices the trade of sex in all its forms, directly and indirectly. Giant corporations and establishments are established on this, under the name of art, entertainment, tourism and freedom, and other deceptive names you attribute to it.

All nations are run differently and all view issues differently just as all religions also do. Each of us is allowed to live in a country that fits our beliefs.

(viii) And because of all this, you have been described in history as a nation that spreads diseases that were unknown to man in

the past. Go ahead and boast to the nations of man, that you brought them AIDS as a Satanic American Invention.

The Europeans were the first to bring diseases to the Americas long before there ever was an America. We did not create or invent AIDS, and while AIDS is spread by acts that are disapproved by God.

(xi) You have destroyed nature with your industrial waste and gases more than any other nation in history. Despite this, you refuse to sign the Kyoto agreement so that you can secure the profit of your greedy companies and industries.

Nothing destroys nature, it will heal itself. The Kyoto agreement is another agreement that will not be upheld by all countries just as all the other agreements are never upheld.

(x) Your law is the law of the rich and wealthy people, who hold sway in their political parties, and fund their election campaigns with their gifts. Behind them stand the Jews, who control your policies, media and economy.

You have studied in America, but you never learned, you have seen, and yet you still do not understand our ways. How sad that makes me feel.

(xi) That which you are singled out for in the history of mankind, is that you have used your force to destroy mankind more than any other nation in history; not to defend principles and values, but to hasten to secure your interests and profits. You who dropped a nuclear bomb on Japan, even though Japan was ready to negotiate an end to the war. How many acts of oppression, tyranny and injustice have you carried out, O callers to freedom?

You have studied in America, but you never learned, you have seen, and yet you still do not understand history. Those without ears cannot hear and those without intelligence cannot understand.

(xii) Let us not forget one of your major characteristics: your duality in both manners and values; your hypocrisy in manners and principles. All manners, principles and values have two scales: one for you and one for the others.

All people view the world through their they eyes alone, and just as you see everything is wrong except for the view of life that you carry as hatred in your heart.

(a)The freedom and democracy that you call to is for

yourselves and for white race only; as for the rest of the world, you impose upon them your monstrous, destructive policies and Governments, which you call the 'American friends'. Yet you prevent them from establishing democracies. When the Islamic party in Algeria wanted to practice democracy and they won the election, you unleashed your agents in the Algerian army onto them, and to attack them with tanks and guns, to imprison them and torture them - a new lesson from the 'American book of democracy'!!!

You have lived and went to school in the U.S.A. yet you never learned anything about democracy or the people that you lived with.

(b) Your policy on prohibiting and forcibly removing weapons of mass destruction to ensure world peace: it only applies to those countries which you do not permit to possess such weapons. As for the countries you consent to, such as Israel, then they are allowed to keep and use such weapons to defend their security. Anyone else who you suspect might be manufacturing or keeping these kinds of weapons, you call them criminals and you take military action against them.

The weapons of mass destruction that we have are for use only against those who would use those types of weapons against innocent people. Iraq, who has weapons of mass destruction has used them against their own people, and those who are in control of Iraq are terrorists who help terrorists for control over others.

(c) You are the last ones to respect the resolutions and policies of International Law, yet you claim to want to selectively punish anyone else who does the same. Israel has for more than 50 years been pushing UN resolutions and rules against the wall with the full support of America.

Israelis are not the problem in the land of Israel, the Palestinians who are terrorists are the problems.

(d) As for the war criminals which you censure and form criminal courts for - you shamelessly ask that your own are granted immunity!! However, history will not forget the war crimes that you committed against the Muslims and the rest of the world; those you have killed in Japan, Afghanistan, Somalia, Lebanon and Iraq will remain a shame that you will never be able to escape. It will suffice to remind you of your latest war crimes in Afghanistan, in which densely populated innocent civilian villages were destroyed, bombs were dropped on mosques causing the roof of the mosque to come crashing

down on the heads of the Muslims praying inside. You are the ones who broke the agreement with the Mujahideen when they left Qunduz, bombing them in Jangi fort, and killing more than 1,000 of your prisoners through suffocation and thirst. Allah alone knows how many people have died by torture at the hands of you and your agents. Your planes remain in the Afghan skies, looking for anyone remotely suspicious.

Each will face his day of judgment in front of God. Allow God to punish those who He sees fit.

(e) You have claimed to be the vanguards of Human Rights, and your Ministry of Foreign affairs issues annual reports containing statistics of those countries that violate any Human Rights. However, all these things vanished when the Mujahideen hit you, and you then implemented the methods of the same documented governments that you used to curse. In America, you captured thousands the Muslims and Arabs, took them into custody with neither reason, court trial, nor even disclosing their names. You issued newer, harsher laws.

Have not the Muslims nations committed acts against Human Rights? Do you allow others to choose their own religion?

What happens in Guatanamo is a historical embarrassment to America and its values, and it screams into your faces - you hypocrites, "What is the value of your signature on any agreement or treaty?"

I know nothing of Guatanamo, so therefore I cannot reply to this question.

(3) What we call you to thirdly is to take an honest stance with yourselves - and I doubt you will do so - to discover that you are a nation without principles or manners, and that the values and principles to you are something which you merely demand from others, not that which you yourself must adhere to.

I ask you to review your religion and to see where it came from; did it come from God or Muhammad? Who's hand wrote your Bible that you call the Qur'an?

(4) We also advise you to stop supporting Israel, and to end your support of the Indians in Kashmir, the Russians against the Chechens and to also cease supporting the Manila Government against the Muslims in Southern Philippines.

You have no right to tell the American people what to support or what not to support. You are not God but merely a man just as I. We cannot make others do what we think they should do.

(5) We also advise you to pack your luggage and get out of our lands. We desire for your goodness, guidance, and righteousness, so do not force us to send you back as cargo in coffins.

You do not speak for the people but only yourself. You do not like the Americans in lands that you call your'. God owns everything and that includes all the land. He has allowed the Americans into those lands and you have no right to tell or force them out of any part of the world.

(6) Sixthly, we call upon you to end your support of the corrupt leaders in our countries. Do not interfere in our politics and method of education. Leave us alone, or else expect us in New York and Washington.

The American education was good enough for you, is it too good for other Muslims? Do you wish to be smarter than all other Muslims?

(7) We also call you to deal with us and interact with us on the basis of mutual interests and benefits, rather than the policies of sub dual, theft and occupation, and not to continue your policy of supporting the Jews because this will result in more disasters for you.

America deals with those who are in charge of other countries. What country are you in charge of?

If you fail to respond to all these conditions, then prepare for fight with the Islamic Nation. The Nation of Monotheism, that puts complete trust on Allah and fears none other than Him. The Nation which is addressed by its Qur'an with the words: "Do you fear them? Allah has more right that you should fear Him if you are believers. Fight against them so that Allah will punish them by your hands and disgrace them and give you victory over them and heal the breasts of believing people. And remove the anger of their (believers') hearts. Allah accepts the repentance of whom He wills. Allah is All-Knowing, All-Wise." [Qur'an9:13-1]

Know to who you worship, and know what you asked of Him because He may grant your request. And Monotheism is not religion that places Allah above all other Gods, Monotheism is believing in one Supreme Being above all others, and those 'others' includes Allah!

The Nation of honour and respect:

"But honour, power and glory belong to Allah, and to His Messenger (Muhammad- peace be upon him) and to the believers." [Qur'an 63:8]

"So do not become weak (against your enemy), nor be sad, and you will be*superior (in victory)if you are indeed (true) believers" [Qur'an 3:139]

The Nation of Martyrdom; the Nation that desires death more than you desire life:

If Muslims desire death more than life, why do you hide from the Americans?

"Think not of those who are killed in the way of Allah as dead. Nay, they are alive with their Lord, and they are being provided for. They rejoice in what Allah has bestowed upon them from His bounty and rejoice for the sake of those who have not yet joined them, but are left behind (not yet martyred) that on them no fear shall come, nor shall they grieve. They rejoice in a grace and a bounty from Allah, and that Allah will not waste the reward of the believers." [Qur'an 3:169-171]

If 72 virgins await each Martyr in Heaven, what is the Heaven for each virgin?"

The Nation of victory and success that Allah has promised:

Victory and success has always been givien to the winner and the winner is always America.

"It is He Who has sent His Messenger (Muhammad peace be upon him) with guidance and the religion of truth (Islam), to make it victorious over all other religions even though the Polytheists hate it." [Qur'an 61:9]

Muslims cannot understand that their religion may not be the last religion formed from God. Yes, Muhammad did communicate with God's Angel, but so have I and many others since the time of Muhammad. And He has not told us the same things that people 'claim' that He told Muhammad.

"Allah has decreed that 'Verily it is I and My Messengers who shall be victorious.' Verily Allah is All-Powerful, All-Mighty."

[Qur'an 58:21]

I am also a Messenger of God's. On a daily basis I see and communicate with the Angels Gabrael, Michael, Joleen and Jesus.

The Islamic Nation that was able to dismiss and destroy the previous evil Empires like yourself; the Nation that rejects your attacks, wishes to remove your evils, and is prepared to fight you. You are well aware that the Islamic Nation, from the very core of its soul, despises your haughtiness and arrogance.

If a war between all other religions and Islam is what the Muslims desire, then by the Power of the All Mighty God that is what it shall be.

If the Americans refuse to listen to our advice and the goodness, guidance and righteousness that we call them to, then be aware that you will lose this Crusade Bush began, just like the other previous Crusades in which you were humiliated by the hands of the Mujahideen, fleeing to your home in great silence and disgrace. If the Americans do not respond, then their fate will be that of the Soviets who fled from Afghanistan to deal with their military defeat, political breakup, ideological downfall, and economic bankruptcy.

Who taught you to fight the Russians? May God's mercy be upon the Muslims, Amen.

This is our message to the Americans, as an answer to theirs. Do they now know why we fight them and over which form of ignorance, by the permission of Allah, we shall be victorious?

It is a non-believer to end his letter as bin Laden did by asking if they (the Muslims) shall be victorious or not. For I know that God's glory will prevail.

Muslims See War as The New World Crusade

Wed Mar 12, 1:33 AM ET
By GEORGE GEDDA, Associated Press Writer

WASHINGTON - *Not many Muslims, regardless of nationality, buy into President Bush's contention that war against Iraq may be needed as a self-defense measure against a potential aggressor.*

Some Muslims are more vehement in their opposition than others. Islamic scholars at Cairo's Al-Azhar University, for example, believe that no provocation can justify an American military presence on Arab soil.

The scholars, members of the university's Islamic Research Academy, argue that Islamic law holds that "if the enemy steps on Muslims' land, jihad becomes a duty on every male and female Muslim."

What does Islamic law say about how to react to a Friend who came to help, steps on Muslims Land? The scholars and members of the university's Islamic Research Academy, are carrying what they think was said in the Islamic Religion and thinks of one who is a friend as an enemy without just cause?

They believe the U.S. military buildup in the Persian Gulf and the expected invasion of Iraq are part of a new "Crusade" by the West against Islam.

The Crusades were a series of wars fought more than 1,000 years ago as Christian armies traveled to the Holy Land to attack the armies of the Muslim sultans who then controlled Jerusalem.

The Christians Crusades occurred because Muslims would not allow them to visit and worship in Jerusalem, who believed they must make the journey to their Holy Land Jerusalem, at least once in their lives. Is it asking to much to be allowed to visit land that one believes to be Holy?

Non-Muslims tend to view the Crusades as an aberration from a bygone past. Muslims, particularly fundamentalists, believe that little has changed since that period. They maintain the West's thirst for control of the region persists to this day, and they cite as evidence Bush's war on terrorism and the Persian Gulf troop buildup.

If the Christians would have wanted to have control of the region, they would have continued the Crusades that occurred in the bygone past, they needed not to wait until today to do so. The Crusades were meant only to be allowed to travel in peace to the land they considered Holy.

Among crusader theorists is Osama bin Laden,, who sees the presence of "infidel" American troops on the "sacred" soil of Arabia, the birthplace of Islam, as evidence that the West is intent on subjugating Muslims.

Bin Laden is confused and would be confused in any religion that he attempted to follow. He truly is trying to carry more than he can handle as he tries to control people in what belief systems they follow."

According to U.S. counterterrorism officials, bin Laden's al-Qaida operatives plan to strike U.S. and allied forces if Bush orders an attack on Iraq.

Bin Laden is Oblivious to God and should be oblivious to us. I shall not allow him to force me to carry his burden.

Attempts by some Muslims to depict the West as colonizers in disguise frustrate those who see history in a far different light.

Confused Ones see Light that is not Light, it does not matter if that Light was in History or in the Present.

In a recent issue of Foreign Affairs magazine, for example, Middle East expert Barry Rubin wrote: *"During the last half-century, in 11 of 12 major conflicts between Muslims and non-Muslims,*

Muslims and secular forces, or Arabs and non-Arabs, the United States has sided with the former group."

It is not the concern to the United States what the religion of the people who need their help, and therefore, their help is directed to those who are in need of help, and that is righteous. The U.S. has allowed others to place their burden upon them, and therefore, they are allowing others to control what they need and want.

The exception, of course, is the Arab-Israeli conflict, in which Washington's support for Israel has been a source of anguish for Muslims for decades.

Israel is indeed in need of help, so therefore, the U.S. helps them.

Among episodes when the United States sided with Muslims against non-Muslims are the U.S.-led bombing campaigns of 1999 in Serbia and of 1995 in Bosnia. American troops intervened to help beleaguered Muslims in both areas.

The Muslims who are on the wrong side in these conflicts you describe are Confused and do not know the truth nor will they accept the truth.

Rubin accuses anti-American Arab radicals of "ignoring all the positive examples and focusing only on U.S. support for Israel."

But many Muslims disagree. European decolonization of Africa and Asia meant an end to the European presence but, as former intelligence analyst Keith Mines has noted, Westerners have stayed in the Middle East, "compelled by new political and economic interests in cheap oil, and a homeland for the Jewish people," among other factors.

In this comment, at least three different issues are put together into one thought; that the U.S. is in different places and helping people in different places, who need help, at different times, total confusion.

All this has created a backlash among many Arabs, which is fed by media disinformation, none more glaring than the widely reported - and widely held - myth that 4,000 Jews who worked in the World Trade Center took a holiday on Sept. 11, 2001.

The Bush administration takes some comfort in the knowledge that, whatever reservations many Muslims may have about Bush's policy toward Iraq, there is common ground with some Muslims.

President Bush is Christian and as will all Christians Bush does not believe in the Muslim religion, and therefore, he sees all that are not Christians as lost; he wishes that all people would convert to Christianity.

"It's not a question of us versus Saddam Hussein," State Department spokesman Richard Boucher said Monday. "Nobody likes Saddam Hussein. Nobody believes that the region is better for having him there."

Richard Boucher believes he is speaking for all the people of the world, and therefore, he is trying to carry the world's burden of who they like or is trying to force his beliefs upon all others.

Whether that sentiment will diminish the terrorism threat if Saddam is ousted is open to question. One who believes use of force will have the opposite effect is Libyan leader Moammar Gadhafi, who told a French newspaper: "The day America launches a war, it should expect the worst. ... Terrorism risks becoming a general scourge."

Gadhafi thinks he is speaking as a Muslim for all Muslims. He cannot know what all other Muslims feel inside. Therefore, he also is trying to force his beliefs of what all Muslims believe and think and will do.

You see that "Only take what you can Carry," does not imply only to money and wealth; it refers to all that we do in life.

Now, back to the subject of the treasure that the Angels will show me; if I go and retrieve my part of the treasure what would I do with it?

Would I give it to people who are without? They may need food for starving or they may need a place to get in out of the cold, but money given to them to continue their same life style will not help them. They need words of Wisdom that inspire them with self-respect that raises them to where they can take care of themselves and to provide for themselves.

Sure I could put the money from the treasure into promoting my Ministry, but if my Ministry is truly a Ministry of God, His Angels will help me spread the words of God.

No, I would not put the money into something that does not need it.

I would use the money to pay off my bills; house mortgage, credit cards and such that I had promised to pay when I received those things. For I do not want to place my promises upon my wife or children, and thus force them to "carry my burden" - the things I thought that I could carry, but didn't.

And whereas, do not allow others to burden you with things they "think" you should carry.

Make sure that the YOKE that you wear is yours and that it does not belong to another - Do not be concerned what others think and do. You are not responsible for others, for you can only find peace for yourself within you.

Muslim Terrorists Do Not Follow Their Religion

And the Angel Gabrael said to me, "Tell the people that Muslims Terrorists do not follow what their Prophet Muhammad laid down for them, and what he quoted from God was wrong and it was from his inner human feelings instead of from God. Those who truly believe in and follow God's words will fight and defeat the terrorists, for it does not matter what religion they follow for all are the children of God. For you (humanity) are the body of God, and the Body shall not deny or persecute any part of Itself. Only those who follow evil persecute and deny others, and all terrorists follow evil. Terrorism shall be defeated because it is not the Anti-Christ that has yet to emerge."

The two primary sources of knowledge in Islam are the Qur'an and Sunnah. The Qur'an consists of the Arabic text revealed to Muhammad over a period of 23 years. The Sunnah refers to Prophet's sayings and deeds, also known as Ahadith. The Ahadith are collected in different books, mostly named after the scholar who collected it. The following hadith is from the book, Sahih Muslim, named after the scholar whose (short) name was Muslim.

It is narrated on the authority of Abu Huraira that the Messenger of Allah observed: "He who killed himself with steel (weapon) would be the eternal denizen of the Fire of Hell and he would have that weapon in his hand and would be thrusting that in his stomach for ever and ever, he who drank poison and killed himself would sip that in the Fire of Hell where he is doomed for ever and ever; and he who killed himself by falling from (the top of) a mountain would constantly fall in the Fire of Hell and would live there for ever and ever."

When it comes to the Islamic conduct of war, some of the verses of the Qur'an that have often been mis-quoted by Muslims to "prove" Islam promotes violence and bloodshed are found in Surah 2 verses 190-194:

2.190. Fight against those who fight against you in the way of Allah, but do not transgress, for Allah does not love transgressors.

2.191. Kill them whenever you confront them and drive them out from where they drove you out. (For though killing is sinful) wrongful persecution is even worse than killing. Do not fight against them near the Holy Mosque unless they fight against you; but if they fight against you kill them, for that is the reward of such unbelievers.

(It is interesting to note: Before Muhammad began his conversations with God during the 7th century there was no Musilms or Islamic Religion, and the Romans gave Israel to the followers of Jesus - "Christians", after they exiled the Jews from Israel, this occurred around the 3rd century. The Muslims during or after the 7th century drove the first Christians out of Israel, and yet today Muslims claim Israel as theirs.)

2.192. Then if they desist, know well that Allah is Ever-Forgiving, Most Compassionate.

2.193. Keep on fighting against them until mischief ends and the way prescribed by Allah prevails. But if they desist, then know that hostility is only against the wrong-doers.

(Muslim terrorists are fighting to make the world one country without boundaries. Contrary to the Qur'an, they want to take land from others, then who are the wrong-doers?)

2.194. The sacred month for the sacred month; sanctities should be respected alike (by all concerned). Thus, if someone has attacked you, attack him just as he attacked you, and fear Allah and remain conscious that Allah is with those who guard against violating the bounds set by Him.

The Historic Context and the Nature of the Qur'an

The Qur'an comprises of revelations from God to Muhammad

over a period of twenty three years (610 C.E. - 632 C.E.). The first 13 years of the prophethood of Muhammad were at his hometown of Makkah (Mecca), where he and his fellow Muslims were severely persecuted by the pagans of Makkah. During that time, Muslims were not ordered to fight back, but bear the persecutions. Finally, God ordered the Prophet and his fellow Muslims (known as Sahabah) to emigrate to the city of Madinah, about 400 kilometers away.

This emigration, known as the Hijrah, marked the beginning of an Islamic society in Madinah, in which Muhammad became the head of the state. It was not long before the polytheists of Makkah marched towards Madinah to wage war against Muslims and destroy the Islamic state of Madinah. This battle is known as the Battle of Badr. The verses 2.190-2.194, above were perhaps the first injunctions from God to Muslims to prepare themselves for fighting. It was obviously a war in the defense of their homeland and their Faith.

In verse 2.190, God instructs Muslims to fight back, but not to transgress, and remain just even during the battle. They are told, "Material interests should not be the motivation for their fighting, that they should not take up arms against those were not in opposition to the true faith, that they should not resort to unscrupulous methods or to the indiscriminate killing and pillaging which characterized the other wars." The excesses alluded to in this verse are acts such as taking up arms against women and children, the old and the injured, mutilation of the dead bodies of the enemy, uncalled for devastation through the destruction of fields and livestock, and other similar acts of injustice and brutality. Muhammad prohibited all these acts. The real intent of the verse is to stress that force should be used only when its use is unavoidable, and only to the extent that is absolutely necessary.

Commentary on verse 2.192: God, in whom the believers have faith, is forgiving and ready to pardon even the worst criminals and sinners after they have renounced their arrogant defiance towards Him. It is suggested that this attribute of God should be reflected in the behavior of the believers as well. Hence, whenever the believers have to resort to armed conflict, they should do so not for the sake of quenching their thirst for vengeance, but in the just cause of their defense. Their conflict with any group should last only as long as that group is fighting them. As soon as it gives up this fight the hostility should cease. (These statements indicates; Muslims must fight until they win and their enemy is defeated. Interesting...)

It should be emphasized that so many revelations in the Qur'an came down to provide guidance to Muhammad based on what he was confronting at that time. Therefore, it is important to understand and know the historic context of the revelations for a proper understanding of these verses.

Muhammad was a peace maker for his time. He endured torture, hunger and the killing of his loved ones by his enemies, but he remained a merciful person while his followers "preached" his words with the sword.

Suicide

And the Angel Gabrael (his name is not spelled Gabriel) said unto me, "Blasphemies against the Father and Heaven may be forgiven on earth and in Heaven. Blasphemies against the Son and earth may be forgiven on earth and in Heaven. But Blasphemies against the Holy Spirit shall not be forgiven on earth or in Heaven."

I asked the Angel Gabrael, "What is an act that is so unforgiving that God will not forgive? What is the differences between the Blasphemies that you speak of?'

The Angel Gabrael answered, "Blaspemies against the Father, the Heaven, the Son and the earth are not against the Creation, but are merely against part of the creation.

(Please note and understand the difference between the words "Creation" and "creation.")

"Suicide is Blasphemy against the Holy Spirit. It does not matter what form or what reason one takes his own life, it is still Blasphemy against the Holy Spirit while also, Blasphemy against the Holy Spirit is convincing another that there is nothing in the Creation worth living for, thus death does not need to come to the body, but can also be of the spirit of the individual – spiritual death."

SUICIDE IS A GRAVE SIN

It is my understanding that a church named, International or Worldwide Church of God located in Texas claims; Suicide is forgivable by God. They make this statement because the Bible says, "Nothing is impossible with God."

Do you recall the true story, "The Onion Field Killings?" After being stopped by two policemen for a traffic violation, the two men in the car, takes hostage the policmen and decide to drive them north to Bakersfield to kill them because at the time, you would receive the same penalty for taking hostages as murder. Now this law has been changed, the penalty is less for taking hostages than murder. Thus, suicide is the same, the Church needed to add and/or declare suicide is forgivable by God.

The two primary sources of knowledge in Islam are the Holy Qur'an and Sunnah. The Holy Qur'an consists of the Arabic text revealed to Prophet Muhammad over a period of 23 years. The Sunnah refers to Prophet's sayings and deeds, also known as Ahadith. The Ahadith are collected in different books, mostly named after the scholar who collected it. The following hadith is from the book, Sahih Muslim, named after the scholar whose (short) name was Muslim.

"It is narrated on the authority of Abu Huraira that the Messenger of Allah observed: He who killed himself with steel (weapon) would be the eternal denizen of the Fire of Hell and he would have that weapon in his hand and would be thrusting that in his stomach for ever and ever, he who drank poison and killed himself would sip that in the Fire of Hell where he is doomed for ever and ever; and he who killed himself by falling from (the top of) a mountain would constantly fall in the Fire of Hell and would live there for ever and ever." (Sahih Muslim, Chapter 48, Book 1, Number 0199).

There are same or similar ahadith in Sahih Bukhari.

Life is sacred by the teachings of Islam.

The following excerpts are from Dr. Ahmad Sakr's book, "Muslims and Non-Muslims, Face to Face" (isbn: 091119-31-9).

A deputation from the Christians of Najran (Yemen) came to see Muhammad in Madina. They came into the Prophet's Mosque (Masjid Nabawi) as he prayed the afternoon prayer. The time of prayers of Christians having come, they stood and prayed in the Prophet's Mosque, and the Prophet said that they were to be left to do so. (see The Life of Muhammad by A. Guillaume).

During the life of Muhammad, the Jews in Madina had a

synagogue and an educational institute, Bait-Al-Midras. The Prophet preserved the institute and gave protection to the Jews.

The Prophet respected the autonomy of the Christian churches. The nomination and the appointment of bishops and priests was left to the Christian community itself. Muhammad promoted cooperation between Muslims and Christians in the political arena as well. He selected a non-Muslim, 'Amr-ibn Umaiyah-ad-Damri, as an ambassador to Negus, the King of Ethiopia.

The Prophet sent a message to the monks of Saint Catherine in Mount Sinai:

"This is a message written by Muhammad ibn Abdullah, as a covenant to those who adopt Christianity, far and near, we are behind them. Verily, I defend them by myself, the servants, the helpers, and my followers, because Christians are my citizens; and by Allah! I hold out against anything that displeases them. No compulsion is to be on them. Neither are their judges to be changed from their jobs, nor their monks from their monasteries. No one is to destroy a house of their religion, to damage it, or to carry anything from it to the Muslims' houses. Should anyone take any of these, he would spoil God's covenant and disobey His Prophet. Verily, they (Christians) are my allies and have my secure charter against all that they hate. No one is to force them to travel or to oblige them to fight. The Muslims are to fight for them. If a female Christian is married to a Muslim, this is not to take place without her own wish. She is not to be prevented from going to her church to pray. Their churches are to be respected. They are neither to be prevented from repairing them nor the sacredness of their covenants. No one of the nation is to disobey this covenant till the Day of Judgment and the end of the world." Jihad (unholy war)

Jihad in arabic means to strive, to do one's utmost. There are two types of Jihad in Islam.

1. Jihad against one's own self (to keep one on a straight path)
2. Jihad in the Path of God which includes but not limited to fighting to defend one's property, life or Faith.

Terrorists can declare Jihad and call it Jihad, but their Jihad is in the path of Satan, NOT in the path of God.

If the word Jihad is used in its Arabic meaning, then the officers and volunteers working in the relief effort are doing a Jihad, *as they are doing their best to find life and bodies in the rubble of WTC.*

Those people who are grieved, angry and feel rancor are doing Jihad to contain their anger and rancor and remain just. This is Jihad against one's self.

Satan is happy to see the instigators at work. May God contain Satan and protect us all from his evil.

Palestinians Against The Israelis

I have been closely watching the events unfold in Israel, and this has caused me to study the Islamic Religion.

The Islamic Religion speaks of one Muslim nation with no borders nor boundaries. That indicates to me, if there are no boundaries or borders to their nation, they are speaking of one nation that covers the world. And yet, today the Muslim countries have different leaders.

Also, they speak of a nation that has no man-made laws. Can you imagine, a country with no man-made laws... where no one is in charge... everyone does as he wishes.... no one needs to work, if you need money, just take it from someone who has money. The stores would be open only the hours that it wishes. And if you wanted to have a store, just kill a storeowner and take it, no laws to stop you. God nor Allah wrote the words for Islam, man wrote the Islamic bible, so whose laws do they follow?

Equal rights for all the people of the Islamic Religion... there is none. They believe that Muhammad will be born to man, and women will be the beast of burden again. Also, they state, "No formal education or medical care for women." Even today, Muslim men buy and sell women.

The Palestinians speak of their suicide bombers as martyrs, a martyr as one who dies, suffers or gives up everything for his religion. Also, a martyr is one who is persecuted. The Israelis are being persecuted, not the Palestinians. Palestinians are not dying for their religion; they are dying for control over Israel, and for control over the people of the world. The Islamic religion is racist, and Yasser Arafat is racist and pushing policies for ethnic cleansing of the Israelis.

The present Palestinian uprising started over 11 months ago because the now Prime Minister of Israel, Ariel Sharon, visited a Holy site. The Palestinians cast the first stone while Israelis reacted in self-defense. And now the Israelis retaliate only to the ugly acts of gorilla warfare from the cowardly Palestinian leaders who tell their people that if they die fighting the Israelis, they will go to Heaven. The Palestinians officials cry out that they are sending in suicide bombers and killing the Israelis because the Israelis killed Muslims first. The Palestinians were the first to kill Israelis at the start of this uprising, but does it matter who died first? This is not a Holy war or a war for freedom; this is a war by man for ownership of land and a power trip of a few Muslims.

Muhammad was given God's words, but his followers and the Palestinians have turned those words into words of the dog. After Muhammad died, his followers demanded others to join their religion, and if they refused, they were put to death. Even today, those who convert to Christianity from the Islamic religion are put to death, if found out.

All the people of the world need to rally behind the Israelis now, because the Palestinians will not stop their fighting until they have control over Israel, and if they do defeat Israel, someday soon we too, will be fighting the Muslims in our home lands, for the fall of the Israeli people will be the beginning to the end of the civilized world.

Yes, I believe as told to me by the Angels, "Taking of a life is not the answer." But if the Israelis cannot Inspire the Palestinians to live in peace, then the Palestinians must be dealt with as needed. Because we cannot let a group of people that do or do not call themselves a nation, and who are backed by terrorist, dictate to any other group of people. We cannot allow the Israelis to become enslaved as they were during World War Two under the dictation of Hitler.

May the one God who is above Muhammad, Jesus and Moses, who is the God that Abraham, Isaac and Jacob embraced, have mercy on the Palestinian's and the Muslim's Souls.

Islamic Terrorist

And the Angel Jo said unto me, "Did you not warn them? For in your Messages you have warned what was coming, even the Message that you gave last Sunday in Ohio, indicated what was to come. Also, did not We - God's Angels warn many, and did not some heed our words? We cannot save everyone because one's actions are their individual decisions. And if We forced them to listen and follow our Knowledge, then they would be under our domination. And all, including the evil must have their freedom of choices to live in God's Concept of Life - 'To learn and experience through the experiences of others through endurance of life.'

"Many died because they thought terrorist could not harm them in their country. What makes their country any better than the rest? Does the fool who smokes a cigarette, think he will not get cancer? People are all the same. Countries are all the same. What happens in one can happen in another.

"Once again I say to you, 'This is the beginning to the end.' And yet, this is not the end, because every step forward is getting closer to the end. Every step is another part of learning and experiencing life and deciding what is best for you. What is best for you is what is best for all the people - children of God.

"Remember, 'A Love for a Love is the answer, but one must receive a slap if one delivers a slap to another. Taking of a life is not the answer if one can be inspired to change, but if one will not change, then they must be removed. Do not allow the corrupt to destroy the good.'

And I said to the Angel Jo, "The people only rally together and/or seek God whenever something bad occurs that affects their lives. They refuse God and do not recognize or speak to Him daily. And when something bad happens to others like it has to the Israelis, they say and do nothing, so why should He bother Himself with them? Let the dead bury the dead, God does not need their pain and suffering of those who cannot see or hear."

And the Angel Jo replied, "All are God's children. God is Love...whenever one wishes to speak to Him, or have Him in his life, He is there. He will not dominate His children...He does not demand anything of them. If the Father does not make demands on His children why should a child make demands on his siblings? You will not fully understand until you arrive here on The Other Side, until then, Love your brothers as you love yourself. Feel the pains and hurts that your brother feels, for you too, as they are part of the total body of the human race. Do not condemn others for their actions or their thoughts. Do not hate those who try to dominate others, and do not be angry at those who seek God only in their time of need. Anger comes from the Dog, hate grows from evil, dislike comes from love and God is Love. Dislike the actions of those who try to dominate. Dislike the actions of those who seek God only in their time of need. Try to Inspire them to repent, but do not try to dominate them and do not allow others to dominate you. Mourn for the decease of the cycle, but cry forever for the dead."

Fighting Terrorists

I have been told by Jesus to speak in words and terms used today. Thus, I do not "preach" the old from the Bible, I speak of God in today's living. He is with us now just as He was throughout the pages of history. Therefore, this Message is about Evil - Terrorism that is surrounding us, and how to combat it. Remember His touch - seek Him and He is there.

In fighting any group of terrorist, one must understand what they believe and what is driving their terrorist actions.

Muslim Terrorists are driven by their belief in Islam and Allah. They have given up everything including their lives, children and families to their god - Allah. All is for him. Therefore, they believe that they are fighting a war for him.

When the Terrorists blew up the U.S. Embassies located in Africa, bin Laden said concerning the civilians killed, "It was Allah's will." That statement indicated he and his terrorists did not intend to kill civilians but they were after the U.S. Embassies and the civilians died because they were there.

In the Islamic Terrorists thinking, this is the same thing that happened on September 11th. The terrorists were not trying to kill Americans; they were after the World Trade Center and the U.S. Military - the Pentagon.

Even the Anthrax was meant for the U.S. Government and for

the U.S. news media that bin Laden and his followers hate. Contamination from the letters sent to our Government and news media could contaminate our personal mail, but this was not the terrorist main intention, but our health and safety is not their concern. (Personally, I microwave all mail that we now receive, not only for Anthrax but also for the de-contamination of other organisms and diseases.)

The accusations from the Taliban of us bombing civilians in Afghanistan has stepped up the war to include the terrorist killing Christians such as in the massacre of 15 Protestants worshipping at St. Dominic's Church in Behawalpor, Pakistan the other week. Now, we as Americans need to be more aware that terrorists could and may strike in our hometowns and against civilians just as the Israelis are persecuted by Palestinian Terrorists.

When one is fighting a war, one must keep in mind and understand the differences between guerrilla, terrorist and army warfare, and whom we are fighting. And one must call upon those who have fought terrorists for stratagem, therefore, we must learn from the Israeli people. They do not have terrorists taking over their airlines and flying them into buildings, and also, they are not threatened with Anthrax, but face terrorists every day.

Of course, we as children of God, should not fight, but when one approaches and tries to dominate, we must defend ourselves. And when our opponent has killed those that he has fought in the past, we must understand that he plans to kill us as he defeats us, therefore, we must try to destroy him first.

God's Angels say, "A Love for a Love." But if terrorists approach and chant, "Blood for blood," an enemy must be fought on the terms that they fight. We cannot raise our enemies to our level of intelligence - standards of life.

Understanding Our Enemy

(Story first appeared in St. Louis Riverfront News)

Abhaseen Barikzy sits alone in the bare living room, still as a wounded lion. His eyes are hidden by dark glasses and his chest is covered by a Forest Park Balloon Race T-shirt, but on his brown forearms, huge blotches shine pale pink where the acid splashed. He holds his head stiffly to one side, his left shoulder hunched close to his neck, drawn by tightening scars. His skin shows thick in patches, hard with the collagen his body flooded over untreated wounds.

Barikzy dutifully checks in at the BJC medical and psychiatric clinics, but he's uninterested in his own healing. "This is not my terrible face," he tells them. "This is the terrible face of Islam."

The Barikzy family (not their real name) has been in St. Louis since April, but the house the family is renting is still sparse and immaculate, with mattresses on the floor of the dining room for the six kids and a prayer rug on the wall. A gift from the local mullah, the rug is a reminder of the other, kind and temperate face of Islam, and Barikzy's wife still uses it to pray. Abhaseen cannot. Every morning he walks the older children to the school bus, then sits in a large donated chair in the dim living room. There, backlit by the window, his face in shadow, he slowly -- with the help of a translator he barely trusts -- releases the story he's waited two years to tell.

Barikzy grew up in the dusty village of Khak-raiz, in the

southern desert province of Qandahar, Afghanistan. He was Pashtun, the ethnic majority, and like 99 percent of his countrymen, he grew up Muslim. At 11, he started noticing the contradictions between school, "where we learned about the world, about luck, humor, love, progress, technology" -- and the village's strict mosque, "where we were told we shouldn't live for this world, this is just for two days. They said the technology in the world was for pagans but for Muslims there was another world: paradise."

Barikzy was too interested in this world to dismiss it so easily. Nor could he accept the way his father treated his mother, lavishing love and kindness on a second wife (traditional Islamic law allows as many as four) and leaving Barikzy's mother to do all the housework, take his beatings and gratify his desires. "When I was 12, she died because of too much suffering," he says, "and that bothered me a lot. I felt like an orphan."

Two years later, a young woman in his village left her father's house and went to the house of the man she loved. "When they brought the girl to the mosque, people gathered to see how the mullah would punish her," recalls Barikzy. "He said she should be put in a bag, and they put a cat with her and tied the bag and started beating her." Barikzy says they struck her 80 times: "When they finally opened the bag, she was covered in blood, and the cat was dead. So was his faith in God. He decided that conservative Qandahar, birthplace of Afghan kings and, more recently, the Taliban, was full of "dark-minded" people. The next year, 1966, his family moved the Afghan Communist Party was beginning to take hold. As soon as Barikzy heard the Communists start talking about women's issues and progress, he joined them.

The party handpicked Barikzy to study journalism at its institute in Kabul. By the time they took power in 1978, he was an officer in the army, writing for the defense ministry's army newspaper and, often, the party's paper as well. A few months after the takeover, he says, he attended a huge party meeting at the Kabul headquarters, where officials accused Pakistan's ISI (Interservices Intelligence Directorate) of assassinating a party leader. Originally they'd blamed the king. Now, someone had produced a note allegedly written by, and implicating, the ISI.

While the party was sorting out its suspicions, it was continuing to welcome Soviet advisors at various government offices. Their alien, heavily accented presence stung Afghans loyal to Islam and to their traditional governing council. Fundamentalist rebels, or mujahideen, banded together to oppose the godless Communists. In 1979, the Soviet military entered Afghanistan in force.

The Soviet Union, alert to the millions of Muslims within its own borders, could not risk the contagion of chaos in a client state. The U.S., about to elect Ronald Reagan president, could not sit still while the Soviets bolstered their "evil empire." We backed the mujahideen, pronouncing them "freedom fighters" and channeling arms to them through Pakistan, the bordering Islamic country where democracy had never quite taken hold. Busy opposing communism, we failed to notice the growing religious extremism our support was fueling.

Barikzy spent these years as a Communist war correspondent. "Whatever the party commanded me, with passion and with love I accepted," he recalls. Notebook in hand, he traveled to the ever-changing "front," villages along the jagged Hindu Kush mountains (elsewhere known as the Himalayas), where the God-fearing, U.S.-armed mujahideen battled his party, fighting both a holy war and a proxy war between the Soviets and the U.S.

One crucial battle site was Khost, a garrison city 34 kilometers from the Pakistan border, cross-hatched by several routes to the Afghan interior. In Khost, the taxis are horse carts, and instead of running water or electricity, there is symbolism. Two men had fought hard for this strategic town: Gulbuddin Hekmatyar, whose rebels received the bulk of U.S. arms, and Jalaluddin Haqqani, who scoffed at political negotiation, insisting that "only jihad (holy war) will produce an Islamic government in Afghanistan" (New York Times, April 16, 1991).

In April 1991, after 16 days of fierce battle, the mujahideen took Khost. Barikzy traveled there, "wearing the cloth of the local people" and taking cover with a friend who worked for the mujahideen. Haqqani and Hekmatyar had come to Khost to receive a reward from Pakistan for their victory, says Barikzy, and once there, they announced a fatwah against the people of the town, promising their soldiers, "You can kill 160 men, and you can keep the women and whatever you get from their houses." He says they went to "the center of the city, an area people call a park, but there was no grass on it. They put the men in a line, and one of the leaders said, 'Whoever kills them, God will praise and reward.' Then they machinegunned them, and all the men fell down dead.

"Some cut a special part of the women's bodies, an abdominal part," he adds. "Then a general in ISI came and rewarded the commanders for their victory."

Barikzy had seen enough. He fled to Kabul and wrote accounts of the massacre for both the army paper and the Communist paper.

A month or so later, someone threw a warning message into the walled garden of the house in Khushul Mina, the green, well-kept suburb of Kabul where Barikzy lived with his wife and children. "It said, 'According to Islamic law, you must be executed, because you talk against Islam,'" he says. "I hid it and didn't tell my family, just went to the office and reported it. I became a little careful."

In April 1992, the Communist government fell, leaving Afghanistan to a scattered array of fundamentalist groups. For Barikzy, "careful" was no longer enough: "I had friends who were working with the mujahideen, and they told me I was safe," he says, folding his arms high and tight across his chest. "Unfortunately, the different mujahideen groups started fighting against each other." They were divided, as the country always had been, by geography and tribal ancestry -- but the old harmony, the old unifying council, was gone.

For the next two years, the mujahideen fought each other, bombing even residential areas into rubble. In 1994, the Taliban (from taleb, "religious student") entered the fray, promising to destroy the corrupt mujahideen groups and win Afghanistan back to the 1,000-year reign of pure Islamic law. The Taliban's version of Islamic law, promulgated by a few fiery-eyed mullahs, proved the harshest and bloodiest the world had ever seen -- but it would take years for the world's powers to notice.

In spring of 1995, the war brought Barikzy's enemies to his door. When his neighborhood, Khushul Mina, became a battleground for two of the warring mujahideen groups, he took his family to live with his in-laws, then took a taxi back to his house. He wanted to gather up any papers that showed his Communist activities.

The houses on his street were dark, empty shells -- their occupants had fled, and the electricity had been cut. The only people he saw were mujahideen with guns on their shoulders. Swiftly unlocking the garden gate, Barikzy went straight to his bedroom and rifled through drawers and files, pulling out his article on Khost, another article about Pakistani intervention in Afghanistan, his party-membership card, photos of him with Russian journalists, his army-officer ID, a medal from the Communist government. As he stuffed them into his big black fake-leather briefcase, he heard the rocketing coming closer, until the explosions shook the windows. He couldn't leave now, he realized. He'd have to spend the night.

He found an old oil heater, brewed some tea and, around midnight, went to bed. "I was almost asleep when I heard someone knocking at my gate very violently," he says. "Suddenly the door broke and a large group of people carrying guns came in. 'Are you Abhaseen Barikzy?' they said. 'Is this your own house?' I said, 'Yes, this is my own house.' Then the commander commanded the other people to close my eyes with a turban. They wrapped it very hard, beating me with their fists and also with guns, and pulled me to the room where I'd been sleeping. The commander said to search around the house to find out if I had guns."

Barikzy wasn't worried about guns -- he was worried about the briefcase, which he'd set carefully in the corner, ready to take with him the next morning. One of the men found it almost immediately. "There's lots of papers here," he called.

"I was feeling very terrible and dizzy, thinking, 'I was a clever man, but they took me just when I'd collected all those things myself,'" recalls Barikzy. "We have a parable:

A very clever bird will fly back to the nest." He smiles wryly. "I'm thinking they had already found my house, and maybe someone was looking when I went back."

He says the commander's men briefly translated the articles, first for two Arabs in their party and then into Urdu for a man from Pakistan. Then, he says, they started beating him, saying, "You are a very stupid man. Nobody will flee from Islam. You see that God gave *you to us. We were looking for you in the higher, but we found you on the earth."*

They took him outside and carried miniature paintings and other valuables out to their small Japanese trucks. Shoved into the yard, Barikzy heard the commander tell his men to pour petrol throughout the house and burn it.

They drove for about two hours, north into the mountains, and when his captors untied him from the truck, Barikzy says he heard "very faint moaning, like a sick dog," and smelled a sick-sweet rot. As he walked, his feet brushed against what he knew instinctively were bodies, and they did not move. *"For half-an-hour, there was silence all around me; they went somewhere to pray and worship God,"* he says. *"I was crying, imagining what would happen to me. It was morning now -- I could feel the sunshine -- and because they tied my eyes so tightly I was feeling very much pain in my eyes."* He also felt someone watching him, and then a prickle of alarm heralded the others' return from prayer: *"The commander, whom they called Mullah Anwar, said my eyes should be opened. When they took off the turban, my face was all swollen, everything was cloudy, but after a few minutes I could see everything clearly. The commander was tall, with a long black beard, and he wore a long white shalwar (dress tunic) and a white turban. He told me to look around and see all the different kinds of tortures. I saw naked bodies -- old people, young people, women, children. Some were still alive. Suddenly I started shouting and crying loudly because they had not taken me to a court for any trial; they just brought me straight to the torture place. I said, 'If I am a criminal, why don't you punish me according to the law?' and the commander said, 'This is the law of Islam.' He asked if I knew what would happen to me, and I said, of course, he would kill me. Then he told me, 'Whoever fights with pen against Islam, they should not be killed suddenly. We will kill you gradually.' He told one of his men to get a bayonet and take out my eye."*

Gesturing for his wife to take their 2-year-old, Silsila, into another room, Barikzy removes his glasses. His face is expressionless, the eye socket the bright red of fresh blood. *"They took a syringe and shot acid into the eye that was bleeding,"* he continues, voice dull. *"I started jumping -- it was boiling. Then they put pepper and salt in* there, and I passed out. They said for three days and nights I was passed out."

When he woke up, they brought him a glass of tea and a little bread, gave him a cloth to clean his face and a tablet to relieve the pain and a fresh tunic, because his had been torn and blackened. "They were never friendly; they kept insulting me the entire time," he adds. "I did not understand why they did those kind things until later, when another prisoner told me they offer tea and bread so we survive longer and they may torture more and get more blessing. They think they are doing the jihad for God's sake, so for them, a person like me, a Communist who didn't believe in God, it was a pleasure for them to torture me.

"Later that day, the commander came with two Arab men and said they shouldn't give me a big torture today, just two simple ones. They cut my earlobe off. I said, 'Why don't you cut the whole ear off?' and they said the next time they would. They put the lobe in my hand and said, 'Look at this.' Then they put salt and pepper in the wound, and for almost half-an-hour I was crying and shouting and they were looking at me, laughing." He falls silent, and the muscles in his jaw and arms clench until they quiver. "It was better for me to die than for them to laugh like that."

Finally, he says, "Another man came who had a very terrifying face. He filled the syringe with acid and injected on the inside of the forearm." He holds out his right arm, turning it to show the welt. "I was burning and shouting, 'Please give me water!' but they wouldn't. When they injected it, I felt like they were pounding a bunch of nails into me. Minutes later I was losing the skin, and the meat, the flesh, it was bubbling and there was a big hole, very red, as if a dog had taken out the flesh.

"Then they told me that for one week I could relax."

The interpreter begins the next session with an apology: She has looked and looked for an English equivalent to "the torture place" but cannot find one. Barikzy describes the place as being in a mountain valley north of Kabul, near the village of Shakardara. "They dug holes into the ground about 2 meters and covered it with reeds to keep people from getting wet. There were about 50 prisoners in each hole, and they put a blanket over the door that kept light out, so it was too dark even to see each other. They crossed two big wooden beams over the door so nobody could open it. When they locked the door, we would talk to each other. I soon figured out that all of them were educated people -- not all Communists, but clear-minded, independent people. Even they brought a mullah there, because he had told them, 'What you are doing to women is not according to Islamic commands.' So they tortured him, too.

"I couldn't sleep at all that night, maybe half-an-hour. People were moaning from their torture; one man had his fingers cut off. The next morning a man came in with a lamp in his hand, looking to see who was dead and who was alive. They told us to get out of the pit, and as each of us stepped out they had a rope and made links around our necks, tying us in a line. They led us to an open area, and I saw many people from other pits, most tied with rope like we were. They sat us in a circle around a wood platform, and they brought out the mullah they were going to torture. Actually they had already started: They made a big hole in his nose and put a very big piece of wood inside. The nose was swollen, and they were pulling him by a rope through the wood. They said he was not really Muslim; he'd been trained in America, where they had a school that trained people to come in the cloak of Islam but work against Islam. It was clear for me that everything was false, because I know Muslim people like I know my hand. But the illiterate people could easily believe them.

"Then they said, 'America has two purposes for the world. The first was to destroy communism. The second is to destroy Islam.' They ordered guards to pull at this mullah's hair and beard, and after half-an-hour I saw no more hair on his head, only blood. He was shouting, 'All you say is false; I just told about Islam.' Then they took him away."

Days passed. Barikzy says they were allowed outside only to relieve themselves and for mandatory prayer, when "they made us get water from the wheel and clean our bodies." Asked to demonstrate the ritual, he springs to his feet, takes down the prayer rug and kneels rapidly. "They are doing as if they are doing gymnastics," he says over his shoulder. "There is nothing in their heart." Demonstration finished, he returns to his chair, breathing hard. "For me," he says, "it was another kind of torture."

Days later, he says, they received news that the war between the Taliban and rebel leader Ahmad Shah Massoud had gotten worse: "The group holding us wanted a hiding place in case they were attacked. They gave us spades and told us to dig a trench 2 meters deep and 4 meters wide in the rocky ground. Whoever went slowly, a commander with a long rubber hose was beating them."

The prisoners dug and dug, and then the fighting burst upon them. "Of course, we were not fighting, but a lot of prisoners were dead because of the bombing and rocketing,"

Barizky says. "There was a big deck, and when the prisoners would die, they threw the bodies up there. But for themselves they made graves."

Barikzy says the fighting lasted more than 10 days, and nobody won: "Before that, I had totally lost my hope, but then when the fighting started I was thinking maybe somebody from the opposition might recognize me and be my friend, or the fighting might get worse and we could find a way to escape." Instead, they had to move camp, trudging through the cold for almost a month, heading toward the end of the valley, at the base of a small mountain. "There we started digging again in the rock, using the side of the mountain as one wall and building a stone wall on the other side, with branches for a ceiling. It was so cold that when we were washing our hands to pray, the water would freeze. I told the mullah it was not good for me to wash, because Islam says when you have a wound you cannot wash your body. He said the washing wasn't so I could worship, it was for more torture."

Barikzy says he and many other prisoners caught fevers before finishing the shelter. Luckily for him, one of his captors was from Qandahar, his home province, and their common Pashto language was a bond. "He gave me tablets for the fever and told me that nobody should know. Then we were told that mullahs from Pakistan were coming to meet us. 'Maybe these mullahs will forgive some of you and release you,' they said. 'Maybe some of you will go for execution.'"

Barizky was pretty sure which fate would be his.

The mullahs came two days later, says Barikzy, along with several Arabs claiming to be from Osama bin Laden's party. (Two *years later, bin Laden would become the U.S.'s archenemy, his terrorist network blamed for bombing two embassies in Africa. In an impotent attempt to "get" him, we dropped bombs outside Khost and in Sudan -- succeeding only in fanning the anti-U.S. sentiment he'd helped ignite throughout the Islamic world.)*

Barikzy says he recognized one of the mullahs as Maulana Fazal-ur Rehman, leader of the Pakistani fundamentalist party Jamiat Ulema-e-Islam and an outspoken defender of bin Laden. *(Rehman claims the U.S. is bent on destroying the true Islamic state of Afghanistan; in a rally last year, he vowed to wage war against us, and last month, he opposed the Pakistani government's plan to expel illegal Muslim immigrants wanted for terrorism in their home countries. "Pakistan should protect these people," he insisted, "as they came here as our guests to participate in the Afghan jihad" (Agence France Presse, July 13, 2000).*

"They got the prisoners together in one place," continues Barikzy, "and Fazal-ur Rehman read verses from the Koran and said, 'We will forgive some of you on condition. We have some Muslim prisoners in the U.S. Who can make these prisoners get released? Or find a way that they may escape? That is one condition. Another is, who has relatives in the U.S. and will make some bomb explode there? America is the first enemy of Islam.'

"All of us were crying for them to forgive us," says Barikzy, "but nobody could say, 'Yes, we can do this.' Then Fazal-ur Rehman said to the commander, 'I want to kill a very bad pagan among the prisoners to receive more blessing from Allah,' and the commander said to another man, 'Bring six new prisoners from the Massoud party.' They put the six close to the mountain, and the two mullahs and four other men took Kalashnikovs, lined up and shot them one by one."

A month or so later, Barizky says, the prisoners were told that a representative of the Taliban was coming to talk to them. "This group and the Taliban kissed each other and compromised with each other -- both spoke Pashto -- and the commanders of this group announced that from this moment on, they were Taliban. We were also told that all the expenditures for this group were paid by 'Amir-ul-Islam,' and when we asked who is that (amir means 'leader of leaders') they said, 'Osama bin Laden.' Then we were told that Kabul had been captured by the Taliban and Dr. Najibullah had been hanged."

(On Sept. 27, 1996, Najibullah, the former Communist president -- who'd sought sanctuary four years before in the United Nations compound -- was dragged from the compound and killed. The Taliban placed an unlit cigarette between his fingers and hung his bloodied body in a public square alongside his brother's, announcing from mosque loudspeakers that they had taken control of Kabul. Press reports around the world repeated the Taliban's claim that they had assassinated Najibullah, but Barikzy believes he was already dead when they hung him, killed for strategic and not ideological reasons by Pakistan intelligence. Because Pakistan's ISI is widely credited with training and directing the Taliban, it's almost a moot point.)

"When I was told that Dr. Najibullah was hanged, I washed my hands from life," continues Barikzy. "When we lost Najibullah, we lost Afghanistan.

"From that moment on, it looked like the sky was raining stones. The commander went, and a new one came from the Taliban. This new man got together all the prisoners; he said, 'I want to see each person by name, and I want to know what are their crimes and how have they been tortured.' When it was my turn, the man asked, 'What was his torture?' and they said, 'We burned him by acid and blinded one of his eyes and cut one of his ears.' The man said, 'In all this time you only give him this much torture?' Then he asked them to bring more acid and told me to lie down." In a single fierce gesture, Barikzy mimes the ripping open of his shirt. "They opened the bottle and dumped acid as if pouring water on the ground (he inverts an imaginary bottle and swirls it) all over my chest. He said, 'People, do torture like this, learn from me.'

"The next day I woke up and saw my stomach -- it was just like red meat, and I passed out again. I lost my mind and my emotions. I couldn't stand; when I was standing I was falling down, and my body was bleeding and I was talking in a very bad way. I couldn't control my tongue. The others told me later that I was talking nonsense, but I couldn't remember."

Once again, another Pashtun from Qandahar took pity on him (Barikzy was one of the few Pashtun prisoners) and brought him some ointment, bandages and antibiotic tablets. "He told me to put it on at night and take it all off in the morning so the commander didn't see it. He also told me, 'When you passed out, I did another favor for you, I put water on you; otherwise the acid was very strong and would keep working and make a hole.'

"After one month, I started to hear again; I had been completely deaf. I told my friend, 'If you really want to do a favor for me, find a way that I may escape from here.' He said, 'Be patient until this cruel donkey (the new Taliban commander) goes away.'" Barikzy waited. His friend avoided bringing him out for any more torture, but Barikzy says he saw the Taliban's worst punishments of other prisoners: "For Uzbek people, they wanted them digging in the mountain without having any purpose. Forty people digging a big hole in the side of the mountain. Then they asked them to go inside the hole, and they exploded it, and all of them died in there.

"The Massoud followers, they told them, 'Because you live in a mountainous area, you are used to cold weather,' and then tied them upside down on trees and put lots of water on them. By the next morning they were all dead, their bodies iced.

"Then there were 50 or 60 Hazara (an ethnic minority from central Afghanistan). They tied their hands and feet and put them in line, and a man had a hammer and nails, and he was beating the nails into the heads of the people. As soon as the nails got in, the blood rushed from their mouth and nose and they died."

Last he describes a military pilot suspected of being a spy. "They put a butcher's hook in his throat and hung him, pretending that he was a sheep and calling out, 'Who wants to buy sheep meat?' and the others were mocking him, saying, 'I want 2 kilo of the leg,' and they would cut the leg and pretend to sell the meat."

More than two years passed. Finally, in the fall of 1998, his friend came to him and said, "Congratulations, the cruel donkey has left." Barikzy wasn't heartened; he couldn't imagine anyone decent replacing the commander. But a mild "middle mullah" arrived, and soon Barikzy's friend was back, asking, "Is it possible for you, if I talk to this new commander, to give him some money?"

"I told him, 'As much as he wants, I can find.' But he wanted 500,000 Pakistani rupees. I said, 'I can't -- they burned my house, so I cannot sell it, and I don't even know where my wife and children are.

Then I said 100,000 rupees, and he accepted." They sent someone to the house of his uncle-in-law, a friendly shopkeeper in Kabul, where he hoped (correctly) his wife was staying. "When they brought my uncle-in-law back with them, he didn't recognize me," Barikzy says ruefully. "Then he started crying. I said, 'Don't cry now, just go back in a hurry, tell my family I am OK and borrow 100,000 so they will release me!'"

The family sold his car, a dilapidated '73 Volga, and his wife's Iranian gold, a dowry present from his family. His in-laws donated some money, and they borrowed the rest. In October 1998, Barikzy was released.

When his wife saw him, she froze. Then she fell to the ground and started beating herself, crying and shouting. "Before prison, I was a very healthy man, a handsome man," he explains matter-of-factly. "I came back with a terrible face. My body was smelling very badly because of the wounds; my hair and beard were long; my nails were like an animal's. My in-laws all started crying and shouting, and I told them to please stop, we were still in Taliban area; they shouldn't know that I was there."

A doctor came to the house every day for a month, changing dressings and giving periodic blood transfusions. Then, barely strong enough to walk, Barikzy arranged passage for his family across the border to Quetta, Pakistan.

It took one year for Barikzy to regain enough strength to discuss his future with the United Nations High Commission for Refugees, which had granted him shelter and treatment in Quetta. Finally, two men came to the shelter and asked his plans for the future. "I told them to send me overseas," he says. "They asked where I wanted to go, and I said, 'To the United States, because there is good security there and I feel safe.' So they sent a transcript of their interview with me to the American counsel in Islamabad."

That winter, an officer at the U.S. Embassy sent for him and interviewed him in person, took photographs, told him they would be sent to the United States but that the family would have to wait some time. Barizky says, "They put us in a shelter in Islamabad and told us we shouldn't go outside the shelter. It looked like it was run by Pakistani people, but the U.S. Embassy was in charge -- I think they *rented the house for political refugees."*

On April 4, the entire Barikzy family boarded a Pakistan International Airlines flight to New York. (The U.S. government had to contract with PIA, explains Barikzy, because terrorist hijacking had made KLM, the Dutch airline that usually flew the refugees, nervous enough to cancel.) One hour after they landed in New York, the Barikzys were on a TWA flight to St. Louis, one of the nation's major resettlement centers for refugees.

They've had a strained three months, trying to feel their way into safety in a new culture and be honest about their experiences without hurting devout Muslims who would not dream of swirling acid onto pagan flesh. Barikzy's wife is terrified of reprisals against their family; her thin, elegant face lined with pain and fear, she brings bread and tea but refuses to speak for the article. Barikzy is terrified, too, yet speaking is the only healing he can fathom.

From Afghanistan's tortuous history comes a parable: "As long as the root touches the water, there is hope." Barikzy insists he has no hope. "I believe that nobody can cure me, heal me. All I know is, I need to be in a kind of front against Islamic terrorism and torture."

The week he arrived, he begged the International Institute to arrange a meeting with a U.S. politician -- "not from the White Palace but a small one. I have lots of ideas about terrorism and torture that would be helpful for the U.S. government."

That mission, spliced by physical pain, nightmares and burning waking memories, has replaced virtually everything else. "I had a strong love for my family before I got tortured," he says. "Right now I have interest in them; I can't say love. The torture took the place of love in my mind."

Joy also vanished. "I was very happy as a young man, in the hope that our party would gain power in Afghanistan, and I had a great time with my family and friends, my thoughts and beliefs, my work. When I came here, disappointment took hope's place in my heart. There is a parable: 'The voice of a drum is interesting from a distance.' This is my parable for America. From a distance, the name of America is a glory. People think when they arrive they will suffer no more. But I see many other difficulties here. It is like honey in a bottle, and the bottle is very tight, and we cannot open it."

He occupies his days caring for his family, making the obligatory clinic visits, worrying about family back in Afghanistan and writing a book, *The Role of Fundamentalism in Terrorism*. He is trying to make sense of the atrocities, fit them into his mind's compartments so they do not dance in front of his eyes forever, like macabre corpses there's no place to bury. But before he can put the memories away, he needs some sense of justice.

"It is not enough," he says abruptly, "if people read this and say, 'Oh, sorry.'"

For more information, see The Official Story
Related Links:
Taliban's own official site: www.taleban.com Human-rights reports (Amnesty International site): www.amnesty.org
Counterterrorism data (U.S. State Department site): www.state.gov/www/global/terrorism/index.html
Transcripts from the July 20 Senate subcommittee hearing available through the Federal Document Clearing House.

Afghan camps hunting ground for human organs
Dawn, Nov.11,1998
By Ahmad Hassan

PESHAWAR, Nov 11: An American human rights organization has claimed that extraction of human organs, mainly kidneys from refugee children, is rampant in the Afghan refugee camps in Peshawar. Moreover, it says Afghan children of eight or nine years of age are subjected to sexual violence, are beaten up and forced into child labour. Girls of up to 10 years of age are bound in wedlock against heavy dowers, the organization's report says.

The report alleges that not only the local police but also officials of Afghan refugees commissionerate are involved in these coercive and criminal acts.

It is learnt that a three-member delegation of the Washington-based 'Women Alliance for Peace and Human Rights' paid a visit to the NWFP a few months back. The UNHCR provided guidance and hospitality to the delegation which visited various Afghan refugee camps in and around Peshawar and obtained information about the state of affairs obtaining there. They used other sources of informations as well.

The organization prepared a detailed report following this exercise in which horrific disclosures of sexual violence against and gross maltreatment of were made. Their report claims that the arrest and unlawful detention of Afghan children and elders is routine affair. The report has been sent to the provincial home department which has sought explanation from the concerned agencies, the sources said.

Monday, OCT 29 2001

We the people from Hazara OnLine highly and strongly condemn the inhuman, insane, idiotic and barbaric act on the innocent civilians of New York and Washington. Our tearful prayers and wishes go out to the victim's families in this attack by the Taliban Islamic Militia and Saudi native, terrorist Osama Bin Laden and all of his followers. We wish the victims families and loved ones of the horrible act on September 11, 2001, our best wishes as the Afghan Hazara community mourns a loss to humanity.

Hazara OnLine is a non-political site that focuses on bringing people's attention to the horrible crimes committed on Afghanistan's ethnic groups, on the women of Afghanistan and about the horrific living conditions in Afghanistan due to the Taliban Islamic Militia and the Civil War. We also bring a cultural and informative news site for our visitors on the current situation in Afghanistan.

We the Hazara people have never and will never support any act of terrorism or any act that would take the lives of innocent victims and challenge the greatness of freedom, justice and democracy. We the Hazaras support freedom, democracy, justice, equal rights and human rights no matter what gender, no matter what religion, no matter what ethnic background, no matter what language and no matter what skin color.

Terrorists and the Taliban have committed similar acts of cruelty to the Hazara people of Mazar: 1998 8,000 men, women and children massacred, Yakawlang, Bamiyan: more than 500 massacred, in Herat, in Kabul, in West Kabul, in Bamiyan again and other places. The Taliban themselves are a terror network.

Once again, may the victims of the dark and horrific day of September 11, 2001 rest in peace as our deepest thoughts and prayers go out to the victim's family.

Please visit our condolences to an American brother

Taliban Islamic Militia (composed of Arab and Pakistani Fundamentalists and Radicals) + Osama Bin Laden DO NOT = Afghanistan

We the Afghans, stand for peace, justice and democracy for all peoples but could never achieve it due to warlords and civil war.

Letter from Hazara

To a fellow American.

The true Afghan people of Afghanistan highly and strongly condemn the horrible, inhuman terriost attacks that took the lives of thousands of innocent civilians on a Tuesday morning. Saudi native, Bin Laden and his supporters are radicals and fundamentalists that are taking refugee in Afghanistan due to the civil war in the war-torn country. With the present civil war, Afghanistan has been a safe heaven for Bin Laden and his terriost supporters from the support and high cooperation of the Taliban Islamic Militia that is composed of Pakistani, Arab and Afghani Islamic fundamentalists that are uneducated, barbaric and pre-historic militiamen claiming their killings in the name of Islam. Please understand that in Islam, suicide bombing attacks or any attacks that would take the lives of innocent people is not tolerated nor preached. Islam is a peaceful religion just as Chrisitanity, Judaism, Buddhism, etc. is as well. It is the work of these insane terrorists that have given all of us, as the human race, a bad name for their sicking crime.

Please visit other non-political Afghan websites to share the tears of mourning such as:

www.hazara.net
www.afghanistans.com
www.hazaragimagazine
www.afghan-web.com/aop/today.html

Hazara is a major tribe and ethnic group in Afghanistan that has been oppressed, discriminated against for hundreds of years due to beliefs and ethnic origin. Afghanistan is a diverse country composed of more than 25 ethnic groups.

From The Holy Qur'an:

Whosoever kills an innocent human being, it is as if he has killed all of humankind; and whosoever saves the life of one, it shall be as if he has saved the life of all of humankind. (Chapter 5, Verse

32)

The World's 1,300 Year Old War

During this time of confusion that is spreading around the world, we need to reflect back over history to understand how people battle and make war against each other.

From the date in time that man first walked upon this earth, he has battled others because of their different beliefs. The present is a reflection of the past and the future will be the same as the past if we do not learn from our mistakes.

We live in a western world society in a mindset of Christianity. If when one of our police officers approach a suspected criminal, the officer will unlock his weapon from its holster, in case the suspect becomes hostile, but if the suspect is cordial as friendly, his weapon will remain in its holster; i.e. Whenever two or more people do battle, the fighters must fight in the arena of concepts of the one with the lower intelligence. Whereas, presently, we - the U.S. and Isreal are fighting a war against Muslim terrorists. We fight in the arena of concepts of fairness while the Muslim terrorists fight in the arena of mentality of the 8th century. Therefore, we must remove our concepts of fairness and fight on their level.

This war that we fight against Muslim terrorists really began when Muhammad first started to spread his evil religion upon the people, for he, Muhammad, was the first terrorist. But this section of the war against Muslim terrorists actually started during 1947, after

Arafat first created the terrorist actions against Isreal and started his push to force all Isrealis out of Isreal. Whereas, this is the longest war (1,300 years) that the world has ever known, and this section of the war is 57 years old.

As you review wars of the 8th century, you will find that no prisoners were taken except those they wanted for slaves, and the losing country and all it has became property of the winner.

We need to remove all TV and radio communications from Iraq and allow our armies to fight the war against terrorists and the Muslim world. Our soldiers need to fight as the Russians did as they approached Berlin during World War 2; they killed every man, woman and child who they came in contact with.

And at the end of W.W.2, we used two Atomic bombs in Japan, because it was common knowledge that all of the Japanese would fight in hand-to-hand and in house to house combat against our troops if we sent them into Japan and thus, more people would have died on both sides than what died by our dropping Atomic bombs and therefore, our two nukes saved many lives on both sides. Our nukes were designed to be a deterrent for aggression against us as they did in the cold war against Russaia. We need to flex our muscles and at least, detonate one in the desert of Iraq, but whenever their people die in one of their suicide bombings, they say, "It was Allah's will that they died." But still, we need to allow them to see the power our God has given us.

Many of us are preparing the path for the one who will come and bring peace to the world. He will not preach Christianity or Judah or Islam or any other religion.

The monotheism that Islam proclaims says, "Allah is the Supreme Being," but the true Supreme Being above all others including Allah is the Father, because ALL the people are His children.

And He, that we pave the road for, is coming and He shall rebuild King David's Temple for the Father and the Muslims will allow it because by then, they will know that the Father is the Supreme Being.

"Allah in NOT great, for the Father IS great for He is All."

World Conflict

On the evening of 23rd of November before I went to bed, I was online checking out the internet news. The news headlines told about two American soldiers in Iraq that were shot, beat on their heads with concrete blocks, and then pulled from their car and dragged in the streets by Muslim teenagers. This happened to them as they drove their unmarked vehicle from one headquarters to another.

After I read the story, I became angry and thought; the U.S. should declare open season on ALL Muslims and give bounties for each set of ears cut off dead Muslims that the people kill. Then I thought about how the Muslims try to live as if this is still the 7th century when their evil god - Muhammad, founded Islam. We are in a losing battle in Iraq, it is the same kind of war that we found ourselves fighting in Nam, and what I said back then still applies today; "We need to drop a few nukes there and tell the rest of the world, 'If you don't like it, we have some for you, too.'"

As I laid down that night, I realized to where I had come - the things that I had just thought about killing all Muslims came from the dog, the human, but now I am surpassing human feelings and knew I had come to the threshold of understanding and living God's Will.

(The next day, the 24th, the news media was still reporting the two soldiers were shot and killed, but they reported that all else about their deaths was false.)

To live God's Will you must understand what God's Will is, and over the past few weeks, I had asked people what is God's Will? (For back then, I knew where I was being directed (inspired) by God's Angels to live God's Will.) No one could give me the complete answer, only bits and pieces.

God did not create anything that He did not appove of. Therefore, each of us as individuals, are exactly were we are suppose to be in time, and geographic location, and knowledge.

Each of us as individuals are exactly where God wants us to be. We were created to experience the unknown of our personal decisions. The experiences of our personal decisions should be pleasant but most of the time our decisions are driven by feelings of the flesh. But no matter which direction our decisions take us, or the experiences that we have, they are part of God's Will and part of His Master plan, that places each of us at this correct time, and in the correct geographic location, and in the exact location of knowledge, for God does not make mistakes.

Christians nor Muslims nor Jews can change what is to come, each state the end of time is coming, but each claim they will triumph and its the true religion of God. The end of time is coming because man has chosen to place himself as god above all others and including the Father. (Man need not state that he is god for his actions indicate his thoughts.) This cannot be stopped because it is God's Will, but as individuals, we can change the place we are when the end of time comes. And if you honestly look at "the end of time," you will see that each of us face our "end of time" at our individual human death because human death is part of God's Will. In this plane, which is God's Will, nothing last forever, everything will die someday, and therefore, we cannot stop our individual human death. We can only change the place we are when our human death comes. And once our individual death comes, we cannot go back and change our past life, for human death is permanent. Our experiences of our actions are chiseled unto our Souls and will live in the others memories and with God forever.

I shall practice living God's Will; allowing all others to chose for themselves, love all others as I love myself, treat all others as I wish to be treated, embrace God - love the Creator for all that He has created (including us and our lives) for us to enjoy and experience. Do not try to judge others because we have not walked in their shoes - we have not experienced the things that they have experienced nor the things that their parents or their ancestors experienced; the things that made them who they are. But we should judge the things that others do and say to decide if those actions are correct for us. And we should try to inspire others to do better with our words and the things we say and do concerning other people and things.

I am here to guide people to the God that they need. I am Spiritual Monotheist, I embrace the true Father (Creator) above all gods and not Allah, Jesus or Yahweh for they are also man-made Gods. I inspire others to know that part of the Scriptures from the different religions is true and was given by the Father, but also that most parts of the different religions was conceived by man who wanted control over of the majority. The words truly given to man from the Father always states "Love all others and have no domination toward them," and this has been written into the three major religions by God - the Father and Creator of life itself.

I am not here to persude you to worship the Father. I am here to inspire you to embrace a better life, that you feel is righteous with Love for all, with God that fits your needs.

Violence in The World

First of all, let's look at the church. In the Christian Bible it says Jesus will knock on the door of the church and will be refused entry.

What is the church?

Is it a building or is it a religion or is it a group or teachings that people follow?

The word "church" should mean the body of Jesus and/or religion but instead it means a group or teachings that people follow.

The word "church" should mean a religious structure as the complete teachings and not the individual thoughts or ideas of a select group of people. This select group of people that I speak about is the leaders of individual churches and not the body of Jesus. Keep this definition in mind of what a church is while you read this.

The Christian churches are preaching that to be saved you must go through Jesus. If that is what they believe, for them so be it. But these Christians will argue and fight over who's God is the true God. These churches are condoning Violence when they fight and/or argue over God.

The Christian Bible says there shall be Violence in the world, and we do see the Violence in the world. Just as predicted in the Bible.

Nothing can be done to change the outcome of what God has intended to happen. His intentions were written into the Bible. We must learn and experience life while we live out His intentions.

Yes, God's written intentions of what will happen is for us to understand that He is in complete control of all life, but our lives of learning and experiencing was not written into the Bible, therefore, it is His intentions for us to all "Live" - experience and learn with Love - grow without domination toward others- become adults.

The people who live as described in the paragraph above are truly God's children. They need not be Christian to belong to Him while all others are of Satan.

So one can claim to be a Christian and still be one of Satan's.

Violence comes out of most religions, but not from God's children. Violence comes from Satan's children who claim to know God. Violence mostly comes from those who seek God only on Sundays or in the church and its building.

Love from God comes from those who know God in their daily lives. These are those who show God to others in their daily lives.

Only a small percentage of people truly know God and these are His children, and therefore, we are surrounded by the Violence of Satan from people who are not God's children daily.

God has given everyone of us the choice to decide who and what to follow. He will not demand you to follow Him. But He wishes that you would.

Demands and Domination are of Satan. Any church or person that places these upon you, are of Satan. Does your church place demands upon you? Is your church a true Church of God?

We shall be surrounded by Violence until the end of time. We cannot and will not stop all the Violence, and therefore, we must all stand fast on our beliefs and with the true God above all other gods.

Remember, a Love for a Love also means a slap for a slap.

As the Angel Joleen told me, "Cry for the lost children of the world."

We all should cry for the lost (dead) children of the world (the children that Satan dominates).

Terrorism

Mon May 6,12:27 PM ET
By IBRAHIM HAZBOUN, Associated Press Writer

BETHLEHEM, West Bank (AP) - The outlines of an agreement to resolve the 35-day standoff at the Church of the Nativity were taking shape Monday, but the sides remained at odds on several issues, including how many of the wanted Palestinians holed up in the Christian shrine would be deported.

There is no agreement and there is no standoff. Those who are hold-up inside are evil and should be destroyed as one would destroy any enemy that one faces in battle. Acts of terrorism should not be rewarded.

The Palestinians want no more than eight of those in the church sent into exile in Italy, while Israel reportedly insists that at least a dozen be deported. Another 30 Palestinian militiamen would be sent to the Gaza Strip (news - web sites), according to the Palestinians.

The Palestinians have no say in whatever happens to the terrorists hiding in the Church of the Nativity. Only the Israeli Army holds the fate to those terrorists.

A U.S. official confirmed media reports that a senior CIA official - identified by the Maariv daily as Tel Aviv station chief - was involved in the talks, and would also take part in negotiations

Monday evening. The U.S. official, who spoke on condition of anonymity, said a resolution was not likely before Tuesday.

Prime Minister Ariel Sharon, meanwhile, arrived in Washington for talks with President Bush. Israel and the United States agree on the need for radical reform in Yasser Arafat's Palestinian Authority, but differ on Arafat's place as its head. Sharon wants Arafat kept away from future peace talks.

Ahead of the meetings, Bush said on Monday he shared Israel's disappointment with Arafat.

"He has disappointed me," Bush said as he toured a school in Southfield, Mich. "He must lead. He must show the world that he believes in peace."

Bush wishes to convert Arafat over his ideology which is the theology of the Christian Baptist Religion.

In new fighting, three Palestinians, including an activist in the Islamic militant group Hamas, were killed early Monday in clashes with Israeli troops in the Gaza Strip.

The Israeli military, meanwhile, said Israeli soldiers who opened fire from a tank Sunday, killing a Palestinian mother and two of her children, ages four and six, were spooked by the sound of a tank tread coming loose. The army initially said that a mine blew up near the tank, but said on Monday no traces of an explosion were found. The army said it regretted the deaths. A 9-year-old Palestinian boy also was killed by Israeli fire in the West Bank on Sunday.

Palestinians children of all ages and of either sex can be terrorists, and some of both are terrorists. Age does not matter to Muslim terrorists.

Also Monday, the director of the U.N. Development Program in the West Bank and Gaza Strip, Tim Rothermel, estimated that it would cost between $300 million and $400 million to repair the damage done by Israel's recent large-scale military offensive against Palestinian militants. The Israeli military declined comment. Rothermel said it would take a year to 18 months to complete repair work.

The standoff in Bethlehem began April 2 when more than 200 Palestinians, including several dozen gunmen, fled into the Church of the Nativity ahead of invading Israeli forces, at the height of Israel's large-scale incursion into the West Bank. About 75 Palestinians have since emerged from the besieged compound, which marks Jesus' traditional birthplace, while last week, 10 foreign pro-Palestinian activists sneaked into the shrine. Several dozen members of the clergy have been staying inside the compound as well.

The Israeli Army should kill anyone trying to sneak food, weapons or medical supplies into the Church of the Nativity, for anyone entering the Church believes in terrorism.

Officials from both sides were reviewing a list of 132 names of Palestinians inside. Palestinians said most of those would be freed.

Hassan Abed Rabbo, a senior member of Arafat's Fatah movement in Bethlehem, said the outlines of a deal were in place.

Israeli Defense Minister Binyamin Ben-Eliezer said he hoped the "saving formula" would be found by the end of the day. "The problem lies in the careful sorting of who is who and what, and I have a feeling that we are certainly moving in a positive direction," he said.

Under the deal outlined by the Palestinians, some of the wanted men would go into exile and others would be sent to Gaza, where they could be imprisoned under the watch of American and British jailers in a deal similar to one brokered last week that led to Arafat's release from 34 days of confinement by Israel.

All who entered the Church of the Nativity while fighting the Israeli Army, should be treated as enemies of Israel and dealt with as the followers of terrorism.

Abed Rabbo said the Palestinians wanted no more than eight men sent into exile, while Israel Radio said Israel is demanding the deportation of about 15. Yarden Vatikai, an adviser to Ben-Eliezer, confirmed that the size of the group of deportees was one of the sticking points, but would not say what Israel's minimum was.

Palestinian officials said the deal was being worked out with representatives from the United States, Britain, the Vatican and the European Union.

The United States, Britian, the Vatican and the European Union have nothing to do in this battle. It does not matter what they say or wish.

The Israeli military provided AP with a list of 10 top wanted men inside the church. Among those named were several members of the notorious Abayat clan, including Ibrahim Musa Salem Abayat, 29, accused of the murders of three Israelis, and Muhammad Salem, a 23-year-old accused of organizing two suicide attacks that killed several Israelis in March.

The Palestinians initially rejected the idea of deportations - a policy which Israel used before the peace process began in 1993. Israel used the tactic both as punishment for political activists deemed dangerous and to distance militants from Israeli targets.

Ben-Eliezer said Monday that once the standoff was resolved, Israeli troops would immediately leave Bethlehem, the last Palestinian city in the West Bank they still occupied as part of a military offensive that began March 29.

After winding down the operation late last month, Israel adopted a new tactic, launching frequent incursions into Palestinian territory to arrest suspected militants. Israeli military correspondents have said the Shin Bet security service has a wealth of new information about planned attacks after questioning hundreds of Palestinians arrested during the military operation.

Early Monday, Israeli troops entered the Tulkarem refugee camp, moving from house to house to arrest wanted men. Tanks also remained in some parts of the nearby town of Tulkarem, which troops entered Saturday.

Israel must fight the terrorists in the terrorists camps and home, and not in the homes or cities of the Israelis.

In the United States, Sharon was due to meet Defense Secretary Donald H. Rumsfeld at the Pentagon on Monday, then hold separate talks Tuesday with Bush and Condoleezza Rice, his national security adviser.

Israeli and U.S. officials said the two sides will seek to define the composition and terms of reference for a proposed international peace conference.

Traveling with Sharon, Israeli Education Minister Limor Livnat said Israel was trying to persuade the United States and the international community that there could be no viable peace with the Palestinians until they replace Arafat.

Rice said that it is not Washington's role to dictate to Palestinians who should lead them.

"The White House position is that we're not going to try to choose the leadership for the Palestinian people," she said.

Sharon will present to the United States a 91-page booklet of documents that Israel claims prove Arafat is directly involved in funding terrorists.

Arafat is a known leader of terrorists and should be handled as a terrorists.

Palestinian Information Minister Yasser Abed Rabbo labeled the booklet "ridiculous" and said that all the documents "were forged." Arafat, meanwhile, held talks Sunday at his Ramallah office with Egyptian Foreign Minister Ahmed Maher, Arafat's first meeting with an Arab official since his confinement.

Egypt will work with the United States in an effort to work out an end to Israeli-Palestinian fighting and a resumption of peace talks, Maher said.

"The United States, monitor of the peace process, has a very big responsibility to continue working for this peace as long as the basis of peace is still there," Maher said.

Muslim nations differ over suicide bombings;
Malaysia urges end to holy war of `guns and bombs'
Mon May 6, 5:35 AM ET
By JASBANT SINGH, Associated Press Writer

KUALA LUMPUR, Malaysia - Muslim nations took different stances Monday on suicide bombings in Israel, with Malaysia urging an end to them and Saudi Arabia calling Palestinian suicide bombers martyrs.

The differences at the meeting of religious affairs ministers of the Organization of the Islamic Conference showed lingering divisions among Muslim countries since a meeting in March, when foreign ministers were unable to define what constitutes terrorism.

In a speech opening the three-day conference, Malaysian Deputy Prime Minister Abdullah Ahmad Badawi said holy war cannot be won with violence and suicide bombers, which achieved nothing by killing Israeli civilians except to bolster views that Palestinians are terrorists. He added building strong economies were more important in the fight against injustice.

Abdullah said Muslims should not "allow Islam to be hijacked by those who have a flawed understanding of our faith and rally under the banner of militancy."

He also urged Muslim countries to drop the widely held belief that the religion's tenet of jihad, or holy war, meant carrying out militant attacks.

Jihad must "not be pursued with guns and bombs" but should be translated into actions that would help to lift Muslims "from the throes of poverty," he said. "Muslim countries need to develop economic clout and political influence to dispel suspicions against the religion."

"We must abandon mental blocks that we ourselves have erected and embrace knowledge and innovation," Abdullah said. "If Islam is equated with the acts of a minority who have hijacked our faith, the world will continue to fear and loathe Islam." But Saudi Arabia's minister for Islam, Sheik Salleh Abdul Aziz Muhammad al-Sheik, views differed at a news conference.

"The suicide bombings are permitted," he said. "The victims are considered to have died a martyr's death."

The Saudi Arabian minister said that the Palestinians' armed jihad is permissible as a fight for their rightful land.

Before the Jewish people entered their Promise Land, the people living there were not Muslims because Islam was not founded until the late sixteen hundreds. The Bible as historical documentation, states that the Jewish people owned the land before the Palestinians. Therefore, the Palestinians do not have any claim to the land

"Jihad is any effort that requires strength to better the lives of a people. It can range from practicing self-control to defending your country," Salleh said.

The meeting was attended by 42 of the 57 members of the conference and was expected to address ways to counter a negative perception of Islam following the Sept. 11 terror attacks.

It followed an OIC conference in late March where Prime Mahathir Mohamad was unsuccessful in getting foreign ministers to adopt his call to define all attacks on civilians, including suicide bombers, as terrorism.

However, other Muslim countries felt the recent wave of

Palestinian suicide bombings was the only weapon available to people crushed by harsh Israeli occupation.

The Saudi Arabian said that the U.S-led war on terror is targeting Islam because of a misperception of the religion, but said it would only be "temporary."

"After Sept. 11, there has been an upsurge, even in America, to learn what Islam is really about," Salleh said.

Around two hundred years ago, a new Islam Religion was formed, and it was a spinoff of the beliefs of Muhammad, and it is a religion that created a god, who hates the same things it's creators hate. This new thinking of Islam is the Religion of today's terrorists as demonstrated in the statements made by Salleh above.

One major problem that we will soon face; Muslims will not allow any Muslim be humiliated, and it does not matter to them, which Islamic faith their brothers follow.

Now, that Palestinian Terrorists have died fighting in the Church of the Nativity, the Muslims will try to take over the Church as one of their own, and shall fight to make this site an Islamic holy place. They have demonstrated this in the past, as claiming the Dome of the Rock in Jerusalem is holy to Islam. They claim that while Muhammad slept, he dreamed that he traveled to the Rock in his journeys to heaven, but Muhammad never stated the mountaintop that he went to was in Israel, he only said it was to the west. The Muslims convert Jewish and Christian Holy places to that of Islam to "push out" other religions.

Who is Right

The World is Right and I am Wrong, and for the last 6 years, I have been studying under the Angels of God. They were inspiring me to find my Salvation and have taught me things that should help others in their missions of life, but the more I learn, the more I see the world has been corrupted by man's concepts, and I see there is no hope for the world.

The games of rules and regulations played by our governments and society leaves no room for God nor for self-respect in our lives.

Examples: If you wish to be a plumber, you must learn how to and have a license to screw pipe together, roughly an 8 hour course. And if you wish to be a Hypnotist, you must study under a licensed hypnotist for about 6 hours. And if you wish to be a minister, you must go to some type of theology school for 4 to 6 years, and there you learn their religious doctrines to preach about, you cannot have nor follow your own beliefs, only theirs.

A few months ago, I learned that the city owns the first 6 feet of our front yard and I cannot place any fence on their property, and also the fence on my property cannot be over 3 feet tall.

We must have a license to get married, but none is needed to have children.

We are outlawing smoking, but we are heading toward legalizing pot.

Most bars have parking lots, but we cannot drive after we have been drinking.

Others who think they know what is best for us control everything that we do, and have, and think.

Do you remember back in the early sixties when Russian Premier Khrushchev said, "We do not have to fight the Americans. They will turn communist by themselves." And that's what we have become.

I have truly tried to be the person the Angels asked me to be, but I cannot do it.

Therefore, I have come to the conclusion that the world is right and I am wrong. My conclusion comes because I am tired of trying to help people find their happiness. Most of you, just like the rest of the world have come up with your own off-the-wall beliefs. You don't care about God because the only thing that concerns you is YOU!

The Christians don't Sin, they merely back slide, and they can't do anything wrong or evil because their Christ died for their sins. But Jesus never said he was Christ, some fool said that about him.

The Catholics are blind and being lead by the blind.

Muslims have 72 virgins waiting for them in Heaven.

Is that Heaven for the 72 virgins?

The Jews, who believe they are God's chosen people, are waiting for their Messiah to come and deliver their religion and laws to the rest of the world who must follow their religious doctrines completely.

The Jewish people think they were chosen by God to be at the center of all the turmoil.

BUT WHO CARES?

I know you don't care, and I sure don't! Let the world and all in it go to Hell! Its heading that way in a hand basket anyway.

I lay down my title of "Bishop" and I cannot wear the collar anymore because if I do, I am labeled a Catholic clergy child molestor.

The people of the world are so confused that when I die, I will not go to Heaven or Hell. I will place signs up all around me that reads, "No Trespassing, Keep Out!"

The world was a beautiful place but all humans have destroyed it.

"After God had created His thought of the universe, He was content with the conception of matter and Energy in One. And from that moment forth, all - even time was laid out before Him. But He was sad because of what He saw that would occur during the time to come; the pollution that men would create and spread across the land, and the corruption that men would place in their thoughts.

"And even the concept of evil was in His creation of the universe. But men created the actions of evil, and they envisioned images of themselves that they named Satan and Lucifer."

As we view the events that occur around us, you surely can see that we have refused God by allowing others to control our freedoms; we have designed our governments and created a society to place rules and regulations upon us, thus we have openly accepted a few to say what we are allowed to do and even think.

On occasions, God's Angels have been in "body form" and have ridden around with me in my car. Whenever someone cuts me off or does anything that we would consider stupid, the Angels never seem to mind; they are busy looking around and talking about how beautiful everything is. They are completely content to allow others to do whatever they wish, but God's Angels could command us to do exactly what He desires us to do, but they don't. Therefore, should I care what others do or say? NO WAY!

I shall not worry about what others do and say, and it is not my concern if they wish to kill one another, and it is not my problem if they do not wish to better themselves, for these things belong to them. But I will not allow people to remove my happiness, and I will not allow them to nurture evil within me.

People believe they have found their Heaven in their man-made religions and gods while the Knowledge that God's Angels have revealed to me gives me Salvation. I shall not try to force my Knowledge of God upon others, and I shall not allow others to force their beliefs upon me, for I am free and they are not.

I will allow the world and all in to go to Hell if that is what they wish, but my words about the Knowledge of God will help those who find and reads what I have written, for they are at the correct place in time that they are suppose to be, and those are the ones my communications with God's Angels shall help.

I had thought God wished that I would spread His words and help others, but I was wrong because most were not listening. Therefore, I am exactly what God and His Angels wants me to be, I am FREE! For my Salvation does not come from forcing others to believe in God. Salvation can only come from peace within oneself.

The Enemy Within

A while back, the Angel Joleen appeared as if smoke, and she wore a blueish-white gown and God's Love flowed from her as she spoke to me, and she asked me, "Can you sit and have supper with your enemies?"

I answered, "Yes."

She replied, "I do not think so." And then, we dropped the subject, but for many days, I thought about her question, and then one day, I told her, "I have the answer."

She responded with, "What is your answer?"

I said, "Yes, I can because I have no enemies, for my enemies are within me."

She smiled and said, "Now you are learning."

At that time, I was satisfied with my answer, but my "learning" continued, and later I learned who or what are my enemies within.

Our enemies is the energy of evil and bad feelings that we allow to grow within ourselves. And our only enemy is the thing that will keep us from Heaven.

When Jesus was being crucified, those who were killing him could not stop him from returning to the Father, only his feeling of hatred toward them would have stopped him from his Salvation. Thus, Jesus did not allow hatred to enter into his thoughts, therefore, he remained loyal to God as he kept God's Love is his heart.

These bodies that we wear are nothing. They shall return back to which they came - the dirt, and the earth will grow new life, and new life will live from our flesh and blood as our blood, too, will return back into the waters that flow from the fountains of life. We came from the dead and we shall return to the dead. But the energy of our Soul's shall remain written on the Angels within our body forever.

The energy of our Soul's is all the experiences and endurances that we have faced throughout our lives. This is the reason for life. We live for this second, and the future is always coming, but the past is Forever. Your past is your Heaven or Hell, for once you are gone, you can never change what you felt, said or did. Repent from your past feelings that were negative - recognize your mistakes and learn from them so that you do not make the same mistake again, thus moving yourself toward your Heaven.

We cannot change the past, but we can change our feelings of the past.

The Angels have said, "All the things that we tell you are for your Salvation." But all those things can also be used for others Salvation as well. I do not push God upon you.

You must decide for yourself if what the Angels have told me are true. I will not lead you to God, I only guide you toward Him, for your Heaven or Hell is of your design.

God's Angels Words are The Truth

Over the last few months, I have been trying to help a young man and woman, who have two young children, with their marriage. Their problems are small and should not be reasons for divorce. But, as people do, these disagreements are breaking up their family.

Recently as I talked with the Angels, I asked if they would accompany me to visit the people involved in this family dispute.

The Angel Jo asked me, "Why do you wish to help?"

I answered, "They are taking away the choices of the children, for kids only wish to be with both, their father and their mother, and because children need and want both parents, one parent should not make that decision for another (their children). For another person will not raise a child as a true parent would."

She then asked, "What do you feel?"

As I answered her question with, "Love for all people and have no domination toward others," she asked, "No domination? No domination? No domination?"

I replied, "No domination...I have no domination toward them, I want what is best for their children."

Then I said, "This is my last mission and after this I want to come Home...will you help me come Home?"

She replied, "You have more missions, this is only one of them...You know the way to come Home. We cannot destroy what we have said and written."

I then asked, "I would like Jesus, Michael and Gabriel to come with us."

She answered, "As you wish. The man refuses us and he will not see us, but the woman believes. Tomorrow, he will have questions for you, You will Inspire him. Diana (my deceased daughter) and Paul (a deceased young friend of the man) will come with us, also."

Then the room began to glow in a light blue as Jesus, Michael, Gabriel, Diana and Paul appreared. I laid down to sleep so that I could leave my body and travel with them, as we did many times before.

(Since then, the man has asked me many questions...I feel that I am helping him, and the family is beginning to come back together again, but my help with them continues.)

The "Love for all peoeple and no domination toward others;" if I force my beliefs upon others, then I have placed them in domination. Whereas "Inspiring others" is allowing them freedom of choice.

Jo's statement of "We cannot destroy what we have said and written," All that I have written and relayed to you about "Love for all and no domination toward others" is destroyed if I tried to force my beliefs upon the couple. Therefore, I can only try to inspire others.

Jo's response to my question of, "Will you help me to come Home?" The Angels have inspired me into finding the way to come Home when my time comes. My Salvation is my repenting (changing my views of the past) and that is my direction toward Home (Heaven). When I go Home, I will have freedom of righteousness thoughts; "Love for all Others, and No Domination toward others." Whereas, they will not help me die, for the time and event of my death is written into God's Master Plan. And whereas forced death is suicide and I nor the Angels will have no part of it.

Individual Feelings

And the Angel said upon me, "You walk in the valley (world) of the dead because the ground that you walk upon IS the deceased of the world. All the ground may not be that from human life, but it did come from plant life, or sea life, or even from the water that gives you life. The earth does recycle itself.

"And thus, the body leaves both, the Soul and Angel-within, because the Angel-within which is of God is Energy and energy does not fade away, and because the Soul is the recorded events of the life, only the body decays back into that from which it came, and while the Soul, which is the memory of the human life, and the Angel-within that is part of God, lives forever for they are Energy. Therefore, your actions are forever engraved as your Soul, but that is okay because everyone is wrong at time(s) during their lives, and it is their God given right (to each individual) to repent (change their ideas from the past).

"The Father is mericful and embraces His children with Love, and this is how His Creation should feel about itself and about those other things in His Creation, for what is righteous for you may be also righteous for all others.

"The Supreme Power of the Father could force Itself upon life but the Father does not desire that, He desires Love from you as He embraces and loves you. He did not want to create slaves, He created all life with its personal and individual feelings. You have become confused and do not see the truth about life. Your wants and desires have replaced the meaning of 'Need', whereas Life is 'Needed', but What is Life? and why do you think it is 'Needed'?

"Every living thing has its individual feelings. The plant feels and the littlest to the biggest animal feels, too. Also, humans each have individual feelings, and while the human can comprehend and understand, plants cannot and most other animals cannot. You are the ones who the Father designed intelligence into, for intelligence was created for human needs, and where everything was placed (created) for use in all of the Father's Creation.

"The 'use' may not be any more than to enjoy its beauty, but whatever, all is there for your use, and everything was created for all living things needs. The Father's Creation is Complete and without abstinence. For all is yours if you desire it, but your 'wants' may outweight your 'needs', and when this occurs, you are not part of God's Congregation.

"Is human life more important than all the other animal life? Is human life more important than plant life? Is human life more important than insect life? Is human life more important than germ life? To the human, 'Yes, it is,' but in Creation, 'No, it is not,' for all is balanced and all belongs to each other.

"Is belonging to the Congregation (Righteousness) needed? 'Yes.'

"Is Evilness needed? 'No.'

"But both are needed to balance Creation, and Life is part of Creation.

"Righteousness attitude and actions are needed. But being Evil and doing Evil things (actions) are not needed, but both are needed by the human for him to understand the difference between them. Whereas, Evil actions was created by man, but all was Created by the Father. You cannot understand and enjoy Heaven if you do not know or understand Hell.

"Can Jesus reign over the world for 1,000 years after the end of the world?

"Yes, He could.

"Will Jesus reign over the world for 1,000 years after the end of the world?

"No, He will not because you would not know and understand evil if it is not present.

"But Jesus will reign over Heaven for (as you say) 1,000 years because evil is not needed there. And God reigns over ALL including Heaven, but Jesus alone will reign over Heaven but the Father reigns over Him, too."

We Lead You Not Into Temptation

And the Angel said to me, "Throughout the last years, you have learned much and you have helped many. You need to enjoy and experience the final days of your life; Feel free, Love free, Live free, Touch free and Be free, and this you have done, but it is now coming for your time to sing and rejoice with us.

"We love and embrace you for when the job was ready for you, you were ready for the job, and that brings us happiness for you have learned well.

"You will not be placed on a pedestal, nor will you be worshipped while you are alive or when you are dead. We would not and did not allow you to become corrupted by power, but you will be remembered as a person who communicated with the Father's Angels, and what you said was told to you by Us, His Angels, therefore others will know that He is still alive, and He is the Supreme Being who has complete control of His Creation, and everything and every human is part of that Creation.

"Many will learn and understand, through your writings, that each should embrace the rest of the Father's Creation with love as you do now.

"Did you change the end of time?

"No. For the end shall come as it was recorded, but you did change the final destiny of others as it was planned to be in God's Master Plan.

"No one will change what is meant to be for all is laid out in God's Will. Whereas you must experience the choices that you made while your choices were known by Us. Experience the known future with Love in your heart and then you shall live in Heaven forever.

"It does not lower one's self-esteem when one Loves and embraces the Creator - God. It defeats the purpose of life when one becomes a slave to a god placed above a religion because all religions are designed by man to control its believers, and NO religion is the true beliefs of the Father. The Creator created the concept of religions, but He did not create the religions, man created religions for control of others. Rules and laws placed upon humans through beliefs from other humans is slavery and that lowers self-esteem.

"Do not fret or worry about another's beliefs, for they are only confused and they are exactly at the place they are suppose to be at this time, for that was their choice. Enjoy and experience your life for you are in control of your actions and your beliefs alone, for you, too, are exactly where you are suppose to be at this time. Allow them to follow their beliefs as they allow you to follow yours."

The Choices of God's Angel within

Throughout each individual life, the Angel-within stands beside its selected human. God has given you the choice of allowing your Angel-within to lead or to follow your humanly desires, for all choices in your life are yours.

But, the Angel-within is your "pathway" to God. This Pathway, if selected by you, is your Soul's vehicle to God after your demise. If, during your life, you refuse God, then your human feelings are your road to everlasting Hell - self-inflicted torment after your demise. The Heaven or Hell that you shall find in your afterlife is whichever lifestyle you led during your life here on earth, for the lifestyle you presently demonstrate is what you will carry over into everlasting life.

Salvation is the continuous activity of selecting the righteous over the corrupted. When one finds Salvation, he has merely made the correct decision for the moment. For Salvation is like a multilane freeway with many exits and entry ways, where one can continue to drive straight onward toward God or take exits (detours), and then later, and before life's end, finds his way back toward God. The choices (exits - detours and the on ramps) are our personal decisions that we made throughout our lives, for they are the personal gifts that God has granted each as individuals. Therefore, God does not dominate our decisions or us, but He does demand that we find our individual ways to Him in order for each to secure our independent concept of Heaven. And after your death, Knowledge of All that you shall receive will inspire you into the understanding of the righteousness or the evilness that you have done here on earth, and this shall be your Heaven or Hell. For if you contain afterthoughts that cause you torment - Hell, you shall not go to God because you will be ashamed of what you had done. But if you have lived a life of righteousness, then you shall want to rejoice and sing with God in Heaven, and then you shall venture to God.

Therefore, throughout one's life, his experience of either good or bad that he inflicted upon others, shall become part of his Angel-within. While his experiences cover the Angel-within as veils which either allow the Angel to glow brightly or become dim, depends on whichever God's Angel that is assigned to the human, considers as righteous, and shall determine the Angel's actions in the afterlife.

For God created the concept of Evil, but man created the actions of Evil, and after death, if actions that you have placed upon your fellow man were Evil, then Evil shall be placed upon your Angel-within as you have learned and taught your Angel-within to know. Whereas God merely created the concept of Evil while humans created Evil, there is no Evil in God. Only in parts of Him (His Angels that were corrupted by evil human actions) and only parts of His Creation (Humankind that He created), that He does not allow (the memories of Evil actions done to others) to join with Him in Heaven.

We are the teachers or corrupters of God's Angels that are within us. Our experiences of either good or bad are placed upon our Angels-within forever unless they can "live" another life in which Salvation is found. And what we have placed upon the Angels-within shall help inspire or pollute the next person's life that they experience. For we do not experience reincarnation, we only experience what the Angel-within experienced that the Angel-within had brought, from a previous life, with it when it first entered our bodies.

The Soul is merely our experiences recorded on energy, and that is the part of us that shall live forever with God in Heaven - the Heaven that we had made for ourselves here on earth. And while the Angel-within each of us, may, carry Soul(s) from other lives before entering our bodies, those other Soul(s) either help our Angel-within to glow brightly or cause him to glow dimly, and those feelings (conditions of Heaven or Hell) reflect into our personalities. But the conditions of what was placed upon our Angel-within shall not be an excuse for our actions. We have final control over our actions and the actions that we allow our Angel-within to demonstrate.

I have seen people who' Angels are covered in Evil, these are the ones whose auras glow dimly, and are the ones who at sometime during their lives refuse God completely. I have also seen those who were with God, then changed and became dim, these have lost sight of God and have corrupted their Angels-within so much that their Angels have left them for the present. These people treat the Angel-within as badly as they treat other humans. But the Angel may return if he chooses too, for as with all, the gift of choice is his, also.

Gift of Choices

To help illustrate "the Gift of Choices" in the "chain-reaction" of life, imagine if you will, setting dominos in a formation so that the first row of dominos contains only one domino, the second row has two dominos side by side, the third row has three side by side, and so forth and so forth until millions of millions of dominos are arranged in this order, and think of each domino as representing an ancestor (person and/or animal) in the evolution of human life. And think of this domino formation as the span of total life here on earth, and near the end of this formation and onto the end of this formation, these dominos represent humans.

As we knock over the first domino at the beginning of this formation, it will touch another and knock over the next row of two others, and in turn they will knock over more, and this "chain-reaction" of knocking down the dominos will continue until the complete formation of dominos are laying down.

Now, imagine that the distances between each of the standing dominos and the location that each domino will obtain when it falls as the time that each person lives, and during that time all that each domino's (person's life) experiences influence the next domino (next of kin) that follows it.

And once that first domino was sat in place, and as all the others were placed in this formation, and as the first domino was touched as to knock it down, the chain-reactions of all of the other dominos as to what direction, and to what other dominos it would come in contact with, and to where each domino would final lay, is known to God.

We as the dominos, in this chain-reaction, believe that we have control over which direction our individual lives will go, but our life's directions was known by God before the start of time. All of our individual choices as indicated as "Gods Gift of Choice," are merely the things that we do that was influenced and directed by what occurred in our ancestors and our past life up until this present time. The things that we will do in the future are influenced by those things as well as what we presently do, and all is known by God. Therefore, we are at the correct place in knowledge, and location of time, and geological location, that it was planned for us to be.

"God's Gift of Choice" is our experiencing of the unknown, and that is what life is all about - experiencing as we enjoy life. And it is this "experiencing life;" the recorded experience on energy that is the Soul. The Soul is that part of you that will live forever with God, for each person is made up of two parts: 1. Energy that allows solid matter to think and also gives our bodies movement - that is the Soul, and 2. Matter which will return to which it came from - earth. These two things must come together to form a living being.

And while we live, even though our life's adventures are known to God, our choices of doing good or evil will either help our Angel-within to glow brightly or dim, depending on which you chose. And the attitude of your character is influenced by your ancestors and your past life experiences, will be placed upon your Soul. And after your death, it shall be forever engraved upon the Angel-within.

Another way to view the "Concept of Life," is to think of your Soul as being a file that contains your life's experiences, and the Angel-within as a disk, and God as the Master Computer. And after you die, your file (Soul) is transferred to the disk (the Angel-within), and the Angel-within takes your file to God where the Soul (your life's experiences) are downloaded into the congregation of God - His Angels. For God is all Angels in congregation. And therefore, until your life ends, your file is not complete and may be changed, but once life is over, your Soul stands as the Memory of You that will live forever in God, and the feelings that you had toward others will influence your descendants in their life, and that is your everlasting Heaven or Hell that you shall live in forever.

The Light and The Darkness

An acquaintance of mine who's web site is "Welcome Traveler," address: http://www.hcis.net/users/miltozah/h2light.htm, recently posted:

He wrote; *If you have ever wondered which is more powerful, Light or Darkness, be aware that negative forces have been given some latitude here on this physical plane, this material world. They can at times, be allowed by positive forces, to be quite powerful.*

Even here though, on the physical plane there is a simple test that you can perform that will tell you all you need to know regarding which is the source of real power. The test has two parts. Part one will certainly seem silly to you, but when taken with part two, together they make the point. First, walk into a well-lighted room with a container of any size made so that light cannot penetrate, so you know that the inside of the container is dark. Open the container and release the darkness and notice if the room becomes any darker. Naturally it does not, because darkness will not overpower light.

Next, for part two, darken a room completely. Light a candle of any size and take it into the dark room. Does the room become less dark? Of course it does. If "light" has this much power over "darkness", think how much more so "Light" does over "Darkness"!

There are other examples of the power of "Light" over "Darkness". One that comes to mind is in the beginning of the Book of Job in the Old Testament portion of the Judeo-Christian Bible.

Satan can only approach Job with God's permission and even then only within the restrictions outlined by God. This example is not there by accident, and neither is the one that follows. In Milton's inspired works Paradise Lost and Paradise Regained, you see Satan, once again needing God's permission before being allowed certain access. Don't be misled by these examples, however, into believing that no harm can ever come to you from negative forces. If your current life or a previous incarnation, has been one that included negative or harmful acts toward others, lack of caring or compassion for others, or any such indication that your understanding of these matters is less than complete, then you may find that negative forces have been allowed to administer some of the karmic lessons that you have been found to need. This is done, of course, so that you will have the opportunity to learn the needed lessons so that you can make wiser choices in the future.

Are you beginning to see that there are very good reasons for living by the Golden Rule? This isn't intended to mean that the one who has the gold makes the rules; the pendulum has already swung much too far in that direction. We must return to the way of life that subscribes to the idea of treating others the way that we would want to be treated. Interesting perspective on life, however he missed the greatest point about Light and Darkness.

Whenever you walk into an un-lit room, the darkness hides the things you cannot see that surround you. But when you enter into an illuminated room, then you have knowledge of all that surrounds you. For when you stand in a dark room, only your inner-feelings suggest the evils that may surround you. This fear of the unknown that surrounds you as being evil draws you into believing superstitious concepts of what surrounds you.

The illumination that lights our surroundings is Knowledge, for when we see the things that surround us, then, we know what it is. Therefore, symbolically, Light is Knowledge and is God, for He is all Knowledge, and for Knowledge is without fear.

Fear is your uncertainty of your surroundings because you cannot see nor understand what is near you. Therefore, darkness is viewed as being evil because you cannot see what is near. But darkness is NOT evil, for darkness is merely the absence of Light -

Knowledge of your surroundings and your understanding that you are part of what is in that room. While darkness only brings on the consciousness of your inner-feelings, and when only cultivating feelings directed toward yourself, and not caring for or considering others, is Evil.

Your choice of seeing or not seeing is demonstrated in the Book of Job in the Old Testament; with open eyes you see the truth of God that surrounds you, but if you keep your eyes closed, you only sense the fear of the unknown that dwells within you, as you allow it to conjure up evilness that you believe surrounds you. Whereas, we have no enemies, for our individual enemies live within each of us, and it is your choice, as given to you by God, to follow the road in life that you chose to travel. But yet, it is not God that allows darkness as if evil to harm us, it is the one who believes they have no control over their lives that allow evil to enter into their lives. Therefore, there is no Satan or Devil, but only evil actions that we display against another. For God conceived the concept of Evil while man developed the actions of evil, and he created the image of Satan and the Devil just as he did the image of God. All three created in the likeness of man.

Throughout the Old Testament, the stories contain topics about encounters with God, but each story also tell of people's desires that were turned inward. Even burnt or blood sacrifices to God indicate that people believed they had to give God something for Him to "Bless" them. Therefore, the ritual of sacrifice was performed to enhance the people's life and not God's. Then contrary to the Old Testament, the New Testament, which is about Jesus' life, truly indicates that a life style like that of Jesus, is the will of God. For the life style that Jesus lived, shows his feelings turned outward to others instead of inward toward himself. And as Jesus said, "I do not bring peace to the world, instead I bring turmoil." The "turmoil" that he brought into the world is the concept that we should focus on the needs of others instead of pleasing ourselves, but also, to live in harmony with all others. This concept of "turmoil" places a battle within each person of righteousness against evil because his life style was completely opposite to how people thought and did before and during his lifetime.

And thus, his death upon the cross was to demonstrate that we need to allow others their independent "Gift of Choice" as granted them by God, but we need not let others dominate us. The demonstration of his crucifixion occurred to show us the lifestyle that we should try to achieve, and that is not a lifestyle that we will achieve. Because God knows that we are not perfect as Jesus, and therefore we shall not live as Jesus did.

Jesus was human just like you and I, but the Angel that dwelled within him was different than ours. The Angel within each of us is only one Angel. While Jesus' Angel was made up of different parts of all Angels, and God is all Angels in congregation, and Jesus' Angel came directly from God. And therefore, Jesus is the Son of God.

And while Jesus totally allowed the Angel-within him to lead his life as he controlled (leashed) his human feelings, we humans cannot completely control or leash our human feelings, and so therefore, we must balance the two equally as we see fit for our lifestyle.

To finish out this thought of Jesus, understand that he did not die on the cross for our sins. He died because of our <u>sin of trying to control</u> what he said and did. Therefore, he died because of our sin of Domination, and therefore, each of us is judged independently for our sins and righteousness. For the sin of domination has been prevalently from the dawn of time throughout the ages.

And as Jesus said, "I am the Light of the world." In other words, "He is the knowledge needed to live a righteous life." His lifestyle demonstrated the knowledge that we need to live in harmony. For God is the Light of All, but we need not to have the knowledge of All to live in harmony. And therefore, God is the Light to see His Knowledge - to know and understand what surrounds you.

The Covenant - A Promise Between God and The People

As you now realize that all, including God's Angels, make choices based upon the knowledge that each contains.

The Angel's life may be viewed as eternal, and has been influenced by each human life that it experienced with the human, and is the Angel's attitude that is derived from its previous lives, which flows over onto its human present life. And its human desires that it has obtained by corrupted lives needs to be leashed as each leashes his individual human attitude of human desires. This leashing of the corrupted (evilness) from the Angel-within is seen as removing the veils of darkness from the Angel thus allowing the Angel-within to see what surrounds it - God. And only human knowledge - comprehension (understanding what his actions will bring) is the only vehicle that will deliver Righteousness to the person.

But meanwhile if one continues to allow evilness to lead his life, soon his Angel-within will become so disillusioned by the person's actions that he (the Angel-within) will leave the person. His leaving also may occur because of a person becoming idle and letting life go by without the person contributing anything to anyone. (For when you contribute to another person you have contributed to humankind.) But The Angel-within that has left may return at any time, and will return at the end of the person's life to receive that person's Soul. And those who Angels are full of evilness from past lives, may never enter the person, but stand near as the ones who leave the person during their life. These people without Angels within may be recognized by their auras glowing dimly because they contain only the energy of the animal that they are, and while these people can also be recognized because they may be sickly and/or complains of tiredness during those times they are without the Angel-within.

I have seen many elderly people whose auras glow dimly because they are without missions in life as they only await their own demise, for now life holds no enjoyment or experiences for them. For without Enjoyments and/or Experiences, we have no growth, and then we are not expanding our Souls.

I was one that the Angel-within merely stood near most of my life, and he would only enter when I did things of his desires (things of evilness). The Angels Joleen, Gabrael, Michael and Jesus had to inspire me to remove the veils that covered my Angel-within. They had to inspire me to embrace God. They had to make me aware of the things that surround me. They were my Light, for they were the Light of God that I needed. And it was their concepts of life that they showed me that inspired me to understand, for even when you are in the darkness, you must know that there are other things that are near you. And once you realize that, you can then start to comprehend the concept of life that surrounds each of us.

God gave the choices of life to you, and it is up to you which to choose and what to follow. He does not place demands of domination over you. You have the final say in your life. And therefore, God does not dominate you on which religion you are to do follow and believe in. And while, I am not the only Messenger of God to the Covenant, there are many presently living now as well as there were many in the past.

The Covenants of the past and present have been many, I know of at least four.

The first Covenant was in the Garden of Eden. God gave Adam and Eve all the things that they could enjoy and experience in life, and in exchange, they were told to not eat from the Tree of Life. They accepted what He gave them, but refused what they were supposed to do in return of His Gifts.

The second Covenant was given with Moses when he came down from the mountain and the FOUR tablets: two of the tablets contained the things God was giving to His children and two tablets contained the things that His children were to do. And once Moses saw what the people were doing, he threw down the FOUR tablets and broke the Covenant. Moses then returned back to the mountain top where God gave him only two tablets that contained what we know as the Ten Commandments - these are the things that we are to do without any Gifts (things in return) from God.

The third Covenant came in the form of Jesus' life of which we destroyed. And here as well, God placed Commandments upon the people to follow Jesus instead of Him (God).

And now the fourth Covenant, today many others and I are God's Messengers of the Covenant, bringing Gifts from God if the people will accept them and do as He wishes (Wills).

But most will not believe in what we say. There are few who will be saved because God has left it up to man if he desires to be saved or not. It is man's choice to live or not, just as all choices in life have been left up to the individual. Oh yes, many will read what we have written, but only a few will continue to live a righteous life after the words have drifted back into the deepest parts of their minds. But, we cannot be concerned with their deaths because only our personal commitment to God is our concern.

The Covenant of Living With Others

Try to understand that evilness comes from concepts of righteousness that are corrupted and polluted by ideas designed to control the majority by a few individuals.

This concept of evilness is truly demonstrated in the wars that are recorded in history; an individual has a concept of how society should be, and then he persuades others that his logic is righteous. Then he and those who believe his opinions will stand together and try to change the world's ideas.

Once a person has a few others standing with him on his concept of social science, he has a little power and will use that power of his congregation to convince others to fall inline with his sociology. (The power of a group who's thinking that something is righteous is very convincing to an individual even if their concept is completely incorrect.) But if that individual cannot be convinced to believe the logic of the group, that individual(s) then comes under the threat of domination. But the individuals who come to believe and follow the leader of this evilness are under his domination, for their freedoms of pursuit of happiness and thoughts is controlled by the leader. And as the group's warped perspectives spread out to envelope more people, wars between countries, or religion, or cultures will begin.

While you are walking down a street an outraged man with a knife in his hand approaches you, and says he is going to kill you. You do not know if he has killed others or not, therefore you cannot reason with someone who may be insane and must defend yourself, and as he walks toward you, you must have and be prepared to use a better or more forceful weapon than the knife that he holds. For when one tries to dominate another, freedom must prevail.

The true problems of defending what is righteous occurs because those who believe and follow "Freedom of Choice" stand alone because they believe that its the individual's rights to believe and follow whatever he wishes. The followers of evilness stand and fight in a congregation while the individuals that follow "Freedom of Choice" will not join with others to fight unless he feels personally threatened. This was truly demonstrated by the terrorist acts of 9/11 because before that, we as citizens of the U.S.A., refused to help fight, or to show support for Israel against the terrorists that the Israelis are fighting, but after 9/11, we are willing to fight terrorists wherever they are in the world, for now we too feel and are threatened.

"Turn the other cheek" does not mean to allow one to strike you again. It means to continue what you are doing as if you were never struck the first time, but while keeping up a defense to protect yourself as you pursue happiness (enjoy and experience life). For if you allow one to strike you a second time, you have placed yourself under his domination, but if you go after your enemy as you plan to destroy him, or if you set up a defense against another attack, you have also placed yourself under his domination because he has caused you to do something that you did not want to do; fight or set up a guard against another attack.

Can we live in a world full of evilness?

We have no choice. We cannot force our beliefs upon others, for if we do, we have control over what others believe and follow. We cannot force our beliefs upon others by teaching them our ideas, for teaching others is the same as enforcing our concepts into their logic. Therefore, we can only inspire others to consider that maybe our beliefs might be as righteous as theirs, or maybe ours might be better than theirs, but above all, we must allow others to follow whatever they wish as long as it does not dominate others. But while we are not any better than our brothers or sisters, and therefore we should study and inspect their ideas to see if they are more righteous than our concepts and beliefs.

The silly thing that saddens me is that all people follow the same God (Supreme Being or Entity) and have the same beliefs, but all understand them differently, and symbolically to their comprehension. The world would be a wonderful and peaceful place if all would understand this concept. But presently as in the past, people place their concepts, ideas and thoughts into what God has said concerning how we should live among others.

Living in harmony with others should be our primary concern in life. We cannot worry about which god is the true God, or which religion is the religion that is approved of by God. We cannot dwell on what is to come or where we will be spending eternity; we should only concentrate on pursuing those things that bring happiness upon others as well as ourselves

Tue Dec 16, 7:59 AM ET
World - Reuters
Cardinal Says U.S.
Treated Saddam 'Like a Cow'
By Philip Pullella

VATICAN CITY (Reuters) - A top Vatican official said Tuesday he felt pity and compassion for Saddam Hussein (news - web sites) and criticized the U.S. military for showing video footage of him being treated "like a cow."

Cardinal Renato Martino, head of the Vatican's Justice and Peace department and a former papal envoy to the United Nations, told a news conference it would be "illusory" to think the arrest of the former Iraqi president would heal all the damage caused by a war which the Holy See opposed.

"I felt pity to see this man destroyed, (the military) looking at his teeth as if he were a cow. They could have spared us these pictures," he said.

"Seeing him like this, a man in his tragedy, despite all the heavy blame he bears, I had a sense of compassion for him," he said in answer to questions about Saddam's arrest.

Martino was referring to the videotape released by the U.S. military which showed a grubby, bearded and disheveled Saddam receiving a medical examination by a military doctor after his capture in an underground hole Saturday.

Martino was one of the Vatican officials most strongly opposed to the U.S.-led invasion of Iraq.

"It's true that we should be happy that this (arrest) has come about because it is the watershed that was necessary... we hope that this will not have worse and other serious consequences," Martino said. *"But it is not the total solution to the problems of the Middle East,"* he said.

Martino said the Vatican hoped the arrest of Saddam *"can contribute to promoting peace and the democratization of Iraq."*

He added: *"But is seems to me to be illusory to hope that this will repair the dramas and the damage of the defeat for humanity that a war always brings about."*

The Vatican did not consider the war in Iraq *"a just war"* because it was not backed by the United Nations and because the Vatican believed more negotiations were necessary to avoid it.

Martino said the Vatican wanted an *"appropriate institution"* to put Saddam on trial but he did not elaborate.

U.S. forces were keeping the ousted 66-year-old dictator at a secret location for interrogation before he is put on trial in the months ahead. He could face the death penalty.

The news conference was called for Martino to present the World Day of Peace message, in which Pope John Paul took a swipe at the United States for invading Iraq without the backing of the United Nations.

Where was Cardinal Martino when it was discovered that his clegry were sexually abusing the children of the world?

And since he said, "The Vatican did not consider the war in

Iraq "a just war" because it was not backed by the United Nations," does that mean he or the Vatican does care about the welfare of the Iraqi people? For that statement also it means; "The Catholic church does not back the American people and their concerns about their children," who are still being abused by his clergy.

As it is written into the Book of Daniel, "The Catholic church has fallen, as it was only a matter of time before its pieces were consumed by the vultures who attempted to conceal their desires of the flesh under the words of their Gods." And now, we can see the belief system of the Catholic church - the major player in Christianity, begin to crumble.

God's Messenger to The Covenant

From October 1996 to present, I have been in communication with an Angel named Joleen. She has introduced me to the Angels Gabrael, Michael, Jesus, and then to God. Most of our conversations are documented on video and audiocassette.

And Jesus said unto me, "Tell the people of your pains and hurts as I once did. You recently asked me, why I did not return now? I answered, 'I would be ineffective.' For I know that the people of the world today would not believe in what I said, sure some would, but most would not. You can tell the people of your pains and hurts, for you understand them and speak their language. They will believe in what you say, if you speak to them from your heart."

I believe that Jesus nor His Disciples ever actually had a building that they called their church. They spoke to whomever, whenever and wherever they could. I am following the directions that He gave me, to tell people of the things that cause pain and hurt in my heart.

The basis for the foundation for Jesus' House of Jacob came directly from the Christian Bible, John 15:16, Luke 1:33 and Romans 11:26.

John 15:16; Ye have not chosen me, but I have chosen you, and ordained you, that ye should go and bring forth fruit, and that your fruit should remain: that whatsoever ye shall ask of the Father in

My name, He may give it you.

I was ordained by God to write what His Angels have told me, and I was ordained by the Universal Life Church to place "Bishop" in front of my name. The title "Bishop" signified that I am the housekeeper of Jesus' House of Jacob. It does not stand for rank, I am no closer to God than you.

Luke 1:33; And He (Jesus) shall reign over the House of Jacob forever; and of His Kingdom there shall be no end.

The Angels Joleen and Gabrael instructed me, David, to start the House of Jacob. Then, Jesus said unto me, "Speak to the people and tell them of the pains and hurts within your heart as I once did. For you are one of the stones in the foundation for My House, the House of Jacob."

The House of Jacob belongs to Jesus and God. I am merely the housekeeper for Jesus and God. His House of Jacob shall live forever, for we Honor Jesus and His House of Jacob, but we Worship God alone.

Romans 11:26; There shall come out of Sion the Deliverer, and shall turn away ungodliness from Jacob.

The Deliverer - the Angel Joleen is the one who delivers the deceased children to God, she has removed all ungodliness from Jacob, the Angel that dwells within me. For during the last days of January in 2000, the Angel Joleen told me, "Fast for the next 40 days from corruption." This I did, thus, the Deliverer removed ungodliness from the Angel Jacob who dwells within my body.

Therefore, the Foundation for Jesus' House of Jacob is the Knowledge God's Angels has delivered to me, and includes the Messages that I have written and gave verbally, which totals over one million words.

Jesus' House of Jacob is a true House of Jesus. This house - a Body of God that has been forgotten throughout time until God revealed the Master Plan of His Spiritual Covenant with the living once again.

The practice of Jesus' House of Jacob declared as instructed by Jesus, and the Angels Gabrael, Michael and Joleen;

All living, deceased and future humans are members to Jesus' House of Jacob.

All gods referred to in the different religions are above all man-made religions, but under the true One - the Supreme Being - the Creator - God.

All religions are God's.

All religions are of God if they show and practice Love for all and do not condone Domination of others.

To pick up your cross and follow Jesus - to show and tell the other people of the World of your pains and hurts within your heart - tell people about God if they seek God from you.

To follow Jesus - live the lifestyle that He has shown us in the Bible to be Righteous - To live with an open heart for all people and not to Dominate others.

Read and understand your Bible for the historical content that it contains, which includes that God, Angels and Jesus are alive and that they did and do still communicate with the people.

Understand, and respect, and follow the 10 Commandments.

Understand that God is a Loving God who contains no Domination to anyone or anything.

Understand that God does not demand but wishes that all people would live His Concept of Life; "TO LEARN AND EXPERIENCE FROM EXPERIENCES OF OTHERS THROUGH ENDURANCE OF LIFE."

Jesus' House of Jacob understands that God has given all people their individual choices of life, and from these individual choices, we will all someday judge ourselves. Then at the end of time, God will judge all of us individually.

Jesus' House of Jacob recognizes and understands that we need to live by God's Concept of Life, and the laws of our society, and the laws of our nation.

The main purposes of Jesus' House of Jacob is to help:
1) Spread the word of God to those who wish to know
2) Understand God
3) To direct people for the Salvation of their Souls
4) Glorify and Embrace God.

Our goal is to help others recognize all choices of life are theirs alone regardless of race, gender, background or church affiliation.

The Beginning of The Guider

And the Angel Joleen said to David, "You once learned, 'You know you have created your god when he hates the same people you do.' That also applies to your god liking the same things and people that you do. We have told you many things that you did not agree with, through Divine Love, We have inspired you to know those things were true, therefore, God created you. For God has allowed mankind to create religions and place their individual god above them, but God is above all religions and all man-made gods.

The intent of The Guider is to bring into reality that all people are equal, and that all religions are under one God. Our concepts are the steps about life between your church and the Supreme Entity, usually referred to as "God," and to give you comfort in your faith.

Follow Jesus' Way of Life

What I am talking about is following God's or Jesus' words, and not following what you "think" or "believe" their words meant or what you "think" or "believe" they were trying to say.

There is a group or organization that its headquarters are located in Tyler, Texas, who (claim) they have over 500 churches around the world in their organization.

A man who said he is the leader of this organization sent me a pamphlet the other day. His pamphlet was written about his beliefs and thoughts, and his churches ideas about what is an unpardonable sin.

The reason he sent me his pamphlet was because of an e-mail conversation we had concerning his false concepts about what are Blasphemes against the Holy Spirit. He claimed that there were no sins or crimes that are unpardonable. He believes an unpardonable sin or crime is one where one does not ask for forgiveness. He "thinks" that no matter what one does, if one asked for forgiveness, it will be granted by God.

First, we must get an understanding of what is "Blasphemy." A Blasphemy is not only words, but it is also all thoughts and actions against the Holy Spirit, the Father or the Son.

Blasphemes against the Holy Spirit are sins - thoughts, actions or words spoken against the combined things that God has created. It is against Creation. If one commits suicide, one is saying there is nothing worth living for. Think of that, nothing that God created is worth living for. Not even one little thing is worth living for is a Blasphemy against the Holy Spirit.

Another sin of Blasphemy against the Holy Spirit; is a sin that has forced another unto thinking or believing nothing is worth living for, thus the person is talked into committing suicide. This Blasphemy against the Holy Spirit is causing another to commit suicide.

Suicide is either ending a human life and/or ending the spiritual life of another person or yourself.

Another sin of Blasphemy is murder. If one murders another, the murderer is saying that person did not have one thing in the world worth living for.

These are just three of the many sins of Blasphemes against the Holy Spirit.

The church leaders have written into the Christian Bible about all sins being pardonable, because it is the same as with the story/movie of "The Onion Filed Killings." The story/movie told the story about two crooks who kidnapped two police officers, then out of fear of receiving the death penalty for kidnapping, they decided to kill the police officers, but instead of murdering both officers, they killed one policeman and the other got away.

Therefore, the church leaders wrote into the Bible about pardonable sins. This allowed the sinner off the hook, for the sinner would not kill more after he thought about how he could be pardoned for just one killing.

Well, what about the mass murders?

What about Hitler? Do you think that he was pardoned by God? NO!

One death is just as bad as many deaths. The number does not matter. The action is what matters. But why should the church, you or I worry about unpardonable sins? Just live by following what Jesus did, and all will be fine.

Do not write into your bible your thoughts or beliefs.

Do not follow your preacher's thoughts and beliefs.

Follow what is in your heart, and then you are following Jesus in His life style.

Let us Pray:

"My Lord, the True and Righteous Holy God above all, guide Your children in the correct way of life that You intended them to travel. Show them that their gods are not the True and Righteous One that You are. Teach them their religion is no different than their brothers. Show them the things they claim, and do, and say is for their god is not for You but instead is for themselves. Make them understand that their religions are not the same but all religions belong to You just as they, also, belong to You. I mourn and cry out for them. I love them. Have mercy on them. Amen."

And The Angel Michael Said unto Me...

In the early hours before morning, I was awaken by a bright light in my bedroom. As I turned over toward the light, I saw a person whom I have never met, but knew him to be the Angel Michael. He stood about 5 feet 8 inches tall and appeared to be very muscular and was wearing some kind of soldier's uniform as if from the ancient Greek or Roman era and similar to what the Angel Gabrael wears. The Angel Michael also drifted like smoke and his face seemed blurred, too.

The Angel Michael said unto me, "Yes it is I, Michael, the one believed to be God's warrior, and yet, I am also a Guardian as with all Angels of God. And for now, I am the Guardian of your youngest son. I will guard, protect and guide him as others have done so in the past and as We try to do with all people in the world. Yet, the people in the world who are of the world refuse our help, they do not have eyes to see us with, or ears to hear us with, for they have been taught to believe only what others tell them.

"People believe me to be God's warrior because they have been taught there is rank in Heaven, but Heaven is the peace within one's self, and all are equal in God, for all are part of God. And people in the world who are of the world use rank in their religions to hold domination over others.

"Fear not, for I will take care of your son as God has promised to guard, protect and guide you and your family. Non-believers words will not harm you or your family, nor will their stones touch you or your family. We shall stand beside you forever. For you have followed God's request - You have laid the foundation for Jesus' House of Jacob - the Son's House of Jacob, for you are David, but the Angel within you is Jacob. Therefore, your body is a House of God - the Father and the Son's House, as should be with all people.

"The Angel Jacob that dwells within you may not be the Jacob indicated in the Christian Bible, but it is irrelevant to you who He is, for the Christian religion, too, has been twisted by domination toward others and much of the Truth cannot be found there.

"Blessed are the ones who truly believe and follow the Father and the Son, and yet, do not tempt God, but follow the Angel-within with Love for all and no domination toward others. For the Angel-within you is part of God as with all others."

Then the Angel Michael was gone.

To the Father - the true God of Abraham, Isaac and Jacob I pray:

"My Lord, the True and Righteous Holy God above all, thank you for another day and all that you have allowed us during this day. Forgive me of my sins and help me understand them so that I will not make them again tomorrow. Thank you for letting your Angels help and guide my family and me. Amen."

Do Not Fear...

The other evening around midnight, while sitting in the gazebo located in my back yard and viewing my back yard that is mostly gardens, I thought how beautiful this garden is for it is a place of peace, love and serenity.

The Angel Jo appeared, and she sat down in the wrought iron chair beside me, and she said unto me, "We were here as We watched and helped you design and put together this garden, for this is a garden of God. And you have seen and felt me and other Angels bring not just the children, but the 'children' of God through here as we help them travel on to the Light.

"As it is written in Exodus, 20:25-26, you have done as We have guided you to do so. For you did not know about God's 'church' until after you completed it. And yet, there are many others of God's 'churches' around the world constructed in the same manner of these, We also use them in the travels of God's 'children' to the Light.

"You have placed two statues of Angels in this garden; one is the Angel's Offering, it is a reminder to you that God has offered many gifts to you. The other is an Angel in prayer, it is a reminder that you should give thanks to God for all that He has given you. And yet, these statues are not to be worshipped, for you should embrace God and not His Angels or icons. But you should Divinely Love His Angels, for they are part of Him, and you should like the icons for they are also gifts of beauty from God to you.

"Most in the world build what they think are 'churches' of God, but instead they build 'houses of the dog' that dwells within themselves. For the foolish ones pull from their own 'bibles' what interest them alone, and not what God desires. And yet, God does not stop loving them but instead turns His back on the foolish ones and waits for them to repent.

"When one of Jesus' disciples brought and showed Jesus money that someone had given him, Jesus instructed him to return it. The 'houses of the dog' demands money from their congregations, but God did not delegate them to be His banker or His tax collector. Nor did God instruct them to press their Spiritual understandings upon others, but yet, most force their beliefs on their neighbors, while some are put to death if they do not conform to what the suppressors believe to be true.

"Yea, though you walk in the valley of death, do not fear others, but show love to all others and have no domination toward them, for they are equal to you."

Then the Angel Jo was gone.

To the Father - the true God of Abraham, Isaac and Jacob I pray:

"My Lord, the True and Righteous Holy Father above all, thank you for another day and all that you have allowed us during this day. Thank you for letting your Angels help, guide and protect my family and me. Forgive us of our sins and help us understand them so that we will not make them again tomorrow... Have mercy on us. Amen."

Blessed are Those Who...

The Angel Jo said unto me, "You once asked Jesus, why he does not return, and he replied that he would be in-effective today.

"Did you think that the lives of those that are written into the bibles were exactly the way they lived? Did you not think that they also had feelings of the 'dog' that dwelled within them? Did you truly believe that they never became angry, displeased or unhappy about the actions of others including themselves?

"Life was not designed to be without let-downs. And yes, you do have the final decision of matters in your life, but also, not only does an Angel within you dwell, but a 'dog', too. Therefore, you will do good, but you must try to control the 'dog', because all choices are yours.

"Did you think life today is any different than in the times of living during the writings of the bibles stories? Did not the people in Jesus' time murder him? Not all believed him then, so why do you think that the people would believe him if he would return today?

"In the bibles stories, people saw and talked to Angels, Jesus also seen and talked to Angels. Do you think that all the people that were alive back then, believed them? Why should all the people of today believe you or the others who see and talk to Angels now?

"Jesus never said he was the only Son of God, people wrote that he talked to and about His Father. When the people created the 'Trinity' they decided that Jesus was the Son and is God. Jesus or God never made that statement, human conceived the thinking that He is both - the Son and God. Now as you see, you are learning that people have set in stone their concepts of Him and God.

"If Jesus would return today, He would not 'live' under false conditions, and some would believe the end has come because others have written into the Christian Bible that when Jesus returns, all men would fall down on their knees and praise Him because His appearance means the end of time.

"Love not only the Wise, but also, the foolish for they all are humans and each has a part of God - an Angel within.

"Blessed are those who leash the 'dog' and follow God."

Then she was gone.

Final Secrets of Fatima

I wish to share with you a letter that I received on June 18th. The letter was in response to a communiqué that I e-mailed to Prime Minister Ariel Sharon.

My e-mail was in condolence and of our sorrow from the congregation of Jesus' House of Jacob. Therefore, this letter is to you, also.

LETTER FROM THE OFFICE OF THE PRIME MINISTER

Dear Bishop Haven,

On behalf of Prime Minister Ariel Sharon, please accept our heartfelt thanks for your message of condolence in the wake of Friday night's tragic bombing at a discotheque in Tel Aviv, where 20 young people were murdered in cold blood, and dozens more were wounded.

The people of Israel are determined not to allow the terrorists to break our resolve, and are making every effort to continue with routine in the face of the brutal violence being perpetrated against innocent Israeli civilians by the Palestinians.

The Support and friendship of many religious communities worldwide is greatly appreciated.

(signed) Raana Levy, Advisor to the Prime Minister on World Christian Affairs

FINAL SECRETS OF FATIMA

During the week of June 10th, I watched a television program on the History Channel about the Final Secrets of Fatima. For those of you that do not know about these Prophesies, they were foretold in a 1917 vision of the Virgin Mother to three Portuguese shepherd children.

(The first that The Angel spoke of; "Whenever you see someone who is dying and is truly heading toward Hell and they think that they are heading toward Heaven, do not tell them. Let them believe in what they wish." The second Secret, The Angel spoke of was the the wars that would come.")

The third Prophesy was released by the Vatican on May 13, 2000 by Pope John Paul II during a meeting with Santa Maria Lucia of the Immaculate Heart. Now at the age of 94, she is the only remaining of the three Portuguese children.

In her recollection of the third Prophesy, "We saw an Angel with a flaming sword in his left hand; flashing, it gave out flames that looked as though they would set the world on fire; but they died out in contact with the splendor that Our Lady radiated toward him from her right hand. Pointing to the earth with his right hand, the Angel cried out in a loud voice: 'Penance, Penance, Penance!' And we saw in an immense light that is God: (something similar to how people appear in a mirror when they pass in front of it), a Bishop dressed in white, (we had the impression that it was the Holy Father). Other Bishops, Priests, religious men and women going up a steep mountain, at the top of which there was a big cross of rough-hewn trunks as of a cork-tree with the bark; before reaching there the Holy Father passed through a big city half in ruins and half trembling with halting step, afflicted with pain and sorrow, he prayed for the souls of corpses he met on his way; having reached the top of the mountain, on his knees at the foot of the big cross he was killed by a group of soldiers who fired bullets and arrows at him, and in the same way there died one after another the Bishops, Priests, religious men and women and various lay people of different ranks and positions. Beneath the two arms of the cross there were two Angels each with a crystal in his hand, in which they gathered up the blood of the martyrs and with it sprinkled the souls that were making their way to God."

If you recall, it was in St. Peter's Square during 1981, that Turkish guman Mehmet Ali Agca made an assassination attempt on the Pope's life, and that was on the anniversary date of one of the visions seen by the three shepherd children.

The Pope, John Paul II, believes that is was the Virgin Mother, the Madonna of Fatima, that saved his life, and he claims that it was a mother's hand that guided the bullet's path and in his throes the Pope halted at the threshold of death. He believes and claims this because he thinks the third Prophesy was about him as the "Holy Father".

After seeing this program, the Angel Jo and I discussed this topic about the third Prophesy of Fatima.

And the Angel Jo said unto me, "Prophesies cannot be changed because they are what will be. Interpretations are just that, can one see mountains if there are only clouds in the sky? One must say what one sees and not what one 'thinks' or 'wishes' are behind. One cannot interpret the word 'stop' to mean 'run', as one cannot interpret the word 'killed' for 'saved from death', when referring to what you consider as 'life'. The man who calls himself, pope john paul the second, is just that... a man. His name is not John or Paul for he stole those names from others. He is trying to keep his church together and has placed not only his church, but also himself above God, for he is trying to hide corruption from others.

"Once you found out that the Angel Jacob is the one who resides in you, you asked, 'Should I change my name to Jacob?' I replied, 'No, for you were born David. Do not change what is rightfully yours. Your Mother and Father named you David...keep it.'

"The third Prophesy, tells symbolically of the end of time as We, too, have written about; after all have fallen down dead, the Angels will approach and pray for the 'dead' - lost souls, will try to harm the Angels as they near the leader of the end of time. Then, the Angels of God, who Santa Maria Lucia saw as Bishops, Priests, religious men and women, will symbolically sprinkle Everlasting Life - Righteousness on the Souls of those who are making their way to God - the Light.

"Enjoy life, for what you have experienced during your life has made life for you. Do not think about what will come, but cherish what has been, and then, you shall have life.

"Blessed are those who Inspire and do not dominate, but Love all others."

Then the Angel Jo was gone.
And I prayed,

Christine J. Haven

"Father, hold my hand and lead me for I cannot see, guide me for I do not completely understand. Amen."

Leash The Dog

And I said to the Angel Jo, "You and the other Angels have fulfilled your mission with me, for I have written the book as you requested and instructed me to do, and yet, I have failed... myself."

And the Angel Jo said unto me, "All people have the right to their individual choices, and from the start many have tried to dominate others, but they always end in violence.

"Are you sad? You have not tried to dominate. We become sad whenever we see you unhappy for the anger that you display at another' actions causes you sadness. The actions that anger you are their individual choices, and yet, they do not see their actions are forcing their beliefs upon you or others, for they have no eyes to see with.

"We have told you, 'practice what you have learned,' and yet, your anger comes from not liking some actions of others. Understand that you cannot control the 'dog' every time and sometimes the 'dog' will become unleashed.

"Remember, you are not an Angel, but instead a human that contains an Angel within. Therefore, sometimes you cannot control the 'dog', but you should always try to control him. And yet, do not try to be what you are not.

"When others seek your advice, give it freely without conditions. It they use your advise, feel no greater than they. And if they use your advise and overcome their problems, and then return to their old life style, do not feel anger, or have resentment toward them, for you were there when they needed your words, for it is not your concern if they return to their old ways.

"You are only an instrument of God, all that you do is His, the words that you speak to others are His, and if, and when they return to their old ways after you have spoken the words to them, they have not only turned their backs on you, but also on God. And yet, did the words you speak come from God or you? For you alone have the right of your individual choices of the words that you use. Humans try to dominate each other while God does not try to dominate, for if He wished He could dominate all, whereas, God has given all their individual choices in their lives.

"From the dawn of time, people seek God whenever they are in need of Him, then afterwards, they turn their backs on Him as they return to the feelings of the 'dog'.

"Do you remember the night that you sat near the top of your bed and leaned against the head board while I sat near the foot of the bed, and you asked me to remove the dog feelings from you? I answered, 'I cannot.' Then you said, 'Jesus healed the sick, can he not remove these dog feelings that dwell within me?' Then Jesus manifested in front of you as other Angels appeared as little lights and flew around the room. He raised His hands toward the ceiling, and then, placed His hands upon your chest as all the Angels followed His lead, and flew around you as they darted in and out of you. Jesus then said, 'Are you sure you wish to remove these feelings? I can only help you remove the dog feelings but only you can remove these feelings.' As He said this, you felt His love - God's love flow through your body. Christine, who had been asleep beside you then awoke and saw Jesus, She wept as she extended her arms toward Him, for this was the first time that she had seen Jesus. He extended His hand to her and touched her hand and then, she too, felt the warmth of God's love flow through her.

"The dog feelings are part of... as you say, the dog.

"Without these feelings you would not be human. The choices of those feelings are part of your individual choices that God has given you. You should use those feelings to learn and experience in the endurance of your life. And yet, you need to control them.

"We will not control you or your feelings but we will Inspire you - help you learn to control them, if that is what you wish.

"Blessed are those who continue to keep God in their hearts and their thoughts daily."

Then the Angel Jo was gone.

And I prayed,

"Father, thank You for helping me understand even though I do not fully understand yet. Please continue your guidance and teachings for I wish to learn. Please help me leash the dog. Amen."

And if Anyone Wishes to Move a Mountain...

In the middle of May, I became concerned about crabgrass trying to take over our front lawn, and also, I never put as much time into making the front of our home as beautiful as I did with the back garden. Our front yard is not very large, only around 1,000 square feet, but with my health as bad as it is, I knew that I could not do much yard work any more.

The inside of my home and the back garden (yard) are for the deceased children of the world. For many Angels bring the children through here on their journey to God. Thus I felt, the front must be part of the Altar for God that we had created in my back yard, as described in Exodus 20:22-26 of the Christian Bible.

During the first days of July, after workers had removed our old front lawn, my wife, son and I finished God's Altar.

Late in the evening of July 10th of 2001, Jesus said unto me, "We Inspired you to make the Father's Altar for His children in your back yard, did you not think We would help you finish the job that now includes the front?

"My Brother, you built this garden because you wished it to be, we only inspired you, and We carried you when you were tired. And yet, you did not tempt God by taking breaks, you knew your limits, but We were there if you forgot. And when a neighbor said to you, 'Get someone to do this front yard for you... I don't want to look over and see you laying dead.' You answered, 'I will not die working on this yard for God is on my side... His Angels help me.' Do not look down on yourself for you have not failed yourself or the Father.

"How true are the words that you spoke. And if anyone wishes to move a mountain, all they need to say is, 'move mountain,' and it shall be done."

Then Jesus was gone and I cried.

And I prayed,

"Father, thank You for helping me, I am getting old and tired and my heart will not allow me to do much more. I know that if I do not tempt You, I shall not live one second more or less than I am suppose to, for all is in Your Master Plan. All that I do is for You. Amen."

Live a Righteous Life

And the Angel Jo said unto me, "Life was not designed to be prefect. Life was made to experience. Just as Jesus once told the people that he did not come to bring peace, but instead to bring conflict into the world.

"All lives are innerwoven, all that you do effects others and all that others do, in some way, effects you. It is not your concern what others think about you, it is your concern what you say, think of and act to others, and yet, it is okay to dislike the actions of others, but do not hate them.

"You will not fully understand all that We say until you join Us on this, The Other Side, but you should try to hear and follow what We say, for We mean only the best for you. We love not only you but all that live.

"We understand that humans only know life as that they live, and yet, We try to show and teach them of God's Love. But most cannot comprehend life until after death, though We continue to direct Our Love toward them, for it is their choice to receive it and return God's Divine Love or not, for We will not dominate you or them.

"Many on this side, what you call The Other Side, call you the Guider for you guide others toward God. It does not matter which religion they prefer because all religions belong to the one God at the top, as long as their religion says to love all people and have no domination toward others, they will do fine. And yet, if they would just lift their Souls - feel free, live free, touch free, love free and above all else, be free, then We will rejoice and sing with them.

"If people would not only realize that they are part of the human race, but that part of God resides in them as the Angel-within is part of God, and to treat others as they wish to be treated and as they should treat themselves, all would be fine. For those who lived a righteous life without the need to have heard or seen are the most rewarded in the Light."

And I prayed, "Father, thank You for giving me the guidance of Jesus and Your Angels. Amen."

We Bring Only Love to All

The other evening as I walked out onto our patio, there stood the Angel Gabrael, and He said unto me, "The war that now rages in Israel demonstrates the evils of man.

"Israel was given to the Jewish people, for they were God's chosen ones. Once they allowed others to roam and live in their land without belonging to their Jewish Religion, they did this from the goodness in their hearts, but now that goodness is gone and they have become the dogs as the Palestinians have always been.

"No, We do not dislike the Palestinians, for they are also human, We dislike their actions which came from the followers of Muhammad. He was a great man who talked with God, but his followers took God's words that were given to Muhammad, and destroyed them, and placed their polluted thoughts and ideas into them. And now, the Israeli are doing the same thing.

"As you have heard, 'Taking of a life is not the answer,' for you - the human race must inspire your children to know the difference between right and wrong. Those that have done wrong, you must decide rather to put them in prison or to inspire them to righteousness I speak of righteousness not as religious or spiritual beliefs, but as doing what is best for mankind and those around them. Cannot the schools and parents teach the children this type of righteousness without preaching religion?

"Jerusalem is a city for all religions, and yet, the Palestinians want all the Jewish people gone, and if they indeed controlled Jerusalem, no other religion would be found there. God gave the Jewish people control over Israel and its land, they gave others the right to come and even live there, if they desire it.

"As it was said that Jesus stated, 'I have come to bring conflict to the world,' this meant that his followers would destroy his words - the Words He spoke from God to the people so that many different branches of 'Christianity' would be heard around the world just as the Jewish and the Islam Religions are also encircling the world.

"Jesus is part of God, and God is in everything, break open a piece of wood and He is there, so is Jesus. God is in Jerusalem, if Jesus brought conflict to the world, is it not in Jerusalem, too?

"Jacob, the second son of Isaac, was the founder for the twelve Hebrew tribes, and now the House of Jacob, Jesus' House of Jacob shall bring those twelve tribes together, for all belong to those tribes. Muhammad and the followers of Jesus polluted God's Words with their own ideas and thought of the twelve tribes as being Hebrew groups of people, the twelve tribes really meant the twelve true religions of God that were spin offs of the Hebrew Religion that also included the Hebrew Religion, for all other religions did not come from God, but yet, those also belong to God for He created everything including them.

"You shall not pollute the Words that We have given you, therefore, you will not speak those Words and destroy them with your thoughts and ideas. Only those who come after you will speak from the books that you have written as instructed by God. Of course, some of those will pollute the Words when they speak, but any who wish to know God shall find Him in the words that you laid down upon paper.

"We gave you the Words of God because you were not polluted by any religion, in that you were pure, but your attitude is still mostly that of the dog, which you do try to control as inspired by the Angel Joleen. Therefore, you guide others toward God, the true One at the top, and allow them to pick and choose the religion of their choice. As long as their religion says to love all people and have no domination toward others, they will do fine.

"We did not bring conflict into the world, the people did that, we bring only Love to all."

And I prayed, "Father, the true and only God at the top above all others that Abraham, Isaac and Jacob prayed to, thank You for giving me the guidance of Jesus and your Angels. Amen."

Foolish People

Over the last year, people have E-mailed me asking where in the Scriptures does it say the things I write about.

I have seen and talked with Angels and Jesus and I still do, and that is where my Messages come from and not out of some old writings that were written by man.

The Scriptures that these foolish people ask about, I guess they are referring to the Christian Religion. For some reason they think the only religion in the world is Christianity, but in reality it is merely one of the minority religions in the world.

I really do not care what is said in the Christian Religion or Bible, because I speak the truth from God and only Him. I speak of things that the Angels and Jesus have told me, and all that they tell me came directly from God.

The Christian Bible was written by men, and yes, even the disciples of Jesus were just humans as you and I. True, they did have Jesus while He was alive to help guide them, but after His death, they thought and did as all men do; they followed their own interest and ideas. I do not follow my human interest; I follow what the Angels and Jesus have told me and continue to tell me. I understand that the human feelings will get in our way. I have learned how to keep my human feelings out of what they tell me. The foolish people of long ago did not understand nor did they do this. Most things that they said and wrote were contaminated with their own ideas and thoughts.

Can we separate the truth of God from the human thoughts that are written into any bible? No!

We can only believe that the Christian Bible contains only some of the many truths from God, but we must understand that the human polluted all bibles with his human's ideas and thoughts.

The Foolish People in today's world will fight and die trying to convince others that their god is the true God. How confused the people are to think God wishes us to dominate our brothers and sisters.

If the true God wanted everyone to believe in Him, all He would have to do is show Himself and demand us all to follow Him and Him alone. But He does not, why?

Because the true one God above all others has given us are individual choices to make in our lives. Therefore, we should not force our gods upon others, but let them decide what belief system that they wish to follow, for all beliefs have the same God that is above all religions and all others are false gods.

I understand that most Christian Religions stemmed from the Catholic Church - the old Roman religion. And since that is so, all Christian Religions are corrupted and evil. Just look at the evil things that occurred from the Catholic Church...wars...killing of innocent people...Sex scandals...removal of many important parts of the Christian Bible, plus many more things that they have done.

Do you truly think the Catholic Religion with all of its injustices is the kind of religion that God wishes us to follow?

Keep in mind that the old leaders of the Catholic Church were the ones who decided what your Christian Bible should say and what it should not say. They are the ones who removed many parts from the true Bible. And as I said earlier; humans that first wrote the bibles polluted it.

Go ahead and follow your corrupted Christian Religion or any other religion that you wish. Kill all the people because they do not follow your religion.

I know and follow the one and true God, for His way is not of Domination, and His way is to Love all people.

Let us Pray:

"My Lord, the True and Righteous Holy God above all, guide

Your children in the correct way of life that You intended them to travel. Show them that their gods are not the True and Righteous One that You are. Teach them their religion is no different than their brothers. Show them the things they claim do and say is for God is not for You, but instead is for themselves. Make them understand that their religions are not the same but all religions belong to You just as they also belong to You. I mourn and cry for them. I love them. Have mercy on them. Amen."

Confused and Ignorant People...

Shortly after I laid down to sleep, the bedroom started to glow as if someone had lit a nightlight. I rose up and looked around the room to find that the Angel Gabrael had entered, and the light came from within him. He drifted like smoke past the foot of my bed and stopped near the side of my bed. He wore what appeared as a Roman Soldier's uniform of long ago. His breastplate and some kind of metal things that hung down from his waist shined as if they were made of gold while thick, well oiled and richly looking leather lay between them and against his body.

And the Angel Gabrael said unto me, "When you first realized that I was near, you thought I was a threat to you, for you did not know of me. Once you allowed your heart to lead, you came to peace within, for then, you knew I was the same as the Angel Joleen - we Love you. Then, you were able to relax and read my story, and yet, what you read about me was not my story but what others had written.

"I am the one who symbolically blows the horn once a day to notify those in the Light of the Home coming of newly deceased ones who have love in their hearts and yet, the number of triumphants grows smaller each day because of the ways of the flesh.

"And yet, all Angels including myself are Protectors and Guardians of man, but most refuse us because they cannot open their hearts to God, but instead they rely on selfishness for their enjoyments and experiences. But if they listen, we would Inspire them to the higher Enjoyments and Experiences of God.

"You are not special or different than any other. We try to communicate with others but they refuse us, you did not, for they are caught up in their lives with beliefs that contain their man-made gods.

"And yet, if you view the Christian Bible as the Gospel (truth) instead of as gossip, you would believe that only a few Angels exist, but in reality many exist, including the Angels Joleen and the one who people refer to as 'the Virgin Mary,' while neither of these are named as Angels in any Bible. But many who claim to be Christians, say they have seen the Virgin Mary. But one person had to have seen the Virgin Mary first, is that any different than you being the first to have seen and communicated with the Angel Joleen?

"Foolish and ignorant people think Jesus died on the cross for their past, present and future sins. Boy, what a way to 'live' - not caring about how your actions hurt and harm others while believing that another' death saved you. Those people think they are special, but instead they are insignificant. God does not dominate, He allows all to have their individual choices in their lives. Domination comes from humans that demand placement of their man-made gods above all.

"Blessed are those who have open hearts for their fellow humans. For we love you."

To the true God of Abraham, Isaac and Jacob I pray:

"My Lord, the True and Righteous Holy God above all, thank you for allowing me this life to experience and enjoy. Forgive us for our sins and give us the knowledge to know what our sins were. Grant us the intelligence to understand the truth so we do not commit the same sin again. Guide and protect us as we travel through this life and bless those who Love You. Amen."

"Love Them"

In the early hours before sunrise on a spring day during the year of 2001, the Angel Joleen in a beautiful flowing 'ice blue' gown drifted like glowing smoke in front of me as I stood in my backyard garden as a cool gentle breeze swayed the branches in the nearby tree.

And the Angel Joleen said unto me, "Joan of Arc, heard from us as God, telling her that she was to lead the French into battles that would crown Charles as King, that was her mission. After she had done that, her mission was over, and yet, she continued, but she was not guided or protected by God, for then, she did things for the 'dog' that dwelled within her.

"We instructed you to write two books, that you did, and after you had finished, you then asked, 'What shall I do with these books?' I answered, 'Nothing,' for it is not your job to spread the Words of God that you have written, for others will do that after you have gone, but you should keep helping others, for many from this, The Other Side, as well as from the human side will continue to come to you and seek your help.

"Then you asked, 'Should I start a church?'

"I replied, 'If you wish to do so, but not many will come, instead use your electronics to lay the foundation for 'Jesus' House of Jacob,' for you are his housekeeper, and many from around the world will read your website, and what you say there will help them.'

"As I have told you before, enjoy and experience life, for We have made you whole once again. Do not make life difficult for life is one of the gifts that God has given you. Understand that life is not prefect, and many will do things that you as the 'dog' will not approve of, but that is their choice for individual choices is also another gift from God. Love all people for who they are - a human (dog) that contains an Angel-within, do not judge them but judge their actions for all actions are energy of good or evil. And people mostly demonstrate actions of evil for their actions come from the 'dog.' Do not become angry at 'born again Christians' when they try to force their religion or beliefs upon others, but you may dislike and show concern for their actions. Anger is from the 'dog' and not God, nor from the Angel that is within, for anger is evil energy that is from the 'dog.' Love them for they are like you - all have an Angel-within. And yet, it is okay to fight another for the protection of the gifts given to all by God. And yet, do not concern yourself when others say they own the true Jesus' House of Jacob, for all will be revealed when the time has come. For no human owns or rules Jesus' House, he selects his own caretaker(s).

"You need to tell others to embrace the one and only God and not to worship Jesus for he is the Son of God, and Jesus dislikes being placed above the Father.

"You once asked me should you continue to place messages upon your website. I replied, 'Do you have more that you wish to say?' For God did not ask you to write those messages for Him, you are their author and you speak them from an open heart, and when you feel that you have said enough, then discontinue. Follow what is in your heart for I Love you."

Those who truly understand God and His Will shall be Blessed and may you become re-confirmed to God again.

Do Not Brood...

And the Angel Joleen said unto me, "Do not brood over the wisdom of the world. For wisdom and intelligence are fulfilled at the level desired and needed by the individual for all are born equal. The need and desire to learn are inspiration that one seeks in his life. You cannot inspire those that do not wish inspiration, nor can you push learning onto them, for pushing knowledge onto others is domination, and that we will have no part of.

"Your world is presently full of people pushing their concepts of God and ideas about God onto others. You are to speak with Love in your heart for all. You are to have no domination toward others. The things that we instructed you to write along with your life style that you now demonstrate will have impact on some. The Love that you show will inspire others to follow God's way of life - Love for all and no domination toward others.

"There is a certain man that you know of, he once had high expectations of life and was working very hard to achieve them, but now he has lost his way because of his marriage to a certain woman and their expected unborn child. You nor I or can God change what will come in his life for he has final decision of his choices, and yet, his wife has pulled him down to her level of wisdom, and that is wrong for he should have inspired her to climb in intelligence. He should have guided her to Heaven in her thoughts, but instead she has led him into her Hell.

"God does not call for or ask for wars, murder or suicide of His children. For those things are of the dog. Teach as to inspire others not to make war, to kill or to commit suicide in the name of God or for God. And yet, tell them to protect themselves and fight if needed to preserve their individual rights of choice.

"All people have individual choices in life, and their choices may not be the same as yours for their wisdom and intelligence may not be the same as yours, and they may not have the same priorities as you, therefore love them for who they are - a human that contains an Angel within. But you need not love their actions for they may be different than yours.

"The certain young man and his wife that I spoke about, you nor I cannot prophesize with accuracy if their unborn child will live or not, nor what their lives will bring for only God knows that. Love them, but you may be sadden at their decisions that they have made as one. For they will someday stand in front of God to be judged as one for their actions during the time they spent together.

"And yet, this certain couple are only two of the billions of the world that do not have the wisdom or intelligence to know or understand God, let alone life. And their actions are not your problem, for you are to enjoy and experience life, as they also should do.

"Repent of your past actions of unkindness toward others - Forgive yourself as you ask God to forgive you of these past sins. Climb higher with wisdom of life as you learn as inspired by God's Concept of Life - To Learn and Experience through the Experiences of Others through Endurance of Life.

"Blessed are you who faithfully follow the Father and Son with wisdom in your hearts that show Love for all and no domination toward others. We shall forever guide and protect you, for We love you, too."

Marriage and Family

Throughout the last eight years, the Angels helped me understand the Creator (Father) and about life. And through their teaching, I learned that ALL people, including me, are or will become confused about creation, or its purpose, or understand our part in creation (life) during some time in our lives. Creation is like a ball of many individual strings, you cannot remove one to examine it and expect to understand all about life.

God is Love. Love is God. God is the congregation of Angels, therefore Love is a verb and a noun.

Angels are Energy that is intelligent, but on a higher plane of consciousness than us, for we are part of its (God's) Creation. Love is giving (sharing) your life experiences with another, whereas Love is your Spirit (Soul) freefully (is Heaven) sharing your life's experiences with all Angels. Love is not demanding anything from another but accepting and sharing experiences of life from another, whereas on The Other Side, Love is giving and sharing life's experiences with all others. Whereas Love Is Not Give and Take!

When we are younger and during our breedable years, since we are mammals, our natural animal scents indicate to the opposite sex if our Generic make-up would help strengthen his or hers off-spring. But while with human concepts, we cover our natural odors with smells that we think makes us more attractive and thus added with our young beautiful bodies, we see only the skin-deep beauty of our partner while our animal thoughts turn to personal self-gratifying sexual climax. And once the female becomes pregnant, her body changes and most likely, she will gain weight, and maybe she will never lose that extra weight. Her body has changed from that sexy desirable beautiful young girl into a woman who has beared your child.

Two people blend together to become one.

If your partner does something that you do not agree with, you must discuss that issue so that both agree on the action. If you accept their actions then you are just as responsible as your partner for their actions. Whereas, if you become sexual active with a person but do not agree with his or hers actions, you have disgrarded all of your beliefs and thought merely of your self-gratifyications.

When one becomes two

After a man and woman become one in marriage (when two become one), usually they will have children, and each child is another person, (one becomes two). Each child thinks and acts independently from its parents. (The child's parents may do things that the child does not agree with, and the child is NOT respondsible for its parents actions.) And thus, one becomes two. The parents are merely respondsible for teaching the child. It does not matter if the teachings took or not. For the child is responsible for his or her actions alone when he or she becomes older because all people are capable of knowing the difference between right from wrong.

The child is an indepentent entity from its parents. It has its own needs and wants, it cannot support or protect itself. The parents' duty is to take care of the child and to oversee, and teach, and to guide the child through his or hers younger life. Whereas, the parents must put their wants and desires on hold through the years of raising their children.

What are the wants and needs of a child?

Younger children do not want much, sure they need a livable surrounding like a well maintained home, food and clothing and an education, but their wants are easily fulfilled. They mostly want to be near their mother and father in a home setting, and merely want to be loved and to be happy as they see their parents happy, too.

People forget about their children as they divorce and think only of their present day wants and desires. We expect others to treat us as equals while we treat our children as no-things. People do what they think is best of themselves and forget about their children's needs and wants. Well, guess what... if your partner is not good enough for you to live with, do you think he or she is good enough for your children to live with? Your child is an extension of you...he or she will carry your DNA, blended with your partners' DNA, into tomorrow...as you both live through your child and his or hers DNA into the future.

People need to know that if they were compatible before they procreated life, what happened to change things after the birth of their child?. People should not wait until after having a child to decide if they are compatible or not. Our children will replace us here on earth after we go Home. We need to teach our children to comprehend and understand life better than what we did and we need to give our children a better life than what we had, or we are no better than the animal that we are.

In a marriage, getting a divorce is the same as saying, you are giving up on your children (an extension of yourself), and you think someone else (another man or woman, which ever you are) will do a better job of raising your children then you.

And the Angels said to me, "When a woman and man join together as husband and wife, they give up their individual rights of choices for now they are only part of One while the other part of the One is their spouse. Therefore, they must put into account the desires, and wishes, and wants of their partner before they make any decision and above all before they make any decision that concerns their partner or their children. And while they must live for the rights of their children because it is the birth-parents obligation to their children to do the upmost to raise their children in an environment that includes both parents in the growth of the children, and while the growth of the children is a 24/7 job, whereas, both parents need to be in the home in which the children live. No other can or will direct a child's life as his or her own parents.

"The child did not ask to be born unto you, you decided to procreate life and you should and shall stand accountable for your actions. And when you decided to have children, you then decided that a child's life was more important than your rights and choices. Only an animal and a fool decides after the fact of procreation that his or hers rights and choices are more important than a child's life. Therefore, it is your duty as a parent, to provide happiness to the child, and to provide all the child's needs and wants until he or she is of age.

"Whenever one decides to divorce, that one is saying his or her life is more important than his or her spouse and their offspring, and his or her rights and choices are more important than the child's.

"Men have placed into his religion that women are less than men mainly because what of happened to Adam and Eve in the Garden, We do not agree with that, but one partner needs to lead in the direction of marriage in life. Should not the one who protects his or her family be the leader?

"Your husband's or wife's body will waste away...it will grow old, the body will wrinkle as their hair turns gray and as their skin begins to sag and their body will not do what it used to do. But is it not the same person that you desired and loved before? Has his or her body become old and ulgy while yours stayed young? Is his or her body all that you loved?

"Two women came in front of their King because they where in an argument about who was the mother of a child and who should have the child. The King ruled that the child would be cut in two and half given to each woman.

"One of the women stood up and said, 'Please do not cut the child in two, she can have him, I do not wish to see the child dead.'

"The King gave that woman the child and said, 'She truly does love the child while the other woman does not.'

"Doing what is best for a child is Love for the Child. Getting a divorce maybe the best for you but doing what is best for you - LOVE FOR YOURSELF is not the best for your children."

Going Back

Last week I took a trip back to Wooster, Ohio to where I was born and raised. I also visited Marion, Ohio, the place the Angel Joleen in her last life was born and died, and also the place that we had our love affair in 1965.

Going to Marion for researching of Jo's life as a child was easier than going back to my hometown. When I say, "GOING BACK." I am talking about going back to your old homestead and friends; old memories from which you have come.

On this visit, my oldest brother, Jim, was dying. I wanted to assure him of what his life has been about. I remember a time, years ago when I was not even a teenager, that caused Jim to become very upset. It was in one discussion Jim had with another brother. One of my other brothers told Jim the world would not build a monument to him because he was nothing to the world.

I came back home to tell Jim that he did build a monument of himself through his children, whereas he would live forever through his children. My message made Jim feel better about his life and of the thoughts of him dying.

After visiting with my oldest brother, I looked over the area of town that I was born and raised in. I was sad to see that the town had decided to build a Library that is going to take the entire block in which our old home once stood, even though years ago our old home was torn down and replaced by a parking lot. A Few of the old beautiful houses still stood on that block, but now were empty and ready to be demolished.

Many thoughts entered my head; Why would any town tear down those wonderful old homes to build a Library? Why would they do this? What could I do to keep those old houses?

Then, I realized that over the years I had changed too, so why shouldn't this town also change?

What was the true reason that I came back? Was I looking for my childhood? Did I lose something there that I must find? Joan Lee Harris had died years before. Did I think that I would find her standing there waiting for me to return?

We cannot go back and change the past. Whatever happened and what we have done in the past is forever, and therefore, it cannot be changed. We are presently making our past now. We should try to do things correctly now, do not wait until it is too late to change or correct our actions. If we do things correctly now, we can cherish our past and not regret it.

Then I remembered once when I was talking with the Angel Joleen, she had stated that she did not want to go back to her hometown for a visit. Now I understood what she really meant; She did not want to see the changes in the place that she grew up in. She wanted to remember her old home town the way it was when she was alive.

The world is changing daily, we are also changing, we should not expect others or the world to stop and remain the same for us.

God has given us all the choices of change. We must all grow into the future. No one or place should stop and wait for another to come back.

The choice of change that God has given us can move us to better or worse things, the condition and direction of our changes are opinionated, as also, we must allow others to change in the direction they wish to travel. We are not our brother's keepers; We must allow others to have their opinions and change, too.

God promised each of us three things in life;
1) birth
2) life you can experience
3) death

For one to live, one must go through all the of these times. This life that we live as individuals is nothing when compared to Eternity; all livies are very short. When life is over, our lives are over. Afterlife is not life continuing as we live here. The Soul is the recorded experiences of this life. Heaven is the ability of your Angel to re-live your past life that the Angel within may share with all other Angels as the congregation of Angels that makes up God. Hell is the knowledge of your life's experiences that you do not want to share with others.

And the Angel Jo said, "Do not be unhappy when you see others change in life. Be happy when you know someone has lived and went back Home."

Whenever you see someone, realize that they had to be born. You may be able see the things that they experienced through their life, then you know that they had succeeded in life and are presently preparing to go Home. And when you see someone dead, know they are once again back Home with God.

Stand fast on your opinions and convictions unless you truly see that someone else's ideas are better than yours, and if you decide that theirs are better, then repent and move with them. But do not try to stop others from doing what they desire unless their ideas are destroying or dominating others.

Love all others as you love yourself and as you desire to be loved. Try to guide all others as you wish to be guided. Help all others, as you desire to be helped. Say nothing as you wish others would say nothing. Then you are living a life style as Jesus showed us was righteous, and that life style is what God intended us to live.

The Dog Returns to Its Vomit

And the Angel Jo said to me, "If you see something that another is doing wrong - below your standards, and if you tell that person about it, that person may change his actions and do what pleases you for a while, but then, he may return to doing the things that displeased you. Therefore, the actions of another person that sicken you did not sicken that person, only you telling him about his actions sickened him.

"So then, who returned to his vomit? The person who repeats the action or the one that told the person about not liking his actions?

"Others will not truly change because you do not like their actions, they will only change their actions if they are inspired to do so. God has given you individual choices in your life. Has He not given all others their individual choices, too? You should not try to place domination over them. Therefore, if you see something that is not likable in your opinion, why not inspire them to change or remove yourself from the situation. For most will not allow you to inspire change in their lifestyle. You do not control the world, only yourself. Therefore, if you happen to meet someone who cannot be inspired to change, leave before they turn you into what they are, unless you are of the dog who wants to returns to its own vomit.

"Removal of yourself from another' life is not death, life goes on, but without that person near you. There are many in the world that you have never met, and yet, your life continues. Does one life out of the millions on earth, have that much impact on you that you cannot live without them near? You and all others do not really care about the people that are being terrorized and persecuted or killed daily around the world. Did God intend the world to only revolve around you?

"Life is all innerwoven, and yet, all lives are individualized. What makes one sick may not make another sick. And yet, when we talk about 'the dog returning to its vomit,' we are also talking about one sick in spirit - Soul. One following an evil concept, thoughts or ideas, may not know that he is following evil and continue to follow it, therefore, he returns to what made him sick. This returning to one's vomit also applies to family members. Respect family members and love them as you do your friends if they respect and love you. Allow no person in your circle of friends, to abuse you or refuse to respect your lifestyle. You need not compromise your lifestyle with any other unless you cannot live without them. And if you cannot live without this individual near, you are of the dog and dead - without God, and no more than this individual's slave.

"Once, I asked you if you could sit and have supper with your enemies? You answered, 'yes.' I replied, 'I don't think so.' After thought, you returned and said, 'Yes, I can sit and have supper with my enemies because I have no enemies, my enemies are inside of me.' I answered, 'Correct, now you are learning.' Your thoughts of enemies made you sick in spirit. I inspired you to seek God, Whose truths removed your sickness.

"Those who try to abuse you or refuse to respect you are not your enemies, they are their own enemies and allow their enemies to dwell within themselves that the inspiration of God would cure if they did not refuse Him. If one refuses God's gift of individual choices, one is refusing God.

"Teach others - plant the seed in others as I have done with you, and if they refuse the inspiration, forget them, for they are of the dead and will not help themselves. Do not force God upon them. Allow the dog to return to its vomit, if that is what it wishes."

The Transition Continues

In the evenings, occasionally I go out onto the front porch to smoke a cigarette or two, even though I have had 8 heart attacks I still enjoy a cigarette once in a while, and as I stand on the porch, I will gaze upon the small statue of Joan of Arc that stands in the middle of our front yard, seeing the statue reminds of the directions of our missions in life.

Joan of Arc was directed by God's Angels to fight and win the crown of France for Charles VII. After he was crowned King, her job was over she continued to fight, but God did not grant her the mission of her continued fight, she was on her own and she lost because of her reasons for fighting.

The other day, I asked the Angels, "Should I go to Israel, I could bring peace to the land."

They answered, "No, that is not your mission, when the time is right, someone else will do that."

We all have missions as directed by God, and if we continue after our mission is over, we must continue in the same directions as God intended or face the consequences, we cannot allow our human feelings to ovetake our missions. All have missions of God if they do not refuse Him. And our missions may seem small and you might not even be aware of them, but they are important to God.

The "same directions as God intended" may be to go a different direction as Joan should have returned home instead of her comtinued war. We do not know what God desires, therefore, we cannot and should not put our words or thoughts into Him. The only thing that we can do is follow our hearts, and hopefully, it will be the right decision.

"All that we have told you are for your Salvation," is what the Angels have told me. But they also have said, "Speak and write of the things that we have told you, for your words will help others."

The statue of Joan of Arc that stands in my front yard reminds me that I am human, too. And it also reminds to be patient, for soon my knowledge of God will be needed by me and by others.

I cannot base my life on what others say about God. I can only base my life on what I know about God. It is not fair to my intelligence to believe what others have written about what they "think" God desires. All that is written in the Christian Bible was conceived and wrote by man. Thus, he - man had placed his thoughts upon God.

"Let the blind lead the blind," and, "Those who have not heard or seen, shall be the most rewarded in Heaven." "Be as children; play and enjoy life."

Do not dwell on others actions. We all are One, and therefore we need to help carry our brothers and sisters burdens, but allow them the dignity of humanity - inspire them to help themselves, and do not become their servants, for you are not only the servant but also the master, for above all; you are their equal.

To God and His Angels, the length of our lives is a merely wink of an eye. Enjoy life as you lift your Soul, for they are part of you.

A few months ago, the Angel Jo said, "There is a transition taking place within you, for this is the symbolic death of David. Allow the Angel Jacob, who dwells within your body to lead." (This is not the Jacob as mentioned in the Bible).

Slowly this transition has been taking place for well over three months now. The bad and evil feelings that I allowed to live and grow within me are being removed. I am conquering my Enemy Within. God does not command us to live as He desires, He allows us to live as we desire.

Understanding Prayer

Prayer is no more than a one-sided conversation between you and God; You doing the talking while God listens. God knows everything that will be, you are included in His Master plan. He already knows your needs and what you will do, we live merely to experience and to enjoy or to not enjoy our actions and reactions of our decisions, for we are responsible for the choices of our actions. Therefore, Prayers are to give God recognition as the Father of Creation - the Creator, and to give Him thanks for all that He has created for us and that includes creating us and life.

When the disciples asked Jesus to teach them to Pray, Jesus responded with what we now call the Lord's Prayer:

"Our Father, who is in Heaven, Holy be Your Name. Your kingdom come. Your Will be done, on earth as it is in Heaven. Give us this day our daily bread. And forgive us our trespasses, as we forgive those who trespass against us. And lead us not into temptation, but deliver us from evil. For Yours is the kingdom, and the power, and the glory, for ever and ever. Amen."

His disciples requesting help in Praying indicated that they didn't understand how to Pray. We seem to think we should know instinctively about Praying, but from their question we see that even the disciples -- who were with Jesus every day, witnessing his life and seeing him Pray -- still needed help with Praying. But yet, their question shows us the common human tendency is to want a correct relationship with God.

Jesus responded to their desire, but with the very first words of the Prayer he signals a basic truth: Prayer and communicating with God is not about rules but about relationships. Jesus did this often when someone asks for rules.

Jesus told them to begin their Prayers with, "Our Father who art in Heaven." That first word; "Our" reminds us that we are not alone; we are all God's children - His Creation, that we are linked with God and to one another as one family. And by telling us to call God "Father," Jesus restored images from a man-made God to an image of God as the Creator within us, who is part of us and who we are part of. "Heaven" is the place of all Knowledge in a place of no time or location, for Heaven is the past, present and future - it stands beside and within us, but as humans we stand apart from it.

Then we are to Pray, "Holy is Your name," acknowledging God's holiness as the Creator. This may seem a contradiction, to acknowledge that we are family and then immediately to acknowledge God's holiness (in contrast to our lack of it). But "holy is Your name" reminds us that the basic posture of Prayer is awe -- awe that grows from seeing God's greatness and yet knowledge that One who is The Creator desires for a relationship with us, and while "holy is Your name" expresses He is the Father while we are merely His children who are trying to learn and that He is all Knowledge. That is why we Pray; Giving Thanks to Him and to deepen the relationship and Knowlwedge of our Father. This is the essence of Prayer; embracing the Father and naming Him as God.

Thus this encounter changes us, little by little, and allows us to experience freedom of choice.

This Prayer that Jesus offered begins, "Our Father," acknowledging our close relationship with God as He is the Creator and we are His children (creation). The Prayer then moves to acknowledgment; "Your Kingdom come, Your Will that will be done on earth, as it is in Heaven" This calls for a radical reordering of our individual lives and priorities, but yet, His Will - His desire - is done! For His Master plan is in play, we are only living - experiencing and enjoying or not enjoying the decisions of our actions. We shall all arrive at the correct place and knowledge that we were suppose to at the correct time, and while some will be closer to God than others because that is where each of us are suppose to be.

"Your Kingdom come" asks that your daily consciousness - the individual, to be toward the concepts of God and that you will be transformed into a place where God reigns - where things are done by God's standards, but yet, presently all is done by and to God's standards. We know that our human ways are not God's ways nor our thoughts and concepts God's thoughts or concepts. This reverses the usual human order where those who have more make the rules, and that our lives as individuals nor as a group are more important than the Creator and the Afterlife - Heaven. We ask for all in our personal world to be for the Father, for "the kingdoms (our individual lives) of this world to become the kingdoms of our Lord - the Father."

Like most of Jesus' teachings, this one is personal - Prayer is given from one individual to the Father. When we pray for God's Will to be done "on earth as it is in Heaven," we do well to remember that we are made of earth. When we ask for God's Will to be done "on earth," we invite God into us - into the matters of our lives. This opens the door for God to guide us at the deepest levels of our being so that we come to desire what God Wills. Then we embody our prayer by opening ourselves to receive and to choose God's way and allow God to work through us - we accept (embrace) God's Love. (Love is to give and receive.)

"Give us what we need." Many of us find it difficult if not impossible to pray for the human race instead of for ourselves and friends. But in telling us to Pray, "Give us this day our daily bread," the Lord's Prayer indicates that we are to ask God for the things we as the human race needs to sustain physical life. Though Jesus said rightly that we do not live by bread alone, he also made it clear that we are to look to God for the literal bread that we need. Jesus shows us that God is concerned with the details of our lives.

"Give us this day our daily bread" reminds us also that like the caveman gathering each day in the wilderness, we cannot store up what we need from God. Yesterday's experience with God was for yesterday; today we must come to God again for this day's nourishment, reassurance and direction. God sustains us one day at a time.

Praying for specifics pertaining to our individual lives is wrong. For many times when we Pray, what we ask for is not given; People around the world go hungry in spite of Praying for food, loved ones die even when we ask God to heal them. Our relationship with God does not depend on the benefits from our personal request from God. We need to leave the outcome of life to God.

But the Prayer that Jesus gave us also does not say, "Give me today my daily bread." It says, "Give us today our daily bread." We are bound together with all God's children, and God's provision for us is to be shared. There is enough food on the planet to feed everyone; there is enough energy to keep all of us warm; there is enough wealth to supply everyone's basic needs - if we are willing to work for it and not take it from others - giving handouts to others will only make them expect "life" from others. In these words about daily needs we can hear Jesus again calling us to a new way of living - LOVE.

What comes to us is the answer to others' Prayers - if we are willing to open our hearts.

Christians receive when Muslims Pray, and Jews receive when Christians Pray, and Muslims receive when Jews Pray because all are Praying to the same God but referring to Him with different names. As we allow God's love to flow through us, the needs of God's children can be met.

In what we call the Lord's Prayer, Jesus taught us to begin Praying by naming our relationship with and our dependence on God. We are to acknowledge God's holiness and thank Him for meeting our needs. But then it directs us to consider our own sins and to mend our relations with others, telling us to Pray, "Forgive us our sins as we forgive those who sin against us."

Forgiveness often does not come easily. We may berate ourselves endlessly for our failures, unable to forgive ourselves even after we have asked God to forgive us. And many of us find it difficult to forgive others. We so enjoy a good grudge, and must at all cost win! After all, if we think someone hurts us, we naturally want them to suffer for their actions. But Jesus said that if we do not forgive others, we cannot and should not expect God to forgive us.

Some are reluctant to forgive because doing so seems to discount the seriousness of the wrongs that others do; actually, forgiving says the opposite. Forgiving requires first acknowledgment in your opinion that the act is wrong. If you did not think it was wrong, then forgiveness would not be needed. When we forgive, we are saying, "In my opinion what you did was wrong, but I release you from its penalty." We also release ourselves when we forgive those who we believe have harmed us. If we do not forgive, we remain bound to the one who has wronged us and we are allowing hatefullness to grow within us. Only by forgiving can we put the past behind us. Nursing hurts from the past takes energy, and forgiving frees us to use that energy to experience and to enjoy in the present.

Forgiveness is the door to freedom, and Jesus reminds us to make forgiving and being forgiven a matter of Prayer as he opens that door to forgiveness and love for us.

We know that God does not "lead us" into temptation, and so this Prayer is not a plea for God to refrain from doing that. This Prayer asks God to direct us from our human feelings that pulls us away from God. Jesus' teachings here shows us that he understood what it is to be human. He understood that we want to do what is right, but we also want to do what is wrong because of our animal feelings. He reminds us to make this conflict a matter for Prayer, just as in other parts of the Lord's Prayer we offer praise and bring to God our thankfulness of His filling of our daily needs. In teaching his followers to Pray about their struggles, Jesus showed that God wants us to ask for help in the areas where we struggle and sometimes fail. The same God who supplies our "daily bread" offers strength to change our direction when we go where we know in our hearts we shouldn't be.

When we struggle to change our behavior and Pray for help, we find ourselves facing the situation that challenged us. We should tell ourselves, "This is the moment of choice," and realize we have always choosen to do what we have always done and now we will choose to do what we feel God wants.

My daily Prayer is;

"Dear Father, Thank You for another wonderful day, and all the things that You have given us in this day. Thank You for taking care of my family, friends and all those who try to make this a better place in which to live. Thank You for guiding me and allowing Your Angels to come into my life who help guide and teach me, also. I know that I became angry again today and hurt others with my words or actions, I will try to control my animal feelings better tomorrow. I ask You for Your forgiveness and I shall also ask them. I shall continue to sing praises to You until my last moment of life, and then I shall sing and rejoice with You and Your Angels in Heaven forever. Amen."

Confession and Forgiveness

And the Angel Jo said unto me, "Confession of Sin does not remove the Sin unless the Sin does not occur again.
"Asking the Father for forgiveness of a Sin does not receive Forgiveness unless the Sin does not occur again.
"One must be able to self-judge in order to repent from one's past thoughts, ideas and concepts. One should know the difference between the right and wrong actions they reflect upon others, in order to self-judge. The knowledge of right and wrong comes with maturity - growth.
"This self-judgment is not only for a spiritual level, but for all things that are involved in your daily life.
"The Father will not hold it against you if you happen to carelessly repeat the Sin, but you should try not to repeat the Sin, for if you repeat the Sin, you have forgotten God. But God does not forget you, for you live in His heart as He should live in yours.
"People think of Sin that which is only against God, but all things against the Father, Son or Holy Ghost - Spirit are Sins. The Father, Son and Holy Ghost are all things in life and including all life. Whenever you do anything against another or human society or man-made laws, you have committed a Sin, for that act is against life as God has intended life to be, and against the things that lifted you from animal.

"Those who repeatedly confess about committing the same Sin shall not be forgiven. Those who repeatedly ask forgiveness for the same Sin shall not receive Forgiveness. For if one admits to committing a Sin, then he knows the difference between right and wrong. And those who knowingly do wrong are of the dog and not of God.

"The Father is very loving to His children and does allow them to lie to themselves, but He is very adamant on his stance and will not allow them to lie to Him when they try to enter His Kingdom."

And Jesus said unto me, "Do not fear, for you shall not be judged for other's actions against humanity. For when the times comes, God - that part of God within each that you refer to as the Angel within, shall judge the life that he has lived. The gate to Heaven is narrow and not many will enter, less than one of one percent of one percent shall be saved, and those saved shall come from all religions. Even most who claim to be Christians - the ones who say they follow Me do not, and they shall not be saved either. Proclaiming repentance in confession or asking for forgiveness will not save them unless they truly change. We have given each their individual choice to Heaven, and most have refused Us. You as well as all others shall be judged for only what each individual have done. Enjoy life and raise your Soul, find the Salvation that you need and allow others to follow theirs."

And I pray, "Dear Father, Thank You for another day and for all that You have given me to use during this life. Help me rise above the dog with the knowledge of You. Guide me to Your Kingdom and everlasting Love. I try to hold You in my heart constantly and control the dog, but if and when I fail, please forgive me as I repent. Amen."

A World Without Santa Claus

We are heading into a world with a Santa Claus or The Christ or without Jesus.

Reuters

December 11, 2003

South Africa Pulls Plug on Santa Claus Mail

JOHANNESBURG (Reuters) - For South African children there is no Santa Claus this year -- and that's official.

South Africa's Advertising Standards Authority has banned an advertisement for the country's Post Office that gave children an address to write to Santa Claus with their Christmas wishes.

In a ruling this week the Authority said the Post Office was "profiting from the natural credulity of children."

"It creates the impression, in the mind of the credulous child, that by writing to the given address she/he will be writing to Santa Claus, who, according to the Santa Claus myth, will then bring him/her the requested presents," it said.

The Authority banned the advertisement, upholding a complaint which said it encouraged "a falsehood that could break the fragile spirits of the already disillusioned youth of South Africa."

Is it wrong for people that are not religious, to wish for "Peace on Earth" during the Christmas Season?

At Christmas, when we pray for "Peace on Earth," do we really think God will grant us our prayer?

I know the blame for "fragile spirits of the already disillusioned youth of South Africa," should not fall upon Santa Claus because of the idea of him giving gifts, the Disillusion of their Fragile Spirits are the outcome from them being taught that they should be given wealth for not working for it. But yet, all Children need to live their young lives with the hopes of greater and better things in their lives. Society will not prosper without dreamers who work hard for better and greater things, for all who lives need to be dreamers.

During this Season, we need to lay aside religious concepts and consecrate (treat as if Holy) on Loving our children. The love of Santa does not know religion and his love should be shown to all the children of the world. And all people are the children of the world.

The other day, I heard a Jew who turned Christian say, "Christians are the only children of God and they are my brothers."

All the people of the world are God's children. It does not matter which religion they follow. For all religions belong to Him!

It is written, while Jesus was inside a home and talking with some people, a servant came to him and said, "There are people at the door saying they are your family and asking for you to come out." Jesus replied to the servant as he looked toward the people inside, "They are not my family, you are my family."

There are two families of God's children; one follows God while the other follows the desires of the flesh.

It is time for people to wake-up and realize they are all fighting a "holy war" for their beliefs against all other religions and those who do not follow any religion. Walk out of your church and forget those who preach the words of their man-made god; Those who proclaim they know the words of the Father while merely teaching their religion are liars and are not your brothers. For they only want to dominate you and force others to live under their control, and fellowship (brotherhood) of a religion, does not mean placing those of other religions into slavery.

Santa Claus is Coming to Town

Around this time of the year, I hear people talking about how their parents wrongly told them about Santa Claus.

These people do not understand that parents raise their children the best that they can, and perhaps these people who do not condone the way they were raised, think children should not be told fairy tales.

The song "Santa Claus is Coming to Town" has the line, "He knows if you been bad or good...," this line or any line of any song should not be quoted to children as if it is true. Many people do not wish to include Santa in their Christmas celebration because they were told Santa would not bring them gifts if they were bad, but then, they saw other children receiving better presents from Santa, who they knew were not as nice. Therefore, if you use this type of line on children, you must be prepared to deliver a Christmas to their expectation.

I am 57 years old, and Santa still comes to our home every Christmas. When I learned that Santa as a person, did not exist, I could not tell my parents because I could not shatter their dream, for I thought they believed in him, too.

My sons, ages 18 and 24 years, both know there is no Santa Claus, but every Christmas morning there are gifts from Santa under our Christmas tree. To us, Santa is not a person who brings only gifts of earthly goods, for he is one who shares the joy of the birth of Jesus by giving gifts of love and out of love. The gifts from Santa Claus are symbolic of the gifts given to Jesus at his birth that people of all religions can enjoy, and is symbolic for God's love that we share. Therefore, Santa is the symbol of love for the season. But retailers commercialized this holiday, the same holiday created by the old Roman Church when it merged the birth of Jesus and an old pagan holiday to force a Christian Holiday upon people. Now our twisted concepts of Christmas cause us to think of giving earthly gifts instead of giving love as God gave to us when He gave us His only begotten son, as demonstrated by the birth of Jesus.

This year, my oldest son who is in the Marines, and on a ship heading for Afghanistian. This year he will not be home for Christmas. But we shall celebrate Christmas with him when he returns next August, but for now, we sent him a few little things that he can use on his trip.

This Christmas as with the previous 5, the Angels of the deceased children excitedly wait for gifts that the Angel Joleen brings for them in our home. The toys that the Angel Joleen delivers to them are of love. They will not keep their presents because of their earthly matter, but they will play with them, and next year, we will set them out for the children that will spend Christmas here before going on to God.

Santa lives in our heart as surely as God lives.

I hope that this Christmas you tell your family that you love them. Show your love to family and friends by giving little gifts out of the love in your heart.

And the Angel Jo says to you, "Merry Christmas to all, AND A SPECIAL MERRY CHRISTMAS TO YOU! For you are Special to God!"

The Christmas Season

As we enter into this Christmas Season I would like to say; this is the time of year that should unite the people into wishing for peace on earth.

One needs not be Christian to want peace on earth. Nor does one need to be Religious or Spiritualist to want peace on earth. The peace and love that people seek for the world is not only for all others, but also it is for themselves. This season is not just for the few that believe and/or follow God or Jesus. This season of love and peace is for all people. Even if you do not have a God or Religion to follow, you still should want to have love and peace with your fellow man.

A Few years ago, during the Christmas Season, Jesus said to me, "I do not see why the big fuss is over December 25th, I was born March 13th two years prior to when it is recorded that I was born."

It is not the date or the celebration of Jesus' birth that matters, but instead it is the idea of all people coming together with love in their hearts for all. Yes, in fact we do use this time to remember Jesus' birth while we play music of His Glorious Birth, but still we need to use the season to remember His lifestyle and what God was trying to teach us with Jesus' life - His life was to show us how we should live and treat each other, and God gave us this Holy Season for us to review what life should be throughout the year.

Whenever you give a gift to another, you are showing as an example of God giving His Love to us. The Christmas Season expresses this example of what God has given to all humans of the world.

Our lives are symbolic for the Love that God has shown upon the world. The gifts that we give each other also are symbolic for God giving us His Love. Our individual lives are God's gift to each of us. God did not need a Christmas Season to give us our gifts of life - Love.

Therefore, at this Christmas Season, I give you my blessings and myself - all the Love that God has given me. I hope and pray that all of your days be merry and that you prosper throughout the coming new year.

Christmas Love

As we near Christmas Day, we should see and understand what Love is as well as to know what Christmas is all about.
Christmas is not just for remembering the birth of Jesus, it is also for refreshing our thoughts and understanding what Love is. The birth of Jesus was meant to show us Love - God's Love for us.
The birth of Jesus was God re-writing his Covenant with His children, us. It was to correct the injustices and prejudices placed in God's Bible by humans, thus proving His Divine Love for us.
Love - to give yourself to another.
In the Bible, Jesus in conversation with (I believe) John, asked John three times if John loved him. Each time John answered, "Yes."
Jesus asked John three times because John did not understand His question, just as we did not, and still today, do not understand Jesus' questions.
Jesus said in the Bible, "The only way to the Father is through me." We still do not even understand His statement, but it states in the Bible that God is Love, for Love is God. If you break open a piece of wood and I am there, overturn a rock and I am there, God is inside everyone of us, His is Everything and also in the Bible, it states we are His children.
Therefore in the Bible, God and Jesus both are saying; everything is One, we are all together as One, and Love is uniting all together as One. So, if God and Jesus are not lying to us with these

statements, we are part of God and Jesus, by accepting that Jesus is part of you (giving yourself to Jesus) as well as giving yourself to all things, is the way to the Father, for then you have accepted God - the Father.

Whenever a religious person or group places demands on you, such as you must believe in and follow their religious beliefs, they are going against God's Will. These people are also antichrist because they are going against Christ.

The birth of Jesus that we celebrate as Christmas was to demonstrate God's Love to us.

God will not dominate us, He allows us to follow and do as we wish. But He is demanding because if we do not Love All, He will deny us.

Follow the Love that is in your heart, then you are following the Angel that dwells within you because that Angel is the part of God that is in you. Then you are allowing God to direct your life as is His Will.

My Christmas with The Angels

I would like to share with you the true story of my Christmas spent with the Angels this year.

Every Christmas Eve at the stroke of Midnight, the Angel Joleen appears and we take a walk in our back yard or around our neighborhood. This year I had decided before hand that we would walk down the sidewalk in front of our home.

Precisely at Midnight Joleen appeared as I sat at our kitchen table and waited for her. We stood up, hugged and kissed each other, and we wished each other a Merry Christmas.

Seeing the Trinity Cross that I wear, the Angel Joleen bent down and kissed the Cross hanging from the chain around my neck. Then She smiled at me.

Hand-in-hand we preceded out the front door into the night air. As we walked from the porch into the night, she stopped and looked into the darken sky, and for a minute Joleen stood still, and did not say a word, and then she said, "How beautiful."

As we continued our walk down the street, Joleen kept saying how beautiful all the Christmas lights on the houses were, and how beautiful the star lit sky was. We stopped as she gazed up at the stars and pointed to a distant star and said, "We have been past that one." Then, she said, "Listen...do you hear that... the Love... all the people praying... all asking for Peace and Love on earth."

I, too, could feel the Love of their Prayers, but I could not actually hear their words.

Standing there in the cold night air as I held the Angel Joleen's hand, I said to Her, "This year I have no gift such as diamonds, gold or silver to give to you... this year I present you and God with me... I give you me. I wish for peace on earth for Christmas in a world where there's not one hungry child. A day when hope and faith concurs fear and hate... all I'm asking for is a little more love."

She looked at me and smiled.

After we had returned back into my home, Joleen placed a stuffed Santa, two stuffed snowmen and a Santa sleigh in front of our Christmas tree that she had bought. As She did this She said, "These are my gifts to the Children this year... the deceased Children that we have brought here before we take them Home to God, they will love these gifts."

I asked, "Should I leave them set out all year?"

She answered, "No, just tomorrow Christmas Day, if you like...you can leave them out until the New Year as you do with your other Christmas decorations, and just set them out under your tree next year."

I held the Angel Joleen in my arms as we once again wished each other a Merry Christmas, and then She was gone.

Within a few minutes after the Angel Joleen had left, I picked up my 35mm camera and took pictures of the gifts that she had left for the Children under our Christmas tree.

On Christmas Day around 6:00pm the Angel Joleen once again appeared unto me. As the night before we hugged and kissed while we wished each other a Merry Christmas. She told me the children were happy with their gifts that she had gotten them. The Angel then asked me to telephone my wife's sister, and then she told my sister-in-law that she had a beautiful Christmas tree, the children at her house were very happy, and how her (my sister-in-law) New Year would be (things to come) and wished her a Merry Christmas. The Angel Joleen handed me the telephone receiver and left as I talked to my sister-in-law on the phone.

Yes, I had a wonderful Christmas.

Christmas 2001 with the Angels of God

During the afternoon on Sunday, the 23rd of December, the Angel Joleen appeared and asked me to take her shopping for Christmas presents for the Children.

As we drove toward our local Toys "R" Us store, the Angel Joleen sat beside me and we talked about there being too many cars on the streets today and about how beautiful the houses and landscaping looked.

Upon entering the parking lot of the store, we saw many people trying to navigate their cars into parking spaces, while others were trying to leave the parking lot, and pedestrians hurriedly walked by. When we exited our car, the Angel Joleen grabbed my hand and held it tightly as we cautiously headed for the store.

After entering Toys "R" Us, her grip on my hand eased as she marveled at the toy displays that surrounded us. And within 15 minutes of walking around inside the store and gazing at all the toys, she selected a box containing a Rudolph and the Island of Misfit Toys figurine collections, and the video, Rudolph. And then, she turned to me and said, "We must go to a store near where we live to buy two sleds to place Rudolph and his friends on for the Children, I do not know the name of the store, but I will give you directions to it as we drive."

Once we had drove to and entered the Savon Drug store, the Angel Joleen led me directly to an isle where we found the sleds, and after I paid for them, we headed home.

The Angel Joleen asked, "Can we have McDonald's for dinner?"

I answered, "Yes, but its too early now, lets wait until around 5 before we go there."

She agreed, and after parking in our garage, we left the presents in the car, and went into the house where we passed the time away as we talked.

I asked her, "Won't the Children see the presents we bought?"

"No," she said, "I won't let them near them until Christmas morning."

I replied, "That's mean." And she smiled.

At 5 o'clock, my son, Dan drove the Angel Joleen to McDonald's.

When they returned from McDonald's with our dinner, the Angel Joleen said, "We did not have to go inside, we got the hamburgers and fries and never got out of the car. Things sure have changed."

As we sat at the dining room table and ate, she bent down close to the table and smelled the french fries. And I said, "dead animals, the fries were cooked in dead animal fat."

She replied, "Food! They smell good."

When we had finished eating, the Angel Joleen wrapped the rest of her hamburger up in its wrapper. Then, she came and sat on my lap and said, "Its time for me to go. I love you," and then, gave me a kiss.

I replied, "I love you, too."

We hugged, and then, she collapsed as if dead, and she was gone.

(On Thanksgiving Day of this year, I had told my oldest son, who is in the Marines and would be on a boat and heading for Afghanistan on Christmas Eve, that the Angel Joleen and I would visit him on Christmas Eve at midnight.)

In keeping with my promise, at 4:00 AM Pacific Time on the 24th of December, the Angel Joleen entered my bedroom and I raised up out of my body and took her hand as we headed for my son's ship somewhere near Australia.

There inside the ship, we found my son asleep in his narrow bunk, too tired to await for our visit. We stood there and watched him sleeping for a while as I sensed the coolness of this long "room." Then I felt the sounds of this ship and the feelings of all those who occupied it; many were sad to be away from their homes and families at Christmas, some who were sad because they had no homes or families to miss, and those of who were happy doing what they desired - traveling the world as a U.S. Marine. Then, we returned home.

On Christmas Eve, approximately 10 minutes before midnight (Pacific Time), the Angel Joleen appeared. After we placed all the gifts under our Christmas tree, we went for our usual but very special Christmas Eve walk. We strolled the streets near our home as we held hands and talked about how wonderful the Christmas lights looked on all the houses, and about how beautiful the stars and moon were.

Without looking at her, I said, "I am just about ready to come Home. And my body is getting old and it is tired, too. I won't be long."

There was no need for me to look at her, for she squeezed my hand as I felt her Love as her loving smile flowed over me.

Once back inside of our home, we hugged and kissed, then gazed at our Christmas tree with all the presents under it, and she said, "I like the feelings of your hugs and kisses, but it is time for me to go. Hold me," then she collapsed in my arms and was gone again.

Christmas morning, when I awoke and throughout the day, I felt the presence of the Children, the Angel Joleen, Gabrael, Michael and Jesus, for this was all for the Glory of God. I hope your Christmas was as wonderful as mine.

And I pray, "Father, Thank You for another wonderful day and for this life. Forgive me for the things that I do wrong, I will try not to commit them again, as I forgive those who do wrong to me. And thank You for allowing me to know Your Angels as They have guided me to You as I guide others toward You. For my life is nothing without You. Amen."

Christmas 2002 with The Angels

As I sit here, a few days before Christmas and write the Message for December 29th, 2002, and as the world's conflict over religions heads us towards another World War, my Message is of both; hope and displeasure of things to come.
A few years ago, as a few friends, my oldest son, and I sat in our kitchen and talked, my son and I told of visions of things to come; we had seen the war in Kosovo in which pulled China into it, American Armed Forces fighting in South and Central America as well as islands (their locations, we did not know), Korea and Japan fighting (we did not know if it was North or South Korea, or if they joined together in the fight against Japan), an Atomic American Submarine and an Australian Submarine colliding together and both sinking somewhere in the seas (or waters) around Japan, a country in Asia or China "Sucker Punches" the United States (I do not think this was the 9/11 terrorists act, I think this will happen somewhere in the northwestern United States) because our forces will be too thinly spread around the world in different conflicts, an American civilian 777 airplane going down somewhere between the Hawaiian Islands and the western coast of the U.S. and the U.S. Navy will be needed to retrieve the wreckage because of its depth. All these things we both, my son and I saw, but while I also saw alone; mountains rising quickly where no mountains are now found, mountains that now stand

disappearing, water as oceans or seas in places where we now find land, towns, villages and cities fighting over food and drinking water as even family members fight among themselves for the necessities of life, people who are injured laying outside of hospitals because their beds are full inside, drought and famine and terrible weather conditions in different parts of the world. But I also saw a world where these things did not cover the complete world but only parts of it while other parts remained the same as they are now. But this is not the end of the world. They are only things that we were told that will come to pass. The people of the world have plenty of time to repent (change their views of the past) before the End of Time comes. But whereas, I see many that this will be the last Christmas Holiday for them to celebrate during their lifetime. Many, of all religions, will fall during this coming year as the Muslims find their Messiah that they seek, is recognized and coming into power, and the Catholic Church falls farther away from God as its new leaders direct the Pope as they continue to hide the final secret of Fatima which was pointed directly toward the corruption of the Church.

Whereas, not all that will occur in this coming year is directed by some people trying to dominate the majority, many of our friends and family will pass on from old age, disease and accidental death, for the Angels of death walk firmly on the earth as they have done throughout the passage of time. But yet, we should look upon death as a blessing to seek Eternal Life with God in Heaven. Rejoice for those who have crossed over, for a job well done, but cry as you miss their presence here in body with you. And recognize that some of those who you wish "Merry Christmas" to this year will not be present next Christmas Season as you Cherish the memories of Christmas' past.

And while I write this Christmas 2002 and 2003 New Year's Message, I see hope for each person to find his individual Salvation and his direction toward God. And once again as with all Christmases, I see the miracles shown to me by God's Angels.

After my wife, Chris, our son and I had spent the evening of December 24th of this year together, and after "Santa's" presents were placed under our tree, Chris and I walked out onto our front porch, it was around 11:30PM. We gazed around at our neighbors' Christmas Lights in the crisp night air and we smoked a cigarette as we killed the time before our Christ-Mass. At precisely 11:45, the Angel Joleen entered into Chris' body as the Angels Michael, Gabrael, Jesus and others gathered around us.

I said to them, "How can one stop evilness without trying to dominate others? Is it wrong if one knows and allows another to kill people or to place them into slavery, without trying to stop the terrorists? Is it right to defend yourself or to let another take what is yours without trying to stop them? Can I stand by and watch terrorists destroy others without trying to warn them or even help them? You do not have the same compassion as humans, you know what will happen, you know all that happens is because of the things that we have decided to do has led us to where we are. But the human does not know that; he does not understand that what is happening is what will happen. He does not know what will happen as it is known by God. I know that if I say something sometimes, and it is not to be known, no body will listen to what I say, but if I speak, and 10 people are to listening that will be saved, then they shall hear my words and be saved, for if that is what is to be, it will be. I know that I cannot change the future just as I cannot change the past. But yet, I am sad because of all the people who are being killed or who are being placed into slavery daily. Can I allow this to continue? But yet, if I kill to keep others from being placed into slavery or murdered, then am I as bad as the evil ones?"

The Angels looked at me as they spoke in unison, "You cannot change what will be, do not try to change the future. Stand where you are, you need not kill or dominate, for others will do that. Allow all others their choice as you too allow yourself your personal and individual choice. Speak if you feel that is what you are supposed to do. Follow what is in your heart. For if you speak and others listen to what you have said, then it was meant for them to hear."

Then at the stroke of midnight, the Angel Joleen took my hand and we walked into the yard, she said, "Pray with me..."

Then she looked up into the star lit sky and said, "Do you hear all the prayers...they contain so much unhappiness." And I heard the prayers flowing throughout the world. And then, she pointed to a place to the right of the moon and near a shining star, and she said, "That is where all the prayers first go, and then they spread out and throughout the Heaven." All the Angels that surrounded us and embraced us as we wished each other a Merry Christmas.

Afterward, we entered back into our home and placed a tiny Santa and sled beneath our Christmas tree. And the Angel Joleen said, "The Children are happy with it, see them playing with it?" I took a few pictures of the smoke-like images of the deceased children that drifted and/or raced around the room; these children had stopped by here on their way to God.

After a few minutes, the other Angels left us standing alone in our living room, and Joleen turned to me and said, "It is time for me to go."

We hugged and kissed as we said our goodbyes, and then she went limp in my arms as if she had died, and then within a few seconds, then she started breathing again as my wife, Chris, retrurned back into her body once again.

I hope that you had a wonderful Christmas, too.

The Glory of Christmas

And the Angel Jo said to me, "Jesus is the Son of God. He is everything that is good in God and all that is good in people as well, for all that is good in humans is God, too.

"Jesus does not want to be worshipped, for he is not the Father, embrace the Father alone. And as you celebrate this 'Christmas' season, think of him and the lifestyle that he demonstrated. But realize that humans can be evil and cruel toward each other as demonstrated by and in the death of Jesus.

"Enjoy this 'Christmas' season and show love toward all others, and be pleased with all as God is pleased with you.

"Presently the Glory of Christmas is the foundation of the Christian religion, for without Jesus' birth and death there would have been no Resurrection after his death, for without it, Christianity would not exist. But the foundation to the true Glory of Christmas is; 'Love all others and have no domination toward them,' as demonstrated by Jesus. He laid the foundation to Christianity, and now he has inspired the foundation to his house - Jesus' House of Jacob. And yet, Jesus' House of Jacob is not a Christian religion; it is the religion of God that states, one God above all. Therefore, the true Glory of Christmas is the knowledge that God allows humans to follow whatever religion they wish, as He continues to welcome them Home into the Light - the Knowledge at the end of their mission - life, for all has been recorded and is known in the Master plan by the Father."

And I pray; "Dear Father, thank You for the wisdom that You have allowed Your Angels to share with me. I continue to follow You even though I do make mistakes and constantly ask for Your forgiveness, but I shall try not to make the same mistake twice. And I know You, Your Angels nor I can change the world, but please give thoughts of thankfulness to all people. Show them Your Glory of Christmas, and maybe some will truly change, for I know that they are Your children, too. Amen."

My Last Christmas here on Earth

As we moved into December this year, I had a feeling that this was my last Christmas. I didn't understand how or why I knew this, but I knew something is going to happen in the near future. And during the time from December 14th through December 21st of this year, I was given the opportunity to view the future to understand my life, for now I was allowed to prepare myself to die.

My life was needed to be as it was because I needed to experience all the things that I had chosen during my life, and from those experiences, I was able to live the transition from human to Angel that I am presently living.

My life had no impact upon many, but the things that I have written, will have great influence, and will give direction to many, after I am gone. I cannot discuss the future that I saw, I do not wish to change what is to come, or to change the things that people do freely. But, I will not live to see another Christmas.

I have come to live God's Will, Jesus said, "I see what the Father sees." I as Jesus in other words, "I do not look for good or evil, for the Father does not judge what others do."

While learning, we need to to judge the actions of others to see if their actions are righteous for us, and then once we have learned what is righteous for us, we need to stop judging others and KNOW what is right for us as we live with what is right for us - God's Will;

Live only to enjoy and experience the righteous.

　　I shall soon be gone; Home to the Father, where I will sing and rejoice with Him and His Angels in Heaven forever, and in the mean time, I will continue to sing praises to Him.

The Angels Final Teachings to Me

God has allowed us to create the different religions of the world.

God has allowed us to place the god that we made above our creations. In the Christian Bible, God states; "Do not place any God above or in front of Me." He is really saying, "You can have any god that you wish that is below Me."

Then God also states; "Do not worship any other god or idols." Again, He is clearly stating, "We can have gods below Him, but do not worship our man-made god, only Him."

All religions have been created from vision or other communications with God and/or His Angels. These religions are on an imaginary line just above man in the triangle.

Why do people not see miracles and God's Angels today like those reported in the Old Testament and New Testament? I see them, my family sees them and many of our friends do, also, for we are embracing the true God. All people who claim to be religious of the world are not embracing the true God, for if they did, they would also see God's miracles and His Angels, too. I believe a few other people of today that I do not know of are also seeing the same as we because they are also embracing the true God as well.

If you, the one with ears would truly hear what I say, then you too would see Jesus and the Angels, and you would be communicating with them, and see God's miracles in your daily life. For if you, the one with ears would stop following a man-made religion and its god, but instead follow the true God, then the riches that my family, friends and I share also would be yours.

Because of their latest teachings to me, I have been Ordained a Bishop Of God. Thus, I am now ready to ordain others as Ministers (Workers) of God to spread God's true word of Love to others in the world. The word "Bishop" placed in front of my name does not mean I am higher than you, we are all equal, it is to signify that I qualified to be a servant to God through His Angels teachings.

Let us Pray:

"My Lord, lead me in the direction of life that Jesus has shown me to be righteous. Teach me a Love for a Love as I walk through this world of the Dead. I know that when I remove this clothing (my body) then I shall be "born again" and not until then. Help me to live a life without corruption in this world of corruption. Help me to try to replace my eyes with eyes of my heart, replace my hands with hands of my heart and replace my feet with feet of my heart, so then I can see Love, hold Love and walk in Love with You and also as You did and still do. Allow me to use my ordination to help spread Your words of Love to others. Amen."

And I prayed, "Why..."

Approximately three years ago, and after learning that the Angels, Jesus and God were real and now they were part of my life, as part of my prayer one night, I prayed,

"Dear Father, why have You told me all these things and continue to have Your Angels tell me more? I am not worthy to speak with You nor Your Angels for I am a Sinner. I have committed almost every sin there is because I was one who lived for the things that I enjoy in life. No one will believe in or listen to what I say. People won't believe that I have communicated with You through Your Angels just because I smoke cigarettes and I have a bad temper and get mad at people all the time, and that is not including all the other bad things that I have done throughout my life. I am not a religious person, and I never believed in You until now. And I always quit before the job is done - I am just a loser... just a nobody. And I can't talk in front of people, I get too nervous. I can't even write what You wish me to tell people because I am nearly illiterate. And I don't even know the Bible. If You need someone to speak Your words, surely You can find someone better suited for the job than I."

Later that evening after I went to bed, and shortly after midnight, the Angels appeared and we went into our backyard where we talked.

And the Angel Joleen said unto me, "God does not make

mistakes. He knows exactly what His Master Plan holds. He knew what your life must be for you to be where you are today, thus, He knew the only place and time for me to enter into your life and then into your heart. For when you were ready for the job, the job was ready for you. But you will not fully understand until you are here beside me on The Other Side."

And Jesus said unto me, "It is written, 'I take the stone that the mason discards and use it for my foundation.' Therefore, is it better for the Father to use the one who thinks he knows Him or of one who He teaches? For those who think they know God only speak of their religion and not of the Father."

And the Angel Gabrael said unto me, "It is said that Moses had a speech impediment, and yet, God instructed him to speak to the pharaoh of Egypt.

"The people referred to as Prophets are ones whose lifes that did not include God until they were introduced to Him. God uses those who are not polluted as His speakers - Prophets. For you are one of Jesus' foundation stones.

"Repentance cleanses the past, it is not your concern if others do not believe in what you say. Therefore, do as you were instructed to do, speak of the pains and hurt in your heart to others and also, write the things that you were told. For when you return Home others will speak the things that you have written. And yet, do not walk upon the Altar as if pretending to be closer to God than others, for if you do, they shall see your nakedness - they shall see that you too are human with human faults. Your life may not seem grand but to God all life is grandeur. And every human living or dead or yet to be born is a child of God.

"When people ask you, 'Why does God speak to you and not me?' Reply, 'All that is, is suppose to be.' "

My Final Message

     Frustration comes upon a person when he is seeking God but cannot find Him.
     Contentment comes when a person finds what he is seeking.
     Which God he finds does not matter if he is content with the God that he finds. But one must be careful not to create his God. For if you have created your God, he also hates the same people and things that you hate, thus he is no better than you.
     Frustration comes when a person who is seeking God, but cannot find a God who hates the same people and things the person hates. Therefore, for a person to seek God, he must be opened minded and seeking a God that is for all people because all people are the children of the true God. The true God is the Father, who is the Creator of all things, including all people. A god that is the father of a few, or only the father to his creator, is merely a man-made god and not the true God of all.
     A man-made god can bring contentment to an individual for a little while, but this contentment cannot and will not last because the individual will loose interest in his god, and then, continue his search to seek the true God.
     The true God who Abraham, Isaac and Jacob worshipped is the only one God above all other gods and religions. And once an individual finds Him, he shall have everlasting contentment.

Those who have found the true God before their lives end dwell in Heaven, and shall live in Heaven with the Father forever.

We should not force God upon others, allow them the time they need to search. For each step in our lives is learning and is needed for us to be at specific places at certain points in time throughout our lives. Each of us grow - increase with knowledge individually at a personal rate, therefore, we cannot force knowledge upon others. We must allow them to grow at their own speed as we have learned at our own pace. But we should guide them whenever they ask for our help. Then, contentment is yours for you have found the true God, for you are following Him as indicated by your actions, to your everlasting life with Him.

Present day established Religions are all man-made and are frustration makers because they lead to man-made gods. They are this because men have removed the true God from them and have replaced Him with their ideas, thoughts and concepts. God does not hate, only human hates. Yet, men have created their gods to their likings - one who hates.

Does One create something to hate?

Only man creates a god that hates the same things that he hates, and then when seeing that his god does not destroy what he hates, he looses interest in his god and searches for another god that fits his needs and does his bidding.

Happiness comes when you find the true God who teaches you all life is innerwoven and that you are not the center of the universe, but merely a part of it. And all life is grandeur, and all life is to be protected by living with love for all and to have no domination toward others. Once you stand beside God, you shall have what you search for along with eternal Contentment.

People have compromised their god into money. Today, less people than what you can count on one hand care about God or truly know Him, all live in frustration. The Jew, the Christian and the Muslim, all lust for the dog wants. And yet, repentance would change the course of history, but it is written what will be, for God does not lie. The gate to Heaven is narrow and not many will enter, the "not many" come from all times that have been, not just from this time and nor from just one religion.

I shall not change the world, and we shall not save the world. We must live the duration of our lives as set forth by God without self-destruction. We need to raise our individual Souls with freedom - feel free, touch free, love free, live free and be free.

Once you care not just for yourselves but the Angel-within you and all others, then you have found self-contentment and everlasting life with God.

I cannot repent for you. You drag me down to your hell. I must let loose of you and allow you to drown if that is what you wish. If you desire everlasting life with God, then follow not me but the God that I follow, then you have found contentment with the Savior - GOD! For there is no other Savior than Him!

Surely by now you know God. I need not say anymore about Him to you. Remove yourself from the idiosyncrasy of man-made gods and seek the true God of Abraham, Isaac and Jacob.

We do not know everything. We have taken the first steps from when our ancestors, the first one-cell animal, walked upon the earth, and we will learn until the end of time. Nothing is real in our reality, everything was created by and for the Creator; we came from nothing and will return to nothing. The only thing that will remain is the Energy that lives within each individual. And the Energy is the individual's life experiences that will live forever with the Creator.

Neil deGrasse Tyson
Astrophysicist American Museum of Natural History

Recognize that the very molecules that make up your body, the atom that costruct the molecules are traceable to the crucibles that were once the center of high mass stars that exploded their chemically enriched guts into the galaxy enriching pristine gas clouds with the chemistry of life, so that we are connected; to each other biologically, to the earth chemically and to the rest of the Universe atomically. That's kind of cool. That makes me smile. And I actually feel quite large at the end of that. It's not that we are better that the Universe, we are part of the Universe. We are in the Universe and the Universe is in us.

And I pray, "Dear Father, Thank You for another day of life and all that You have given us to use during this life. Forgive us when we stray and guide us back into contentment. I once asked the Angel

Jo, 'Should I continue my web site?' The Angel Jo replied, 'Do you have more to say?' I then answered, 'Yes.' But now I answer, 'No!' I am finished. I have done the work that You have asked of me. I pray that our communications continue. I shall live in the peace and contentment that all people should have, for it is not my concern if they seek or find You. Amen."

www.ingramcontent.com/pod-product-compliance
Lightning Source LLC
Chambersburg PA
CBHW021129230426
43667CB00005B/74